COLLECTED WORKS OF ERASMUS

VOLUME 73

COLLECTED WORKS OF
ERASMUS

CONTROVERSIES

APOLOGIA DE
'IN PRINCIPIO ERAT SERMO'

APOLOGIA DE LOCO 'OMNES QUIDEM'

DE ESU CARNIUM

DE DELECTU CIBORUM SCHOLIA

RESPONSIO AD COLLATIONES

edited and translated by
Denis L. Drysdall

University of Toronto Press

Toronto / Buffalo / London

The research and publication costs of the
Collected Works of Erasmus are supported by
University of Toronto Press

© University of Toronto Press 2015
Toronto / Buffalo / London
Printed in the U.S.A.

ISBN 978-1-4426-4894-4

Printed on acid-free paper

Library and Archives Canada Cataloguing in Publication

Erasmus, Desiderius, –1536
[Works. English]
Collected works of Erasmus.

Includes bibliographical references and indexes.
Contents: v. 73. Controversies.
ISBN 978-1-4426-4894-4 (v. 73)

I. Title.

PA8500 1974   199'.492   C740-06326x

University of Toronto Press acknowledges the financial assistance
to its publishing program of the Canada Council for the Arts
and the Ontario Arts Council, and agency of the Government of Ontario.

 Canada Council   Conseil des Arts
for the Arts   du Canada

ONTARIO ARTS COUNCIL
CONSEIL DES ARTS DE L'ONTARIO
an Ontario government agency
un organisme du gouvernement de l'Ontario

University of Toronto Press acknowledges the financial support
of the Government of Canada through the Canada Book Fund
for its publishing activities.

Collected Works of Erasmus

The aim of the Collected Works of Erasmus
is to make available an accurate, readable English text
of Erasmus' correspondence and his
other principal writings. The edition is planned
and directed by an Editorial Board, an Executive Committee,
and an Advisory Committee.

Contents

Illustrations

Introduction

The works translated in this volume of the *Controversies* do not have a substantial common theme, method, or form that enables us to treat them as a related group. Nor do they have a common opponent or an important common historical link. They all arise from the early editions of the *Annotationes* of *1516* or *1519* and, with the exception of the *De esu carnium*, concern textual criticism and opposed theories of translation. In most cases they contribute to expansions of the *Annotationes* in the later editions from *1522* to *1535*. The first work (1520), defending Erasmus' use of *sermo* instead of *verbum* in John 1:1, results mainly in an increase in the number of authorities quoted to support a purely philological argument. The second (1522), defending his choice of the only reading he found in Greek sources for 1 Corinthians 15:51, involves Erasmus in a defence against a charge of heresy and entails doctrinal argument and protests about the attacks. The last work (1529), also involving a serious charge of heresy, grows out of and feeds back into a large number of the annotations on the Epistle to the Romans. The odd item is the third one here: the *De esu carnium* (1522) grows out of an annotation on Matthew 11:30, 'For my yoke is sweet,' which was much enlarged in *1519* but does not appear to feed back into the annotation later. It is not philological or exegetical in character, but rather pastoral, an appeal, in the form of an open letter, for sincere practice as opposed to empty ritual in Christian life, using the topics of abstinence or fasting, feast days, and clerical chastity as examples, and constitutes at the same time a consideration of the validity of church regulations in these areas. All of these works also have associations with the faculty of theology at Louvain. The first version of the *Apologia de 'In principio erat sermo'* (there are two versions, referred to here as *1520a* and *1520b*) begins, overtly at least, as an answer to the Englishman Henry Standish, but was probably a more immediate response to the actions of Edward Lee. The second version is mainly targeted at the faculty and in particular perhaps at Nicolaas Baechem (Egmondanus) and a protégé. The *Apologia de loco 'Omnes quidem'* is also directed at Baechem and Standish. The *De esu carnium* responds to attacks by a group of Louvain Dominicans. The *Responsio ad Collationes* is a reluctant answer to the Louvain theologian Frans Titelmans, whom Erasmus suspected of being manipulated by Jacobus Latomus (Jacques Masson) – but these works all provoke and draw in other opponents too.

Apart from these links with Louvain and with the *Annotationes*, however, the works presented here are isolated items in the history of Erasmus' controversies, deal with a variety of subjects, and are disparate in nature. This introduction therefore will not attempt a general description of Erasmus' philology or theology, his method of defence, or exegesis in his controversies but will provide a separate introduction to each item, describing the immediate historical circumstances of each, and point by way of conclusion to one or two shared features.

APOLOGIA DE 'IN PRINCIPIO ERAT SERMO'

The word *sermo*, replacing *verbum* 'Word' in the opening verse of the Gospel of John, first appeared in the second edition of Erasmus' New Testament, published by Froben in March 1519. *Sermo*, in the sense of the Word of God or Son of God, occurred already at numerous places in the Latin Vulgate, but Erasmus had not introduced it here in the first edition of his New Testament, fearing, as he remarked in the annotation of 1519, that he would 'offend the weak.'[1] The reaction following the change seems to have been a veritable storm, but the critic whom Erasmus appears to target as the author of the attack on this particular point was the Franciscan Henry Standish, bishop of St Asaph.[2] The attack came during a sermon delivered at

* * * * *

1 Erasmus' annotation on *Erat verbum* consisted in 1516 of half-a-dozen lines citing Jerome's remark that various translations of λόγος, including *sermo*, could be applied to the Son (see 10 below). In 1519 he added: 'But since this [word, ie *verbum*] had always been the usage up till then, I did not dare to change it for fear of immediately offending the weak' (Reeve I 218n). This phrase was replaced in 1522 and subsequent editions by 'for fear of giving a handle to those who criticize anything at any opportunity' (Reeve I 218). The rest of the annotation at this time was concerned with the significance of the definite article in Greek before λόγος. For the annotation, see LB VI 335–7 (this phrase at 335A–B); Reeve I 218–21; CWE 46 15 nn16 and 19. The *Annotationes*, in the original editions and in LB, are keyed to the Vulgate text that was the object of his revisions.
2 For Standish see CEBR III 279–80; and Rummel *Critics* I 122–7. Erasmus' correspondence paints a picture of unrelieved malice and stupidity. The remarks in letters of 1515 and 1516 about unnamed English Franciscans, which have been taken as connecting Standish with criticism of the edition of Jerome, may

St Paul's in London, perhaps shortly after the second edition of the New Testament reached England in the spring of 1519.[3] Another attack was made by an unnamed monk, to whom Thomas More responded in a letter written probably between May and September 1519.[4] A third attack came 'at about the same time' as Standish's from Brussels, where a Carmelite, allegedly instructed by the persistently hostile Nicolaas Baechem, also spoke from the pulpit, and some unnamed enemies in Paris raised a simultaneous outcry on the subject. An additional cause of irritation was that these attacks were verbal ones made from the pulpit and in public gatherings, a procedure that Erasmus found particularly damnable because, as he explains at length, it exposed what he claimed were only scholarly suggestions, not demands for changes, to the reactions of the ignorant.[5]

However, although Standish was one of the originators of the criticism, his attack was not perhaps the immediate motive for the initial publication of the *Apologia*, and his role in the affair may seem to be more important than it was. His outburst in the churchyard of St Paul's, the offending sermon preached at St Gudula in Brussels, and the tumult that occurred in Paris, reported to Erasmus by letters, all took place some time before Erasmus published his response. He had probably known about Standish's attack for perhaps eight or nine months before he wrote a letter to Wolsey at the beginning of February 1520, in which he complained of Standish's behaviour and expressed the wish that the cardinal might arrange with the pope to silence him.[6] The curious point here is that, during all this time, he

* * * * *

in fact, as Professor Rummel has pointed out, refer to Edmund Birkhead, his predecessor as bishop of St Asaph. Standish is first explicitly named in Ep 608 of July 1517, where Erasmus expresses his gloom over the current situation of theology: 'Some black theological planet must now be lord of the ascendant, so much do our Master Doctors rule the roost everywhere: Standish in England . . .' This was written before Standish became bishop of St Asaph, so it is clear that he was already vocal before his elevation.

3 Copies were sent to Cardinals Campeggi and Wolsey in England on 1 and 18 May 1519 respectively (Epp 961 and 967).

4 Kinney 237–49. More does not mention Standish in this letter. The monk has been identified as the Carthusian John Batmanson.

5 In Ep 777:15–6, c 22 Feb 1518, Erasmus seems to say that his response would be different if Standish had made his attack in writing: 'If Standish had assaulted me like that [like Lefèvre], the beast would have had a very different reception. Lefèvre I answered with the greatest reluctance.' Then, still during the period before publication of the *Apologia*, Erasmus recounts an absurd dispute between Standish and an Italian friar in a long addition of 1517/18 to *Adagia* II v 98 *Esernius versus Pacidianus*, which is about two gladiators.

6 Ep 1060

had not thought of a written reply, perhaps precisely because it had been an oral attack or perhaps because he believed that the criticism did not deserve it. As he suggested later: 'I thought their argument was such that I never suspected anyone could be so impudent as to make a case against me on that basis.'[7] By mid- or late February 1520 it seems necessary to look for another cause for the decision to publish a written response. Even then he apparently found it necessary to do so twice, in two versions of his *Apologia*, composed in February and August 1520.[8]

The motivation for the first response may have been provided by Edward Lee, whose *Apologia* and *Annotationes* Erasmus finally obtained, after a long delay, about the middle of February. The dispute with Lee had begun soon after he and Erasmus met in Louvain in July 1517.[9] Lee seems to have hoped at first to contribute to the work on the New Testament, but Erasmus rejected his criticisms as trivial, and Lee became hostile. In May 1518 Erasmus went to Basel to supervise publication of the second edition and, on the way, composed what appears to be a response to some of Lee's criticisms; this appears in a letter addressed to Maarten Lips, probably intended for quick publication by Froben in the *Auctarium*.[10] The dispute continued after Erasmus' return to Louvain in September 1518. Lee withheld his

* * * * *

7 *Apologia de 'In principio erat sermo'* (1520b), 14 below
8 See the bibliography xli below. The Louvain and Nuremberg editions of *1520a* contain Ep 1072; the Cologne, Antwerp, and Mainz editions contain Ep 1072 and the *Apologia qua respondet invectivis Lei*.
9 The earliest allusion to Lee in Erasmus' letters is in Ep 607, 17 July 1517. See also Ep 765 to Lee, introduction, 15 July 1519, Ep 1037 (Lee's preface to his *Annotations* published in February 1520), Epp 1053, 1061 (Lee's *Apologia*, his own account of the course and nature of the dispute), 1074, and 1080; CEBR II 311–4; and CWE 72 introduction. Lee's attack was mainly directed at the first edition of Erasmus' *Annotationes* and even in the twenty-five notes that he added to the second edition, he did not comment on the substitution of *sermo* for *verbum* in John 1:1. More than half of Erasmus' annotation in 1519 concerned the significance of the definite article in Greek before λόγος, which was a point argued at length by Lee (it marks λόγος as the subject of this phrase). For more on the latter's standing, see Wallace K. Ferguson's introduction to the *Apologia qua respondet invectivis Lei* in *Opuscula* 225–34; and for his attack on the *Moria* and the seriousness with which Erasmus treated it in view of the possible accusation of Montanism, see M.A. Screech *Ecstasy and the Praise of Folly* (London 1980) 164, 193, 201–2.
10 Ep 843, 7 May 1518. For a different view of this letter, see Kinney vii–xli. The reference to 'a certain Franciscan' at line 599 is usually taken to be a reference to Standish, but see n2 above. The *Auctarium selectarum aliquot epistolarum Erasmi Roterodami ad eruditos et horum ad illum* was published in 1518.

Annotationes, despite Erasmus' attempts to see them or to persuade him to publish. Thomas More also wrote to Lee, on 1 May 1519, attempting to dissuade him from attacking Erasmus.[11] Lee's work finally appeared in Paris in early or mid-January 1520.[12] But what links the first version of Erasmus' *Apologia de 'In principio erat sermo'* most clearly to the dispute with Lee is that it has a preface in the form of a letter, 'To the reader' (Ep 1072), which states, without mentioning Standish, that Lee's book has just appeared, that Erasmus has answered Lee's *Apologia* (ie Ep 1061) three days before, and that he is about to publish his answers to the *Annotationes*. This version was first published by Dirk Martens in Louvain towards the end of February. Other printings followed, extending over the period between March and July, all apparently with Ep 1072 and some with the *Apologia qua respondet invectivis Lei*, which was also published independently in mid-March.

Given the period of perhaps eight or nine months between Standish's sermon at St Paul's and the appearance of *1520a*, the prefatory letter about Lee, and the closely associated responses to his *Apologia* and *Annotationes*, it seems likely that the immediate motivation for this publication was not the dispute with Standish but that with Lee. The latter was perhaps irritating Erasmus by repeating verbally the criticism of his principal supporter in England,[13] though he had not included it in his *Annotationes*. Lee may well have been the principal 'emissary' who was spreading the 'conspiracy' that Erasmus alleges repeatedly in *1520b*[14] and was using this criticism as ammunition. He was a continuing cause of irritation during the months from February to August and is said to 'continue to stick at nothing to secure my undoing.'[15] The argument against *sermo* had apparently become more insistent and more demanding of a response than Erasmus had thought.

* * * * *

11 Kinney 152–95
12 *Sunt in hoc volumine. Apologia Edouardi Leei contra quorundam calumnias. Index annotationum prioris libri. Epistola nuncupatoria ad Desiderium Erasmum. Annotationum libri duo, alter in Annotationes prioris æditionis Novi Testamenti Desiderii Erasmi, alter in Annotationes posterioris æditionis eiusdem. Epistola apologetica Edouardi Leei: qua respondet duabus Desiderii Erasmi epistolis.* Prostant Parrhisiis: In edibus Egidii Gourmont ... [1520]. The *epistola apologetica* ends *Vale Louanii. Calendis Februa. An.* M.D.XX.
13 CEBR II 311–14
14 15 and 39 below
15 Ep 1127A:2–3. See also the passage on Rom 5:12 in the *Responsio ad Collationes*, which dates from 1529 (see 201 nn25 and 34 below).

Beyond the immediate stimulus that provoked *1520a*, however, *1520b* is a response to the increasing hostility at Louvain and the character assassination carried on there. This was certainly in part sustained by Lee; there are continuing complaints in this period linking him to Standish and John Batmanson.[16] This second edition, almost three times as long as the first, was published by Froben in August 1520.[17] It no longer has Ep 1072, but the work is accompanied by the *Epistolae aliquot eruditorum virorum*, which also attack Lee. The *Apologia de 'In principio erat sermo'* is now clearly intended mainly for the faculty and in particular perhaps Baechem.

The most detailed account we have of the initial episode came five months after the publication of *1520a* in a letter of 31 July 1520 to Hermannus Buschius,[18] who at that time was supporting Erasmus in his dispute with Lee. In the letter Standish is said to have delivered a sermon in St Paul's churchyard, in which he digressed from his chosen subject of Christian charity and 'began to rave against my name and reputation . . .' Things had become intolerable, he said, since Erasmus had the effrontery to corrupt the Gospel of St John; for where the church for all these years had read *In principio erat verbum*, he was now introducing a new reading, *In principio erat sermo*.[19] Subsequently Standish is described as having debated the question, during a dinner at court, with two men whom we later learn are Thomas More and John Stokesley, the royal chaplain,[20] until the king himself intervened to save Standish from further embarrassment. A shorter version of the story, with slightly different detail, is given in the *Apologia de 'In principio erat sermo'* itself, and a third version, in which a 'Spanish Franciscan' propounds the 'syllogism' incorporated by Erasmus in the second version, is recounted in a letter dated July 1520.[21]

who

* * * * *

16 Ep 1099 to Richard Foxe, Ep 1113 to Philippus Melanchthon, Ep 1126 to Hermannus Buschius. See n4 above.

17 The corresponding part of the annotation on the NT was doubled in length in *1522*, which refers the reader to the *Apologia de 'In principio erat sermo'* and reproduces much of the material from it. Subsequent additions to the annotation on this particular point, in *1527* and *1535*, were minor.

18 Ep 1126:15–245

19 3 below

20 Ep 1126:15–245; CEBR II 456–9 and III 289–90 respectively

21 Ep 1127A, addressed to Luther; see 33 and n83 below. Erasmus continued to grumble about Standish in letters to Buschius (Ep 1126:15) and to Thomas More (Ep 1162:167–78). His letter to Vincentius Theoderici (mid-March 1521), Ep 1196:687–99, recalls the scene before the king. Other attacks on this *Apologia* followed. The letter to Wolfgang Faber Capito (6 December 1520), Ep 1165:19–24, talks of a Dominican and a Carmelite (identified as Jacques and Julien

Both versions of the *Apologia de 'In principio erat sermo'* also relate that similar, almost simultaneous verbal attacks occurred in Brussels and in Paris. No names are mentioned in connection with these critics, but in *1520b* the attacker in Brussels is further described as 'a certain Carmelite and bachelor of theology,'[22] and alleged to have been 'instructed by his teacher who is popularly known as the "Camelite" because of his dull-wittedness,' that is, Nicolaas Baechem.[23] The latter will be described in the introduction to the second item in this volume, since he is more directly concerned with that debate; but he is certainly in Erasmus' mind on this occasion. In a manuscript addition of 1522 Erasmus overtly vents his contempt for the faculty, inserting

For some years now no one has been admitted to the theological fraternity in Louvain without giving some proof of his worth, such as this attack, nor are people initiated into the most sacred mysteries of theology there unless they have declared themselves to be egregiously shameless sycophants. (m[1]v 134; 16 below)

Erasmus' introduction and his concluding tirade against the dishonest and rabble-rousing methods of his attackers are both considerably expanded in the second version. In the body of his text, additional material from Cyprian, Hilary, and Augustine, along with evidence from authors not previously mentioned – Tertullian, Ambrose, and Lactantius – add weight to the main argument that the Fathers used the word *sermo* of Christ frequently and

* * * * *

Hasard) who sent him a pamphlet, 'the maddest thing you ever saw.' In the *Catalogus lucubrationum* (Ep 1341A:857–64) Erasmus repeats his suspicions about a conspiracy to force the chancellor to drive him out of the University of Louvain, naming the *Apologia de 'In principio erat sermo'* as part of the evidence against him. Later, in April 1525, he complains to Noël Béda about the abuse of Pierre Cousturier (Petrus Sutor), who 'challenges me to produce even a single authority who has adopted the reading *In principio erat sermo . . .*' (Ep 1571:58–60). In another letter to Béda in the same year, he repeats Standish's three accusations (Ep 1581:380–92), and in 1529 he still recalls Standish as one of the Franciscans 'who constantly attack the name of Erasmus in their sermons and public addresses' (Ep 2126:160).

22 Tentatively identified as one Jan Robyns, but otherwise almost unknown. See Rummel *Critics* I 142; Ep 178:9n, letter to Jan Briart, 22 April 1519), Ep 946 4n, possibly Ep 948:167–71, Ep 1040 n7, Ep 1046, Ep 1317 n4, and Ep 1341A n240; CEBR III 166. This Robyns is not to be confused with Jan Robbyns, dean of Mechelin, Erasmus' friend who played an important part in the founding of the Collegium Trilingue.

23 Identified in Ep 1165

show that it was used in John 1:1 in versions of the Latin Bible circulating in their time. Condescending further to his audience of scholastic theologians,[24] he also adds to his list of medieval authorities – Aquinas, the *Glossa ordinaria*, Nicolas of Lyra, Hugh of St Cher – Anselm, Remigius, and Durandus. After this he ridicules his opponents with a sample of the sort of 'syllogism' they put forward against his emendation. The syllogism, attributed in Ep 1127A to a 'Spanish Franciscan,' is here credited to 'a theologian distinguished in the judgment of a few others, and in his own in particular' (33 below). Although this argument may have been propounded first in England, as the letter says, it is introduced here as if taken up by someone at Louvain. The theologian in question may well be the notoriously vain Baechem, the 'Camelite' who, 'if he were as pleasing to Christ as he is to himself, would be a better man than St Paul.'[25] However the bulk of Erasmus' amplification, in both the introduction and the conclusion, is taken up with heated protests against the 'conspiracy' that he is sure is being mounted, against the blatant use of misrepresentation in the pulpit to rouse the ignorant public on the subject of proposals that should be calmly treated in private discussions, and against the envy and malice that seeks to destroy the reputation of one who is, in his own view at least, entirely innocent and well deserving.

The additions to his witnesses do not involve any doctrinal exegesis of John 1:1; the *Apologia* confines itself to a philological defence of the use of *sermo* in place of *verbum*. Doctrinal implications, as Marjorie O'Rourke Boyle has shown,[26] are dealt with in the relevant part of the *Paraphrasis in Joannem*, which appeared in 1523 and do not need to be rehearsed here. As Erasmus himself says at one point, 'I am not discussing now what weight should be given to the interpretation of Augustine here. It is enough for my purpose that he should not shrink from the term *sermo*.'[27] It is the philological nature of the discussion, however, that constitutes the value of the work as a sample of Erasmus' controversies, for it was, in large part at least, his philological methods that raised the ire of the traditionalists and the establishment.

* * * * *

24 And perhaps not only the scholastics: Thomas More catches Lee in a contradiction when he (Lee) reproaches Erasmus for allowing too little authority to the 'moderns' and at the same time claims that Erasmus has dishonoured him by observing that he supports his annotations with the opinions of the moderns. See Kinney 185.
25 16 below; and Ep 1162
26 Boyle 22–4
27 23 below

The philological nature of the discussion also creates a problem for the translator, for Latin words themselves are in question, not ideas. Since there is no set of English words that have an exact one-to-one correspondence to the Latin series *verbum, sermo, oratio, ratio,* it is necessary either to leave these and occasionally some other terms in the text, with translation in brackets, or to add the Latin in brackets to indicate which term is translated by 'word.' It is also clearly unsatisfactory in some cases to use 'speech' (or 'statement' or 'speaking' or 'discourse' or 'utterance') for *sermo* – for example, 'In the beginning was [the] Speech.' English by long tradition uses 'the Word' in this special sense. But it is occasionally necessary to use two different terms in order to follow Erasmus in translating the distinctions he is making, so, where necessary, 'speech' or 'speaking' has been used for *sermo.*[28] A similar problem, though without the added difficulty of translating a set of words, is encountered in the *Apologia de loco 'Omnes quidem,'* and again frequently in the *Responsio ad Collationes,* where the semantic group *curare / cura, affectus,* and *sensus* in Rom 8:5 and 27 also poses a special difficulty.

APOLOGIA DE LOCO 'OMNES QUIDEM'

Erasmus reported in a letter to Hermannus Buschius (31 July 1520), Ep 1126:127, that Henry Standish had accused him, *inter alia,* of 'doing away with the resurrection' on the basis of his emendation of 1 Cor 15:51. However, he indicates in the opening of his defence that this *Apologia* of 1522 is directed not against Standish – he now regards that as an 'old affair' (fol HH3 r) for which Standish has been suitably shamed – but against a Carmelite of Louvain. Though unnamed in the first edition of the *Apologiae omnes* of February 1522, this person is identified both in a manuscript note in Erasmus' own hand in the copy held in Cambridge University Library (see the list of editions below) and in a letter to Joost Lauwereyns (14 July 1522) as Nicolaas Baechem.[29] Standish is also named in a manuscript note on the same page.

* * * * *

28 For more on this, see CWE 56 255 on Rom 9:9.
29 Ep 1299:10. See the article by Marjorie O'Rourke Boyle in CEBR I 81–3; Rummel *Critics* I 135–40; Bentley 55–6, 94–5, 155–8; Hamilton, which all give valuable general context. For Baechem, see De Jongh 152–4; he is caricatured in the *Colloquia,* which were revised and expanded in 1522. See Ἰχθυοφαγία 'A Fish Diet' CWE 40 703:39–40 (where he is called *Lemantius* 'blear eyed') and 720:40–1, and *Apotheosis Reuchlini* 'The Apotheosis of Reuchlin' CWE 39 246:6–14 (where he is also nicknamed 'the camel'; see n28 above). See also Craig Thompson's note on *De votis temere susceptis* 'Rash Vows' CWE 39 41–2 n14.

The hostility of the director of the Carmelite house at Louvain seems to have been aroused as soon as the *Novum instrumentum* was published; the 'libellous Carmelite' referred to in Ep 483 may well be Baechem.[30] According to a later letter to Petrus Mosellanus, Baechem began his attacks in the autumn of 1516, threatening the coming of Antichrist, though claiming that he had never read Erasmus' book.[31] There are persistent complaints of a conspiracy among Carmelites and Dominicans, and insinuations of collusion with Franciscans in England,[32] but Baechem is first named in Ep 878, where Erasmus reports a meeting between him and the inquisitor Jacob of Hoogstraten, remarking acidly: 'Thief knoweth thief and wolf to wolf is known.'[33] Baechem, who became assistant inquisitor in the Netherlands in 1520 and helped to publish the bull *Exsurge Domine* (15 June 1520; proclaimed in the Netherlands on 28 September), 'said more about me in his sermon than about Luther'[34] and persistently accused Erasmus of inspiring Luther's ideas.[35] A colourful account of a meeting in the presence of Godschalk Rosemondt, the successor of Jan Briart as rector of the faculty, which Erasmus had requested in order to protest at the attacks made on him from the pulpit and to try and settle the dispute, is given in a letter to Thomas More of November 1520. It is a stinging portrait of impenetrable obstinacy, vanity, and venom. In the discussion Erasmus teases Baechem wickedly and concludes humorously that, tiresome as he is, the man is not deceitful, is wholly consistent in his belief that he is a pillar of religion, and that what he does is for the good of the church.[36] This *Apologia* is Erasmus' response to the particular attack on his reading of 1 Corinthians 15:51. A more general complaint about Baechem's attacks was sent to 'the theologians of Louvain' in an early version of Ep 1301, July 1522, and a longer version of this letter (CWE 9 129–36) was published in 1523 with the first edition of the *Catalogus lucubrationum*, which also retells this story.[37] Baechem and Standish each receive a paragraph in Erasmus' defence of himself to Noël Béda in 1525.[38]

Unlike the *Apologia de 'In principio erat sermo,'* this dispute is not a purely philological matter. Erasmus explains his textual procedure, taking

* * * * *

30 9 November 1516
31 Ep 948:141–9, 22 April 1519
32 See the indexes to CWE 4, 5, and 6.
33 19 Oct 1518. Cf *Adagia* II iii 63.
34 Ep 1144 to Francesco Chierigati, 13 September 1520
35 See eg Ep 1153 to Godschalk Rosemondt, 18 October 1520.
36 Ep 1162, November [?] 1520. See also Ep 1173.
37 Ep 1341A:928–75, 30 January 1523
38 Ep 1581:380–422

Jerome as his chief authority for the variants; his main discussion, however, is not concerned with the ridiculous accusation that he had 'done away with the resurrection' but with the doctrinal acceptability of all the variants.[39] None of them is in fact heretical, and no authority has suggested that any one of them is. He disagrees with Jerome, whose preference for reading A ('We shall all sleep, but we shall not all be changed')[40] – on the argument that in B 'we shall all be changed' is superfluous – carries no weight with him. He explains the distributive or approximative meaning of 'all,' and rejects the 'spiritual' tropologies of people like Origen, for whom the 'living' means the just and 'those who sleep' means sinners. His main concern, and his reason for choosing reading B ('We shall not all sleep, but we shall all be changed'), is to understand the verse in the context of Pauline thinking. The Apostle is saying that those who are overtaken in their lifetime by the second coming of Christ will not die but will be changed ('we' means present believers, including perhaps himself since he expects the second coming to take place soon); the dead will rise again, and all believers will be transformed to immortality in the same instant. Paul is speaking only of believers, not of unbelievers, and says that all those living at the time of the second advent will not die ('sleep'), but will be taken up into immortality ('will be changed') with those who have already died. As Erasmus says near the end of his theological arguments and before his polemical epilogue, 'This is the only way to attain to the real meaning of Scripture, by paying careful attention to what the writer is talking about.'[41]

The third edition of Erasmus' *Annotationes* appeared at about the same

* * * * *

39 Ep 1235 to Pierre Barbier, 23 September 1521, dated just before the *Apologia de loco 'Omnes quidem,'* gives a preliminary sketch of the defence eventually presented.
40 In the following and in the translation, in order to make the argument clearer, references to the three readings will be inserted as A, B, and C following Asso:
     A *Omnes quidem dormiemus, non autem omnes immutabimur* 'We all indeed shall sleep, but we shall not all be changed' (Greek reading, cited and preferred by Jerome, but known to Erasmus only in Latin codices; known also to Augustine and Aquinas).
     B *Non omnes dormiemus, omnes autem immutabimur* 'We shall not all sleep, but we shall all be changed' (Greek reading known to Jerome and adopted by Erasmus).
     C *Omnes quidem resurgemus, non autem omnes immutabimur* 'We shall all indeed rise again, but we shall not all be changed' (VG; according to Jerome not found in Greek sources but known to him; known also to Ambrose; translated as in DV).
41 22 below; Asso 330–1

time as this *Apologia* in 1522. The long addition to the end of the annotation
that was included at this time is half concerned with the explanation that
omnes may refer to 'all believers' but half with protest at the actions of
Standish and Baechem – not named there either but identified in the same
way as here, with an additional sly reference to Louvain theologians. The
material is much the same as some of the *Apologia*, and though not verbally
similar, it is a notable example of the way in which Erasmus allowed his
polemics to overflow into his annotations.

    This translation is based on the edition of the text of 1522 published
by Cecilia Asso. However it does not seem necessary to suppose, with
Dr Asso, that Erasmus is mistaken in his reading of Jerome's letter in the
way she alleges.[42] He may have made a confusing or confused statement in
his original annotation, and there may be some perhaps deliberate fudging
or ambiguity, or merely looseness of reference in the *Apologia*. However,
neither the Cambridge copy of 1522, which has manuscript marginalia in
Erasmus' own handwriting, nor the slightly expanded version that appears
in 1540 provide any indication that he wished to correct anything referring
to this question. These two facts support the suggestion that no real error
remains there,[43] and the translation is made on this assumption.

DE ESU CARNIUM AND
DE DELECTU CIBORUM SCHOLIA

Although nominally a letter and not initially intended, according to Erasmus, for publication, this small treatise exceeds the usual length of even his
longest letter, and he directed, in the *Catalogus lucubrationum*, that it should

* * * * *

42 Asso asserts that Erasmus is guilty of 'several basic inconsistencies that un-
    dermine the validity of the argument' (171 and 176–9). In her opinion 'the
    source of this inconsistency is a mistaken interpretation of the principal text
    discussed, Jerome's Epistle 119 . . . concerning the interpretation of 1 Cor 15:51'
    (170–1). Specifically she alleges: 'Erasmus states that at the present time Greek
    codices have only B and Latin ones A, but he does not specify what the two
    ancient Greek readings were, and makes A and C coincide. In this way he
    confuses the antithesis Vulgate / Greek codices (that is his main problem here)
    with the ancient discussion reported by Jerome, who had set the supporters
    of the two different Greek readings against each other and did not consider
    the Latin one' (176–7).
43 See 'Editions of the Texts' and 'Translator's Note' 52 below. The principal
    addition of 1540 is indicated on 49 n25 below. For a detailed discussion of the
    problem, see Denis L. Drysdall 'Erasmus' alleged error in the *Apologia de loco
    "Omnes quidem resurgemus"*' ERSY 27 (2007) 76–82.

be classified with his *Apologiae*.[44] However, it differs from the other apologetic writings in this volume in that it was not primarily a direct response to an attack on his *Annotationes* on the New Testament but a reaction to his personal situation in Basel when a challenge to Lenten practices aroused a public uproar. It does, however, reproduce views that he had expressed earlier in his annotations. It also led him into one of his more prolonged controversies with opponents in Louvain and was an element in his disputes with Josse Clichtove, Noël Béda, and Alberto Pio, giving rise eventually to the publication of a second edition with scholia defending his position.

There were several important factors influencing Erasmus' move to Basel in 1521: most obviously the hostility of the theologians in Louvain, the need to be present for the printing of his works by Froben, and the existence there of a circle of humanist colleagues. One of the chief factors, however, in his eventual decision to stay there, despite considerable hesitations, seems to have been his regard for the bishop of that see, Christoph von Utenheim, a man committed to humanistic learning and ecclesiastical reform, whose patronage Erasmus could value.[45] When he went to Basel in 1514 to attend to the new edition of the *Adagia* and to work on the New Testament and Jerome's letters, Erasmus had taken a letter of recommendation to the bishop from Jakob Wimpfeling.[46] Subsequent letters show that Utenheim not only had treated him on a later visit most generously, trying to persuade him then to stay with him (in later letters he is said more than once to have offered 'half his kingdom') but had approved of the *Novum instrumentum* and authorized its publication in his diocese.[47] Another invitation came in a letter of 13 July 1517, to which Erasmus replied that he thought it advisable to spend some further months in Louvain, but that he was seeking a suitable subject for a tribute to the bishop.[48] This has been taken to be possibly the first mention of the *De esu carnium* but is more likely to allude, if it alludes

* * * * *

44 Epp 1341A:1306–13. For the place of these ideas in Erasmus' work as a whole, see the introduction by C. Augustijn to his edition of the *De esu carnium* and the *De delectu ciborum scholia* in ASD IX-1. This translation is based on that edition, and the notes are heavily indebted to it.

45 Christoph von Utenheim (1450–1527); see CEBR III 361–2 and Rummel *Annotations* 146–52.

46 Ep 305:243–6

47 *Novum instrumentum* is the title of the 1516 edition of the *Novum testamentum*. See the letters to Thomas More, Ep 412:10–14, to John Fisher, Ep 413:21–5, to Andrea Ammonio, Ep 414:15–18, to Leo x, Ep 446:63–4, and to Henry Bullock, Ep 456:159–78.

48 Ep 598, 13 July 1517 and Ep 625, c 23 August 1517

to anything definite at all, to the *De immensa Dei misericordia*, which Erasmus eventually wrote as a tribute and token of appreciation.[49]

When Erasmus finally left Louvain on 28 October 1521, arriving in Basel on 15 November, he had still not decided to stay. A letter from Basel of 10 November 1522 reveals that he had abandoned a proposed trip to Rome to meet the new pope Adrian VI and was contemplating a move to France.[50] In January 1523 he expects to move but has 'decided to stay here until March'[51] and is still hesitating even then: 'I have almost decided to stay here until next August, and then to go either to Italy . . . or to France . . .'[52] It is not known when he eventually decided to settle, but if it was tranquillity he was hoping for, he was soon disappointed.

On Passion Sunday, 13 April 1522,[53] a deliberate challenge to the rules governing feasting during Lent was mounted by a local doctor, one Sigismund Steinschnider, who invited his guests to eat pork. The incident is first mentioned in a letter of 24 June 1522 to Bonifacius Amerbach, where it is said to have caused an 'astonishing uproar.'[54] Later missives give further details, including the fact that Hermannus Buschius was involved in the affair, to Erasmus' great disappointment.[55] The later account in the *Scholia* shows that the incident took place in a context of more general public protest and that Erasmus deplored the gruesome punishment meted out to the man.[56] That passage goes on to say that there were some who pointed the finger at Erasmus – who benefited from a papal dispensation that allowed him to eat meat for health reasons – and to state that, as a consequence of this, he wrote a defence addressed to the bishop; though not originally intended for publication,[57] this defence appeared eventually – that is, in August 1522 – as the *De esu carnium*.

* * * * *

49 Ep 1341A:782.
50 Ep 1319
51 Letter to Utenheim, Ep 1332:38
52 Letter to Zasius (23 March 1523), Ep 1353:272–5
53 Palm Sunday, according to the text of the colloquy Ἰχθυοφαγία 'A Fish Diet' CWE 40 707. This colloquy touches on many of the themes of the present text. See also Allen Ep 1353:160n.
54 Ep 1293
55 The scandalous dinner is described in the letter to Udalricus Zasius (23 March 1523), Ep 1353:179–210. This letter also treats similar themes to the *De esu carnium*. For Buschius, see n18 above. Cf also Ep 1496 to Melanchthon, 6 September 1524.
56 See 105 below.
57 Cf letter to Béda (15 June 1525), Ep 1581:798–807.

Erasmus had broached these subjects at some length in the New Testament of 1519 in an annotation on Matthew 11:30 ('For my yoke is sweet and my burden light').[58] In 1516 this note consisted of only two lines on the meaning of the Greek χρηστὸς, which the Vulgate translated as *suave* 'pleasant' (DV 'sweet'), while Erasmus preferred *facile, commodum,* or *humanum* 'easy.' He used *commodum* in his text. In 1519 the annotation was made the occasion for a lengthy plea on fasting, the growth and weight of humanly devised rules, and the danger of turning Christ's 'easy' yoke into a heavy burden of Judaizing law, a burden that not only exceeded that of Jewish law but threatened evangelical freedom.[59] These, with the addition of the question of the celibacy and morals of the priesthood, are the essential themes of the *De esu carnium*.

The annotation seems to have been subject to almost immediate verbal attack in Louvain. A Dominican, Vincentius Theoderici, the 'Vincent' of the colloquy *Funus* 'The Funeral' and the *magister noster Bucenta* of Ep 2205, had written an invective but was prevented from publishing it.[60] The contents of the *De esu carnium*, initially intended for the bishop's eyes only, became known, and it was published in August 1522.[61] No response to this work appeared in print until March 1525 when Erasmus' treatise on confession, *Exomologesis*, provoked a hostile attack published under the pseudonym Godefridus Ruysius Taxander.[62] Erasmus eventually

* * * * *

58 LB VI 63–5 n44. For the continuity of Erasmus' positions and some detectable changes, see J. Coppens 'Les Scolies d'Erasme sur l'*Epistola de interdicto esu carnium*' in *Colloquia erasmiana turonensia* ed J-Cl. Margolin (Toronto 1972) II 829–36.

59 It was expanded by nearly one hundred lines in the 1535 edition; see Reeve I 53–6. Additions in 1522 and 1535 were minor. For a fuller account of the annotation and a comparison with the *De esu carnium*, see Rummel *Critics* I 180–4 and Rummel *Annotations* 72 and 146–51. The subject of the superstitious, Judaizing nature of some modern regulations is raised again in the annotation on the word *assumite* in Rom 14:1.

60 For Vincentius Theoderici, see De Jongh 171–2; CEBR III 317–18; for an account of Erasmus' difficulties with Theoderici, Ep 1196, March 1521; for the banning of his invective, Ep 1585:71–7 and Ep 1603:40–5 with n15. Vincentius is mentioned in the colloquy *Funus* 'The Funeral' CWE 40 768 15 and n14.

61 Letter to Béda (15 June 1525), Ep 1581:798–807. He also claimed in this letter that the work was read twice by the Paris theologian Ludwig Baer and published at the request of Utenheim.

62 *Apologia in eum librum quem ab anno Erasmus Roterodamus edidit ...* (Antwerp: S. Cocus 1525). The volume had a preface addressed to Edward Lee (see Ep

worked out that this tract, 'so silly and unscholarly that one would expect a higher level of scholarship from a pig,'[63] was produced by four Louvain Dominicans, including Theoderici, who seems to have been particularly responsible for a second tract in the volume, *Libellus quo taxatur Delectus ciborum sive liber de carnium esu ante biennium per Erasmum Roterodamum enixus*. Like other responses to the *De esu carnium*, especially those of Béda and Pio, this one ranges more widely than the declared subject and persists particularly in linking Erasmus' name to Luther.[64] Erasmus sketched a response entitled *Manifesta mendacia*, which he decided to suppress.[65]

A second attack from Louvain, more covert and at the same time more serious, came from another old enemy, Latomus, whose *De ecclesia et humanae legis obligatione*, also of 1525, was the third part of a work nominally directed against Johannes Oecolampadius and his views on confession, but which frequently criticized Erasmus without naming him.[66] Here Erasmus recognized that Latomus was attacking a passage in his *De esu carnium*, about church regulations, that was based on Gerson's *De vita spirtuali animae*.[67] He made no reply to this criticism, nor did he

* * * * *

1571 n14). Erasmus immediately suspected Theoderici, and later found it was written, in addition to him, by Cornelis of Duiveland, Walter Ruys of Grave, and Govaert Strijroy of Diest. See Ep 1603 to Willibald Pirckheimer, 28 August 1525.

63 In Ep 1571 to Béda, 28 April 1525

64 See Rummel *Critics* II 3–4.

65 Professor Rummel, who identified this fragment, has provided the text in 'An Unpublished Erasmian *Apologia* in the Royal Library of Copenhagen' *Nederlands Archief voor Kerkgeschiedenis* 70 (1990) 210–29 and the translation in CWE 71. She has argued that it may originally have formed part of Ep 1581 to Béda, 15 June 1525. For the background, see her articles '*Nihil actum est sine authoritate maiorum*: new evidence concerning an Erasmian letter rejecting the accusation of apostasy' *Bibliothèque d'humanisme et renaissance* 54/3 (1992) 725–31 and '*Manifesta mendacia*: Erasmus' Reply to "Taxander"' *Renaissance Quarterly* 43–4 (1990) 731–43.

66 Latomus (Jacques Masson) was a determined opponent at Louvain from 1518 onwards. He was one of those who were asked by Erasmus to comment on any errors or points of possible disagreement in the first edition of the *Novum instrumentum* when he was preparing the second in 1519, but who apparently had said nothing. From about 1520 Erasmus considered him his principal enemy, and Luther described him as his most formidable opponent. See De Jongh 173–80; CEBR II 304–6.

67 See Rummel *Critics* II 8–12. Latomus' volume containing *De confessione secreta. De quaestionum generibus quibus Ecclesia certat intus et foris. De Ecclesia et humanae*

publish an immediate answer to criticism from a former colleague of Lefèvre d'Etaples, Josse Clichtove in Paris. This scholar had come under the influence of the syndic of the faculty of theology of the Sorbonne, Noël Béda, and now attacked Erasmus in his *Propugnaculum ecclesiae,* which appeared in May 1526. He treats the objections of the adversaries whom he calls Lutherans and seems to focus on Erasmus in this category. Erasmus' answer, not published until 1532, was the *Dilutio.* He states there that he considers the criticisms Clichtove made of his *De esu carnium* to be sufficiently answered by the scholia attached to the new edition of this work, which appeared in the same volume, but he does add some general remarks on priestly continence and marriage. Erasmus also responded to the criticisms of the Paris theologians concerning fasting and the choice of foods in his *Declarationes ad censuras Lutetiae vulgatas.*[68]

The confrontation with Noël Béda and the examination of Erasmus' works by the Sorbonne also included, of course, criticism of material in the *De esu carnium.* There is a general allusion to 'Taxander's' tract in Ep 1571, addressed to Béda, but particular reference to criticism of the *De esu carnium* first occurs in Ep 1581 to Béda, 15 June 1525, where Erasmus claims that his views on the celibacy of the priesthood, fasting, and the prohibition on eating meat, as expressed in the *De esu carnium,* were read and approved by both Ludwig Baer, a former pupil of Béda, and the bishop of Basel.[69] In his reply on 12 September, Béda simply disowned Baer, declared his support of Clichtove and Pierre Cousturier (Petrus Sutor), and warned Erasmus that the *De esu carnium* gave ammunition to the Lutherans.[70] The accusation

* * * * *

legis obligatione was published at Antwerp by M. Hillen. The passages of the *De esu carnium* attacked by Latomus, Clichtove, Béda, and Pio will be noted, in so far as they are answered by Erasmus, in the translation and that of the *De delectu ciborum scholia.*

68 Clichtove's *Propugnaculum ecclesiae* was published in Paris by Simon de Colines (Colinaeus); the criticisms of the *De esu carnium* are found in book 3, chapters 22–8. See Rummel *Critics* II 74–9. Erasmus' views on fasting had been attacked earlier by Clichtove in his *Antilutherus* (III i 3) published in 1524. See the letter from Béda (21 Oct 1525), Ep 1642:9–12. The *Dilutio* was omitted from the *Opera omnia* of 1540 and from LB; it was not published again until 1968 by E.V. Telle. An English translation is to be found in CWE 83 112–51; for the reference to the *De delectu ciborum scholia,* see 144 n129. The *Declarationes ad censuras Lutetiae vulgatas,* published in Antwerp and Basel in 1532, are in CWE 82 31–47.

69 Ep 1581:798–807. On Baer, see Ep 1571 n6; and CEBR I 84–6.

70 Ep 1609:20–41, 63–9

of Lutheranism occurs frequently in Béda's *Annotationes*, published in May 1526, where this text is also censured. In the *Prologus supputationis*[71] (August 1526) Erasmus lists fifteen objections made by Béda to the *De esu carnium* and appends his justifications.[72] The first of these objections is a general statement, making the same charge, though using the word 'schismatic,' and suggests that the others are made under the same heading. The censures of the Sorbonne included one of the *De esu carnium*, citing the question, 'But what cause for offence is there now in practices the Gospel does not forbid? Nay rather whose censors the Apostle's Epistles condemn when, as he says, they "forbid ... foods that God created to be received." '[73] This the Sorbonne claimed was heretical and not in accordance with the Apostle's intention. Erasmus answered, pointing out that, as so often happened, the question of fasting was confused with the question of abstinence or choice of foods, and that he had in fact said nothing heretical. Nevertheless he concluded by saying that his remark was 'uncircumspect' and that, for the sake of weaker brethren, he would modify the passage. He does not appear to have done so.

The accusations of Lutheranism persist in the dispute with Alberto Pio;[74] indeed this opponent seems almost to have confused the two enemies in his own mind, since large parts of his *Responsio paraenetica* of 1526, a response to Erasmus' letter of 10 October 1525 (Ep 1634), are clearly and admittedly attacks on Luther rather than Erasmus.[75] The latter did not reply until 1529. Pio, who at this stage had apparently not read the *De esu carnium*, took a further two years to read more of Erasmus' works and prepare his rejoinder, the *Tres et viginti libri in locos lucubrationum variarum D. Erasmi Roterodami*. Although Pio died before he could be answered again, Erasmus nevertheless considered it necessary to defend himself against the allegations of this very powerful critic. This he did in the *Apologia adversus rhapsodias Alberti Pii* published by Froben in 1531, answering Pio's objections to four passages or statements from the *De esu carnium* on fasting (Pio book 4) and four statements on rituals (Pio book 6). For the benefit of readers

* * * * *

71 This is the prologue, published with the *Divinationes ad notata Bedae* and the *Elenchus in censuras Bedae*, to the *Supputatio* which appeared a year later (March 1527).
72 LB IX 484D–489A
73 94 below
74 For the *apologiae* against Pio, see CWE 84. For Erasmus' answers to the objections, see CWE 84 181–91 and 212–13.
75 See Rummel *Critics* II 119.

who could only be bothered with the summary provided by the index, he annotates two more items in the tract entitled *Brevissima scholia* attached to the scholia of the *De esu carnium* of 1532. In that year Erasmus seems to have made something of an effort to answer all his critics. The publication in July 1531 of the official condemnation of the Sorbonne, promulgated originally on 17 Dec 1527,[76] led him to publish the *Declarationes ad censuras Lutetiae vulgatas*, with a response to the censure of the *De esu carnium*,[77] and then to reprint that tract complemented by fifty-seven scholia. These answer particular objections made mainly by Clichtove, Béda, and Pio to statements about fasting and choice of foods, the celibacy of the priesthood, and rituals but usually avoid the more general and misplaced charges of Lutheranism or schism. This volume also contains the *Dilutio* against Clichtove and the scholia on 122 items in the index of Pio's *Tres et viginti libros*.[78]

RESPONSIO AD COLLATIONES

It is important to recognize when reading Erasmus' irritated and often withering rejoinders to Frans Titelmans that the latter was not in all respects the impertinent tyro that the great humanist would make him appear. He had completed his master of arts in 1521 at the age of nineteen with a brilliant result: *primus in artibus*, that is, best of all the students of the four colleges in Louvain.[79] He shows some knowledge of Greek in his *Collationes* and claims to have used Hebrew sources in some *Adnotationes* first published in 1531, but he always adhered in his lectures and publications to a strictly medieval technique. He continued his studies in theology while teaching philosophy, and though he does not seem to have taken a doctorate in theology, he taught scriptural exegesis to his fellow monks after joining the

* * * * *

76 See Rummel *Critics* II 43–55.
77 *Declarationes ad censuras Lutetiae vulgatas* (Antwerp: De Keysere March 1532); two editions, one octavo, the second a revised quarto edition, were also published by Froben in 1532. LB IX 813–954 reproduces the latter with a slightly different title.
78 For the full titles of the works in this publication, see the list of editions, xli–xliii below. The text of the *De esu carnium* is changed in only minor respects.
79 For Titelmans and a detailed analysis of his *Prologus apologeticus*, see Paolo Sartori 'La controversia neotestamentaria tra Frans Titelmans ed Erasmo da Rotterdam (1527–1530 ca): linee di sviluppo e contenuti' *Humanistica Lovaniensia* 52 (2003) 77–135; this article gives the bibliography of older sources. See also CEBR III 326–7; and Rummel *Critics* II 14–22 and 159–61, with a useful summary of the *Prologus*.

Franciscans in 1523. His first published works, the *Elucidatio in omnes episto-las apostolicas* and three tractates on the mass, appeared in 1528, and he continued to produce works of exegesis and meditation until his early death in 1537; many of these works were popular enough to warrant multiple editions up to the 1580s.[80]

At the age of twenty-seven in 1529, therefore, he may still have been young and inexperienced, but he could not be fairly regarded as ignorant; he did not, like Baechem, refuse to read Erasmus' works, and he was not to be dismissed like 'Taxander' as worse than a pig. It seems that Erasmus thought it necessary to treat his attack rather more as he had that of Edward Lee, finding it advisable to answer at least some of it point by point. It is also possible that some of the heat with which he answered his critic may be explained by the long-delayed and much-cherished project of a commentary on the Epistle to the Romans, which would have been for him the most important text of the New Testament for theological purposes. He had first conceived of this project in 1501 and had even made a vow to complete it in 1514. Several friends, including John Colet and Thomas More, had encouraged him, and he was still promising it in the early editions of the *Annotationes*. After 1522, however, the last occasion on which he repeated this promise,[81] he seems to have been content to let the *Paraphrasis in Romanos* stand in its place; the commentary was never published, despite being listed in the *Catalogus lucubrationum*.[82] The material he had had in mind for the commentary would have nourished his annotations, and it was in part this material that he was defending against Titelmans. The investment he had in it may account to some extent for his reaction.

Titelmans' method and his manner of addressing his opponents was, it must be admitted, ponderous and patronizing. Erasmus was warned in 1527 by friends at Louvain[83] that, though Baechem was now dead, a certain Franciscan was attacking his reputation in his lectures. Erasmus immediately

* * * * *

80 Titelmans is a figure of minor importance for the history of Aristotelianism in the Renaissance, producing a *Dialecticae considerationis libri sex* and a *Compendium naturalis philosophiae*, which fused humanist methods with Franciscan religiosity and remained popular throughout the sixteenth and into the seventeenth centuries. See the *Cambridge History of Renaissance Philosophy* ed Charles B. Schmitt and Quentin Skinner (Cambridge and New York 1988) 227, 795–6, 838.

81 See Reeve II 334, where the last mention of the project is recorded.

82 See CWE 42 xiii–xiv; and the catalogue at Ep 1341A:1333, 1585 with n329, and 1638–9.

83 Ep 1815 to Mercurino Arborio di Gattinara, 29 April 1527

wrote to Titelmans, reminding him of the papal and imperial injunctions forbidding such attacks.[84] Titelmans replied in a letter that foreshadows the nature of his arguments.[85] The next year Erasmus learned that manuscript copies of a book criticizing him were circulating.[86] The *Collationes quinque super epistolam ad Romanos beati Pauli apostoli* were printed by Guilielmus Vorstermann at Antwerp in May 1529.[87] They consist of some 318 articles of greatly varying length, some dealing with emendations made by Lorenzo Valla or Lefèvre d'Etaples only, but most addressed to Erasmus, who is clearly the main target. All the longer articles and all the more virulent reproaches are directed at him, though as Titelmans declares and Erasmus' sarcastic responses show, the title is meant to evoke friendly consultations and modest suggestion.[88] They are in the form of conversations, ostensibly taking place on five separate days, in which Erasmus, Valla, and Lefèvre are made to quote passages from their works, not without distortion on occasion, and are answered by Titelmans.

* * * * *

84 Ep 1823:3–5. For the initial interventions, see Rummel *Critics* II 5–7.
85 Ep 1837A. See also Sartori 82–3.
86 Ep 1994 from Gerard Morinck, 8 May 1528
87 The title page of Bibliotheca Apostolica, MF 11-1986 reads: Collationes quinque super epistolam ad Romanos beati Pauli apostoli, quibus loca eius epistolae difficiliora, ea potissimum quae ex Graecis aliquid habere videntur difficultatis diligentissime tractantur atque explicantur, ita ut etiam a graece nescientibus facile capi valeat emphasis graecarum dictionum, simul et ecclesiastica Novi Testamenti latina aeditio rationabiliter defenditur. Idque ex authoritate veterum interpretum, caeterorumque probatissimorum patrum, latinorum pariter atque graecorum. Per fratrem Franciscum Titelmannum Hassellensem, ordinis Fratrum minorum, sanctarum scripturarum apud Lovanienses praelectorem. Antuerpiae apud Guilielmum Vorstermannum. Anno M.CCCC.XXIX. Mense Maio. Cum gratia et privilegio.
88 *Collationes* 5r–v. The word *collatio* was used in the modern sense of 'critical comparison' in the title of Valla's notes (*In Novum Testamentum, ex diversorum utriusque linguae codicum collatione annotationes*), by Erasmus and correspondents in the description of his own work (Ep 270:67), and by Titelmans himself (eg *Collationes* prologus [b4]r, [c5]v). However Erasmus also used it as an equivalent of Greek *diatribe* 'discussion' or 'argument' in the title of his *De libero arbitrio diatribe sive collatio*, where he certainly meant a peaceful discussion (CWE 76 5 with n1). Titelmans clearly had the same intention, though there is also perhaps an echo of the use of *collatio* to mean the informal discussions held in medieval schools in the afternoon or evening after the formal classes of the morning, a usage deriving from the monastic practice of readings at meals. See R.W. Southern *Scholastic Humanism and the Unification of Europe* (Oxford 2001) II 45–6. Cassian's *Collationes* are usually translated as 'conferences,' but both 'collation' and 'conference' in English would be misleading here.

The work is preceded by a prologue, occupying sixty-eight pages, which declares the writer's intention to defend the received text at every point. Paolo Sartori has shown that it is not simply the prolix and reactionary text that Erasmus may have wanted his readers to think. It is, when viewed objectively, a systematic and balanced defence of a position that is not without connections to other participants in an important contemporary debate and not without some originality. This is not the place to rehearse the whole argument or to discuss Titelmans' sources, but there are two points essential to a fair assessment. First, Titelmans starts from a conviction that the Latin Vulgate of his time represents a translation of the Greek originally made by a translator, the *vetus interpres*, who was divinely inspired, and that this was emended in a minor way by Jerome, whose authority came from the commission he received from Pope Damasus. The Vulgate is therefore authoritative. In connection with this, he argues that the Greek manuscripts to which Erasmus resorts cannot be more reliable than the received Latin text. Erasmus' position here, of course, is that the Translator is unknown, and that a translator in any case, as Jerome declared, is not the same as a prophet (*vates*). Titelmans read Jerome's remark, nevertheless, as not excluding divine inspiration for the Translator.[89] Erasmus believed that Jerome's translation was lost. Second, Titelmans argues that it is inappropriate to apply the standards of classical Latin to a text that was not only divinely inspired but was also composed for readers who did not expect and could not understand the 'elegancies' of that language, whatever its value may be for other sorts of oratorical or literary discourse. The 'barbarisms' and 'solecisms' that Erasmus condemns are therefore to be respected (with the exception of the very few solecisms that may be due to the negligence of copyists). With respect to this point, it may be remarked that Titelmans' position is certainly the more appealing to a modern student, and that Erasmus' desire to accommodate the Latin text to the erudite standards of a humanist readership (see xxxiv–xxxv below), despite his clear recognition of the intention and method of the old Translator, constitutes the most serious weakness of his position. On the other hand, Erasmus insisted, in defending himself, that he was providing a clarification of the accepted text, not a replacement.

Erasmus rehearsed some of his complaints about the attack in a letter of 19 August 1529 to Johann von Botzheim[90] – who had apparently requested a sample of his proposed response – asking him whether he was right in

* * * * *

89 Following the practice of CWE 56 xv, I have capitalized 'Translator' when referring to the translator of the Vulgate.
90 Ep 2206

thinking it better to be silent than to reply. We learn from a subsequent letter to Pieter Gillis that he also sent a copy of his work to 'friends' in Antwerp. To his great displeasure, these 'friends' apparently forestalled his intention and had it published by Petrus Sylvius in October 1529, a publication not only that he judged cheap and inaccurate but that, as he feared, provoked a noisy response.

I wish my pamphlet had not been published there, not only because I appear in a form both shabby and badly corrected but also because, as I understand, what I half feared has happened: I have taken a grasshopper by the wing.[91] Since I thought this could be better considered by friends living there, I submitted to their judgment whether they thought it should be published or suppressed; for if it had been for me to decide to publish, I could have done it here more conveniently, more quickly, and more correctly.[92]

Much of the letter to Botzheim became a part of the preface to the *Responsio ad Collationes*,[93] but Erasmus evidently felt it necessary to do more and to answer at least some of the criticisms in detail, though it is difficult to see on what criterion he could have made his choices.[94] Irritation seems at times to have played as great a part as reason. Of the 318 articles in the *Collationes* he answers 145 and chooses not to answer 173. Most of his answers are short, many dismissive, but some, and notably the one on original sin and the associated accusation of Pelagianism (in Romans 5:12),[95] are substantial.

* * * * *

91 The proverbial expression is in Greek, adapted from *Adagia* i ix 28.
92 Ep 2260:123–9
93 See 141 below, from 'In the long-winded preface.' In LB this preface is printed before the *Responsio ad Collationes* (965D–968E) but separated from it, so that it appears to be the end of the preceding work.
94 Erasmus' work was initially entitled *D. Erasmi Roterodami ad colllationes cuiusdam responsio*. For subsequent variants, see the list of editions, xliii below. The word *gerontodidascalus* did not appear in the title until 1540, though it appears early in the text (138 below). The Greek γεροντοδιδασκάλος is the title of one of the lost Menippean satires of Varro (*M. Terentii Varronis saturarum menippearum fragmenta* ed Raymond Astbury [Leipzig 1985] 32–4), who borrowed the word from Plato (*Euthydemus* 272C). Erasmus may have seen it in Plato or in Nonius Marcellus, who preserves the surviving fragments; it is not, however, in the list of Varro's works given by Jerome, who records simply: '150 books of Menippean satires' (Ep 33 CSEL 54/1 253:18). Cf *Adagia* III iii 10 *Ante barbam doces senes* 'Before you've grown your beard you teach old men.'
95 For Pelagianism, see the article by S.J. McKenna in NCE 11 58–60; and for the context of the dispute with Luther, see Charles Trinkaus' introduction

The published work remained a hasty collection of disparate notes, which Erasmus evidently felt were not worth further work, though some additions and emendations of *1540* lead one to suspect that this may have been among the works for which Froben is known to have possessed corrections made by Erasmus.[96] Nevertheless certain recurring topics are apparent, most of a philological nature, a few touching on matters of doctrine.

A fundamental philological matter for Erasmus is the notion of correct Latin, and it is a notion that distinguishes his practice sharply from modern textual standards. Despite recognizing that the Gospels and Epistles were written in and translated into the popular language of the times, Erasmus prefers to suggest corrections to the Vulgate by the standards of classical Latin, not biblical or patristic, removing what he considers speakers of 'correct' Latin would regard as solecisms.[97] His version of the Scriptures was intended for the Latin-speaking elite of his day, not for the ordinary public – for which he would have advocated a vernacular translation – and was therefore to be in what the elite would accept and understand as correct Latin. For this purpose Erasmus demands the usage of those he refers to as 'Latin speakers'[98] – that is, people who speak correct Latin, including himself – or 'the standard authors of the Latin language.'[99] In this work he names as examples of such authority Cicero, Horace, Pliny the Elder, Seneca, Quintilian, Terence, Suetonius, and the jurists: 'whose authority allows us to excuse a solecism' (237 below). But the Fathers of the church, even the earliest, Tertullian, even the much-admired Jerome, are not to be taken as witnesses of correct Latin. They may have been 'Latins,' but they wrote for a popular audience, whose usage was

* * * * *

to CWE 76. For the dispute with Titelmans, see 186–205 below. The texts referred to by Erasmus and Titelmans as the *Hieronymiana* or 'possibly Jerome's' were, unfortunately for both disputants, mainly by Pelagius who lived before Jerome, with interpolations by a later Pseudo-Jerome. See Souter II 225 (Pelagius) and III 43 (Pseudo-Jerome), where he separates the two texts. See also CWE 56 155 n22. Migne's edition in PL 30 reproduces Erasmus' edition (Froben 1516) of Pseudo-Jerome but, according to Souter (I 6), unsatisfactorily.

96 See the General Introduction ASD I-1 ix.
97 See the prologue of the *Responsio ad Collationes* 142–3 below.
98 See, for an example among many others, the note on *confundit* and *pudefacit* (Rom 5:5, 184 below).
99 For example, at the end of the note on Rom 6:23 (211 below), where he accuses Titelmans of having no experience in the *probatis auctoribus Latinae linguae*.

often contaminated by Greek, or they wrote at a time when Latin was in decline.[100]

A closely related question is that of the authority of the Translator, that is, whether he is to be regarded as inspired by the Holy Spirit, and whether his language may be corrected. Erasmus deals with the question at some length in his preface, countering Titelmans' charges that he, Valla, and Lefèvre have treated the Translator, who should be regarded as divinely inspired, with disrespect and have 'trampled' (141 below) his translation. Erasmus points out that it is not known whether he was 'a Jew, a pagan, or a Christian, a heretic or a believer, a cobbler or a soldier, a youth or a veteran, a man or a woman,' that he was not known to the church, that a translator does not perform the same sort of interpretation as one who expounds the spiritual meaning,[101] and that the language of the New Testament is in any case quite simple. If he, Erasmus, is guilty of such disrespect, other interpreters, including Jerome, should also be regarded as guilty in the same way.[102] Erasmus, however, does not accept that the Translator was divinely inspired at every point and feels no compunction at accusing him on occasion of error and of 'dozing' (164 below). The *vetus interpres* was providing only a translation of the apostles' Greek, which was inspired, of course, and he 'speaks to common folk.'[103]

An example of the sort of linguistic subject on which Titelmans repeatedly attacks Erasmus is that of *copia* or variation of vocabulary. Erasmus, who was well known for his commendation of *copia* in literary composition and not averse to it in his own translation of the New Testament,[104] nevertheless criticizes the Translator of the Vulgate on several occasions

* * * * *

100 For particularly clear examples, see the notes on *imputare* and *reputare* in Rom 4:3 (174 below, where his one reference to Plautus is based on an unauthorized interpolation) and on *auditus* in Rom 10:16 (236 below). For the list of *Soloecismi* and *Loca manifeste depravata* added to the second edition of the *Annotationes*, see LB VI *5r–**[1]v.

101 Cf the *Capita argumentorum contra morosos*, which formed a preface for the fourth (1527) and fifth (1535) editions of the *Annotationes* (LB VI **2r–***[4]r). See also Sartori 110–12.

102 143 and 144 below

103 Cf the note on Rom 2:15, 164 below. For a discussion of the point, see Eugene F. Rice Jr *Saint Jerome in the Renaissance* (Baltimore 1985) chapter 7 and especially 181–2.

104 See Germain Marc'hadour 'Phobie de la répétition chez S. Jérome, Erasme et Tyndale' in *Les problèmes d'expression dans la traduction biblique* ed Henri Gibaud (Angers 1988) 43–56; Hamilton 103–5.

for rendering the same Greek word with different Latin ones. Titelmans objected, and in his *Responsio ad Collationes* Erasmus counters: 'Variety in translation is not a fault, dear boy, but translating good Greek with bad Latin is an elementary fault, and the affectation of variety where it serves no purpose is inept.'[105] Regarding Romans 4, where Lorenzo Valla had complained that one Greek word (λογίζεσθαι), occurring seven times in verses 3–11, had been rendered in the Vulgate in three different ways (*imputare, accepto ferre,* and *reputare*),[106] Erasmus not only agrees with Valla, using *imputare* every time, and speaks of the Translator's 'childish striving for variety,' but dismisses Titelmans' attempt to defend the Translator by making silly distinctions.[107]

In Romans 8 a recurring subject of dispute is the Greek verb φρονεῖν and the noun φρόνημα, which have a range of meanings around the ideas of thought and feeling and cannot be rendered by the same Latin word in every context, for example: 'For they that are according to the flesh *mind* the things that are of the flesh, but they that are according to the Spirit *mind* the things that are of the Spirit' and 'Because the *wisdom* of the flesh is an enemy to God . . .'[108] Titelmans had attempted to turn Erasmus' strictures on the Translator's love of *copia* against him because Erasmus had used *curare* to translate the verb and *affectus* for the noun. Erasmus justifies himself on the grounds of good Latin idiom: 'It is not a question of meaning but of the appropriateness of the language . . . I can give reason for my variety.'[109] This particular criticism continued to annoy Erasmus, as can be seen in the letter to Pieter Gillis (Ep 2260), where he expands his argument over nearly four pages of Allen's edition.

The long response about the phrase in Romans 5:12, 'inasmuch as all have sinned,'[110] includes elements relating to the question of good Latin but is mainly concerned with a charge of exposing the church to the attacks of Pelagian heretics and a charge of heresy against Erasmus himself. The annotation started life in 1516 as half a dozen lines on the Greek expression ἐφ' ᾧ, which Erasmus translated initially as *in eo quod* 'in this that' and subsequently as *quatenus* 'inasmuch as.' The Vulgate translates the expression as *in quo*, which, like ἐφ' ᾧ, could mean either 'in whom' or 'in

* * * * *

105 See 153 below.
106 Valla I 856 2
107 See 153–4 below.
108 Rom 8:5, 7; my italics
109 See 216 below.
110 For the annotation, see LB VI 585B–590B.

which' but was generally taken to mean 'in Adam.' Erasmus' translation and initial short note immediately evoked the criticism from Edward Lee that, allowing as it does the possibility of reading the verse as referring to individual sin rather than original sin, he was attacking the latter doctrine and opening the text to that Pelagian reading against which St Augustine had fought so hard.[111] Erasmus responded in 1519 with a reference to supporting interpretations of Ambrose (Ambrosiaster) and Origen, and added Chrysostom, Theophylact, and the commentaries of Pseudo-Jerome to these in 1527. Titelmans renewed the attack at much greater length, making four points. Two of these Erasmus dismissed as editing or printing mistakes. The third, in which Titelmans tried to distinguish between the verbs *pertransire* and *pervadere* 'spread through,' he answers briefly, pointing out that he had responded on this point to Lee.[112] The main discussion in both the *Responsio ad Collationes* and the annotation, as consequently expanded in 1535, is concerned with the translation and implications of the conjunctive phrase ἐφ' ᾧ as *quatenus*. Titelmans would have it that this translation excludes the possibility of understanding the passage as referring to original sin and removes from the church its most effective defence against the Pelagians, who deny original sin. Erasmus' reply, in summary, is that he said no more than that ἐφ' ᾧ can be understood differently; that this passage is not the most effective proof of original sin; that Augustine, lacking as he did a knowledge of Greek, cannot be regarded as authoritative on this point; that scholastic theologians propound doctrines on this subject that would have shocked Augustine; that he, Erasmus, is far from being the only one to interpret the passage in this way; that Pseudo-Jerome, Origen, Chrysostom, and Theophylact all support his reading; and finally that the context of Romans 3 and 4 has nothing that refers to original sin. The argument is powerful, but we may suppose that the length of the response suggests Erasmus was seriously worried by the charge and was perhaps even aware of the delicacy of his position. He had, of course, faced the same charge from Luther.[113]

Titelmans sought to continue his assault with an *Epistola apologetica*,[114] which was a further defence of the Translator of the New Testament, then

* * * * *

111 For the context of the disputes with Lee, see Erika Rummel's introduction to CWE 72, with Erasmus' response to Lee on this point in *Responsio ad annotationes Lei* 2 'Concerning note 141' CWE 72 269. See also 201 below nn25 and 34.
112 See *Responsio ad annotationes Lei* [2] 'Concerning note 142' CWE 72 270–1.
113 See Rom 5:12, 201 below n29.
114 Vorstermann 1530. Part of the text is Ep 2245.

turned his attention to the canonicity of the book of Revelation and the identity of 'St John' in *Libri duo de authoritate libri Apocalypsis*,[115] which Erasmus had questioned in one of his annotations.[116] Fearing that his response would only provoke an even noisier reaction from his opponent, Erasmus did not reply to either, though he continued to grumble about Titelmans in his letters to others.[117]

CONCLUSION:
THE FEEDBACK INTO THE *ANNOTATIONES*

The three apologiae in this volume, having been provoked by attacks on the earlier editions of the *Annotationes*, furnished substantial material in turn for the later editions. The *De esu carnium*, though it amplifies material found in the annotation on Matthew 11:30, does not lead to a further expansion of that note. The enlargement of the annotation on the word *verbum* in John 1:1 from 1522 consists mainly of the additional references to patristic authorities for the use of *sermo*; they characterize this apologia as a good example of Erasmus' philological method, the note being increased by as much as three pages in 1535.[118] Both patristic references and the exegetical argument of the *Apologia de loco 'Omnes quidem'* make for a similar expansion of the annotation in the 1522 and later editions. But Erasmus is not satisfied in most cases with amplifying the philological and exegetical material of his annotations. He obviously feels impelled also to continue replying to the personal attacks that have been made on him.[119] In the case of the *Apologia de loco 'Omnes quidem'* he concludes with a defence against the methods of his attackers, added in 1522 and, with some minor additions in 1527 and 1535, occupying forty-two lines of this last edition.[120] He refrains from naming his attackers here, but makes it quite clear, for his contemporaries at least, who they are and includes at the end a sly reference to Louvain theologians in a purportedly casual example. In the

* * * * *

115 Hillen 1530. The preface is Ep 2417. See Rummel *Critics* II 20–2.
116 LB VI 1123E–1126A
117 Epp 2260, 2275, 2807. In the first of these he says that one of the reasons for his reluctance was that he may have 'taken a grasshopper by the wing'; see the *Adagia* I ix 28.
118 See Reeve I 218–21.
119 Cf Rummel *Annotations* 126 and *Critics* I 189–90.
120 LB VI 741F–743F; Reeve II 518–19

case of the largely rewritten annotation of 1535 on Romans 5:12, he concludes with an attack on 'modern theologians,' which is clearly a reflection of his response to Titelmans' concluding attack on those who question everything and seek nothing but novelties,[121] that is, of course, the
humanists.

Two items provide excellent examples of an important feature of Erasmus' critical method: that is, the resort to context to determine the meaning
and intention of a passage.[122] In both the *Apologia de loco 'Omnes quidem'*
and the *Responsio ad Collationes* he mentions the point explicitly. In the first,
as we have noted above, we read this conclusion to the argument about the
meaning of Paul's assertion 'We shall not all sleep': 'This is the only way
to attain to the real meaning of Scripture, by paying careful attention to
what the writer is talking about.'[123] In the *Responsio*, among many other references to the importance of context, Erasmus responds at one moment to
Titelmans' claim of support from Origen: 'He is allowed to philosophize in
allegories; it is something he does freely, even to the point of strain. My
task is to expound those things that are appropriate in the context of the
present passage.'[124] And in the major discussion on original and personal
sin we read:

For this is now my interpretation: Paul is not speaking here of infants who, as I believe, were not customarily baptized at that time but of adults, as he does almost
everywhere. This is made likely by the very context of the discussion. In chapter 3
'They have all turned aside, together they are become unprofitable' cannot be referred to original sin. Likewise the preceding passages in the first and second chapters where he reproaches the gentiles for their evil deeds. And it does not refer
to anything else when he concludes against both [Jews and gentiles], 'For all have
sinned and fall short of the glory of God.' Nor does there seem to be anything that
refers to original sin in the fourth chapter whose conclusion is 'Who was delivered
for our offences and rose again for our justification.' When this conclusion is followed by this statement 'Therefore being justified by faith . . .,' it is very clear that
this too refers to the sin of action. And what follows shortly – '[Christ] died for
the ungodly' – cannot be referred to infants; they are said to be exempt from justice and cannot be said to be unrighteous. And so since up to this point the whole

* * * * *

121 Cf 197 below; *Collationes* 132r–133r; and CWE 56 151 n83.
122 Cf Chomarat II 579–81.
123 See 57 below.
124 Rom 4:17; see 179 below.

discussion has dealt with personal sins and to this is added 'Wherefore, as by one man sin [entered into the world],' does it not seem clumsy to have gone over suddenly to another sort of sin? There is nothing here either to force us to read it in the sense of original sin . . .'[125]

The corresponding annotation was largely rewritten in 1535 and extended to five whole columns of the folio pages of LB, having been only three sentences in 1516 and having occupied no more than twenty lines in 1527. The expansion was mostly based on what Erasmus had said in his response to Titelmans and included an amplification of this argument from context.[126]

Erasmus also expanded, or rewrote entirely, other annotations on Romans for the 1535 edition as a result of the controversy with Titelmans. Of course some changes in this edition have nothing to do with the dispute with Titelmans, some, on the other hand, are responses to Titelmans but do not appear in the *Responsio*. However it is reasonable to say that most of the changes introduced as a result of this dispute were part of a process that appears to have become dominant after 1527. Erasmus claims more than once that his notes, designed originally to help scholars read the Vulgate correctly and fruitfully, were not intended to replace the accepted text or to be discussed before the general, uneducated public.[127] But from edition to edition the *Annotationes* became increasingly an instrument of his polemic against his Catholic critics; and are therefore addressed not only to scholars but to the larger public of actual and potential opponents. Beyond his irritation and impatience with Standish, Baechem, or Titelmans, Erasmus still found it necessary to publish, through the medium of the *Annotations*, a less ephemeral, more considered, and more widely disseminated response on certain major issues than he would achieve with the hasty publication of his apologiae. These issues concern not merely such topics as correct Latin or the need for *copia* but also heresy and the validity of humanist philology. The arguments about the language the Vulgate uses or should use must always be seen as a part of the larger dispute about scholastic[128] and humanist method, and ultimately of the fundamental dispute about the right to interpret Scripture.

* * * * *

125 Rom 5:12; see 199 below.
126 LB IX 587B–589B; CWE 56 144–8
127 See for example the *Apologia de 'In principio erat sermo'* 17 below.
128 For Erasmus' position on scholastic theologians, see his *Apologia contra Latomi dialogum* CWE 71 and Ep 1002:11–24.

EDITIONS OF THE TEXTS

APOLOGIA DE 'IN PRINCIPIO ERAT SERMO'

1520a *Apologia Erasmi Roterodami palam refellens quorundam seditiosos clamo-res apud populum ac magnates, quibus ut impie factum iactitant, quod in evangelio Ioannis verterit, In principio erat sermo.* There appear to have been six booksellers involved in this edition, Dirk Martens (Louvain), Froben (Basel), E. Cervicornus (Cologne with colophon date March 1520), F. Peypus (Nuremberg), M. Hillen (Antwerp) and Jo. Schöffer (Mainz with colophon date June 1520). Copy used: microfilm of BL 3905 ee 128 (Nuremberg; with Ep 1072).

1520b *Apologia de In principio erat sermo* ... bound with *Epistolae aliquot eruditorum virorum* (Basel: Froben 1520).

1521/2 *De in principio erat sermo apologia* in *Apologiae Erasmi Roterodami omnes, adversus eos, qui illum locis aliquot, in suis libris non satis circumspecte sunt calumniati* (Basel: Froben November 1521 and February 1522). Copy of the 1522 issue in Cambridge University Library, Adv.a.5.1, with manuscript marginalia in Erasmus' handwriting. *De in principio erat sermo apologia* is the sixth of the seven works in this volume, occupying pages 133–48.[129] The *1521* issue appears to have contained five works: *In Iacobi Fabrum Stapulensem apologia; In Iacobi Latomi dialogum apologia; In quendam pro declamatione matrimonii apologia; De in principio erat sermo apologia; In Eduardum Leum apologia* (which includes both responses to Lee). In *1522* these are still on pages numbered 1–366⁺ (some final leaves are missing from the Cambridge copy). The other two works added in *1522* (*In Iacobum Lopim Stunicam apologia* and *In quendam de loco* ... *Omnes quidem resurgemus* ... were inserted at the beginning and are on unnumbered pages. Evidently annotating the Cambridge copy in preparation for a further edition, Erasmus has written under the list of titles: *Hi tituli ponantur proxima facie* 'Let these titles be placed on the next page.'

1540 *Des. Erasmi Roterodami Apologia de In principio erat sermo in Erasmi opera omnia* (Basel: Froben 1540) IX 95–104

* * * * *

129 Vander Haeghen 12. H.J. de Jonge has pointed out that not all the manuscript annotations in this volume are by Erasmus himself; 'Aantekeningen van Erasmus in een Exemplaar van zijn *Apologiae omnes* (1522)' *Nederlands Archief voor Kerkgeschiedenis* 58/2 (1978) 176–89. However all those added to this particular item appear to be genuine, since they are all incorporated into the text of *1540.*

LB   *D. Erasmi Roterodami Apologia de In principio erat sermo* (Leiden 1703–
      6) LB IX 111–22

APOLOGIA DE LOCO 'OMNES QUIDEM'

1522   *In quendam de loco, qui est apud Paulum ad Corinth. I. cap. XV. Omnes
       quidem resurgemus etc. Quae recens ab autore profecta, nunc primum om-
       nium in lucem prodiit apolog. II in Apologiae Erasmi Roterodami omnes,
       adversus eos, qui illum locis aliquot, in suis libris non satis circumspecte
       sunt calumniati* (Basel: Froben February 1522). The first issue of this
       edition of the *Apologiae omnes* (November 1521; see xli above) does
       not contain the *Apologia ad annotationes Stunicae* (entitled in this edi-
       tion *In Iacobum Lopim Stunicam apologiae* I) or this text. They are in-
       serted on unnumbered pages as the first and second items in this
       issue, this text occupying ten pages and four lines on fols HH2v–
       A[1]v, and in another issue they follow *Erasmi in Iac. Lopim Stunicam
       ... apologia* (Strasbourg: Huld. Mohardus 1522; 1525).[130]

1540   *Apologia de loco taxato in publica professione per Nicolaum Ecmondanum,
       theologum et carmelitanum Lovaniensem. Locus est in epistola Pauli ad
       Corinthios priore, cap. xv, Omnes quidem resurgemus, sed non omnes im-
       mutabimur in Erasmi opera omnia* (Basel: Froben 1540) IX 359

LB   *Desiderii Erasmi Roterodami apologia de loco taxato in publica professione
       per Nicolaum Ecmondanum, theologum et Carmelitanum Lovaniensem. Lo-
       cus est in epistola Pauli ad Corinthios priore, cap. xv. Omnes quidem
       resurgemus, sed non omnes immutabimur* (Leiden 1703–6) LB IX 433–
       42

Asso   Cecilia Asso 'Erasmus' *Apologia de loco "Omnes quidem resurgemus"'
       Archivio italiano per la storia della pietà* 15 (2003) 165–201

DE ESU CARNIUM **AND** *DE DELECTU CIBORUM SCHOLIA*

1522   *Ad reverendum in Christo patrem et illustrem principem Christophorum
       episcopum Basiliensem, epistola apologetica Erasmi Roterodami, de inter-
       dicto esu carnium, deque similibus hominum constitutionibus. Cum aliis
       nonnullis novis, quorum titulos reperies in proxima pagella* (Basel: Froben
       7 August 1522). C. Augustijn (ASD IX-1) lists six issues of this edition,
       the other five are by H. Alopecius of Cologne, I. Soter of Cologne,
       I. Knoblouchius of Strasbourg, S. Grimm of Augsburg, and V. Schu-
       mann of Leipzig[?]. An edition by Froben of 1523, given by Vander

* * * * *

130 Vander Haeghen 13

Haeghen, is not listed by Augustijn. The latter describes six more issues for this date, two by Alopecius, one by Soter, two by P. Vidoue of Paris for C. Resch and G. Dupré, and one by W. Zuseler of Deventer. The British Library has copies of Lyon editions by S. Gryphius dated 1525[?] and 1529[?].

1532   *D. Erasmi Roterodami dilutio eorum quae Iodocus Clichtoveus scripsit adversus declamationem suasoriam matrimonii. Epistola eiusdem de delectu ciborum, cum scholiis per ipsum autorem recens additis. In elenchum Alberti Pii brevissima scholia per eundem Erasmum Roterodamum* (Basel: Froben 1532). The scholia are on pages 129–75. Augustijn lists an undated issue by S. Gryphius and two other issues without place, date, or printer. There were also German and English editions before 1536.

1540   In *Erasmi opera omnia* (Basel: Froben 1540) IX 982. Does not contain the scholia.

LB   *Desiderii Erasmi epistola apologetica de interdicto esu carnium, deque similibus hominum constitutionibus. Ad reverendum in Christo patrem et illustrem principem, Christophorum episcopum Basiliensem* (Leiden 1703–6) LB IX 1197–1214. Does not contain the scholia.

ASD   *Epistola de interdicto esu carnium* and *In epistolam de delectu ciborum scholia* in *Opera omnia* ... ed C. Augustijn (Amsterdam 1982) IX-1 3–50 and 51–89

RESPONSIO AD COLLATIONES

1529   [Title page] *D. Erasmi Roterodami ad collationes cuiusdam. Opus recens* (Antwerp: Petrus Sylvius 7 October 1529; the colophon reads 15 October 1529). After the prefatory letter the title reads: *D. Erasmi Roterodami ad collationes cuiusdam responsio.* 4 + 54 folios, A[8]–H2. Vander Haeghen records an issue of this edition by Hieronymus Denis of Paris.

1540   *Des. Erasmi Roterodami ad collationes cuiusdam iuvenis gerontodidascali responsio* in *Erasmi opera omnia* (Basel: Froben 1540) IX 786–824

LB   *Desiderii Erasmi responsio ad Collationes cuiusdam iuvenis gerontodidascali* (Leiden 1703–6) LB IX 965D–1016B

ACKNOWLEDGMENTS

This volume has relied heavily on the work of predecessors to whom I gladly acknowledge my debts. Two of the translations presented here are based on recent new editions; that of the *Apologia de loco 'Omnes quidem'* on the text published by Cecilia Asso, and that of the *De esu carnium* and its subsequent scholia on the ASD edition by Cornelis Augustijn. Their studies and annotations, as well as their texts, served as solid foundations for the translations. The *Apologia de 'In principio erat sermo'* has benefited particularly from the work of Marjorie O'Rourke Boyle. A translation of the first short version of this apologia has been added so that the reader can see how the work was expanded. Annotation of the *Responsio ad Collationes* was made immensely easier by the CWE 56 edition of the *Annotationes in Romanos* by Robert D. Sider, John B. Payne, Albert Rabil, and Warren S. Smith. Here the *Responsio* has been set out with Erasmus' translation of each verse and the Vulgate text as rubrics in the same manner as the *Annotationes* in that volume. The analysis of Titelmans' prologue by Paolo Sartori proved to be an essential counterweight to Erasmus' own account of that controversy. Among more general works, the studies by Erika Rummel and Jacques Chomarat have shown themselves on many occasions to be particularly useful. The editions of the *Annotationes* by Anne Reeve and Michael A. Screech and of Erasmus' correspondence in CWE have proved to be invaluable sources of information. Invaluable also were the very detailed comments of Sister Mechtilde O'Mara, Professor John Grant, and other anonymous readers who gave generously of their time and experience to matters of both language and content. Valuable help with certain problematical passages was given by Professor Alexander Dalzell. Any shortcomings that remain are, of course, entirely my own responsibility. In addition to this I wish to publish my thanks to the University of Waikato for the facilities made available to me as a research associate, to the university's librarians for their efforts in obtaining copies of works often difficult to find, and to Philip Abela of the library of the University of Auckland for his patience in helping me to consult that enormously useful electronic resource, the Cetedoc Library of Christian Latin Texts (CLCLT) published by Brepols. Finally my thanks go to those who have collaborated on this volume at UTP, in particular to the late Ron Schoeffel, to Suzanne Rancourt, and to my copy editor Carla DeSantis.

DLD

Translator's Note

The bases for the translations in this volume are as follows:

- for the first, short version of the *Apologia de 'In principio erat sermo'* (1520a), a microfilm of the copy in the British Library (3905 ee 128)
- for the second, longer version (1520b), the 1522 edition in the copy of the *Apologiae Erasmi Roterodami omnes*, Froben 1522, held in Cambridge University Library with marginalia in Erasmus' hand (see xli above), the *Opera omnia* of 1540, and LB. No copy of the 1520 edition by Froben was available.
- for the *Apologia de loco 'Omnes quidem,'* the critical text published in Asso. This is the text published in the *Apologiae omnes* by Froben in 1522. The copy held in Cambridge University Library with marginalia in Erasmus' hand has also been consulted.
- for the *De esu carnium* and the *De delectu ciborum scholia*, the critical edition in ASD IX-1
- for the *Responsio ad Collationes*, the first edition of 1529 and the Basel edition of the *Opera omnia* (1540). The use of an italic font to mark quoted speech in LB was a useful guide in this text where Erasmus often quotes or pretends to quote Titelmans; but it is a guide to be used with caution since it is not entirely reliable. This text has been set out with Erasmus' translation of each biblical verse (ER) and the accepted Vulgate text published in 1527 (VG) as rubrics in the same manner as the *Annotationes in epistolam ad Romanos* in CWE 56 (see also 147 below, n2 of the first article on Romans 1:3 of the *Responsio ad Collationes*).

Biblical texts in English are generally quoted according to the Douay-Rheims version of the Vulgate (DV), unless the Authorized or Revised Standard Versions (AV or RSV) present a relevant variation. All exceptions to this practice are noted. The Douay translation, revised by Bishop Richard Challoner, dates from the eighteenth century, and as a result there is some mixture of old and modern usage and styles; but the gain in consistency and accessibility to the linguistic questions is sufficient to offset this. Biblical texts in Latin are from the standard Clementine Vulgate. In the case of the *Responsio ad Collationes*, references to the Vulgate are to the version of the accepted text published in 1527 (VG), which is likely to be that which Erasmus used. For the cue phrases from the Vulgate here, I usually follow the translations of CWE 56, unless there is reason to give a more literal rendering. English translations of Erasmus' Latin New Testament are made as literal as possible. References to his letters use the letter and line numbering of CWE unless otherwise indicated.

A DEFENCE BY ERASMUS OF ROTTERDAM PUBLICLY REFUTING THE MISCHIEVOUS CLAMOUR OF CERTAIN MEN AMONG PEOPLE BOTH HUMBLE AND INFLUENTIAL TO WHOM THEY DECLARE THAT IT WAS AN IMPIETY ON HIS PART TO TRANSLATE IN THE GOSPEL OF JOHN: *IN PRINCIPIO ERAT SERMO* (1520a)

Apologia Erasmi Roterodami palam refellens quorundam seditiosos clamores apud populum ac magnates, quibus ut impie factum iactitant, quod in evangelio Ioannis verterit 'In principio erat sermo'

ERASMUS OF ROTTERDAM TO THE READER, GREETING[1]

A book by Edward Lee has suddenly appeared.[2] Of its quality, although it is an attack on myself, I express no opinion; the wise reader will decide on the facts. In the meantime I would make one request of everyone: to suspend judgment until the appearance of my reply. I have written an answer to his defences in these last three days, attempting the extremely difficult task of replying to abuse without being abusive myself. I now address myself to his notes, to which ten days at most will be allotted, although he took more than two years. And yet in the old days defending counsel was allowed more time on the clock than the prosecutor.[3]

Reader, farewell, and keep the other ear free and open for my reply.

* * * * *

1 Ep 1072, [end of February] 1520. The 'defences' (apologiae) of Lee are his Annotationum libri duo; Erasmus' first reply is his Apologia invectivis Lei (not published until March 1520), and the reply to Lee's notes was the Responsio ad annotationes Lei (April/May 1520).
2 See the introduction xv and n9.
3 Aeschines In Ctesiphon 197. Cf Adagia I iv 73.

A DEFENCE BY ERASMUS OF
IN PRINCIPIO ERAT SERMO
(1520a)[1]

ERASMUS OF ROTTERDAM TO HIS FAIR-MINDED READERS,
MANY GREETINGS
Homer once expressed wonder that mortals never have a surfeit of the most
calamitous thing, meaning war of course, though they do become sick of
sleep, food, drink, dancing, singing, and everything else that is agreeable.[2]
I myself wonder that there are some who take the most persistent pleasure
in repeatedly stirring up new troubles to harm both scholarship and the
Christian religion. Recently a certain man, respected for his teaching of
theology and religion and distinguished by his standing as bishop,[3] set out at
a crowded sermon in London to speak to the people about charity and then
suddenly began to rant against my translation, making a great commotion
because in the Gospel of John I translated *logos* with *sermo* instead of *verbum*;
and he has represented this passage as if nothing could excuse or mitigate it.

Look (he says), we, who have been doctors for so many years already, will have
to go back again to elementary school. For although the whole church has read *In
principio erat verbum* for a thousand years and more hitherto, now after all that time,
for heaven's sake, some ape of the Greeks will teach us *In principio erat sermo*. But
Augustine, though he informs us that the Greek word *logos* means both *verbum* and
ratio for Latin speakers, nevertheless prefers *verbum* to *ratio* in this passage.[4] For
verbum is better suited to denote the second person in the divine context for the

* * * * *

1 The following is the translation of the first, short version of the *Apologia*,
  referred to as 1520a. For the more familiar longer version, referred to as
  1520b, which appeared some five months later, see 13 below.
2 Homer *Iliad* 13.633–9
3 Henry Standish, bishop of St Asaph
4 Augustine *De trinitate* 15.16 CCSL 50A 500/PL 42 1079, where Augustine opposes *verbum* and *cogitatio*, not *ratio*. Cf Ep 1126:30–1.

reasons that Augustine alleges. But these reasons (he says) are not understood by these imitators of Greeks, and yet they dare to contaminate the Scriptures.

As he thought the point was well made, he set out to invoke the support of the mayor of London (for this person was present at the time by tradition) and of the citizens of London, begging that they should not allow new translations, which would undermine the authority of Holy Scripture, to insinuate themselves any further. At about the same time, in the church of St Gudula in Brussels a certain Carmelite[5] – I won't give his name though he did not withhold mine – said from the pulpit before a large congregation of the people, among other things, that there was a certain Erasmus who dared to correct the Gospel of John. A similar commotion occurred in Paris, as I learned from the letters of some friends. The same nonsense is bandied about everywhere among influential courtiers at their banquets.

In the first place, is it not sheer mischief making to bawl about these matters before the ignorant mass of people, among tanners and petty women? And eminent courtiers differ in the very smallest degree from the judgment of such people in these matters. I wrote those notes for the learned, not for the general public, nor do I read a different text in church from what others read. I did not seek to get the pope to remove the old translation but to enable it to be read more clearly and correctly with the help of my privately compiled version. Now, they not only broadcast seditiously what was intended to be discussed among qualified people, but they deceive the public also to provoke it the more. For when humble people hear that there is someone correcting John's Gospel, they do not understand that my business is with the appropriateness of the translation, but they think I am condemning what John himself wrote. They take it the same way when they hear of someone correcting the Lord's Prayer and the Magnificat and other such things. Nor is it only the common people who take it this way but even certain men who want to be considered rabbis by everyone. I could point the finger, if I wish, for there are some who hardly know that John wrote in a language other than Latin. I am aware that the labour undertaken in refuting these ideas is largely vain, but still, as far as *verbum* and *sermo* are concerned, I shall make a brief answer.

To begin let us suppose that the Son of God is nowhere designated in the Bible by the word *sermo*. Come now, would it be irreverent to call

* * * * *

5 Probably one Jan Robyns. See the introduction xvii n22. Described in *1520b* as a bachelor of theology and a pupil of the 'Camelite,' ie of Nicolaas Baechem.

him by that name, since according to these people the terms *sermo* and *verbum* mean the same whenever we are speaking of human things? For no human terms properly express divine things.[6] Because the Father is called just 'God,' may I not on that account call him 'parent' or 'sire'? Because the Son is always so called, can he not be called 'child' or 'offspring' or something else that has the same force? But if both words, *sermo* and *verbum*, are found in the Bible, as I shall shortly demonstrate, we have only to compare to see which of the two expresses more closely the Greek word *logos*. This word has multiple meanings: it may be 'discourse' [*oratio*], 'reasoning' [*ratio*], 'calculation' [*computus*], and 'speech' [*sermo*], all of which Jerome nevertheless thinks are suitable in some way for the Son of God. However, Latin speakers preferred the term *verbum* or *sermo*. The fact that Augustine states that the word *verbum* is more appropriate than *ratio*[7] to designate the Son of God is irrelevant to me, since I am comparing *sermo* with *verbum*, not with *ratio*, and I suggest *sermo* without rejecting *verbum*.

What we call in the narrow sense *verbum* the Greeks call *rhema* [verb], which I believe is used nowhere in the holy Scriptures for the Son of God. However I do not deny that in Latin authors *verbum* is sometimes used for some short saying, such as a proverb or an aphorism. However *logos* is more correctly and more commonly expressed by *oratio* and *sermo* than *verbum*. Then, if there is no difference between *verbum* and *sermo*, congruency of gender certainly favours the word *sermo*; otherwise I would prefer *oratio* to *sermo* because *sermo* often means conversation when a number of people are chatting in a familiar manner. For just as *sermo divinus factus est homo* [the divine Word was made man] is easier to accept than *divina facta est homo*,[8] so *verbum factum est homo* would be harsher if custom did not make it more acceptable. So the question should not have been thrashed out in an uproar even if the Son of God had never up until now been called *sermo*, especially in private reading.

Now there was even less need that this should happen, because both in Holy Scriptures and in the orthodox Doctors you will find that Christ is called *sermo*. First, the reading in what is called the book of Wisdom, chapter 18, 'Thy all powerful word [*sermo*], O Lord, leaping from heaven,

* * * * *

6 For a full discussion of this point, see the first three paragraphs of the *Paraphrasis in Joannem* CWE 46 13–15. Cf 18 below.
7 See n4.
8 John 1:14. This phrase, which is omitted in *1520b*, *1540*, and LB (114A), should probably be: [*oratio*] *divina facta est homo*. See also 19 n20 below; *Apologia de 'In principio erat sermo'* (*1520b*) n20.

comes from the royal throne,'[9] has been interpreted and chanted by the church as applying to Christ for so many centuries now. Someone will say this is found only once in Holy Scripture. Let us allow this is so – though I shall soon prove otherwise – the fact that the church chants this one example so often makes it apparently a very common expression. But, lest this be for some any ground at all for shuffling, St Thomas brings in this witness about the Son of God too, when he interprets the passage from the Epistle of Paul to the Hebrews, chapter 4.[10] But I think it would be better to give his own words. He says:

That word [ie *sermo*] in itself seems to present some difficulty, but if we consider another translation, it is clearer. For where we have *sermo*, in Greek there is *logos*, which is the same as *verbum*; so for *sermo* read *verbum*. And this is how Augustine expounds the verse in John 12:[11] 'The word [*sermo*] that I have spoken ...' that is, 'I who am the Word [*verbum*].' In the book of Wisdom, chapter 18: 'Thy all powerful word [*sermo*], O Lord, leaping from heaven, comes from the royal throne'[12] and this likewise: 'The Word [*sermo*] of God is living,' that is, 'The Word [*verbum*] of God is living.'[13]

Thus far I have repeated his words, from which it is clear that he makes no distinction between *sermo* and *verbum*. It is also clear from the whole of his interpretation that this passage [ie John 12:48] is to be applied to Christ. In fact the gloss known as the *Interlinear Gloss* interprets this same passage as applying to Christ; it says, 'The Word [*sermo*] of God, that is, the Son of God,' not to add what follows in the same sense.[14] Lyra agrees and Cardinal

* * * * *

9 Wisd of Sol 18:15 *Omnipotens sermo tuus, domine, exiliens de coelo a regalibus sedibus venit*; 'Thy almighty word leapt down from heaven from thy royal throne.'

10 Thomas Aquinas *Opera omnia* ed L. Vives (Paris 1876) 21 614–15; *S. Thomae Aquinatis super epistolas S. Pauli lectura* ed P. Raffaele Cai (Turin 1953) II 383–4; Heb 4:12

11 John 12:48; *sermo*

12 See n9 above.

13 Heb 4:12; Augustine *In Iohannis evangelium tractatus* 54 6 CCSL 36 461/PL 35 1783

14 *Biblia latina* IV [255a]; these volumes have no page numbers and no continuous sequence of signatures. The copy reproduced has page numbers in manuscript, but these are often illegible. They are given where possible in square brackets, but it is sometimes necessary to search at the appropriate biblical book and chapter. The *Interlinear Gloss* at John 12:48 says: 'because I am the Son [coming] from the Father.' The *Glossa ordinaria* has: 'because he himself is the Word

Hugh[15] – since indeed for some the highest authority lies with these people. Nor does the gloss known as the *Glossa ordinaria* disagree; it carries the most weight according to the general consensus of theologians. It says, '"Union" [*compago*] is said of the joining of sensibility and reason, which the Son of God sees.'[16] These passages would perhaps be rather vexatious for scholarly people, but I am dealing with people for whom these sources have more authority than the most scholarly. And in fact the reading of the book of Wisdom, chapter 16, 'For it was neither herb nor mollifying plaster that healed them, but thy word [*sermo*], O Lord, which healeth all things,'[17] is interpreted by both what is known as the *Gloss ordinaria*[18] and by Cardinal Hugh[19] as applying to the Son of God, who is said to be the 'Word' [*sermo*] of the Father.

Add to these that St Cyprian uses *sermo* for *verbum* in several passages, including his second book, *Adversus Iudaeos* chapter 3,[20] showing by several places in the canonical Scriptures that where today we read *verbum*, the church formerly read *sermo*. For since the title of the chapter is 'That Christ himself is the word [*sermo*] of God,' and this title is not separated in the old manuscripts but integrated in the text, it seems likely that it is Cyprian's own. He adds these witnesses: in Psalm 44, 'My heart hath breathed out

* * * * *

[*sermo*] of the Father who has spoken himself.' For the *Glossa interlinearis* and *ordinaria*, see Beryl Smalley *The Study of the Bible in the Middle Ages* 3rd ed (Oxford 1983) 56–66.

15 Nicolas of Lyra's commentary *Postillae perpetuae super totam bibliam* was added to an edition of the *Glossa ordinaria* in 1498: *Biblia latina. Cum glossa ordinaria Walafridi aliorumque et interlineari Anselmi Laudunensis, et cum postillis ac moralitatibus Nicolai de Lyra* (Basel: Johann Froben and Johann Petri 1 December 1498. Lyra says at Heb 4:12 (v1r): 'For *sermo* here is taken to mean *verbum*; this is why in Greek too we have *logos*, which means the same as *verbum*. The *verbum*, however, in divine terms is of the same nature as he of whom it is the word; since therefore Christ is the Word of God.' For a general account of Nicolas (1270–1349), see NCE 10 453–4; Rummel *Annotations* 82–4. Hugh of St Cher 7 f N2r 1 *Epistula ad Hebraeos, caput IV. Vivus enim est sermo Dei.*
16 *Biblia latina* IV [479b]. The text is as Erasmus quotes except that it reads *compages* for Erasmus' *compago.*
17 Wisd of Sol 16:12
18 *Biblia latina* II [739b]: 'id est filius per quem omnia, cuius potestas ubique, qui omnia quaecunque voluit fecit, ipse curat corpora, ipse a spiritualibus bestiis animas salvat.'
19 See n15 above.
20 In Erasmus' own edition, *Adversus Iudaeos ad Quirinum* in *Opera Divi Caecilii Cypriani* ... (Basel: Froben 1520); the passage is in lib 2 cap 3 page 275; PL 4 698A–B.

a good word [*sermonem bonum*]'²¹ – for Cyprian understands these are the words of the Father bringing forth the Son from himself. And another: 'The heavens are made fast by the word of God [*sermone Dei*].'²² Again in Isaiah: 'Fulfilling the word [*sermonem consumans*] and cutting it short in righteousness, because it is a brief word [*sermonem breviatum*] that God will speak.'²³ Again in the Psalm: 'He sent his Word [*sermonem suum*], and healed them.'²⁴ Again in the book of Revelation: 'And behold, a white horse; and the one who sat on it was called Faithful and True, judging rightly and justly; and he²⁵ was about to join battle, and he was clothed with a garment sprinkled with blood; and his name is called the Word of God [*sermo Dei*].'²⁶ In the same place he quotes this passage too from John: 'In the beginning was the Word [*verbum*],' where I greatly suspect that the writer, working from memory, put *verbum* for *sermo*, as often happens. As someone may think this is doubtful, it is certain either that Cyprian must have read *In principio erat sermo* or that he thought there was absolutely no difference between *verbum* and *sermo*. Otherwise this piece of evidence would not answer to his heading when all the others do.²⁷

To make this more convincing I shall add the words of Augustine, where he is explaining the passage from John, chapter 17, 'Thy Word [*sermo*] is truth.'²⁸ He says:

What else has he said but, 'I am the truth'? The Greek Gospel has *logos* here, which we also read where it says, 'In the beginning was the Word [*verbum*], and the Word

* * * * *

21 Ps 44 (45 RSV):1 *Eructavit cor meum verbum bonum.* Erasmus' text here is: *Eructavit cor meum sermonem bonum*, as in the same chapter of the edition of Cyprian.

22 Ps 32 (33 RSV):6. This is also quoted from the same chapter in Cyprian.

23 Isa 10:22–3 as alluded to by Paul in Rom 9:28. Erasmus' text is: 'Sermonem [all editions of Cyprian apparently have *Verbum*; CCSL 3 31 5] consummans, et brevians in iustitia, quoniam sermonem breviatum faciet Deus'; Vulg 'Verbum enim consumans, et abbrevians in aequitate: quia verbum breviatum faciet Dominus super terram'; 'For he shall finish his word, and cut it short in justice; because a short word shall the Lord make upon the earth.' For *sermo* or *verbum abbreviatum*, see Boyle 29–30.

24 Ps 106 (107 RSV):20 *Misit verbum suum, et sanavit eos*; and Cyprian PL 4 698B

25 *praeliaturus*] 1520a, 1520b, and 1540; *proeliatur* Cyprian

26 Rev 19:11 and 13 'And with justice doth he judge and fight.' The first part of Erasmus' text here is: 'Vidi caelum apertum, et ecce equus albus, et qui sedebat super eum vocabatur fidelis, et verus, aequum iustumque iudicans, et praeliaturus'; Vulg *vocabatur fidelis, et verax: et cum iusticia iudicat, et pugnat*; ER *et per iusticiam iudicat, et pugnat*.

27 See *Apologia de 'In principio erat sermo'* (1520b) 20 below; PL 4 698.

28 John 17:17

was with God, and the Word was God.' And we know for sure that the 'Word' [*verbum*] itself is the only begotten Son of God, which was made flesh, and dwelt in us. Hence in the first case we could also put, as there is in certain codices, 'Thy Word [*verbum*] is truth,' just as in certain codices there is in the second case 'In the beginning was the Word [*sermo*].' In the Greek, however, there is no variation: in both cases there is *logos*. The Father therefore sanctifies his heirs in truth, that is, in his Word [*verbum*], in his only begotten Son.[29]

These are the words of Augustine, and it is clear from them that in many codices there were formerly the words 'In the beginning was the Word [*sermo*], and the Word [*sermo*] was with God, and the Word [*sermo*] was God,' just as I conjecture St Cyprian read. It is clear that in Augustine's opinion there is no difference whether you read *verbum* or *sermo*.

It is clear in the opinion of the same man that in the Gospel of John Christ is called *sermo*: 'Thy Word [*sermo*] is truth.' The same Augustine explaining chapter 12 of John the Evangelist writes thus: 'When indeed he said, "He who rejects me and does not receive my sayings [*verba*] has one who will judge him ..." but immediately added for those who were waiting to hear who this would be, "The Word [*sermo*] that I have spoken will be his judge on the last day," he surely spoke of himself; he announced himself.'[30] In this passage again clearly the Son of God is expressed by *sermo*, not *verbum*. I am not discussing now what weight should be given to this interpretation of Augustine here. It is enough for my purpose that he should not shrink from the term *sermo*.

The same authority, in the first book of *De trinitate*, dealing with the passage of the Gospel that I have just quoted ('The Word [*sermo*] that I have spoken, the same shall judge him in the last day'),[31] writes in these words: 'I ask therefore how are we to understand "It is not I who shall judge, but the Word [*verbum*] that I have spoken will judge," since he himself is the Word [*verbum*] of the Father that speaks?'[32] Augustine applies this passage too to the Son of God showing there is no difference between the terms *sermo* and *verbum*. What purpose then is served by seeking examples from the works of other orthodox writers when we have the authority of Cyprian,

* * * * *

29 Augustine *In Iohannis evangelium tractatus* 108 3 CCSL 36 617, PL 35 1915–6
30 John 12:48. Cf n11 above.
31 Augustine *In Iohannis evangelium tractatus* 54 6 CCSL 36 461/PL 35 1783
32 Augustine *De trinitate* 1.12 CCSL 50 66–7:119–27/PL 42 839. All sources cited by CCSL have *verbum* in the first phrase; the quotation is fragmented, and the last phrase may correspond either to *Et ipsum verbum patris verbum esse dicit* (120) or to *Verbum autem patris est ipse filius Dei* (126–7).

who in my opinion comes closer than anyone else to the apostle's thought, and in addition Augustine's and Thomas', not to mention more modern writers?

However, I shall put forward a couple of passages from the works of Jerome, who writes thus when explaining chapter one of the Letter to the Ephesians: 'Not because the one who assumed manhood is one and the Word [*sermo*] who assumed it is another, but because one and the same person for differing reasons may be called now "sublime," now "humble."' Again in the same chapter: 'And just as our Lord Jesus Christ is the Word[33] [*sermo*] of wisdom, truth, peace, justice, strength, let the same Jesus also be glory.'[34] This writer did not scruple to call the Son of God *sermo*, did he?

Then there is Prudentius in the hymn that the choir sings in church: 'Come, supreme Father, whom none has ever seen, and Christ, the Word [*sermo*] of the Father . . .'[35] Was he afraid to call the Son of God *sermo*? 'He is a poet,' they will say. Yes, but one who breathes so much of both virtue and sacred learning that he deserves to be counted among the weightiest Doctors of the church.

But in book 2 of *De trinitate*, Hilary may seem at first sight to say that the Son of God cannot be called *sermo*, though to anyone who looks a little more closely he does clearly so call him, for he writes as follows: 'The sound of a voice comes to an end, as does the enunciation of a thought; this word [*verbum*] is the reality [*res*], not the sound, nature, not talk [*sermo*]; it is God, not emptiness.'[36] Those are Hilary's words. But people do not consider that *sermo* here is taken to mean human speech, which is produced by bodily organs and strikes the eardrum through pulses of air. Such speech is an accident, not a thing subsisting of itself. Christ is not of that sort. On the contrary, nothing prevents Hilary from being able to put *verbum* in the same place: He is nature, not a word [*verbum*]. In fact he calls nature a 'substance' to which he opposes human speech as an accident. And just above in the same place, when he says, 'He was in the beginning, because the "speaking"

* * * * *

33 *sermo sapientiae*] *1520a* (genitive); *sermo, sapientia 1522* and *1540* (nominative). See 30 n66 below.

34 Jerome *Commentariorum in epistolam ad Ephesios liber* Eph 1:3 PL 26 475C and Eph 1:16 PL 26 488C

35 Prudentius *Carmina, Liber Cathemerinon 6, Hymnus ante Somnium* CCSL 126 29:1– 4/PL 59 831

36 Hilary *De trinitate sive de fide* 2.15 CCSL 62 53/PL 10 61A/FC 25 48. See *Apologia de 'In principio erat sermo'* (*1520b*) nn53 and 54. Erasmus there quotes more of the preceding passage.

[*sermo*] of the thought is eternal, since the one who thinks is eternal,' is he not clearly calling Christ the 'eternal Word' [*sermo*], proceeding from the eternal mind?

I do not think it is necessary, in a matter so clear as to be obvious even to a blind man, to heap up any more evidence. Just consider this for me, dear reader whoever you are, how foreign it is to Christian sincerity to rant in public so odiously and without cause against someone else's reputation and with seditious cries to provoke uneducated common folk to throw stones. What if they do imagine that I have made a slip in translating with *sermo* instead of *verbum*! What could be more indecent than to argue about these things in front of an undiscriminating crowd? Or rather not argue but yap? If Christ is called *sermo* in so many places in the Bible and even by[37] God in the Gospels, if this is what is read in public and sung in churches even by those who stone me, if it is recited in schools, if neither ancient nor modern orthodox ears have been shocked by this term, if for such widely approved authors it makes no difference whether you say *sermo* or *verbum* – on the contrary – if the term *sermo* is both more appropriate and more pleasant, and it translates the Greek term *logos* more correctly, will they stir up all these troubles for me over a work that is not read in churches or in schools but only in private studies, where it is lawful to read both apocrypha and the books of heretics, and because I translated as[38] the church in general read it formerly?

If it is impious, if it is blasphemous, if it is a capital offence to call Christ *sermo*, they must condemn before me or with me so many outstanding princes of the church – Cyprian, Augustine, Jerome, Thomas, Hilary – nay rather the whole church. If it is pious, if it is done following the custom of both the primitive and the modern church, if it is done with the authority of the most respected Fathers when we call Christ 'the Word of the Father' [*sermo patris*], think what a dreadful injury it is to hand over a well-deserving man in their public sermons to be stoned by the people and to slay a harmless man. For what difference is there between slaying with the hand or with the tongue?

If Paul is not freed from the charge of homicide because, although he himself did not touch the stones he guarded the cloaks of those who threw them – but rather he committed a more serious crime, as if he were helping the hands of all the stone throwers, than if he had been one of

* * * * *

37 *a Deo*] Omitted in *1520b*
38 *ut olim publica* [adjective] *legit ecclesia?*] *1520a*; *ut olim publice* [adverb] *legit Ecclesia?* in *1520b, 1540*

their number[39] – what shall we say of those who with perverse deliberation
and devout minds rouse the uneducated populace to destroy a man, and
do it from the very place whence the people are accustomed to hear the
teaching of the Gospel? And this is being done by those who claim to be
masters of gospel teaching and pillars of religion in its entirety. These men
are appealing for the help of both princes and people against a deserving
man. I could more justly appeal to the power of these same people against
this sort of factious impudence that, if it is not contained by the authority
of leading men, is a hazard that may sometime break out in serious harm
to the peace of Christianity.

Farewell, reader, and consider from what has happened what credit is
to be given to these people in other matters.

* * * * *

39 For Paul and the stoning of Stephen, see Acts 7:58, 8:3, and 22:19–20. Cf also
Erasmus' *Paraphrasis in Acta* 7, 8, and 22 CWE 50 56 and 131.

A DEFENCE BY ERASMUS OF ROTTERDAM OF *IN PRINCIPIO ERAT SERMO* (1520b)

Desiderii Erasmi Roterodami
Apologia de 'In principio erat sermo'

A DEFENCE BY ERASMUS OF ROTTERDAM OF

IN PRINCIPIO ERAT SERMO

(1520b)[1]

DESIDERIUS ERASMUS OF ROTTERDAM, GREETINGS TO PIOUS AND FAIR-MINDED READERS

Recently as if a preconcerted signal had been given,[2] various people in various places have stood up to oppose me; they are people who are forever contriving some objection to the best sorts of learning and who, making a pretext of Christian religion, fight against Christian piety. In an attempt to calm the tumult as best I could, I answered then on the spur of the moment with whatever happened to come to mind,[3] for the argument seemed to me such that I would never have suspected anyone could be so impudent as to make a case against me on that basis. But these opponents thought they had found a missile that could not be avoided, deflected by any shield, or dodged by any bodily contortion. My friends were scoffed at, a triumph was prepared and even celebrated, I was defeated and dragged along in the victory parade. They kept on asking: 'Where is Erasmus now? Where are those who try to defend his errors? Let them put up some specious argument here to excuse his quite manifest, his quite impious error. At last this fellow has been caught; we have caught him red handed. In the Gospel of John he has wrongly altered the church's reading, and instead of what the church has hitherto read, *In principio erat verbum*, he translates *In principio erat sermo*.'

* * * * *

1 The following is the translation of the second, longer version of the *Apologia*, referred to as *1520b*. Since no copy of the first edition was available, it is based on *1522* and *1540*.
2 On the accusation of conspiracy and the linking of sedition and impudence, see Ep 481 from Thomas More, 31 October 1516. For the suggestion of a Franciscan conspiracy, see Ep 481:44–58; and Boyle 153 n39.
3 A reference to *1520a*, published about five months earlier.

At first the affair was whispered among conspirators, then a strategy was spread abroad through emissaries:[4] everyone together at the same time would start crying out in public that the matter was too dreadful for anyone to tolerate and that all should rise immediately as one and stone the author of such an impious crime. This seemed a cunning idea to everyone; victory was at hand. It does not really matter where Alecto first gave the signal for war on her faint horn;[5] certain it is that the first rumblings came from Britain. The noise was so fearful that it could be clearly heard even here.[6] I shall spare the man's name, and his order, though he did not spare me. For since he was speaking to a public almost all of whom know Erasmus, and since he was attacking a phrase that was mine alone, what point was there in suppressing the name? But this was a man to be respected for his theological qualification, venerable for his religious teaching, and even distinguished by his dignity as a bishop.[7] This man, in London, the most populous city in the whole of England, in the most frequented place in the whole of that city, in the churchyard of St Paul's no less, declaring that he was about to speak on the subject of Christian charity, immediately forgot all Christian charity and began to rant intemperately against my translation of the New Testament, and particularly against this passage from the Gospel of John, *In principio erat verbum.*

Look this shameful thing (says he). We who have been doctors of sacred theology for so many years are obliged to return to elementary school. For although the whole church has read *In principio erat verbum* for a thousand years and more hitherto, now after all this time some ape of the Greeks will teach us, for heaven's sake, that we should read *In principio erat sermo.* But St Augustine (he says) shows that the Greek word *logos* means in Latin both *verbum* and *ratio,* but *verbum* seems better to him than the term *ratio* in this particular passage.[8] For *verbum* is better suited to signify the second Person in the divine context (for these are the words he used) for the

* * * * *

4 The reference to 'emissaries may be an allusion to Lee who was in Louvain at this time. See the introduction xiv–xv with nn9 and 12 there.
5 The Fury or Erinys Alecto, Virgil *Aeneid* 7.324–492. Her horn (Latin *surda bucina*) is mentioned at 7.513; cf Juvenal 7.71.
6 That is, in Louvain. Erasmus did not leave until 28 October 1521.
7 Henry Standish, bishop of St Asaph
8 Augustine *De trinitate* 15.16 CCSL 50A 500/PL 42 1079, where Augustine opposes *verbum* and *cogitatio,* not *ratio.* See n17 below; and cf Ep 1126:30–1.

reasons Augustine alleges. But these reasons (he says) are not understood by these devotees of Greek, yet they dare to contaminate the Scriptures.

He babbled out these and many other things no less ignorantly than provocatively and believed he had made a fine speech of it. With zeal for the Christian faith (as he put it), he started to beg the assistance of the governor of London, whom they commonly call the 'mayor' (for this official by tradition usually attends sermons preached in this place), to beg for the help and support of the citizens of that city, saying they should behave like men and not allow new translations like these, which would undermine the authority of Holy Scripture, to creep any farther. The stupid fellow was laughed at by all the educated people there, and the more sensible among the uneducated were incensed that he should spout such nonsense that had nothing to do with the lives of the people. He was pleased with himself, relying on the admiration of the few who were of the same ilk.[9]

At almost the same time in Brussels, in the church of St Gudula, there was a certain Carmelite and bachelor of theology[10] – I won't give his name though he did not withhold mine. He was instructed by his teacher,[11] who is popularly known as the 'Camelite' because of his dull wittedness and who, if he was as pleasing to Christ as he is to himself, would be a better man than St Paul. In the midst of a crowd of people this fellow said from the pulpit, among other things, that there was a certain Erasmus who was not afraid of correcting the Gospel of St John. (For some years now no one has been admitted to the theological fraternity in Louvain without giving some proof of his worth such as this, nor are people initiated into the most sacred mysteries of theology there unless they have declared themselves to be egregiously shameless sycophants.)[12] Sensible and educated people were for the most part displeased by the stupid audacity of this young man; ordinary, uneducated folk suspected there was some villainy. In Paris, as I learned from the letters of friends, there was a similar commotion. The same nonsense is bandied about everywhere, among mere women, among businessmen, among the foremost courtiers. Among the latter, just as there

* * * * *

9 'The same ilk' (*eiusdem farinae*); cf *Adagia* III v 44 *Nostrae farinae*.
10 Probably one Jan Robyns; see the introduction xvii n22.
11 Nicolaas Baechem; see CEBR I 81–3; and the introduction to the *Apologia de loco 'Omnes quidem.'*
12 The sentence in parentheses, apparently absent in the first edition, was added in manuscript in Cambridge *1522* page 134. It remained in brackets in *1540* and LB.

are some of sound judgment, so there are some whom in matters of this
sort it is not difficult to deceive, especially when they are confronted by that
sort of prophetic refinement (*hieroprepes* 'suitably reverent,' as the Greeks
say),[13] by the severe and frowning brow that might announce a man of some
worth, by the title of 'reverend,' and by the shrewd and false appearance
of piety, which tricks even exceptionally sensible people.

Whether these views of theirs are right or wrong, what could be more
mischievous than to bawl them out before the ignorant mass of people? I
wrote those things for the learned, not for the general public; I wanted them
to be read in private, not in public. The schools still have their translation,
as do the churches. I myself do not read or chant any differently from
the rest. Nor did I ever ask of the Roman pontiff Leo – I first published
this work at his insistence, and I have reviewed it afresh relying on his
authority – that he should remove the old, received translation but that,
with the help of my version compared to it at home, the old might be clearer
and less distorted. If they disapprove of something in it, they should have
either advised me of it in person or sent me a written refutation; but here
they are, broadcasting what was intended to be discussed among scholars
and broadcasting it among tanners, weavers, and mere women. This was
an absurd thing to do, even if they were proclaiming the truth; but here
they are, lying with perverse zeal, distorting, slandering, and deceiving the
people with jugglers' tricks to inflame them more. For when humble people
hear that there is someone correcting John's Gospel, they do not understand
that my business is with the Latin Translator and that I discuss whether
what he translated can be rendered more suitably, but they think I am
condemning what the Evangelist himself wrote. They take it the same way
when they hear of someone correcting the Lord's Prayer or the Hail Mary or
the canticle of the Virgin Mother, which is popularly called the Magnificat.[14]
Nor is it only the common people who take it this way but even certain men
who want to be considered universally as 'wise men' and 'rabbis.' I could
point a finger at them if I wished, for there are some who think they are well
educated but hardly even know that John wrote in a language other than
Latin. There were some who believed, when the volumes of Jerome were
published, that I was not removing errors from corrupt manuscripts but

* * * * *

13 Xenophon *Symposium* 8.40; Titus 2:3 *in habitu sancto* 'in holy attire'
14 The Lord's Prayer is in Luke 11:2–4 and Matt 6:9–13; the Hail Mary is based
   on Luke 1:28–35 and 42–8; the Magnificat is in Luke 1:46–55. Cf the second
   response to Lee, *Responsio ad annotationes Lei* CWE 72 347–8; and Rummel *Critics*
   I 141–2.

altering Jerome's words and trying to make some rather unstylish passages more stylish. I am aware that the labour undertaken in refuting these ideas is largely vain. However, as far as *verbum* and *sermo* are concerned, since there has been such a shameless and malicious outcry, I shall make a brief answer.

To begin let us suppose that the Son of God is designated nowhere in the Bible by the word *sermo*. Would it then be irreverent to call him by that name, since according to these people the terms *sermo* and *verbum* mean the same whenever we are speaking of human things? For no human terms can properly express divine things.[15] Because God the Father is sometimes called just 'Father' (let's suppose this is the case), may I not on that account call him 'parent' or 'procreator' or, if I am writing a poem, my 'begetter' or any other term that expresses the same thing to us as 'Father'? Because the Son is always so called (suppose this is the case), can he not be called 'child,' 'offspring,' 'seed,' 'progeny,' or something else that has the same force? I don't think there is anyone so unfair as to deny me this right. What fault was there then if I had been the first and only person to call the Son of God *sermo*, provided that it is generally agreed that *verbum* and *sermo* mean the same? How much more reprehensible is what they are doing now, when, although both terms exist in the sacred texts, although the church customarily uses both, although both are found in the writings of the Doctors of the church, as I shall shortly demonstrate, they nevertheless try to rouse the world against me with their stupid clamour. And this they do because in a work prepared only with a view to private reading I preferred to use the word *sermo* rather than *verbum*, something that I believe I would be quite at liberty to do even if there were some difference between the two terms. But what if I demonstrate that the word *sermo* is even better suited to express what we want? Will that not make them ashamed of their brainless ideas? But why should they be ashamed? They have no brains.

But it cannot be denied in the very first place that the Evangelist himself, who certainly wrote in Greek, called Christ the *logos*. This word has multiple meanings: it may be 'speech' [*sermo*], 'word' [*verbum*], 'discourse' [*oratio*], 'reasoning' [*ratio*], 'wisdom' [*sapientia*], or 'calculation' [*computus*], each one of which Jerome thinks is appropriate in some way or other to the Son of God.[16] However, Latin speakers liked *sermo* or *verbum* best. The

* * * * *

15 See *Apologia de 'In principio erat sermo'* (1520a) n6; and 28, 30, 33 below.
16 Jerome Ep 53 4:14 CSEL 54 449/PL 22 543: 'λόγος graece multa significat – nam et verbum est et ratio et supputatio [sic] et causa uniuscuiusque rei' (*logos* has many meanings in Greek ... for it is 'word,' 'reasoning,' 'calculation,' and

fact that Augustine states that the word *verbum* is more appropriate than *ratio* or other words[17] to designate the Son of God is irrelevant to me, since I am comparing *sermo* with *verbum*, not with *ratio*, and I shall suggest *sermo* without rejecting *verbum*.

What we call in the narrow sense *verbum* the Greeks call either *rhema* [verb] or *lexeis* [word, diction], neither of which, I believe, can we find in the Scriptures used of the Son of God. However, I do not deny that in Latin authors *verbum* is sometimes used for some short saying such as a proverb or an aphorism. But whenever we mean discourse, we tend to say 'words' [*verba*] in the plural rather than 'a word,' as in *verba facere* for 'to speak' and *multis verbis mecum egit*, meaning 'he dealt with me at length.' I do not have to mention here that *verbum* is often used not for any word but for a particular part of speech, the verb, which, as I said, is *rhema* in Greek. These are trivial matters, I admit, but still, even a slight additional consideration tips the scales one way or the other when a matter is otherwise in balance. Certainly it cannot be denied that the Greek word *logos*, which the Evangelist indisputably used, is more correctly and more commonly expressed in Latin by the word *sermo* than by *verbum*.[18] Finally, if I concede that there is no difference between *sermo* and *verbum*, congruence of gender certainly favours the word *sermo*,[19] otherwise I would almost prefer *oratio* to *sermo* because *sermo* often means conversation when people are chatting in a familiar manner. For just as *sermo factus est homo* 'The Word was made man' is easier to accept, so *verbum caro factum est* 'The Word was made flesh'[20] is harsher if custom, which softens everything, did not make it more acceptable. So the question should not have been thrashed out in an uproar, even if the Son of God had never up until now been called *sermo*, especially as it is done in a book that is read in private and as it does not change the ecclesiastical and public reading.

Now there was even less need that this should happen because in the canonical Scriptures, in the usage of the church, and in the writings

* * * * *

'cause' of anything ...); and Jerome *Commentariorum in epistolam ad Ephesios liber* Eph 1:3 PL 26 475C and Eph 1:16 PL 26 488C (see 30 n67 below).

17 See n8 above.

18 Cf *Annotationes in evangelium Ioannis* 1:2 LB VI 335C; Reeve I 218.

19 *Sermo* is masculine, *oratio* is feminine. As was usual in his time, Erasmus looks for a congruence between sexual and grammatical gender.

20 John 1:14. Some of the corresponding sentence in *1520a* (5 n8 above) has been omitted, and the word *caro* added in the last phrase. The alteration is apparently deliberate, since this new version appears in *1522* and passes without manuscript correction in the Cambridge copy; it is retained in *1540* and LB.

of orthodox Doctors, both ancient and modern, you will find that Christ is called *sermo*, even in the very passage these people are raising an uproar about. If I demonstrate this with perfectly clear arguments, the only thing for them to do will be to admit that they are either unversed in Holy Scripture in not knowing this, or stupid in not having noticed this, or false accusers in criticizing so provocatively what is shown to be validated by so many authorities.

And to start with I shall bring forward one who is no ordinary author but the famous Cyprian, famous firstly for his eloquence, secondly for his holiness, and lastly for his martyrdom. In the work he wrote, *Adversus Iudaeos* chapter 5 of the second book,[21] Cyprian quotes this passage from the Evangelist just as I translate it: 'In the beginning was the Word [*sermo*], and the Word [*sermo*] was with God, and the Word [*sermo*] was God.' Here they have the very passage about which they are making this commotion and in an author so ancient, so generally approved by all those who are most accepted, that no one could possibly disregard him. But, in case they accuse me unjustly of having myself falsified this passage in Cyprian, seeing that I have recently edited this author's works,[22] let them look at the old manuscripts, let them look at the editions of others (there are several), and they will understand that in this passage nothing has been changed by me, either here or elsewhere, except on the authority of ancient versions. Now in the third chapter of the same book, he adduces this same passage of the Evangelist, John, as well as several other passages of canonical Scripture in which Christ is called the Word [*sermo*].[23] The title of the chapter is 'That Christ is this same Word [*sermo*] of God.' And he adds these witnesses: in Psalm 44,[24] 'My heart hath uttered a good word [*sermonem bonum*].' Cyprian understands these are the words of the Father bringing forth the Son from himself. Again in Psalm[25] 22, 'The[26] heavens are made fast by the word of

* * * * *

21 Cyprian *Adversus Iudaeos ad Quirinum* 2.6 [not 5] PL 4 701C. G. Hartel (CSEL 3 1:70) has *In principio erat verbum*.
22 Erasmus' edition of Cyprian (see the following note) appeared in the same month as *1520a*.
23 *Adversus Iudaeos ad Quirinum* in *Opera Divi Caecilii Cypriani* (Basel: Froben 1520) lib 2 cap 3 275 (PL 4 698)
24 Ps 44 (45 RSV):1 *Eructavit cor meum verbum bonum*. Erasmus' text here is: *Eructavit cor meum sermonem bonum*, as in the edition of Cyprian.
25 Psalm 22] Added in *1540*; followed by LB. However it is Ps 32 (33 RSV):6, as Cyprian says correctly (PL 4 698A).
26 The heavens ... in Isaiah:] *1520a*; omitted in *1522*, *1540*, and LB. What follows in *1540* and LB is Isa 10:22–3 as alluded to by Paul in Rom 9:28. Erasmus' text

God [*sermone Dei*].' Again in Isaiah: 'Fulfilling the word [*sermonem consummans*] and cutting it short in righteousness, because it is a brief word [*sermonem breviatum*] that God will speak in the whole earth.' Likewise in Psalm 106,[27] 'He sent His Word [*sermonem suum*] and healed them.' Again in the book of Revelation: 'And I saw the heavens opened, and behold a white horse; and he that sat upon him was called faithful and true, and he doth judge rightly and justly; and he was about to make war. And he was clothed with a garment sprinkled with blood; and his name is called the Word of God [*sermo Dei*].'[28] And before this passage he had put the witness from the Gospel: 'In the beginning was the Word [*sermo*], and the Word [*sermo*] was with God, and the Word [*sermo*] was God.' You see in how many places Christ is called *sermo*, not *verbum*. Again, in case anyone thinks I am seeking to win by trickery, I shall not hide the fact that in some manuscripts even, in this last passage, *verbum* appeared in place of *sermo*. And the same in the second passage, for *sermonem consummans* etc. Even so, it must be clear to everyone that this was the mistake of a copyist who trusted his memory and wrote *verbum* for *sermo*. I shall put forward a double proof of this; first because, unless you read *sermo* everywhere, this testimony will not correspond with his [Cyprian's] heading, where he promises that he will prove 'that the same Christ is the Word [*sermo*].' It will correspond not because some occurrences correspond but because the examples offered throughout the work at every point correspond to his headings. But in case someone argues that this heading was added by copyists, he should know that in the old codices it is not separated from the text but incorporated into it; and in fact Cyprian himself speaks of his headings[29] in the preface

* * * * *

here is: 'Sermonem [all editions of Cyprian apparently have *Verbum*; CCSL 3 31:5] consummans, et brevians in iustitia, quoniam sermonem breviatum faciet Deus in toto orbe terrae' (which is not quite the same as his translation of NT, though he uses *sermo* there). Vulg 'Verbum enim consummans, et abbrevians in aequitate: quia verbum breviatum faciet Dominus super terram'; 'For he shall finish his word, and cut it short in justice; because a short word shall the Lord make upon the earth.' For *sermo* or *verbum abbreviatum*, see Boyle 29–30.
27 Ps 106 (107 RSV):20 *Misit verbum suum, et sanavit eos*; Cyprian PL 4 698B
28 Rev 19:11 and 13. The first part of Erasmus' text here is: 'Vidi caelum apertum, et ecce equus albus, et qui sedebat super eum vocabatur fidelis, et verus, aequum iustumque iudicans, et praeliaturus'; sic *1520a*, *1520b*, and *1540*; *proeliatur* Cyprian; Vulg vocabatur fidelis, et verax: et cum iusticia iudicat, et pugnat; Erasmus' NT *et* per iusticiam iudicat, et pugnat; 'And with justice doth he judge and fight.'
29 PL 4 698

of the work, where he affirms that in two small books he had gathered proofs from Holy Scripture into certain headings and chapters. If anybody distrusts these arguments too, surely one of two things must be true: either Cyprian read *In principio erat sermo* or he believed there was no difference between *verbum* and *sermo*.

This is all very clear, but[30] it will be more convincing if you read Tertullian's book *Adversus Praxean*,[31] for there he calls the Son *sermo* more than once, introducing this very passage from John and proving it was the practice of Latin speakers to read it like this, *In principio erat sermo*, although he himself preferred the word *ratio*. The same writer, in the book *De resurrectione mortuorum*, expresses himself thus: 'because the Word [*sermo*] too was made flesh.'[32] And it is Tertullian, as his teacher, whom Cyprian is usually glad to follow: it is on this point that [Cyprian] quotes from the Psalm,[33] 'My heart hath breathed out an excellent word [*sermonem optimum*].'

Now to make it even clearer I shall add here the words of Augustine where he is explaining the passage from John, chapter 17, 'Thy Word [*sermo*] is truth.'[34] He says:

What else has he said but 'I am the truth'? The Greek Gospel has *logos* here, which we also read where it says, 'In the beginning was the Word [*verbum*], and the Word was with God, and the Word was God.' And we know for sure that the 'Word' [*verbum*] is the only Son of God, which was made flesh and dwelt in us. Hence in the first case we could also put, as there is in certain codices, 'Thy Word [*verbum*] is truth,' just as in certain codices there is in the second case 'In the beginning was the

* * * * *

30 The passage from 'but it will be more convincing ... glad to imitate,' except the sentence 'The same writer ... made flesh,' was added in manuscript in Cambridge *1522*; the latter sentence appears only in *1540*. See also Ep 1000: 164–8.

31 Tertullian *Adversus Praxean* 5.3 CCSL 2 1163–4 / PL 2 183B: *Hanc Graeci λόγον dicunt, quo vocabulo etiam sermonem appellamus* 'This the Greeks call *logos*, which we also call *sermo*.'

32 John 1:14. Probably a slightly confused memory of Tertullian *De resurrectione mortuorum* 6.3–4 CCSL 2 928 / PL 2 848B–C: 'Quodcumque enim limus exprimebatur, Christus cogitabatur, homo futurus, quod et limus, et sermo caro' (For, whatever was expressed as clay [by the creator], Christ was in his thoughts as one day to become man, because the flesh was to be both clay and Word); and of Tertullian *De carne Christi* 19.2 CCSL 2 907 / PL 2 802: *quia ex Dei voluntate verbum caro factum est* 'because it was by the will of God that the Word was made flesh' (my translation).

33 Ps 44 (45 AV):1. See n24.

34 John 17:17

Word [*sermo*].' In the Greek, however, there is no variation; in both cases there is *logos*. The Father therefore sanctifies his heirs in truth, that is, in his Word [*verbum*], in his only begotten Son.[35]

These are the words of Augustine, and it is clear from them that in some codices that the Catholic church used in his time there was formerly written 'In the beginning was the Word [*sermo*], and the Word [*sermo*] was with God, and the Word [*sermo*] was God,' just as we have shown Cyprian reads. From the same words it is clear that in Augustine's judgment there is no difference whether you read *verbum* or *sermo*.

It is clear from the same author that in the Gospel of John Christ is called *sermo*: 'Thy Word [*sermo*] is truth.' This same Augustine explaining chapter 12 of John the Evangelist writes thus: 'When indeed he said, 'He who rejects me and does not receive my sayings [*verba*] has a judge,' but immediately added, for those who were waiting to know who he would be, 'the Word [*sermo*] that I have spoken will be his judge on the last day,' he surely spoke of himself; he announced himself.'[36] Here again clearly, according to the opinion of Augustine, the Son of God is expressed by *sermo*, not *verbum*. I am not discussing now what weight I think should be given to the interpretation here. It is enough for my purpose that such a respected authority as this did not shrink from the term *sermo*.

The same authority, in the first book of *De trinitate*, dealing with the same passage of the Gospel that I have just quoted ('The Word [*sermo*] that I have spoken, the same shall judge him in the last day'), writes in these words: 'I ask therefore how shall we understand "It is not I who shall judge, but the Word [*verbum*] that I have spoken will judge," since he himself is the Word [*verbum*] of the Father that speaks.'[37] These are the words of Augustine, once again applying this passage to the Son of God, and making no distinction between *sermo* and *verbum*.

The same author, explaining Psalm 147, where we read 'who sendeth forth his utterance [*eloquium*] to the earth,' reads 'who sendeth forth his

* * * * *

35 Augustine *In Iohannis evangelium tractatus* 108 3 CCSL 36 617 / PL 35 1915–16

36 Augustine *In Iohannis evangelium tractatus* 54 6 CCSL 36 461 / PL 35 1783; John 12:48

37 *De trinitate* 1.12 CCSL 50 66–7:119–27 / PL 42 839. All sources cited by CCSL have *verbum* in the first phrase. The quotation is fragmented, and the last phrase may correspond either to *Et ipsum verbum patris verbum esse dicit* (120) or to *Verbum autem patris est ipse filius Dei* (126–7).

Word [*verbum*] to the earth.'[38] Where we read 'his Word [*sermo*] runs swiftly,' he reads 'his Word [*verbum*] runs even up to a great speed.' And that he applies both to Christ is shown by the fact that he brings in 'He sendeth forth his Word [*verbum*] upon earth and his Word [*verbum*] cometh upon earth.' But what follows is much clearer: 'This is characteristic of the Word [*verbum*] of God, that it does not exist in part; it is at all times the Word [*verbum*] as such itself, which constitutes the power of God and the wisdom of God, before taking on flesh. If we conceive of God as the form of God, the Word [*verbum*], equal to the Father, is the very wisdom of God . . .'[39] and so on in the same sense.

You will say, this argues against you, for Augustine says *verbum*, not *sermo*. On the contrary, it supports me; for the church calls the Son of God *sermo* and calls him *eloquium*, unless Augustine translates incorrectly[40] or unless church usage employs an impious term. In addition to these points, what we read in the book of Wisdom, chapter 18, 'Thy all powerful word [*sermo*], O Lord, leaps from heaven, from the royal throne,'[41] has been interpreted and chanted by the church as applying to Christ for so many centuries now. If this were found in only one passage, the church chanting this example alone so many times for so many years would still make it apparently a very common expression. And whose ears, pray, are so deaf that they have not yet become accustomed to a word so often repeated and drummed in?

But in case someone turns around and denies that this chant refers to Christ, this is how Thomas Aquinas among others translates when he explains this passage in the Epistle to the Hebrews: 'For the Word [*sermo*] of God is living and ... sharper than any two-edged sword, etc,'[42] clearly adducing this too as evidence about the Son of God. But I think it would be better to give the words of Thomas himself; and I shall not be reluctant to do so, for I do not find the simplicity of the language displeasing. He says:

That word [ie *sermo*] in itself seems to present some difficulty, but if we consider another translation, it is clearer. For where we have *sermo*, in Greek there is *logos*,

* * * * *

38 Augustine *Enarrationes in psalmos* CCSL 40 2157 / PL 37 1931. Ps 147:15 *qui emittit eloquium suum terrae velociter currit sermo eius.* Jerome's translation of the Greek Septuagint has *sermo*, but his translation of the Hebrew has *verbum*.
39 CCSL 40 2158:31
40 See the reference to Psalm 147, n38 above.
41 Wisd of Sol 18:15 *Omnipotens sermo tuus, domine, exiliens de coelo a regalibus sedibus venit*; 'Thy almighty word leapt down from heaven from thy royal throne.'
42 Aquinas *Opera omnia* ed L. Vives (Paris 1876) 21 614–15; *S. Thomae Aquinatis super epistolas S. Pauli lectura* ed P. Raffaele Cai (Turin 1953) II 383–4; Heb 4:12

which is the same as *verbum*; so for *sermo* read *verbum*. And this is how Augustine expounds the verse in John 12: 'The word [*sermo*] that I have spoken,' that is, 'I who am the Word [*verbum*].'[43] In the book of Wisdom, chapter 18: 'Thy all powerful word [*sermo*], O Lord, leaps from heaven, from the royal throne'[44] and here likewise: 'The Word [*sermo*] of God is living,' that is, 'The Word [*verbum*] of God is living.'[45]

I have repeated the passage in its entirety from Thomas because it shows clearly that this author makes no distinction between *sermo* and *verbum*. It is also clear from the whole of his interpretation that this expression is to be applied to Christ. Indeed the gloss known as the *Interlinear Gloss* interprets this same passage [ie, John 12:48] as applying to Christ: it says, 'The Word [*sermo*] of God, that is, the Son of God,' not to go on adding what follows in the same sense.[46] The commentator Nicolas of Lyra agrees and Cardinal Hugh.[47] Nor does the gloss known as the *Glossa ordinaria*

* * * * *

43 See n32 above; *sermo*.
44 See n24 above.
45 Augustine *In Iohannis evangelium tractatus* 54 6 CCSL 36 461/PL 35 1783
46 *Biblia latina* IV [255a]. The *Interlinear Gloss* at John 12:48 says: 'because I am the Son [coming] from the Father.' The *Glossa ordinaria* has: 'because he himself is the Word of the Father who has spoken himself.' For the *Glossa interlinearis* and *Glossa ordinaria*, see Beryl Smalley *The Study of the Bible in the Middle Ages* 3rd ed (Oxford 1983) 56–66.
47 Nicolas of Lyra's commentary *Postillae perpetuae super totam bibliam* was added to an edition of the *Glossa ordinaria* in 1498: *Biblia latina. Cum glossa ordinaria Walafridi aliorumque et interlineari Anselmi Laudunensis, et cum postillis ac moralitatibus Nicolai de Lyra* (Basel: Johann Froben and Johann Petri 1 December 1498. Lyra says at Heb 4:12 (V1r): 'For *sermo* here is taken to mean *verbum*; this is why in Greek too we have *logos*, which means the same as *verbum*. The *verbum*, however, in divine terms is of the same nature as he of whom it is the word; since therefore Christ is the Word of God.' For a general account of Nicolas (1270–1349), see NCE 10 453–4; Rummel *Annotations* 82–4.
Hugh of St Cher 7 f N2r 1 *Epistula ad Hebraeos, caput* IV. *Vivus enim est sermo Dei.* Hugh says: 'id est filius Dei, qui dicitur verbum patris, quia immediate [sic] exiit ab eo, sicut sermo a mente, et postea induit carnem, quasi vocem ad narrandum nobis patrem' (That is, the Son of God, who is called the Word of the Father, because he came directly from him as speech comes from the mind, and afterwards took on flesh, which as it were is a voice telling us of the Father). Hugh's work, first published in 1482, perhaps served to remind Erasmus of other references, for it continues in the same passage: 'Eccles 24:2: I came out of the mouth of the Highest, like a word [*verbum*] from the mind ... John 17:17: Thy Word [*sermo*] is truth ... Wisd of Sol 18:15: Thy almighty word [*sermo*] leaped down from heaven from thy royal throne' (my

disagree; it carries the most weight according to the general consensus of theologians. It says, '"Union [*compago*]" is said of the joining of sensibility and reason, which the Son of God sees.'[48] And in fact the reading of the book of Wisdom, chapter 16, 'For it was neither herb nor mollifying plaster that healed them, but thy word [*sermo*], O Lord, which healeth all things,'[49] is interpreted by both what is known as the *Glossa ordinaria*[50] and by Cardinal Hugh[51] as applying to the Son of God, who is said to be the 'Word' [*sermo*] of the Father. These passages may be rather vexatious for those who have an excessive liking for the more 'polished' authors. However, I am dealing with people for whom these writers have authority; and the consistency of what these writers report from the commentaries of the ancients must be no slight matter for us.

It has been sufficiently proved, I believe, that Christ is also called *sermo* in the old translation that the church both used long ago and still uses. It remains for me to show that holy and orthodox writers too were not averse to using the term *sermo* in their books, something they would in no wise have done if, as these people keep saying, it was not appropriate or not sufficiently appropriate for Christ. First, Hilary in book 2 of *De trinitate*,[52]

* * * * *

translation). For Hugh (1200[?]–63), whose work was also called *Postillae*, see NCE 7:193–4; and Rummel *Annotations* 80–1.

48 *Biblia latina* IV [479b]. The text is as Erasmus quotes except that it reads *compages* for Erasmus' *compago*.
49 Wisd of Sol 16:12
50 *Biblia latina* II [739b]: 'id est filius per quem omnia, cuius potestas ubique, qui omnia quaecunque voluit fecit, ipse curat corpora, ipse a spiritualibus bestiis animas salvat.'
51 See 25 n47 above.
52 Hilary of Poitiers *De trinitate sive de fide* 2.15 CCSL 62 51–2/PL 10 61A/FC 25 47–8. Erasmus' text differs in several respects from the accepted text, which reads:

> *De trinitate* 'Dices enim: "Verbum sonus vocis est et enuntiatio negotiorum et elocutio cogitationum. Hoc apud Deum erat et in principio erat, quia sermo cogitationis aeternus est, cum qui cogitat sit aeternus." *Respondeo tibi* interim pro piscatore meo paucis, dum videmus quomodo rusticitatem suam ipse defendat. Sermo in natura habet ut esse possit, sequens autem ei est ut fuerit; est vero tantum cum auditur.'
> ER 'Dices enim: "Verbum sonus vocis est et enuntiatio negotiorum et elocutio cogitationum. Hoc apud Deum erat. In principio erat, quia sermo cogitationis aeternus est, cum qui cogitat sit aeternus." Respondebo tibi interim pro piscatore meo breviter paucis, dum videmus quomodo rusticitatem suam ipse defendat. Sermo in natura non [sic] habet ut esse possit, sequens autem ei est ut fuerit est vero tantum cum auditur.'

explaining this passage of the Evangelist, 'In the beginning was the Word,' writes as follows:

For you will say, '*Verbum* is sound, enunciation of things to be done, expression of thoughts. This [word] was with God and was in the beginning. It was in the beginning because the "speaking" [*sermo*] of the thought is eternal, since the one who thinks is eternal.' I shall answer meanwhile on behalf of my fisherman briefly in few words, until we see how he defends his lack of sophistication. In nature 'speaking' [*sermo*] does not have the possibility of being: following that, however, the situation is that it will have been

When Hilary says 'the "speaking" [*sermo*] of the thought is eternal, for the one who thinks is eternal,' is he not clearly calling Christ the 'eternal Word' [*sermo*], proceeding timelessly from the eternal mind of the Father?

And again, a little further down, explaining why John preferred to say, 'And the Word was with God [*apud Deum*]' rather than 'in God' [*in Deo*], he writes as follows:

And if you were an unskilled listener and you had missed the first phrase, 'In the beginning was the Word,' why do you complain of what follows: 'and the Word was with God'? Surely you had not heard 'in God,' so that you would understand it as the speaking [*sermo*] of a hidden thought, or had it eluded you in your simplicity that there is an important difference between 'to be' [*esse*], 'to be in' [*inesse*], and 'to be present with' [*adesse*]? For what was in the beginning is said to be not in something else but with something else.[53]

* * * * *

FC 25 47–8 'You will say: "The Word is an utterance of a voice, an announcement of what is to be done, a communication of thoughts. This was with God and was in the beginning. The expression of the thought is eternal, since he who thinks is eternal." For the present I shall answer you in a few words on behalf of my fisherman until we shall see how he defends his lack of culture. A word by its nature has the possibility of being, but the consequence of being uttered is that it shall not be; in fact, it is only when it is heard.'
The fisherman is introduced in *De trinitate sive de fide* 2.13 as an unlearned pupil who raises objections and to whom doctrine is explained. Erasmus was probably quoting from Robert Fortuné's edition of 1511, which he revised and published himself in 1523; the preface is Ep 1334.
53 FC 25 48: 'For even if as an uneducated hearer you did not retain the first statement, "In the beginning was the Word," why do you complain of what follows: "And the Word was with God"? Did you hear "in God" (and not "with God") in order to conceive it as the utterance of a concealed thought?

It is clear in this disputation that Hilary applies the term *sermo* to Christ, though he does not want it to be as accident but as substance,[54] so that, on the argument that it is said to be not 'in God' but 'with God,' we understand that the Word as person is distinct from the Father as person.

But the same author a little later may seem at first sight to say that the Son of God cannot be called *sermo*, though to anyone who looks a little more closely he does clearly apply the term *sermo* to him. For he writes as follows: 'The sound of a voice comes to an end, as does the enunciation of a thought; this word [*verbum*] is the reality [*res*], not the sound, it is nature,[55] not talk [*sermo*], it is God, not emptiness.'[56] That is what Hilary says. When he says, 'not speech [*sermo*] as in nature,' he seems at first sight to deny that *sermo* is Christ. But anyone who is paying attention will easily understand that he is distinguishing the *sermo*, which is the Son of God, from human speech [*sermo humanus*], which is produced by bodily organs and strikes the eardrum through pulses of air. Human speech does not exist of itself – it exists in something else; it is a movement – it does not subsist; it is an accident, not a substance. Christ is not this sort of speech. So let no one be taken unawares by the fact that he said, 'not a *sermo* in nature,' since he could say in the same place, 'It is not a *verbum* in nature,' seeing that before this there is '[This *verbum*] is the meaning, not the sound.' 'Not *sermo*' means it is not speech that makes sound by impulses of air. He calls the substance 'nature,' to which he opposes human speech as an accident.

Again a little lower down he makes an even clearer distinction; he says, 'This is not your mortal speech, because what it speaks of is not a mortal thing.'[57] The mortal thing he speaks of is man pronouncing words by the organ of the mouth or at least human thought representing a temporal thing to itself by means of mental images. This sort of thing was not the Father or his thought; therefore his *sermo* is not temporal like ours but eternal.

Now St Ambrose in his book *De fide*, against the Arians, chapter 2 writes as follows: 'Whatever beginning of the word [*verbum*] you may wish

* * * * *

That which was in the beginning is said to be not in another but with another.'

54 Cf *Paraphrasis in Joannem* CWE 46 17.
55 *natura non sermo*] *1520a*; omitted in *1522* (and not added in manuscript in Cambridge *1522*), *1540*, and LB, obscuring the reference of Erasmus' next sentence. FC 25 48: 'There is an end to the utterance of a voice and the expression of a thought. This word is thing, not a sound; a nature, not a word; God, not a voice.'
56 CCSL 62 53:24–6
57 Hilary *De trinitate* 2.21 CCSL 62 55/FC 25 51–2

to postulate, you will have a disadvantage, because [the Gospel] says, "In the beginning was the Word." Not that we speak of two beginnings arising from a difference of elements, but because the Word [*sermo*] is the Son, he is always with the Father, and was born of the Father.'[58] Has he not without question here called Christ *sermo*? In the *Hexameron* book 1, chapter 9 the same author says, 'The maker of nature spoke light and created it; this speaking [*sermo*] is the will of God, it is the work of God, it is nature, it created light, and illuminated the darkness.'[59] And a little later: 'God spoke, not in such a way that some sound of speech was uttered through the organs of the voice, nor so that the movement of a tongue formed heavenly discourse and some din of words shook the air thereabout, but so that it produced knowledge of his will by the effect of its working.' Again in book 2 chapter 2 he calls the Son *sermo* when saying, 'The Word [*sermo*] of God is the power of nature; through his Son he created all things.'[60] And on this basis Ambrose explains that this *sermo*, which is the all-powerful Son, created all things.

The same author in the *Commentaries* in which he expounds the Epistle to the Hebrews[61] (if the title is not incorrect, it is a book found in a very old manuscript in[62] England) remarks on this passage: 'The Word [*sermo*] of God is living. *Sermo* is the Son of God, who says of himself, "If anyone keeps my word [*sermo*], he will never taste death."'[63] And shortly after: 'For he has said the Word [*sermo*] of God, that is, the providence of God, is a discerner of the thoughts and intentions of the heart.'[64] But to avoid being too prolix in repeating his words, here is the whole of that passage and

* * * * *

58 In ancient times attributed either to Gregory of Nazianzen or to Ambrose, the *De fide* is now assigned to Gregory bishop of Elvira (Gregorius Iliberritanus); CCSL 69 226 §26 / PL 17 584B–C. Erasmus' edition of Ambrose was published by Froben in 1538: *Omnia quotquot extant . . . opera*; the *De fide orthodoxa contra Arianos* is in book 2 209.

59 Ambrose *Hexameron* 1.9 PL 14 153C and 154A

60 This does not appear in Ambrose; perhaps Erasmus is thinking of *Sermo eius finis est operis . . . Firmum est omne quod statuit Deus* (PL 14 158B). Boyle (n110) suggests *sermo eius ortus naturae sit* (PL 14 158C).

61 Ambrose wrote no commentary on Hebrews. The work is now thought to be by Haimo of Auxerre, not Remigius of Auxerre as suggested by Erasmus below, and not Haimo of Halberstadt as it is ascribed in PL 117 849C–D and 850C; see the article by Hermigild Dressler in NCE 6 898–9. The work is entitled *Expositio in epistolam ad Hebraeos* in *In divi Pauli epistolas expositio*. The biblical passage referred to is again Heb 4:12.

62 *apud Anglos*] Added in manuscript in Cambridge 1522

63 John 8:51

64 Heb 4:12

what follows: 'And there is no creature invisible in his sight, etc.' Finally there is this: 'To whom is our Word [*sermo*],'⁶⁵ which he interprets so that it can only apply to the Son of God. And in case anyone objects that the title is suspect, if the book is not by Ambrose, it is certainly by Remigius or someone not very different.

After these there is Jerome, when he explains chapter 1 of the Epistle to the Ephesians, who writes thus: 'Not because the one who assumed manhood is one and the word [*sermo*] who assumed it is another, but because one and the same person for differing reasons shall be called now "sublime," now "humble."' Again in the same chapter: 'And just as our Lord Jesus Christ is the Word [*sermo*], wisdom,⁶⁶ truth, peace, justice, strength, the same Jesus may also be glory.'⁶⁷ Did Jerome feel any scruple here in calling the Son of God *sermo*?

In addition, Lactantius in his *Divinae institutiones* book 4, chapter 8 says, 'First, divine works cannot be known by anyone or told, yet are taught in Holy Scriptures in which it is set down that this Son of God is the Word [*sermo*] of God.' Again in the next chapter he says, 'But the Greeks say *logos*, which is better than our *verbum* or *sermo*, for *logos* means "speech" [*sermo*] and "reasoning" [*ratio*] because it is the voice [*vox*] and the wisdom of God. Nor was this divine speech [*sermonem divinum*] unknown even to the philosophers.'⁶⁸ You see that Lactantius, a scrupulous observer of the Roman faith,⁶⁹ preferred *sermo* to *verbum*; you see that he preferred to say *vox* rather than *verbum*. This name was also used for Christ by Claudianus in a poem: 'The Word [*vox*] and the wisdom of the highest God.'⁷⁰ He uses *vox* in place of *verbum* or *sermo*, *sensus* in place of *sapientia*. And the former is that Firmianus⁷¹ of whom Jerome speaks with uncommon praise.

* * * * *

65 Heb 4:13 *ad quem nobis sermo*; DV 'to whom our speech is'; RSV 'with whom we have to do'; NRSV 'to whom we must render an account.' See also the paragraph on Remigius, 32 below.

66 *sapientia*] 1522 and 1540 (nominative); *sapientiae* 1520a (genitive). The other words in this list are all nominative in all editions.

67 Jerome *Commentariorum in epistolam ad Ephesios liber* Eph 1:3 PL 26 475C and Eph 1:16 PL 26 488C

68 Lactantius *Institutiones divinae* 4.8 PL 6 467A and 4.9 PL 6 469A / FC 49 260. Cf *Annotationes in evangelium Ioannis* 1:2 LB VI 336A/Reeve I 218.

69 *veritatis*] 1540 and LB; *pietatis* 1522; *puritatis* in manuscript in Cambridge 1522

70 *Vox summi sensusque Dei*, the second line of a *Carmen paschale* formerly attributed to Claudianus Mamertus PL 53 788–9 (Ex Collectione Pisaurensi)

71 Lucius Caelius Firmianus, also called Lactantius, that is, the writer quoted above. For mention in Jerome, see *Commentarius in Ecclesiasten* 10:2 PL 23 1146C, *De viris illustribus* 80 PL 23 726A–B. Jerome's remarks about him were not

And there is Prudentius too in the hymn that the choir sings in church: 'Come, supreme Father, whom none has ever seen, and Christ, the Word [*sermo*] of the Father, and[72] kindly Spirit ...'[73] Was he afraid to call the Son of God *sermo*? And it is not that Prudentius was excused by metrical necessity; he could say, 'And Christ, *verbum* of the Father.' Perhaps someone might say, 'He is a poet.' Just because he wrote verse? But on this reasoning Ambrose was a poet too. But what prevents the same person from being a theologian and a poet? Certainly Prudentius breathes such virtue, such theological erudition, that the church has accepted his hymns as sacred and allowed them to be sung by its holy choirs.

And if anyone should object that many concessions are made to these early writers because of their antiquity, although it has already been proved that even modern writers liked the term *sermo*, come, let us bring forward Anselm's witness too and some other writers like him of moderate age whose authority may seem neither obsolete because it is too old nor insignificant because it is recent. So Saint Anselm,[74] explaining this passage in the Gospel, 'In the beginning was the Word,' writes as follows: 'The Son is called the "Word" [*verbum*] because through him the Father became known to the world, or because by uttering him, that is by engendering him, God the Father created all things. For this Son is the utterance [*dictio*] and the Word [*verbum*] and the speech [*sermo*] of the Father. The Father is the beginning, from which all things are made; the Son is the beginning, by which all things are made.' See how such a great man is not afraid to call the Son of God *sermo* and *dictio*, that is, the speaking [*locutio*] of the Father. The same author states that for the Son 'to be born' and 'to be uttered by the Father' are the same thing.

Again in John 17, explaining this phrase 'Sanctify them in truth,' he says:[75]

* * * * *

always complimentary; see for example *Commentariorum in quatuor epistolas beati Pauli ad Galatas liber* 2 PL 26 399C and ibidem *Ad Epheseos liber* 2 PL 26 543A.
72 *et Spiritus benigne*] Added in *1540*; not in *1520a* or *1522*
73 Prudentius *Carmina, Liber Cathemerinon* 6, *Hymnus ante Somnium* CCSL 126 29:1–4 / PL 59 831:1–4
74 As Boyle points out (n114), these passages are not to be found in the modern critical edition of Anselm. They are in fact from different authors. The first is from St Martin of León: *Sancti Martini Legionensis sermonum liber, Sermo quartus in Natale Domini* 2 PL 208 84C. The second is from Augustine *In Iohannis evangelium tractatus* 108 PL 35 1915. See the following note.
75 John 17:17. There may be some confusion here due to hasty composition. Erasmus perhaps knew that this second passage is from Augustine but omitted to

For so they are preserved from evil, as he prayed should be done before.[76] They were already sanctified, being not of this world, but he prays that they should progress further in the same holiness and should become more holy and be freed from the evil of treachery into which the traitor Judas fell. And so they are sanctified in truth as heirs of the New Testament, that is, in Christ; a truth that the signs of the Old Testament foreshadowed. And he expounds which truth he means, saying, 'Thy Word [sermo] is truth,'[77] that is, I who am the Son of the Father, the Word [verbum] of the Father, am the truth.

You see how Anselm is in accord with Augustine and is not afraid to call the Son of God sermo.

And there is Remigius who explains the phrase from the Epistle to the Hebrews, chapter 4: 'For the Word [sermo] of God is living,'[78] and writes as follows: 'The sermo of God the Father and the verbum is the Son.'[79] And shortly after: 'This is the Word [sermo] that never dies and remains always the same.' Again a little later: 'This is the Word [sermo] that says of itself, "If anyone keeps my Word [sermo], he shall never see death."'[80] For if they had kept that same Word [sermo] of God by believing rightly and living righteously, they would have life.' And again a little further on: 'The same is the Word [sermo] of God the Father, who lives always with the Father and through whom he can do all things.' And again after a number of other things, he says, 'Therefore the Word [sermo] of God the Father is so efficacious and sharper than any two-edged sword that it can distinguish between the works of the flesh and the works of the spirit, etc.'[81] And once more: 'What does it mean when it says, "To whom we apply the word sermo"[82] if not "with which Son," because it is to him we are to render account?' How many times does the holy Remigius press on us here the term sermo, which these people are terrified of as being new and unprecedented! Nor do I doubt but that infinite examples could be adduced by which we could show that approved Doctors of the church were not deterred by any

* * * * *

insert the name as the subject of *inquit*. The sentence following the quotation could be read as support for this.

76 John 17:15
77 The second phrase of John 17:17.
78 Heb 4:12
79 Remigius (ie Haimo of Auxerre; see n61 above) *Expositio in epistolam ad Hebraeos* in *In divi Pauli epistolas expositio* PL 117 849B–851B
80 John 8:51
81 Heb 4:12
82 Heb 4:13. See the remarks on Ambrose at n61 above.

scruple from calling Christ the *sermo* of the Father, if anyone had the time to investigate the passages. These have suggested themselves for the moment, and they must be amply sufficient to refute those who clamour that it is impious to call the Son of God *sermo*. For if any try to show by sophistical subtleties that Christ is correctly called *verbum* and incorrectly called *sermo*, what are they doing but making so many distinguished princes of the church blasphemers and lunatics?

But now, if you please, let us listen for a few minutes to see how frigid are the arguments put forward by certain people with such angry shouting. One of them has tried to demonstrate that the statement *In principio erat sermo* is simply untrue by means of the following syllogism: '"*Verbum*," he says, is a silent concept. But if Christ is correctly said to be *sermo*, it will follow that *sermo* too is a silent concept.' This he wanted to appear patently absurd, since *sermo*, according to him, 'is a concept uttered by the voice.' This is the syllogism of a theologian,[83] distinguished in the judgment of a few others and in his own in particular, a syllogism that he was not ashamed to put forward in the company of men of both the highest dignity and the highest learning. For a start, let us concede that *sermo* is something different from *verbum* in this argument; does it follow directly that Christ is not rightly called *sermo* because he is rightly called *verbum*? Is it wrong to call Christ 'light' or 'truth' because it is right to call him 'Word' [*verbum*]? Is it incorrect to call him 'spirit' because it is correct to call him 'Son'? But these designations are applied to persons because of the conventions of human speech, so that our dullness of mind may be more readily led to some knowledge of God.[84] And many terms are used of individual things as if they were literal, which in fact are not literal; nevertheless, because of the way they seize the attention of the human mind, they are used quite aptly to stand for a variety of things. Every time we do this, we necessarily make use of human terms; in any other sense the Son of God is neither a silent concept nor uttered by a voice, but that which is for us a silent concept of the mind is Christ abiding in the Father, with whom he has the same essence; that which is for us a meaning in the mind expressed in speech is Christ eternally born of the Father, from whom he is distinguished by the property of person. Otherwise, if Christ is no more than an internal word [*verbum*], in what sense did John say, 'And the Word [*verbum*] was with God'?

* * * * *

83 Cf Ep 1127A to Luther, where a similar argument is made by a 'Spanish Franciscan,' but quite probably Standish. See the introduction xvi above.
84 Cf *Paraphrasis in Joannem* 1 CWE 46 13 paragraph 1.

Nor does it escape me that Augustine in *De trinitate* book 15, posits a sort of twin *verbum*, one that is pronounced externally and one that is within. He believes that the term *verbum* is better for the latter since what is pronounced is rather the sound [*vox*] of the word than the word, and if the sound is called *verbum*, it is so called because of what assumes that form in order to appear outwardly; this Augustine interprets as meaning that Christ began to be the outward or spoken word only after he assumed human nature.[85] But while on the one hand I admit that what Augustine says is true, yet this is not all that is true. For nothing prevents the same Word from being uttered from the mind of the Father in several ways: it is uttered when Christ is begotten, the truest Word because most like the Father; it was uttered when through it the Father created all things and made fast the heavens with his Word. But it was uttered most plainly and in the way most familiar to us when he took on human form and spoke to us in human speech. Lest I seem with this to stray from my thought so far, I shall offer what Augustine himself relates in book 4, chapter 20 of *De trinitate*. He says, 'So is it any wonder if he is sent not because he is less than the Father[86] but because he is a true outpouring of the brightness of the omnipotent Father'; and shortly after: 'Nor does he flow like water from an earthen or stone outlet but like light from light. For what else does it mean when it is said, "For he is the brightness of eternal light," but that he is the light of eternal light?'[87]

If what in our terms is 'to utter the Word [*verbum*]' is in divine terms 'to emanate from the Father,' since the emanation is eternal,[88] the term cannot be understood literally as meaning the human form he took on. The same author put it more clearly in chapter 4 of his book *De cognitione verae vitae*, for

* * * * *

85 Augustine *De trinitate* 15 10–11 CCSL 51 485–7 / PL 42 1071–2

86 The question of the sense in which Christ is less than the Father was raised by Hieronymus Dungersheim in Ep 554 to Erasmus, March 1517, with reference to Phil 2:6 and Augustine *De trinitate* 1.7.

87 Augustine *De trinitate* 4 20 CCSL 50 196 / PL 42 906

88 Cf *Paraphrasis in Joannem* CWE 46 17: 'This word came continually forth from the Father without ever departing from the Father ... he was *with* God the Father, not an emission in time but before all time, proceeding from his Father's mind without ever departing from it.' 236 n27 adds: *non in tempore prolatus*. *Prolatio*, a patristic translation of προβολή 'emission' (a technical term of the Valentinians who held that the Son is essentially different and separate from the Father). Cf Tertullian *Adversus Praxean* 8 (where Tertullian tries to vindicate the orthodox use of the word). Cf also *Interlinear Gloss* (on 1:1) 185v: 'a word not emitted [*prolatum*] but always remaining by him.'

he recalls that *verbum* has three meanings: the first is when, for example, the word 'man' is enunciated by the voice; the second is when the same word 'man,' without any movement of the tongue, is formed in the mind; the third is when the thing itself, which that word signifies, is conceived as it is by the intellect.[89] Here it is clear that Augustine holds that the first meaning of *verbum* is the sound formed by the mouth; and it is clear that the emanation of the divine Word corresponds to our thinking. But since the thought of the Father is eternal, it follows both that the divine Word is born in another way and is sent forth in another way than by the human form he took on. For what is born in some way is sent forth in some way. Nor does it go against my argument that Augustine says, 'God engendered his Word [*verbum*] by this third way when he spoke himself in thought.' For[90] what he said here about *verbum* he was also going to say about *sermo*. Does he not make it sufficiently clear when he says, 'He spoke himself by thinking [*seipsum cogitando dixit*]' that thought is a type of speech [*sermo*]? In the *Commentaries* in which he explains the Gospel of John[91] he says the eternal Word [*verbum*] is engendered by the Father, as thought is engendered by the mind, declaring clearly enough that it is the same thing for Christ 'to be born of the Father,' 'sent forth by the Father,' or 'emanate from the Father.' I pass over the fact that, in the passage I have just quoted, the purpose of Augustine's argument is to explain the eternal *verbum*; in other contexts, when these terms are used of people according to human speech convention, *verbum* is said rather of what sounds than of what is conceived in the mind. And what is conceived in the mind is not said to be a *verbum* in any other sense except in so far as it sounds in some way.

This is also noted by Durandus, book 1, distinction 17, question 2: 'It must be noted,' he says, '*verbum mentis* does not have the meaning of *verbum* except in so far as it assumes the meaning of a *verbum* expressed.'[92] This

* * * * *

89 Not Augustine but Honorius of Autun (Augustodunus) *De cognitione verae vitae* 14 [not 4] PL 40 1015

90 LB, which normally italicizes words under discussion, reads 'Quod enim hic de verbo *dixit*' here, rather than the correct 'Quod enim hic de *verbo* dixit.' The example is not quoted in *1520a*; *1522* and *1540* make no distinctions with typeface.

91 Augustine *In Iohannis evangelium tractatus* 9 CCSL 36 5–6 / PL 35 1383–4

92 Durand de Saint Pourçain (Durandus a Sancto Porciano) *In Petri Lombardi Sententias Theologicas commentariorum libri* IV. *Liber* 1 *distinctio* 27 [not 17] *quaestio* 2 § 7 (Venice: Typographia Guerraea 1571; repr Gregg 1964) I f 77r 1. Erasmus misquotes slightly; however, *conceptus mentis*, the second of the four modes

is what Durandus says. But since the things the voice expresses are signs of the states that are present first in the mind and one corresponds to the other, each is called *verbum*. And sometimes Augustine makes no distinction between *sermo* and *verbum*. And when modern authors following Augustine argue that the *verbum mentis* is most properly called the *verbum* – conceding that they are right to say this – they nevertheless, when they argue these points, deem that there is no distinction between *verbum* and *sermo*; whatever *verbum mentis* is, so is *sermo mentis*. For someone who is thinking is, as it were, talking to himself.

And in Greek the etymology favours this belief more, because for them *logos* may mean *ratio*, *logismos* may be *cogitatio*, and *logizomai cogito* or *reputo*. *Sermo* seems to come from *sero*[93] [join together], whence also *dissero* [speak, discourse], and comes closer to the meaning of the Greek term than *verbum*, which the grammarians think is so said from the vibration [*verberatus*] of air, just as *vox* is from *boare* [to cry aloud, roar]. In the book *Principia dialectica*, which he wrote as a catechumen, Augustine adduces a fourfold etymology. According to this, for some *verbum* is so said because it vibrates [*verberet*] the air, for others because it vibrates the ear, and these people agree well enough among themselves as far as the etymology is concerned. Then for others *verbum* seems to be said as if it were something true [*verum*]; and again for others as if it were voicing something true [*verum resonans*], as the first syllable *ver-* is found in *verum* and the second *-bum* is found in *bombum*, that is, 'noise.' The first two derivations he does not reject, the last two he laughs at: 'For since,' he says, 'according to the view of these people the word of a liar should not be called a word, I am afraid that those who maintain these derivations are lying.'[94]

So since there is nothing here that does not support me, I should like you now, dear reader, to consider how wicked it is and how foreign to Christian sincerity to rant against someone else's reputation so odiously and without cause, and that publicly in the indiscriminate multitude of men and with seditious cries to incite coarse and uneducated common folk

* * * * *

of meaning Durand ascribes to *verbum*, is said above to be called also *verbum mentis*.

93 Erasmus' etymology is correct on this point; *sermo* derives from the same stem as the verb *sero, serui, sertum*.

94 Augustine *Principia dialectica* 6 PL 32 412. Erasmus was probably using the Amerbach edition of 1506, though this work was first published under the name of Chirius Consultus Fortunatianus in Venice in 1498. Erasmus, who edited the work in 1528–9, had no doubts about its authorship. See the edition and translation, Augustine *De dialectica* trans B. Darrell Jackson, Synthese Historical Library 16 (Dordrecht and Boston 1975) 91–3.

to throw stones.[95] If ignorant people did these things, one could pardon them for stupidity; if lay people did it, although the fault is serious, it would perhaps not be so monstrous. But these are the deeds of men who claim the principal chairs among professors of theology, who promise by the profession of religion a singular holiness of life, whose bicorned mitres make them pre-eminent, and this they do to a man who, having spent so much effort in vigils and labours, deserves the best of them. And yet those who shout these things most irksomely among the populace have not read my annotation on this passage, in which I state briefly that it is not a novelty, nor am I the first to think that the Son of God is called the *sermo* of the Father, but that the term was used in olden times by the orthodox writers Hilary, Cyprian, and Jerome.[96] They have only heard, while they were in their cups, that Erasmus had translated *erat sermo* instead of *In principio erat verbum*. But immediately, between one ladleful and the next, a proscription is declared, immediately they rush to the pulpit, they shout shamelessly, irrationally, nor do they stop to think what poor account they give of their own reputation as they attack someone else's with such stupid arguments. For if anyone shouts without understanding what he says, how little, I ask you, does he differ from a madman?

No one offered me advice, no one counselled me, no one convicted me of error; their whole expectation of winning lay in shouting, in the simple-mindedness and foolishness of the inexperienced mob, which for the most part does not judge. It believes the theologian, it believes the cowl, it believes the sacred pulpit from which they are accustomed to hear the word [*sermo*] of Christ, not the poisons of men. And if they go on in the same way as they have begun, what can they expect will happen but that others in their turn will shout against them from their pulpits, until at last the people come to their senses and drive these blowers of brazen horns off the bridges with stones.[97]

I would not want such a thing to happen, but these people are taking the matter as far as is indeed in their power. Maybe they do imagine that I have made a slip, maybe they do imagine that I was wrong to think Christ is correctly called *sermo*; what could be more unsuitable than to argue about these things in front of an undiscriminating crowd? Or rather not argue but

* * * * *

95 For this accusation particularly against Dominicans and Carmelites, see Ep 597:63–6 and the indexes of CWE 5–8.
96 Only Jerome was named in 1516; Cyprian and Hilary were added in 1519, though this passage was replaced in 1522.
97 That is, to consign them to idleness. Cf *Adagia* I v 37 'To throw the sexagenarians off the bridge.'

yap? If someone brings together errors in the works of St Thomas, Scotus, or Augustine and attacks them loudly in public, are they not going to drive him out of the pulpit as a creator of sedition? But if he objects and cries out, 'Why do you disapprove? Is it not allowed to say what is true?' they will answer, I think, 'What is true, yes, but these matters have nothing to do with ordinary people; they will have their place in the schools.' If Erasmus was less deserving of this honour, it should certainly have been accorded to the order of theologians, whose authority is diminished among ordinary people every time they realize that theologians are in conflict with one another over such divisions. Come, what if someone goes on at length among ordinary people about a hidden crime that this or that Dominican or Carmelite has perpetrated? No one will tolerate him, I think, even if what he was relating were true, either because something must be accorded to the reputation of the order or because these facts are not being discussed in the right place. For the populace expects from a preacher something that will make them wiser and better when they go home. This much could be said against them, even if I had clearly been at fault.

Now, though Christ is called *sermo* in so many places in the Bible,[98] even in the gospel Scriptures themselves and in this very passage they are yapping at, though it may be sung and read publicly in churches, even by those who are stoning me, though it may be repeated in the schools, though neither ancient nor modern orthodox ears have been shocked by this term, though for so many widely approved authors it makes no difference whether you say *sermo* or *verbum*, indeed though the term *sermo* is more appropriate and even more acceptable on several grounds, though it translates the Greek term λόγος more correctly, are they stirring up all these troubles for me simply because, in a work that is not read in churches or in schools but only in private rooms – where surely it is legitimate to read anything? – I have translated it just as the church read it formerly in public?[99] If it is impious, if it is blasphemous, if it is a capital offence to call Christ *sermo*, they must condemn before me or with me so many outstanding princes of the church: Cyprian, Ambrose, Jerome, Augustine, Hilary, Prudentius, Lactantius, and with these Thomas, Nicolas of Lyra, Hugh, the *Glossa ordinaria*, no, rather the whole church.

If it is pious, if it is done following the custom of both the primitive and the modern church, if it is done with the authority of the most respected Fathers, if it is a more appropriate term to use when we call Christ 'the Word of the Father' [*sermo patris*], think what a dreadful injury it is in public

* * * * *

98 Cf *Apologia de 'In principio erat sermo'* (1520a) 11 n37.
99 Cf *Apologia de 'In principio erat sermo'* (1520a) 11 n38.

sermons to hand over a well-deserving man to be stoned by the people – as indeed they can – and further, to slaughter a man who not only does no harm but in fact does real good. For is there not a very small difference between slaying with the hand or with the tongue? If Paul is not free of the charge of homicide on the grounds that, although he himself did not touch the stones, he guarded the cloaks of those who threw them, but rather he committed a more serious crime – on the grounds that he vented his rage through the hands of all the stone throwers – than if he had been one of their number,[100] what shall we say of those who with perverse zeal and devout minds rouse the credulous and uneducated populace to destroy a neighbour and do it from the very place whence the people are accustomed to hear the teaching of the Gospel? And this is being done by those who claim to be masters of gospel teaching and pillars of religion in its entirety.

These men are appealing to the power of both princes and people against the public usefulness of scholarship, against the glory of Christ, and against a man who has done his best to deserve well of everyone by his nightly vigils. How much more justly could we have appealed to the power of these same princes[101] and people against the wicked conspiracy of stupid pettifoggers, against this sort of factious impudence that pursues and assails not only myself, who am nothing, but even the holy Doctors of the church that I have just enumerated and whose authority I have followed in this interpretation! If this is not contained in good time by the authority of those who are at the helm of both administrations,[102] there is a danger that it will finally break out in serious harm to the peace of Christianity, if these shameless, thoughtless people could do whatever they wanted. Indeed it would not be difficult to guess even from this one case what importance we should assign to their judgment in other cases.

Yet those people who, you may swear, have not the human intelligence for honourable actions have still, believe me, a talent for slander. When they are thrown down from all their defences, they resort to scandal: 'If nothing else,' they say, 'you should yet have avoided novelty.' I do not have, I confess, that authority that Jerome had in his time, so that I too may properly despise the pumpkin-farmer[103] gods who rise up together in

* * * * *

100 For Paul and the stoning of Stephen, see Acts 7:58, 8:3, and 22:19–20. Cf also
     Erasmus' *Paraphrasis in Acta* 7, 8, and 22 CWE 50 56 and 131.
101 Erasmus appeals to Wolsey, Ep 1060.
102 Ie ecclesiastical and lay governments.
103 *cucurbitarii* 'empty head, brainless,' from *cucurbita* 'gourd, pumpkin.' Cf
     Jerome Ep 112.22 PL 22 930–1, where he defended his use of *hedera* 'ivy' in-
     stead of *cucurbita* to translate the Hebrew word for 'gourd plant' in Jon 4:6 in

dissent because of some unaccustomed little word. This only I ask: who in the end is hurt by this novelty they speak of? The learned, for whom I wrote the work? But the word *sermo* should not have been novel for them, since it is to be met in so many places in the books of orthodox writers. The unlearned? They hear no such thing in church, nor would they ever have dreamed that I had translated with *sermo* instead of *verbum* if these men had not of their own accord been public criers of this affair among the people. But not even the unlearned would have been harmed, if they had not been deceived by the lies and tricks of these men. For if they were stating the facts: that a certain Erasmus, who is not unskilled in both Latin and Greek, instead of *In principio erat verbum* had translated *In principio erat sermo*, and that the two words have the same meaning and both are found in the Scriptures, that the Catholic church accepted this reading in former times, nay rather that the word *sermo* more aptly expresses the Greek word *logos*, which the Evangelist used, and that this work by a man was approved by the supreme pontiff – who, I ask, even if he were unlearned, could possibly be harmed? And[104] yet if they had said these things, there would not, I think, have been any falsehood, whereas now everything they say is false.

Likewise since in reality there is nothing that can cause harm, since what I bring is not new – and if it were new, it could not cause harm because it is not forced on the ears of the public but is read in private at home – if any occasion for scandal does arise here, it must not be ascribed to any other causes than the factious clamouring with which this opportunity of harming good scholarship has been deliberately pursued. But they do not gain in this way either, for even the most ordinary folk feel that these people are not moved by reason but by hatred and are looking after their own business, not that of Christ. I would be ashamed to recount what they have no shame in blabbing out in large and mixed crowds. And in the meanwhile I shall not invoke on them any other ill than that they should come to their senses, recognize themselves for what they are, and prefer to use their tongues for the glory of Christ rather than misusing them to give a brother a bad name. In this way it will come about that they are pleasing to Christ, not displeasing to good men, and do no harm to one who deserves well. It is easy to do harm to anyone. To do harm to one who does not deserve it is utterly infamous, even among the wicked; but to do harm to one who deserves well is a particular sort of devilish malice.

* * * * *

response to an African adversary. Cf *Responsio ad annotationes Lei* CWE 72 100 n161 and Ep 843:57–62.

104 And yet ... false.] Added in manuscript in Cambridge *1522*

A DEFENCE BY ERASMUS OF ROTTERDAM AGAINST CRITICISM MADE IN PUBLIC TEACHING BY NICOLAAS OF EGMOND OF THE PASSAGE IN PAUL'S FIRST EPISTLE TO THE CORINTHIANS, CHAPTER 15 'WE SHALL INDEED ALL RISE AGAIN, BUT WE SHALL NOT ALL BE CHANGED'

Desiderii Erasmi Roterodami Apologia de loco taxato
in publica professione per Nicolaum Ecmondanum
Theologum et Carmelitanum Lovanii.
Locus est in epistola Pauli ad Corinthios priore, cap XV:
'Omnes quidem resurgemus, sed non omnes immutabimur'

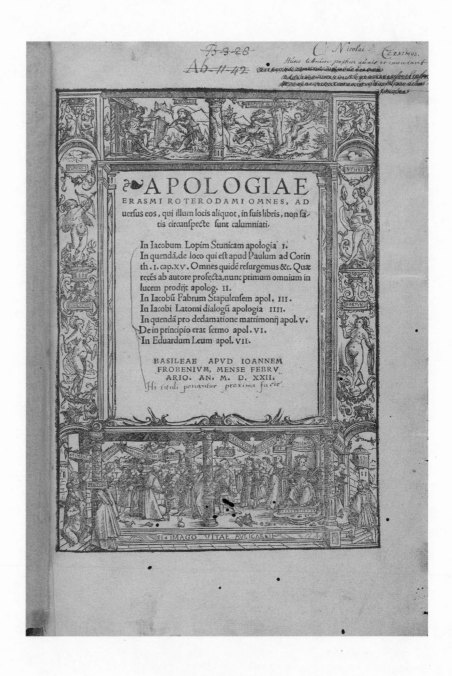

Apologia de loco 'Omnes quidem'
in *Apologiae omnes*
(Cambridge University Library, Adv.a.5.1)
title page

A DEFENCE BY ERASMUS OF
'WE SHALL INDEED ALL RISE AGAIN'[1]

In this passage the Greek codices of former times varied from one to another;[2] those we have now, though agreeing with each other, differ from our commonly accepted reading [c].[3] Indeed in all the Greek codices that I have actually seen (and I have seen not a few) the reading was πάντες μέν οὐ κοιμησόμεθα,[4] πάντες δὲ ἀλλαγησόμεθα 'We all indeed shall not sleep, but we shall all be changed [B].'[5] And there is no modern scholar who claims that he has found a different reading in the Greek versions. Latin codices

* * * * *

1 This translation is based on the text of *1522* as published in Asso, though the variants of *1540*, given there in footnotes, have been incorporated here in the translation. Latin passages have been given here in the footnotes to help in understanding the problem of Erasmus' alleged mistake.
   In the Latin title of this work, *Desiderii Erasmi Roterodami Apologia de loco taxato in publica professione per Nicolaum Ecmondanum Theologum et Carmelitanum Lovanii. Locus est in epistola Pauli ad Corinthios priore, cap XV: 'Omnes quidem resurgemus, sed non omnes immutabimur'*, the words *in publica ... Locus* were added in manuscript to Cambridge *1522*, thus identifying Baechem (and Standish; see n8 below) in *1540*, replacing an original *qui*. On Nicolaas Baechem and Henry Standish, see CEBR I 181–3, III 279–80. In *1540* and LB *Carmelitanum lovaniensem* replaces *Carmelitanaum Lovanii.*
2 *se*] Omitted in Cambridge *1522*; *inter* deleted in Cambridge *1522*; *inter se scripsi* in *1540*, omitted in LB
3 Asso's identifiers A, B, and C are used throughout (see n1 above and the introduction xxi n40 above).
4 See Cambridge *1522*; Asso 183n, *1540*, and LB IX show κοιμησόμεθα, the future middle; the corresponding annotation (LB VI 740F; see Reeve II 515) and the 1527 Froben edition of the NT have the future of a deponent κοιμάομαι, ie κοιμηθησόμεθα; both Greek forms are regularly translated by the Latin future *dormiemus.*
5 On 1 Cor 15:51, see Bruce Metzger *A Textual Commentary on the Greek New Testament* 2nd ed (Stuttgart 1994); and Max Zerwick and Mary Grosvenor *A Grammatical Analysis of the Greek New Testament* (Rome 1996) II 531.

have a different reading, namely: *Omnes quidem dormiemus, sed non omnes immutabimur* 'We shall indeed all sleep, but we shall not all be changed.'[A] But even if it were proved that the Greeks' reading were wrong and even if it had a heretical meaning (which we shall show with very sound arguments is far from the case), I still did not deserve to be assailed with insults, for I am not the author of this reading but the translator only. No, rather I would be to blame if I had translated differently from what the Greek books have, especially as in more than one place I declare, wherever I show that the Greek books have a different reading, that I do not thereby condemn what the published Latin edition has but, on the contrary, I admit sometimes that I prefer what our people read rather than what is found in the Greeks.

In addition to this, although I show carefully in my *Annotationes*[6] that important and orthodox writers recall different readings without disapproving of any, although I show that neither meaning is inconsistent either with Christian piety or the truth of gospel teaching – although, as I say, I made these points carefully, still two individuals, among the leaders and fighters in the vanguard of theologians, have attacked this passage as translated by me, not so as to say I have slipped by human error but so as to shout abroad that I introduce a dangerous heresy; and this, not in their cups or in informal conversations, but one of them[7] in the course of a public lecture in theology in Louvain, the other[8] before the very sagacious king of England and his queen, who is quite the equal of her husband, while a dense crowd of leaders and the most learned men surrounded them. And to make the matter more frightful, he said this prostrate at the knees of these very devout monarchs, eyes and hands raised to heaven, calling on gods and men to come to obviate the great dangers to the church that would shortly collapse if some swift remedy were not provided. Who would not be moved by these words? Especially as, in the first place, they were pronounced so piously by a theologian of many years experience and a man of great age, a Franciscan moreover, though of the sort who call themselves 'Conventuals,' and finally a bishop, not a suffragan or paid bishop, but a real bishop

* * * * *

6 *Annotationes in Novum Testamentum* 1 Cor 15:51 (*Omnes quidem resurgemus*) LB VI 740F–743F
7 Nicolaas Baechem. See the introduction xx and 43 n1 above.
8 Manuscript marginal notes in Cambridge *1522*, *1540*, and a footnote in LB indicate *nempe Joannes Standicius*, an error for *Henricus Standicius*. An account of this incident is also found in Ep 1126.

of rich fortune.[9] If I were to give his name here, I think I would do him no harm, and perhaps it would not be unwelcome; for it is not likely that he wants his declarations in that great gathering of such men to be hidden. But I will suppress his name in this *Defence*, though he did not suppress my name in his calumny. And I would not have added even these notes had I not thought I should take care that no suspicion be spread among many other harmless people. He brought the total of my heresies together in three articles, the first of which he derived from this passage.[10] For he said that I abolish the resurrection – a statement that no one could on the face of it take to mean other than that Erasmus teaches there is no resurrection of the body – and yet he would have understood, because I do not disapprove of the Greek reading [B] that means that those who are caught by the advent of Christ in their lifetime will not die (for only the dead rise again), that I deny resurrection only with respect to those whom I thought would not die. Although I neither attack nor defend this meaning but leave to others the right to judge various meanings given in other sources, and even if I had held tenaciously to this meaning, no one could rightly bring an accusation of heresy against me, as I shall immediately show.

But at the moment I have not undertaken to combat this slanderer in particular: for the affair is an old one, and having been confuted quite conclusively – but not really shamed – in public by the most learned men, he has paid the price of his temerity. Now recently in Louvain – if only I could stop at that! But in case an unchecked suspicion touches some innocent person, I shall indicate this man with a few points so that the others who heard the latest story may recognize him. He is a theologian, a leading one, if not by his qualifications at least by his position, which was given by the

* * * * *

9 The Conventuals are a branch of the Friars Minor founded by St Francis of Assisi distinguished by living together (*convenire*) in 'convents' and sharing goods, income, and property. The other two branches are the Capuchins (distinguished by their life as itinerant, mendicant preachers and their brown habit that has a hood) and the Observants (of the primitive rule; committed to holding no property in common and to renouncing all vested income and accumulation of goods). At this time Standish was about fifty-four years old. A suffragan bishop is the bishop of a diocese that is part of an ecclesiastical province headed by a metropolitan archbishop; see the *Code of Canon Law Annotated* (Montreal 1993) 331–3, Canons 435–7. Such a person might receive a stipend as opposed to the episcopal benefice of the metropolitan bishop.

10 For this incident, see Ep 1126:15–193 and the introduction to the *Apologia de 'In principio erat sermo'* xvi above.

measure of his years, not of his erudition; he belongs to the order called Carmelites – in which connection no one of that order is more unpleasing to me by a single hair[11] (I am criticizing the man, not the order) – and more than fifty-three years old, if I am not mistaken, judging by his physical appearance. When this man came to this passage from Paul in a lecture[12] – and an ordinary public one at that, which he himself wants to be considered deservedly respectable and which he obliges even theology candidates to attend – having been informed privily, I think, by someone over a drink that my edition differs here from the usual reading, he said, 'Here Erasmus introduces a heresy. For he approves a reading that contradicts what the church reads, because according to dialectical reasoning these statements are diametrically opposed: "We shall all rise again" and "We shall not all rise again," "We shall all be changed" and "We shall not all be changed." '[13] Although nothing is more horrible than this insult, still I shall explain in a few words how utterly unreasonably the[14] man, who seems to himself to be a light of religion, has twisted this against me.

So, in the first place – leaving aside for the moment the question of whether Chrysostom too, whose reading [B] is what this theologian here calls heresy, belongs to the Catholic church – if, as I began to say shortly before, the reading of the Greeks unquestionably had a heretical meaning, no accusation could be laid against me, for I claim to be no more than a translator, unless perhaps they will say that Jerome must be blamed for any errors that Origen slipped into his work *De principiis*, since he translated these in good faith for Latin ears as they had been written by Origen.[15] If

* * * * *

11 Latin *nominis Carmelitani, quamobrem nemo huius ordinis mihi vel pilo est iniucundior*. Is there another allusion to Baechem as the 'camel' here? See Asso 168; and Mark 1:6 *et erat Iohannes vestitus pilis cameli*. See also *Adagia* I viii 4 and 12.

12 Sometime in September 1521, just before Erasmus left Louvain.

13 In his biblical text and his *Annotationes* Erasmus did not, of course, say *non omnes resurgemus* 'We shall not all rise again'; he said *non omnes quidem dormiemus* 'We shall indeed not all sleep.' If this is in contradiction with *omnes quidem resurgemus*, it must be that Baechem (and Erasmus) are treating *omnes resurgemus* (c) as equivalent to *omnes dormiemus* (ie A). It seems unlikely that Baechem would have got this from the *Responsio ad annotationes Lei* where the obviously erroneous *non omnes resurgemus* appears. See the article cited in the introduction xxi n40 above.

14 *homo ut sibi videtur religionis lumen*] Added in manuscript in Cambridge 1522 and to the text in 1540

15 Erasmus refers to this translation also in the *Responsio ad Collationes* to Titelmans, 193 below, but says there that it has been lost.

anyone tries to do this, there is no one, I believe, who would not cry that the man should be dispatched to Anticyra.[16] Now how much more dishonest is it to make this accusation against me – I who put forward not this one reading but all the others also, who disapprove of none, who show that this reading, which this man calls heretical, caused no offence to many orthodox and respected authors. Unless perhaps a heretical sense was embraced by Chrysostom and his emulator Theophylact, who neither read anything different from what we read today in the codices of the Greeks nor interpret it any differently – specifically, that those who are overtaken by that day in their lifetime will not die but, together with the resuscitated dead, are to be transformed to the same sort of immortality so that for them the transition to immortality takes the place of resurrection. For I am of the opinion that in this whole discourse, certainly in accordance with the reading of the Greeks, Paul is dealing with the resurrection only of the pious. If anyone distrusts me, both Greek volumes are in the Dominicans' library in Basel, Switzerland. Indeed Origen too, an ancient author and among the most important, in the second book *Contra Celsum*,[17] introduces the following passage using the reading of the Greeks. He says, 'The trumpet will sound, and the dead will rise imperishable. But about the living, who are to be changed and separately from those rising again from the dead, he [Paul] writes thus: "And we shall be changed," which he said in any case when he had previously said, "The dead will rise again."'[18] It is clear enough from these words, I think, what Origen read and how he understood it; namely, that all the pious are to be changed, both those who come to life again having died before the day of the coming and those who are taken up in their lifetime. The latter indeed will not die, but they are to be changed along with those who had died.

* * * * *

16 A town in Phocis, famous for the production of hellebore, which was thought to cure madness. Cf *Adagia* I viii 52.

17 Origen *Contra Celsum* 2.65; Erasmus cites the second part of the verse as in B. See also *Contra Celsum* 5.17 where Origen cites the whole of verse 51.

18 1 Cor 15:52 (Erasmus' rendering of Origen's Greek) 'Tuba, inquit, signum dabit et mortui resurgent incorrupti. De vivis autem immutandis et a mortuis resurgentibus segregatim sic scribit: Et nos immutabimur, quod utique dixit ubi prius dixisset mortui resurgent.' Asso (196 93–8n) refers to Erasmus' edition of Origen of 1536 (IV 37), but see Origène *Contre Celse* I ed and trans Marcel Bourret SJ, *Sources chrétiennes* 132 (Paris 1967) 440:30–5. Asso (lines 95–8) puts *Tuba* [the trumpet] ... *mortui resurgent* [the dead will rise again] in italics, including the initial *inquit*. LB has the initial *inquit* and *De vivis ... scribit* in Roman, as if this were Erasmus' text.

But the authority of the Greeks is of little weight for this man I am dealing with – he was always strangely hostile to Greek studies, frequently crying out that every present evil in the world springs from these sources and ignoring the fact that it was from these sources that Cyprian, Jerome, Ambrose, and Augustine drew almost everything they produced in theology that is worthy of our attention. Before he uttered, or rather babbled, such hateful words as these, he should at least have asked himself – serious man that he is, who demands to be considered a pillar of theology[19] – if Jerome or Augustine or the more modern Thomas or the very widely known commentaries on all the Pauline Letters, which are wrongly reputed to be by Jerome, but which are by no means to be despised, or even the commentary known as the *Glossa ordinaria* had anything to offer in this matter. He is in the habit of claiming to know this text well; there is nothing that he could not have drawn from it as from a cornucopia. In short, if he so despises my *Annotationes* that he thinks they should be condemned without having read them himself, he should have informed himself from the sources of what led me to suggest this reading.

First, in the letter to Minervius and Alexander,[20] Jerome reports that there are two readings of this passage [A and B] and approves the one that is common church usage now [A or C][21] without disapproving the one that is the only one to be found nowadays in Greek books and also in the codex of great age that is in the pontifical library in Rome [B]; so let him [Baechem] not bawl, as he usually does, that my codices are fraudulent. First, as I said, in the letter he wrote to Minervius and Alexander, Jerome states that even in the Greek codices there were two readings, both the one that I have translated on the basis of Greek codices [B] and one that is seen in the usage of the Latin church [A or C].[22] Theodore of Heraclea and Apollinarius follow the former [B], Origen and Didymus the latter [A or C].[23] But on this

* * * * *

19 *theologiae*] In manuscript in Cambridge 1522 and 1540, 'of theology'; *religionis* in 1522, 'of religion'
20 Jerome Ep 119 CSEL 55 446–69
21 Latin *hanc qua vulgo nunc utitur usus ecclesiasticus*. I translate assuming that Erasmus is conflating A and C. See the introduction xxi n40.
22 Latin *eam quam usus habet ecclesiae Latinae*
23 Ie Theodorus Heracleotes and Apollinarius of Laodicea (c 310–90). Quoted by Jerome, CSEL 55 447 and 449. The relevant writings of both these authors appear to be lost. Erasmus refers to Jerome who sets out the arguments for the interpretation of the Alexandrian theologian Didymus (c 313–98) in Ep 119 CSEL 55 449–50: *Didymus non pedibus, sed verbis in Origenis sententiam transiens, contraria via graditur* 'Didymus walks on a different road not in the footsteps but in words [ie metaphorically] crossing into the view of Origen,' ie

matter Jerome prefers the reading that Latin codices have today: 'We shall all sleep, but we shall not all be changed.'[24] [A] I admit this; but[25] in the letter to Marcella, question 3, he simply approves what the Greeks have, namely that those upon whom the advent of the Lord comes in their lifetime will not die but in those same bodies will go to meet the Lord in the air, so that, as he said, the bodies of the living will be transformed into the same substance as resurrected bodies are to have.[26] And not content with this, Jerome removes even those other scruples that can be brought against this opinion from other passages in the Scriptures. So let me repay with the same coin the man who puts up Jerome against me. Let me do without the defence of a second passage and see what reasoning moved Jerome to prefer this reading – though he does express his preference for this one without disapproving of the other. If his reasoning is shown to be invalid, Jerome's authority should have no more weight with us than the reasoning that he followed. Now he thinks, if we read, 'We shall not all sleep, but we shall all be changed,' [B] that what follows,[27] 'The dead will rise imperishable and we shall be

* * * * *

Didymus arrives at the same conclusion as Origen although he starts from an opposite text. Jerome also shows that Origen cites B in *Contra Celsum* (see 47 n17 above) and twice in *Exegetica* 3; see Jerome's citations of Origen on 1 Thess 4:14–17 and on 1 Cor 15:52, CSEL 55 460:9–11, 464:8–9. At the end of the same letter Jerome states unequivocally that the reading of the Latin codices is *omnes quidem resurgemus, non omnes autem inmutabimur* 'We shall indeed all rise, but we shall not all be changed' (C), and that this is not found in Greek books but rather either 'We shall all sleep, but we shall not all be changed' (A) or 'We shall not all sleep, but we shall all be changed' (B; CSEL 55 469:6–11).

24 Jerome reports that the reading of the Latin codices 'will better agree with the truth to read "We all indeed shall sleep, but we shall not all be changed," especially because there follows, "The dead will rise incorruptible, and we shall all be changed"' (*magis conveniet veritati ita legere: 'omnes quidem dormiemus, non omnes autem immutabimur,' maxime quia sequitur: 'mortui resurgent incorrupti et nos immutabimur'* Ep 119 CSEL 55 458:10–13).

25 *sed idem in epistola ad Marcella ... alterius loco patrocinio et* [but in the letter to Marcella ... defence of a second passage and] Added in *1540*; not in manuscript in Cambridge *1522*

26 Jerome Ep 59 CSEL 54 543–4. Jerome does not explicitly say that those upon whom the advent of the Lord comes in their lifetime will not die, but he refers to 2 Cor 5:4 'not that we would be unclothed but that we would be further clothed, so that what is mortal may be swallowed up by life,' and he describes the transformation of the mortal bodies in a manner that appears to justify the interpretation of B.

27 Erasmus quotes Jerome for several lines in the words 'that what follows ... but we shall not all be changed.' See Jerome Ep 119 CSEL 55 449:19–20.

changed,'[28] hardly fits with what precedes. For, he says, if all will be changed and this is the common lot of others, it was unnecessary to say, 'And we shall be changed.' It follows that the reading should be: 'We shall all sleep, but we shall not all be changed.' [A] The facts will show how far Jerome's attention strayed here. First, in this context it fits that 'We shall sleep' is intended to mean 'We shall die.' Then 'We shall be changed' for some means 'We shall be transformed to glorious immortality,' so that it applies only to the just, and for others 'We shall be transferred to immortality of the body' means that it applies both to the just and the unjust. To me it seems that Paul is talking here of the resurrection of the just because of the words that follow: 'But when this perishable puts on the imperishable ... then shall come to pass the saying that is written ...'[29] Also because of the words that have preceded: 'I tell you this brethren: flesh and blood shall not inherit the kingdom, nor shall the perishable inherit the imperishable.'[30] This was the opinion of Acacius, bishop of Caesarea, and of our Ambrose.[31] But if anyone finds it more legitimate to read the statement as general and applying to both classes [believers and unbelievers], I have no intention of doing battle with that idea since it has very little to do with what I am discussing now. Therefore, when Paul was about to explain the nature of the resurrection and had said, 'We shall not all die' (whether this is said of Elias and Enoch[32] or of those whom the coming of Christ will overtake in their lifetime) 'but we shall all be transformed to immortality,' both those who will come to life again and those whom the sudden advent of Christ will overtake in their lifetime, he goes on to explain more specifically what he had suggested in general. For as if someone had asked how it will happen that the living will be transformed at the same time as the dead, he teaches us that it will be done with marvellous speed, truly at a nod of the Deity who can do all things and not by the action of nature, which performs what it does slowly and with effort. He says, 'In a moment, in the twinkling

* * * * *

28 1 Cor 15:52
29 1 Cor 15:54
30 1 Cor 15:50
31 Acacius' views on 1 Cor 15:50–3 are discussed by Jerome Ep 119 CSEL 55 452–4. The reference to Ambrose refers to the commentaries on the Pauline Epistles known now as those of Ambrosiaster but not recognized by Erasmus as such until 1527. See CWE 56 xii–xiii.
32 See 2 Kings 2:11; Gen 5:24; Jerome Ep 119 CSEL 55 447:13–24. 'Elias' is the Greek form of Elijah used in the authorized version of the NT (eg Matt 17:3, 4, 10; Luke 1:17; John 1:21; Rom 11:2).

of an eye, at the last trumpet. For the trumpet will sound,' and both things will be done at once. What are these two things? First, the dead will come to life again; and they will not come to life to die again, but they will now have an imperishable body. 'But nevertheless,[34] a moment before, Paul, you had said that some will not die; what is to become of them?' His reply to this is: 'We also shall be changed,' as if putting himself among those whom the advent of the Lord will overtake in their lifetime or assuming their identity for himself in order to teach. Therefore 'We also shall be changed' is not repeated superfluously, but because the phrase 'But we shall all be changed' was rather obscure, he expands it so that it is clearer, setting out explicitly who those are who will not die and yet will be changed. If anyone argues that this is superfluous, then superfluous too will be practically all mathematical demonstrations that explain by particular examples what a rule teaches in general.

So, since Jerome's argument carries no weight, his authority should not disturb anyone regarding this passage, especially as serious and learned authors would not be at all worried by the scruple that seems to have worried Jerome when, as I believe, he was distracted by some other concern.

St Ambrose appears to deduce the same meaning as the Greeks [ie as B] from a different reading, as far as the first clause of the sentence is concerned. He reads thus: 'We shall all rise again; we shall not all be changed.' [c] These words he interprets as follows: 'Those of us who are found to be dead at the advent of Christ will all rise again. Those of us who are found to be in the body will not all be changed, because the holy alone will attain the glory of blessedness.' And he repeats the same opinion a little later when he says, 'Or at least [Paul] says simply all the dead will rise again, and only the holy, along with those of the living who have been found just, will be transformed into glory.'[35] You see that he thinks some are not destined to die at the advent of Christ; you see that these same people, along with those who had been sleeping before and have come to life again, will be transformed to immortality. So where now

* * * * *

34 *sed*] In *1522*, 'but'; *atqui* in manuscript in Cambridge *1522* and in LB (a stronger adversative), 'but nevertheless'
35 There are interpolations by Ambrosiaster on 1 and 2 Corinthians in certain manuscripts of the Pelagius commentaries. For this passage, see Souter I 53–4:27–40. The text in Ambrosiaster (II 183) is different from that quoted by Erasmus but says essentially the same.

is that 'contradiction'[36] that made a heresy out of an orthodox meaning?[37] Before he burst out with the word 'heresy,' since he wishes to appear a philosopher, the man should have considered whether he has not left out some element or other of a true contradiction – unless perhaps he thinks it is a contradiction if I say of the twelve apostles, 'They are all pleasing to Christ,' and of the Carmelites, 'They are not all pleasing to Christ.' Both propositions are true, both 'We shall all rise again' and 'We shall not all rise again.' 'We shall all rise again' is true if[38] you speak of those who will have died before the Saviour's advent; 'We shall not all rise again' is true if you were speaking generally of the whole human race. Likewise 'We shall all be changed' and 'We shall not all be changed' are equally true: 'We shall all be changed' because we shall be taken from here to immortality; 'We shall not all be changed' because we shall not all attain the glory of immortal life.

But perhaps this man who slanders me, just as he grants nothing to Greek writers because he has with Greek literature 'a truceless war,'[39] so he does not grant much to Jerome and Ambrose because they devoted themselves to Greek. But Augustine, a Doctor so warmly approved by the consensus of all scholars, he will not, I think, despise. In the book that is attributed to him under the title *De ecclesiasticis dogmatibus*, Augustine, stating the opinion of those who say that all will die and therefore will rise again, adds the following: 'But there are other equally Catholic and learned men who believe that those who will be found alive at the Lord's advent will be transformed to the uncorrupted state and immortality with their soul remaining in their body, and that this will be counted to them as a resurrection from the dead because they put off mortality by means of change, not by death. Whichever belief one accepts, he is not a heretic unless he becomes a heretic by his obstinacy. For it satisfies the law of the church to believe that there is resurrection of the flesh from death.'[40] This slanderer, without the least hesitation, calls my translation from the Greek 'heresy,'

* * * * *

36 Greek ἀντιλογία
37 Erasmus is satisfied that he has shown there is no doctrinal fault in using B.
38 *si loquaris*] In manuscript in Cambridge 1522 and 1540; *si loquatur* in 1522, 'if one speaks'
39 Greek ἄσπονδος πόλεμος; see *Adagia* III iii 84.
40 *De ecclesiasticis dogmatibus liber Gennadio tributus* (mistakenly attributed to Augustine) PL 42 1213–22. The Migne editor quotes at the end of his introductory caution the censure of the treatise by the Louvain theologians; see PL 42 2013. Erasmus' text here is PL 42 1215, chapter 7. In LB the last two sentences are not italicized.

and Augustine calls those people 'equally Catholic and learned.' Which are you disposed to believe, Augustine or Suffenus?[41] Let that be the name to use for him for the moment.

Now the man who brought together the commentaries on all the Epistles of Paul attributed, though wrongly, to Jerome was nevertheless, it is clear, a learned man, who stitched them together from ancient sources;[42] he is mindful in this passage of three readings: 'We shall all indeed rise again, but we shall not all be changed' [c] – a reading that, although followed by Ambrose, Jerome says is not found in the Greek codices, since in these are found the other two; the second, which disagrees with this very little,[43] 'We shall all indeed sleep, but we shall not all be changed'; [A] and the third, 'We shall not all sleep, but we shall all be changed.' [B] And it is this last reading that he approves most strongly as best fitting the Apostle's meaning.

Finally, in the commentaries in which he expounds this Epistle, Thomas Aquinas[44] indicates the double reading and not only does not disapprove the one that the Greek codices have but even says that it has no heretical meaning.[45] And Peter Lombard too in book 4, distinction number 43, recounting some extracts on these points from Augustine's *De civitate Dei* book 20, chapter 20,[46] does not reject either opinion but adds of his own accord: 'I would like to hear preferably some of the more learned doctors on these points,'[47] clearly saying that he sees nothing heretical there.

So does old Bleary-eyes[48] see a heresy that men with such good eyes have not seen? What about the fact that this reading is consistent with the

* * * * *

41 Cf *Adagia* II v 12. Suffenus is the poets' stereotype of a conceited fool.

42 These commentaries are now known to have been mainly by Pelagius; see the introduction xxxiii n95. This passage, however, is found in the interpolations of Pseudo-Jerome; see Souter III 43.

43 Latin *altera minimum ab hac dissonans*. The comment is by Erasmus; in the text that he quotes, the second is introduced simply by the word *aliter* 'otherwise.'

44 *divus Thomas Acquinas*] 1522; a 'delete' mark in the margin of Cambridge 1522 indicates *divus* is to be omitted, as in 1540.

45 Thomas Aquinas *Super primam epistolam ad Corinthios lectura* cap 15 lectio 8 nn1003–4 in *S. Thomae Aquinatis super epistolas S. Pauli lectura* ed P. Raffaele Cai (Turin 1953) I 425–6. Thomas speaks here in fact of all three readings, following Jerome.

46 *De civitate Dei* PL 41 688; CSEL 40–2 476; CCSL 48 734

47 *Magistri Petri Lombardi Parisiensis episcopi Sententiae in IV libris distinctae* Spicilegium Bonaventurianum 4–5 (Grottaferrata 1981) II 514–15

48 'Old Bleary-eyes' (*lippus noster*); cf Plautus *Miles gloriosus* 292; Horace, *Epistles* 1.1.29; Martial 12.59; Perseus 2.72.

passage in the First Epistle to the Thessalonians, chapter 4? Since the comparison of like and unlike passages is the surest key to Holy Scripture, we read there as follows: 'We who are alive, who are left until the coming of the Lord, shall not precede those who have fallen asleep. For the Lord himself will descend from heaven with a cry of command, with the archangel's call, and with the sound of the trumpet of God. And the dead who are in Christ will rise first; then we who are alive, who are left, shall be caught up together with them in the clouds to meet Christ in the air; and so we shall always be with the Lord.'[49] Nor does it escape me that certain people interpret 'the living' here to mean 'the just' and 'those who sleep' to mean 'sinners.' This is what Origen and his imitators do, often taking the liberty in obscure passages of Scripture of amusing themselves with tropological figures, especially whenever they exhort people to teach virtue or deter them from vice, and likewise in their commentaries where they want the greatest freedom to put forward different opinions, so that the reader may be supplied with material for thought. But according to Jerome, Apollinarius and Diodorus reject this gloss, preferring to take 'the living' here to mean not 'the just' but all those whom the coming of Christ will overtake in their lifetime.[50]

Otherwise if we interpret *dormientes* to mean 'the unjust' what follows will not accord with it: 'We who are alive ... shall not precede those who have fallen asleep.' For when he says 'we shall not precede' he means that two groups will be caught up together to meet Christ in the air; but the unjust will not be caught up in the air to meet Christ, only the just. When Ambrose expounds this passage from the epistle to the Thessalonians he brings in a cunning argument which is more wordy, in my opinion, than weighty. He says: 'Within this very act of being caught up death will come, and as in a deep sleep the soul, having gone out, is given back in a moment. For when they are taken they will die so that, coming to the Lord, they will receive their souls in the presence of the Lord, because the dead cannot be with the Lord.'[51] And this is what Augustine seems to have followed in the passage I have just quoted, although he evaluates it in such a way that he seems not to trust this opinion entirely but rather to put it forward as if he is reluctant to regard it as certain, but is content if what is suggested does not seem unbelievable.[52]

* * * * *

49 1 Thess 4:15–7
50 See Jerome Ep 119 CSEL 55 458:17–460:4 and PL 33 1545–1628, which preserves some fragments of Diodorus of Tarsus (d c 392). For positive assessments by Basil and Jerome of Diodorus as a commentator on Paul, see PL 33 1556–8.
51 Ambrosiaster III 228:1–5
52 Augustine *De civitate Dei* 20.20 PL 41 687–90

The only matter left now is to investigate a few scruples by which certain people have been upset and have had recourse to petty commentaries of this sort. For certain people think it is absurd, since men are said to be mortal because they must die, to exempt some from this universal law. But this idea does not upset Jerome at all; to Marcella, who asked whether all would die or if those whom the advent of Christ would overtake in their lifetime would be taken up alive in the air to meet Christ, since the Lord himself died and since Enoch and Elias are said in the Apocalypse to be destined to die, he gives the answer that they will not die but will be changed from mortality to immortality.[53] Besides, what is said in the Apocalypse should not be taken literally but in the mystical sense; otherwise people would happily interpret other things that are narrated there about the building of the temple and sacrificing victims in a literal sense, and nothing could be more absurd than that. I am surprised that these interpretations were not obvious to such a great theologian (as my critic wishes to be considered), especially as they are recounted in that very common patchwork[54] called the *Glossa ordinaria*.

St Augustine is particularly impressed by the words of Paul in chapter 15 of the first Letter to the Corinthians: 'As in Adam all die, so also in Christ shall all be made alive,' especially since he adds, 'What you sow does not come to life unless it first dies.'[55] For we seem here to be exhorted by Paul's statements to believe that in the very act of being caught up, the living will die and come to life again instantaneously, although in my opinion there is no need of this. For in the first place, this statement can be taken to mean those who will fall asleep before the coming of the Saviour, as we have shown some orthodox ancient writers interpreted the statement 'We all indeed shall sleep.'[56] [A] In the second place, St Augustine, whose words are quoted in the *Glossa ordinaria*, explains the meaning of this passage and says, 'In Adam all die, in Christ all are made alive, because no one was destined to death except through the former, no one is ordained to life except through the latter; for as through Adam all children of this world

* * * * *

53 Jerome Ep 59 CSEL 54 541–7 and 543:14–544:14 mentions both Enoch and Elias, as does the *Glossa ordinaria* on Rev 11:3–7; see also 50 n32 above.
54 *in vulgatissima rhapsodia*
55 1 Cor 15:22 and 36. For Augustine see n56 below.
56 See Jerome Ep 119:2, where he attests that this reading was known among the Greeks: Theodorus, Didymus, Apollinarius, Origen. Augustine knew two readings among the Latin versions: ' "*Omnes resurgemus*" *vel sicut alii codices habent* "*Omnes dormiemus*," ' *De civitate Dei* 20.20 PL 41 689, CSEL 48 734 49–51. Erasmus finds only the latter version in Latin codices. See the introduction xxii n42 above.

became mortals from his penalty, so through Christ all the sons of God are made immortal in grace.'[57] That is what Augustine says. Those who are born mortals because of the fault of our first parent are said to die, and those who are made immortal by the bounty of Christ are said to be brought to life. Moreover, 'mortality' and 'immortality' apply also to those who for any reason may happen not to die.

Several people bring forward also a verse in the Epistle to the Hebrews: 'It is appointed for all men to die once.'[58] If it is appointed for all to die, it follows that no one does not die. To this two replies can be given. First, general statements of this sort do not exclude exceptions in favour of a few; the holy Isaiah was not a thief and a robber just because Christ said in the Gospel, 'All who came [before me] are thieves and robbers,'[59] but so few were the good prophets and scholars compared to the multitude of the Pharisees and false prophets, that he could say 'all' meaning 'most' and could take so few to be none. Again Peter and Barnabas did not prefer their own profit to the work of Christ just because Paul wrote, 'They all look after their own interests, not those of Jesus Christ,'[60] but he said 'all' referring to the many who were preaching Christ insincerely because there were very few indeed who were preaching as he did. And Nathan the prophet did not go astray and become useless just because the psalmist wrote, 'They have all gone astray, they are all alike useless';[61] nor are the Apostle's words untrue, 'All have sinned and fall short of the glory of God,'[62] just because Christ was free of all sin and through him the Virgin Mother, if we should trust the plausible affirmation of certain authorities.[63] Therefore, since from so many centuries we read of only two,

* * * * *

57 For the general idea, though not the words, see eg *De civitate Dei* 13.24 PL 41 689, CCSL 48 408:111–20. The *Glossa ordinaria* at 1 Cor 15:22 quotes these lines with an attribution to Augustine in the *editio princeps* (Strasburg: Adolph Rusch 1480/81) and subsequent editions (*Biblia latina* IV [333a]). At 1 Cor 15:51 the *Glossa* quotes Jerome's letter to Marcella (*Biblia latina* IV [335a]).

58 Heb 9:27

59 John 10:8

60 Phil 2:21

61 Ps 13 (14 RSV):3 *omnes recesserunt simul conglutinati sunt.* Erasmus has *omnes declinaverunt simul inutiles facti sunt.*

62 Rom 3:23

63 Regarding the sinlessness of the Virgin Mary there were two positions that were hotly debated. In a concise treatise addressed to Pope Leo X in 1515 and entitled *De conceptione Mariae Virginis,* Cajetanus (1469–1534) summarizes the arguments: one side is more probable (that the Blessed Virgin Mary was cleansed from original sin), the other is tolerable (that the Blessed Virgin was

Enoch and Elias, who have been plucked from death – and there will be very few whom that sudden advent will overtake in their lifetime, especially as a good part of humanity will have been annihilated by the afflictions of the Antichrist, pestilence, famine, and earthquake – they will seem to be none in comparison with the immense multitude that has yielded to the tyranny of death in such a long stretch of centuries in the whole world.

Second, these mortals, few though they may be, were still destined to die if chance did not pluck them away from death. This argument, let me say, could eliminate the objection based on the Epistle to the Hebrews (I do not, however, detract from its authority; I grant that it is as valid as if it were written by Paul).[64] The answer could be this: Paul is not talking there about the necessity of dying, something that no mortal can evade, but he is concerned that we should understand that mortals – who by the common law of those who are born do die – die only once, nor does anything remain once they have encountered death unless, through the seed that they have sown in their lifetime, they produce a harvest. And this fact, approved and confessed in all minds, he adapts to the teaching that the death of Christ, by which he redeemed the human race, is never to be repeated; nor is any other sacrifice required for the sins of humankind, nor does anything remain except that he who appeared here in human form and sacrificed himself to the Father in dying on the cross will appear in glory to his own, illustrious in his final coming, to act as the judge of all, having first offered himself totally as the Saviour of all. This is the only way to attain to the real meaning of Scripture, by paying careful attention to what the writer is talking about.

* * * * *

preserved from the stain of Original Sin). The authorities, scholars, and saints on both sides are listed, and special attention is drawn to a decretal (*Extravagantis*) of Pope Sixtus IV (1471–84) who had approved the feast of the Immaculate Conception in 1476. Cajetanus points out that with regard to this issue 'the tongues of preachers and the hands of writers are to be checked and neither ought to condemn the other part as contrary to God, to Sacred Scripture, or to the determination of the church, but they should write and speak soberly according to the precept of the apostolic see by Sixtus IV'; see *Opuscula omnia F. Thomae de Vio Caietani Ordinis Praedicatorum* (Venice: Francesco de' Franceschi 1596) II 1:135–40. See also Hilmar Pabel *Conversing with God: Prayer in Erasmus' Pastoral Writings* (Toronto 1997) 86–90. For Cajetanus, see CEBR I 239–42.

64 Cf 56 at n58 above. For Erasmus' doubts concerning the Pauline authorship of the Epistle to the Hebrews, see CWE 44 353 n3.

With a similar argument we can also remove the doubt of those who are displeased by this statement of Paul: 'What you sow, O man, does not come to life unless it dies.'[65] For Paul is not concerned here either to show that no one avoids death but, using an analogy from human activities that are common knowledge by any standard, to tell us that what evangelical teaching promises is not incredible. For every day we all see cold, dry seed, dead and, as it were, buried, and after it has putrefied it re-emerges as if coming to life again, first as a tender, juicy grass, then as a mature crop, and all this according to the ordinary course of nature; if this is so, why should we doubt God's promises that he intends, by his special power, to call our bodies, though putrefied in the earth, back to life and to an even happier state? So this is what Paul is talking about there, seemingly incredible to many people, that those who have died once will come to life again. Moreover, the question whether a small number will by chance be withheld from the common necessity has very little weight for the majority of the human race.

There are some who even seem to be upset by the idea that, since the resurrection is a special part of the Christian faith, it[66] is not fitting to have an ambiguous reading or meaning here. Would that there were nothing of that sort in Holy Scriptures! But that was not Christ's intention; otherwise there would not be so many enormously learned scholars sweating over so many passages, investigating and rooting out[67] the meanings of the sacred books. But in this passage – to leave aside the reading that the Greek codices have and that ancient orthodox writers indicate [B] – the particular one that the Latin church follows nowadays has an ambiguous meaning, as I have shown above from the divergent interpretation of the ancients.[68] But Augustine dissipated this scruple also, saying that it is not necessary for us to know with certainty every manner of resurrection, that it is enough if we believe that the bodies of the dead will come to life again and will live for eternity along with the soul that they previously had, either to possess

* * * * *

65 1 Cor 15:36

66 *non conveniat*] *1540*; *non convenire* in *1522*. The sentence there is difficult to construe. In Cambridge *1522* Erasmus inserts a caret after *convenire* but does not indicate what he would add.

67 *erudiendis*] *1522* and *1540*, 'elucidating'; but Erasmus indicates in Cambridge *1522* that he would alter this to *eruendis* 'rooting out' or 'eliciting.'

68 48 and 52 above. The reference is to Jerome and others on the one hand (ie to A) and to Ambrose (ie Ambrosiaster) on the other (ie to C). It seems the phrase 'the particular one that the Latin church follows nowadays' must refer to both A and C.

joy or to suffer punishment for the deserts of the life already lived, and that there will not be any other fate for those whom the advent of Christ will overtake in their lifetime, whether they are to die and immediately be transformed to immortality or, without any intervention of death, they are to be taken from mortality to immortality.[69] Would that all we who are called Christians were as sure of this as we may, quite safely, be unsure about what God intends to become of those whom that day will overtake alive!

These, excellent reader, are the thoughts that helped me at this time to fight such an extraordinary and public slander. If the man who proclaimed heresy has read none of them, what could be more contemptible than such indolence in a public, theological declaration? If he has read them, what could be more perverse and malicious than to spew out on a brother such an unconscionable insult? There should be a great difference between the profession of theologian and that of grammar teacher or poet, but who has ever heard such blind petulance in the schools of those who teach the humanities, laughable though these be in your theologians' eyes? This man told me to my face that poets and rhetoricians make lies of everything, but what name shall we give to this theologian's deed? If he had called me babbler or a pettifogger without any reason, what honest person would not have deplored the unbridled abuse of the man – especially as he brought no proof? On the contrary, he had not even read those works of mine that he was condemning. Now does this eminent man, this model of all religion, who thinks the word 'idle talker' and the comment on a certain person as 'a little tipsy' – without misusing that word – after a rather generous meal should be avenged with every sort of punishment, does this man openly, during a holy service, charge his neighbour with heresy, and is he so blinded by hatred that he could not be corrected even by shame?[70]

* * * * *

69 Augustine *De civitate Dei* 20.20 PL 41 689–90, CCSL 48 734–6
70 Baechem's accusation 'You poets are all imagination and all falsehood' is reported in Ep 1162:54–5. 'A little tipsy' in Latin is *subuvidus;* cf *uvidus* in the same letter, translated as 'tipsy' (Ep 1162:134 and 139). 'Idle talker' in the Latin is *mataeologus.* See the letter to Rosemondt (December 1520), Ep 1172:15, where Erasmus complains that his description of Baechem as *mataeologus* was not tolerated by the faculty, but all the 'scurrilous stuff' bandied about against himself is encouraged. Cf Ep 1173:125. The term is used in the NT at 1 Tim 1:6 (ματαιολογία 'vain discussion') and Titus 1:10 (ματαιολόγος 'empty talker'). Erasmus used the former as the pretext for an attack on scholastic theologians. For the dispute caused by the use of this term in 1519 in connection with the *Encomium matrimonii,* see De Vocht 315 n2; see also Rummel *Annotations* 143–5.

Indeed every time he blurts out terms like this (and he blurts them out almost every day) he sees some of his hearers laughing and some of them by their obvious expression of indignation showing that such words are not worthy of a school of theology. Is there anything these people are not ashamed to say in their cups, if they are not afraid to spew out words like these in public theology lectures? Does he want everything he says to seem like an oracle, without holding back words like these – things that even Orestes would hardly give vent to?[71] And does he all the while picture himself as exceptionally saintly? Does he think the Catholic church is on the point of collapse and rests upon his shoulders? Does he think the moral standards of this whole country are made better by his own teaching and life, preaching the Gospel with such a tongue, daily consecrating and consuming the most holy symbol of Christian concord with such a mouth?[72] Personally I do not condemn the fact that he wears a white cloak, but I assert that he would sin less if he replaced the white with black or even green, than if he continues to blacken the reputation of his neighbour with such horrible lies.[73] No, rather he would be less wicked if, instead of Elias' mantle, he put on Labrax's yellow toga or Thraso's purple cloak and waved his sword around, since he hides his intention under a cloak of religion and uses his murderous tongue like a dart tipped with poison.[74] I do not blame him for abstaining from eating meat on Wednesdays, but I believe what this Maevius overlooks in himself is more detestable in the eyes of God.[75] It would be less of a sin if he gnawed hare and chicken on Fridays rather than gnawing and tearing at a quite undeserving neighbour. He does not kill anyone with a sword, but this is a form of homicide, perhaps all the more villainous in that it is more premeditated and less accountable. He does not murder anyone with poison, but this is one of the most damnable sorts of poisoning – to make a foul-tongued attack on a brother's soul. 'Anyone who hates his brother is a murderer,'

*　*　*　*　*

71 For Orestes' madness, see Aeschylus' *Choephori* and *Eumenides* and Euripides' *Orestes* and *Electra*. See also *Adagia* IV i 2.
72 LB IX 440B–D alters the punctuation of this passage radically, removing most of the question marks and breaking up the sentences.
73 The Carmelites wore a white cloak. Black is the symbol of turpitude, green of jealousy.
74 The Carmelites claimed that their order was founded by Elias, who challenged the prophets of Baal on Mount Carmel (1 Kings 18:19). Labrax is the pimp in Plautus' *Rudens*; Thraso is the boasting soldier in Terence's *Eunuchus*.
75 Cf *De esu carnium* 101 n154 below. Maevius was attacked as a bad poet by both Virgil (*Eclogues* 3.90) and Horace (*Epodes* 10); cf *Adagia* III vii 64 and IV v 1.

says John.[76] And is not that man a murderer who is mad with hate and is driven so hard to attack the reputation of someone who deserves well, who raves so wildly about someone else's life (for reputation is more precious than life itself) that he has no fear of the loss of his own reputation as he harms another's? 'Whoever says, "You fool!" to his brother is liable to hell.'[77] If the man who says, 'You fool!' to a fool is liable to hell, what reward does the man deserve who, without any reason, makes accusations of heresy against an innocent person who desires to deserve well of all. This pious man does nothing but deprive me of my authority among scholars and waste the fruit of studies that I labour at not for myself, certainly, but for the public good – and in this I have Christ as my witness and judge. Meanwhile, however, there is the danger that with these arguments he may harm not only his own reputation but even that of the theological profession, if men go on to judge the rest by this spokesman, and that he may stir up hatred for himself among those he is trying to make hate me. Indeed since the things he says are plainly stupid and wicked, who among his hearers will not get angry in his heart and think, 'This man has the worst possible attitude to his hearers, thinking them either so stupid that they do not see what he says is false or so dishonest that they are delighted by such shameless backbiters'? In the schools those who disagree with some author earn praise precisely to the extent that they overcome the arguments of the one they are contradicting with better arguments without insult. The exponents of pagan philosophy too are noteworthy for this moderation, and they were not Christians; but this theologian, who professes a strict religion, restorer of a ruined monastic discipline,[78] allows himself – no, rather applauds in himself – such extraordinary impudence with his tongue, thus misusing an organ intended for a very different purpose. And this is the man who twists bulls and princes' edicts against pamphlets that he himself calls laughable, as if such language were not more noxious than any books. The psalmist wrote of men like this: 'Under their tongue is the poison of vipers';[79] he did not say 'in their medicine boxes' – though there are some who do that too – but 'under their tongue,' where it is most safely hidden and most easily brought forth.

* * * * *

76 1 John 3:15
77 Matt 5:22; 'to his brother' is implied by the preceding phrases.
78 A reference to Baechem's time as regent (1510–17) of the Carmelite house of studies at Louvain? See CEBR I 81; De Jongh 153.
79 Ps 139 (140 RSV):4 *sub labiis eorum*; Erasmus has *sub lingua eorum*.

But let there be some moderation in this quarrel now. I have not written these words with any other purpose than in part to clear myself in case anyone is still so ignorant as to be impressed by such obvious slander and in part, if this is possible, so that he may recognize himself, come to his senses, and be ashamed of himself. His dishonesty deserves that his name should be spelled out, and there is good reason why this should be done, certainly so that suspicion should not fall on some harmless people – which in any case will be avoided if a certain author is made known by name. Among his own, I think, he is already recognized by these indications; to posterity or those far removed from him what does it matter if they learn that some Suffenus or other – let's pretend that is his name – has become so deranged?[80] I would wish the vice to pass unremarked, if only it were changed! If only this man would so conduct himself that he, whom I am now obliged to complain of for his prolonged and unbridled ravings against his neighbour, would oblige me to praise his reform! Away with Christians like these who separate charity from religion, who link an unbridled tongue with the name of piety, contrary to the teaching of James.[81] As for us, let us not trouble ourselves about these people if they cannot be reformed, and let us seek better things. Farewell, reader.

* * * * *

80 See 53 n41 above.
81 James 1:26 'If any one thinks he is religious, and does not bridle his tongue but deceives his heart, this man's religion is vain.'

A LETTER BY ERASMUS OF ROTTERDAM DEFENDING HIS VIEWS CONCERNING THE PROHIBITION ON EATING MEAT AND SIMILAR HUMAN REGULATIONS, TO THE REVEREND FATHER IN CHRIST AND HONOURABLE PRINCE CHRISTOPHER, BISHOP OF BASEL

Ad reverendum in Christo patrem et illustrem principem Christophorum episcopum Basiliensem, epistola apologetica Erasmi Roterodami, de interdicto esu carnium, deque similibus hominum constitutionibus

A LETTER CONCERNING THE PROHIBITION
ON EATING MEAT[1]

TO THE MOST ACCOMPLISHED FATHER AND LORD,
LORD CHRISTOPHER, BISHOP OF BASEL,
ERASMUS OF ROTTERDAM SENDS GREETING.

I can scarcely express, reverend bishop, how seriously upset I am by these disturbances recently created by some people in this city, which I found quite calm and peaceful when I arrived. [1] In olden times the Calydonian boar caused great confusion, but this disturbance among us has been caused, as I hear, by a domestic pig.[2]

[2] I allow that the affair is not a capital matter in itself, but this insolent attitude seems likely to lead to all sorts of outrage, if indeed the case is such as I gather from what many people are saying. We read that among the Greeks the magistrates punished a certain boy who took pleasure in piercing the eyes of birds wherever he could find them, because they conjectured from this irresponsible pleasure in sinning that he would be a destructive and bloodthirsty citizen.[3] We read of another on whom a heavy fine was inflicted because when asked by the magistrate, as was customary, whether he had a wife to his liking, he replied jokingly, 'Indeed I have, but damn it not to your liking!'[4] If this answer had been made by one friend to another at a party, it would have been a witty joke, but when

* * * * *

1 This translation and that of the following *De delectu ciborum scholia* (102 below) are based on the critical edition by C. Augustijn (ASD IX-1), whose notes are an essential source of further information and to whom the translator is much indebted. Numbered markers thus [#] in this text refer to the corresponding scholia.
2 For the Calydonian boar, see Homer *Iliad* 9.538–49; Ovid *Metamorphoses* 8.267–546. 'Domestic pig' is an allusion to the Steinschnider incident on Palm Sunday (13 April); see the introduction xxiv above.
3 The source of this story appears to be unknown.
4 Gellius 4.20.1–6. Modern editions have 'not to my liking.'

said out of place, it showed a frivolous mind with no respect for the public power. It was not the words that deserved the punishment, therefore, but the circumstance in which they were spoken.

A custom reinforced by long usage is an uncontrolled thing, and, even if it were insignificant, still after it has once taken hold, it is difficult to pluck out without disturbance to human affairs and can hardly be removed in any way other than that by which it crept in. Now fasting and abstinence, if one makes proper use of them, are the sort of things that are aids to true piety. In the first place, sobriety and moderate eating make the mind quicker and freer in attending to those things that are relevant to true piety. Then, just as in sinning the body is initially the servant and instigator of evil and the accomplice of unholy pleasure, so equally in repentance it should be the companion of grief and torment and should be subject to the mind as it recovers its reason. [3] Therefore fasting and abstinence are important for two purposes. First, for mastering the licentiousness of the body so that it does not rebel against the spirit. For just as food is taken away and hay given instead of oats to unruly horses who are disinclined to submit to the rider, so when the mind rebels because of an excess of moisture and spirits, nourishment is properly withdrawn from the flesh and replaced by the sorts of food that cause it to kick back as little as possible against its rider. [3] Just as the withdrawal of food diminishes the wantonness of the body, so there are certain foods that nourish the body so that it may live, but without making it wanton. Second, it is conducive to placating divine anger provoked by our misdeeds. Doubtless when he sees that we exact a penalty from ourselves, he puts aside his rod. No penalty in fact is more fitting for each person than when the mind is afflicted by hatred for the sin committed and the body is tormented by abstinence from pleasures. Moreover, this way of pleasing the Divinity is demonstrated in several places in the Old Testament, and Christ himself taught us that there is a certain type of devil that is not driven out except by fasting and prayer.[5]

But although it had been foretold even by the prophets that it would come about that new moons, sabbaths, fasts, abstinences, and other shadows

* * * * *

5 The Law required all Israelites to fast on the Day of Atonement (Lev 16:29), and fasting is associated with penance in the OT in Deut 9:18; 1 Sam 7:6; 1 Kings 21:27; Ezra 10:6; Neh 9:1; Ps 69:10; Jon 3:5. In the NT see Matt 17:20 and Mark 9:28 DV; RSV does not accept mention of 'fasting' in these passages. See Bruce M. Metzger *A Textual Commentary on the Greek New Testament* 2nd ed (Stuttgart 1994) 35, 85.

of the Law[6] would fade away at the dawning of the gospel's light, yet [4] the whole young church of Christ, breathing the new wine of the gospel spirit after her bridegroom was taken up into the heavens,[7] embraced nothing more fervently than fasting and prayer. At that time indeed all fasted, even daily, when they were not compelled to by any teaching. And many among the Christians refrained from eating not only flesh but all living creatures, subsisting on legumes and vegetables, though according to Christ and the apostles each was free to eat what he wished.[8] [5] Finally a custom already accepted and sanctioned by the tacit approval of the whole world was confirmed first by the authority of other bishops and soon after by the Roman pontiff, because charity among the people was, as I believe, already growing cold and many were embracing things of the flesh.[9] So there was added the authority of the bishops as a spur to stimulate the minds of the weak who were already slipping into evil; there was added a regulation that would constrain licence by certain limits so that it would not burst out into every sort of outrageous act. And so fasting and abstinence cannot be entirely condemned on the grounds that they are in no way conducive to piety, if they are used as they should be.

[6] In addition to this there is the important matter of order, without which there is no lasting harmony among mortals. Harmony is maintained either by equality or by each having his given place, each his given office. In the body hands, eyes, feet, and ears are equal; but between the eyes, the

* * * * *

6 Cf Col 2:16–17 'shadow of what is to come'; and Erasmus' paraphrase on those verses, CWE 43 416 and nn51, 53.

7 An allusion to Matt 9:15

8 See eg Matt 15:11; Acts 10:10–16, 11:4–9; Rom 14:17; 1 Cor 10:25–7. See also ASD IX-1 21 47–53n; and 'Fasting and Abstinence' in *Encyclopedia of the Early Church* (Cambridge 1992) I 319.

9 On fast days and their variety in different churches, see Augustine Ep 36 PL 33 136–51/FC 12 138–67, especially chapters 13 and 14 150–1, and Ep 54 PL 33 200–4/FC 12, especially chapter 2 200–1. In these letters Augustine mentions both the Roman custom of fasting on Saturdays as not observed in Milan and Ambrose's advice to follow the custom of the local bishop. For the oldest explicit legislation concerning the priest's fast before celebrating the Eucharist, see canon 28 in *Breviarium Hipponense*, listed as canon 29 of the 'Council of Carthage III' (AD 397) in *Concilia Africae a. 345–525* ed C. Munier CCSL 259 41, 334; see also the *Didache* 8.1 on fasting Wednesdays and Fridays in Kurt Niederwinner *Didache: A commentary* trans Linda M. Maloney, ed Harold W. Attridge (Minneapolis 1998; [German original] Gottingen 1989); and an exhortation attributed to Eutychianus (pope 275–83), addressed to priests and advocating fasts, PL 5 166C.

stomach, and the feet it is not equality that maintains harmony but order. If harmony is taken away, what, I ask, remains of value among Christians, that is, as the apostle Paul teaches, among those who are members of the same body?[10] And so whoever has upset this order has brought a great bane on society, especially if this is done not through expediency or necessity but through heedless zealotries, even over matters that by their own nature do no harm when disregarded. As an example, ecclesiastical usage has it that the Alleluia should not be sung during Lent. And yet to praise God is a pious act at any time, and in place of these words the church has substituted others almost as efficacious. [6] And yet if some parish priest, despising the general custom, repeats the Alleluia in his church and makes fun of the others who do not sing it, will he not seem in everyone's judgment to be committing a fault worthy of a cudgeling? Or if in these last few days of Lent some parish priest should give the order, not by mistake but deliberately, to ring bronze bells, when it is the custom to call the people by means of wooden clappers, will he not seem to deserve to be exiled to Anticyra?[11] 'Why did he deserve that?' someone will ask. There is nothing scandalous in the deed itself, I admit, but there is great scandal in the disregard for public custom and in disturbing orderly conduct. And because public custom could be kept without any disadvantage, the malice of the person committing the fault is less worthy of indulgence.

How much more seriously is this to be deplored here where the example has come down to us from the prophets, from John the Baptist, from Christ and from the apostles,[12] a practice that is commended to us by the extremely long established custom of our ancestors, which is commended by the authority of the Fathers,[13] and which is particularly important both in appeasing God when he is offended by our sins and in preparing our souls for the divine word, for holy prayers, for inspired hymns, and for other pious and truly Christian occupations.

But if custom had led to the acceptance of some practice, which in present circumstances for good reasons might better be abrogated, it would

* * * * *

10 Rom 12:4; 1 Cor 12:12–26
11 See 47 n16 above.
12 For the prophets, see Dan 9:3, 10:3; Joel 2:12; Zec 8:18–19; and Tob 12:8; John the Baptist: Matt 3:4, 9:14, 11:18; Christ: Matt 4:2. The fasting of the apostles is deduced from such passages as Matt 9:14 and Luke 5:33–5; for the fasting of Paul and Barnabas and early disciples, see Acts 13:1–3 and 14:23.
13 See eg Jerome Ep 52.12 PL 22 537; Tertullian *De ieiuniis* PL 2 953B–978B; and *Enchiridion Asceticum* ed M.J. Rouët de Journel and J. Dutilleul (Fribourg 1965).

be appropriate for it to be done gradually so that disturbance is avoided. Although Christ wanted the shadows of Mosaic law to give way to the light brought by the gospel,[14] he himself nevertheless, in order not to give cause of offence to anyone, never omitted anything at all that had been prescribed by the Law.[15] Nor did he ever explicitly teach that those rituals, which the Jews observed too scrupulously rather than allow themselves to be damned, should be rejected. No, rather he did not condemn discourteously even those petty traditions that the Pharisees added of their own accord to the burdens of the Law. He blamed only the fact that in the process of teaching these superstitions they violated serious teachings of the Law, in that they themselves neglected the regulations with which they burdened the people.[16] Nor does he defend the disciples by saying that it is permissible for any reason to violate the sabbath, but he alleges necessity and maintains the innocence of his disciples with the example of David and the priests.[17] But even Paul himself, the strongest advocate of evangelical freedom, to the Jews became a Jew:[18] taking a vow with shaven head, going barefoot, and purifying himself with others in the temple.[19] This same Paul, although he knows that an idol has no real existence and food offered to idols has no special character, yet prefers to forgo meat forever rather than cause a weak brother to be offended by his eating it. He prefers for the time being to accommodate himself to the unbending superstition of the Jews rather than cause the weak to be alienated and cast aside the gospel. He prefers to abstain entirely from eating meat rather than offer to the weak the spectacle of someone consenting to the wicked superstition of idol worshippers.[20] This same Paul wants a Christian slave to heed a gentile master, even one who is sullen;[21] he wants a Christian wife to be

* * * * *

14 Cf Heb 10:1; and Erasmus' 'Argument' of the Epistle to the Hebrews CWE 44 214. See also his paraphrase on Col 2:16 CWE 43 416–18 with nn59, 62.
15 Matt 5:17
16 Matt 23:4, 23; Luke 11:42
17 Matt 12:1–8
18 1 Cor 9:20
19 For vows and Paul's head shaving at Cenchreae, see Acts 18:18, 21:23–4. Jerome mentions in this connection Paul's participation in 'barefoot processions' (*et nudipedalia exercuit*) and describes these as 'very clearly ceremonies of the Jews'; see Jerome *Commentariorum in epistolam beati Pauli ad Galatas libri tres* 407 (on Gal 2:11–13) PL 26 339A. For purification in the temple, see Acts 21:26.
20 1 Cor 8:4–13
21 Eph 6:5; Col 3:22–4; 1 Tim 6:1; Titus 2:9; and Erasmus' *Paraphrases* on these passages: CWE 43 350–1, 424; CWE 44 34, 62. Similar instructions for slaves appear also in 1 Pet 2:18; and Erasmus' paraphrase on 1 Peter CWE 44 92.

respectful to a gentile husband;[22] he wants initiated Christians to satisfy
gentile officials in every way, whether they demand tax or tribute or honour,
so that no obstacle be put in the way of the gospel. If professing Christ
seemed seditious, then offence would be given. Paul was not disregarding
gospel liberty but was explaining that for the work of the gospel knowledge
gives way to charity.[23]

For these people also – so I hear – have alleged gospel freedom as
the excuse for making Luther its defender and advocate. In them I miss
not only a truly evangelical spirit, sober, gentle, and endowed with modest simplicity, but good sense as well. If they want to harm Luther's cause,
they are acting appropriately; but if they support it, there is no other way
in which they could be more hurtful. If they are doing this so that Christians may attain to their original freedom, their rashness only doubles the
yoke, driving magistrates and princes to aggravate their servitude with severe ordinances. But those who defend themselves by claiming the freedom of the gospel should give priority to some considerations that might
persuade them to be indulgent and to overlook these rather less important things. [7] Someone who strives with all his might to be helpful to
his neighbours, who, when injury is inflicted, is so far from retaliating that
he returns benefit for offence, who is always sober and like one who is
fasting, whose character and behaviour and speech breathe purity, who is
wholly concerned with working at purposes that seem to promise some
great and public advantage, he perhaps will be forgiven if he seems less
scrupulous in observing those rituals that are more suited to ordinary weak
folk. But it is those whose whole life is devoted to debauchery and pleasures, whose speech is arrogant and shameless, whose character is so far
from gentle that for a slight insult they are prepared to use their fist or
even a dagger, those are the ones who preach shamelessly about gospel
freedom, though they are the sort who ought to be restrained by Judaic
restrictions until they make progress towards the strength of the gospel
spirit.

[8] Just as the recklessness of these people rightly displeases all good
and sensible folk, so too it[24] grieves these same sensible folk that Christ's

* * * * *

22 1 Cor 7:12–16; and the paraphrase on that passage CWE 43 93–8 with nn31, 33,
      34, 36.
23 1 Cor 8:1; cf Erasmus' *Convivium religiosum* in *Colloquia* CWE 39 190:20–6,
      191:23–9.
24 *iisdem doleat*] Emended version of *1540*, 'it grieves ... folk'; *iidem doleant* in
      1522 and *1532*, 'the same folk grieve that ...'

flock is too involved in some Judaic rituals and oppressed by either the authority or the negligence of certain ecclesiastical leaders. Augustine too complains of this in his letters, declaring loudly that the condition of Jews is almost more tolerable than that of Christians, so extensively had Jewish superstitions of this sort already flooded into general Christian practice by his time.[25] The people themselves almost invite this sort of slavery, like the northeaster drawing clouds, as they say.[26] But it was the duty of prelates to be mindful of the freedom that the flock received from Christ and the apostles. Now, so far from setting free the minds of the people, we often heap burden on burden and add halters to halters, so that we place them more at risk, serving our own rule and our own advantage rather than their salvation.

Paul does not judge one day better than another but considers every day holy, nor does he judge any work profane that is done for the sake of gospel charity.[27] [9] In later times our ancestors wanted the Lord's day to be a holiday for the good reason that the whole people could come together to hear the gospel word.[28] Soon there were prescribed holidays from trades, although [10] sometimes it would have been more pious to take care of manual work when children and a wife were in danger of hunger than to listen to priests in church singing chants they don't understand. Not that I think the solemn hymns the church choir sings in praise of God are to be condemned,[29] but, just as Christ teaches that man was not created for the sabbath, but on the contrary the sabbath was established for man,[30] so I think that such things too should give way whenever the need of a neighbour requires a charitable response. But those who should be teaching people these ideas are frequently the very ones who are forcing them to do something quite different.

Not even this was enough. How many holy days have people been burdened with since and are burdened with more and more every day! For in some communities it is almost customary for each bishop to add a day

* * * * *

25 Cf eg Augustine Ep 55.19.35.
26 *Adagia* I v 62
27 Rom 14:5, 14
28 Cf Erasmus' annotation on Rom 14:5 (*nam alius iudicat*) CWE 56 372, referring to Jerome *Commentariorum in epistolam beati Pauli ad Galatas libri tres* (on 4:10–11) PL 26 (1884) 403B–405B.
29 For Erasmus' view on music in church, see his annotation (*quam decem milia*) on 1 Cor 14:19 LB VI 731D–732C, defended in *Apologia adversus rhapsodias Alberti Pii* CWE 84 215.
30 Mark 2:27

of observance as a sort of private memorial to himself.[31] And this is done sometimes for the most trivial reasons. [11] Perhaps there is someone who had among his favourites a girl called Barbara; so he wants a day to be a holiday for Barbara. Someone else had a mother called Catherine; this is thought to be sufficient reason for a day sacred to her to keep the people from working.[32] Someone else is called William, and for that important reason it is arranged that there should be special holidays for William. These cases should be understood as examples only, for I preferred to use fictitious examples rather than offend anyone. There are both private loyalties peculiar to individuals – this man[33] towards St Erasmus and that one towards St Christopher[34] – and certain public loyalties of social classes, peoples, or cities, as, for example, those who are called Preachers lavishly celebrate their Dominic, the Minorites their Francis, painters Luke, surgeons Cosmas and Damian, cobblers Crispin, soldiers Martin, the Gauls Claudius, the Parisians Genevieve, the Oxonians Winefride.[35] In the same category is the obsession of those who would superstitiously venerate Christ and the saints part by part; it is not enough for them that we recreate the death of Christ so many times by daily commemoration, that two holy days are allocated to the holy cross, but a particular holy day must be devoted to his spilt blood – which they say is preserved in many places – to the nails, to the crown of thorns, to his foreskin – which some worship somewhere or other – and to the milk of the Virgin Mother, which they display in many places.[36]

* * * * *

31 See Erasmus *Manifesta mendacia* CWE 71 125 no 60 n77 replying to 'Taxander' *Apologia in eum librum quem ab anno Erasmus Roterodamus edidit* ... (Antwerp: S. Cocus 1525) sig H i r (see the introduction xxvi n65).

32 See Béda *Errores* 2 ASD IX-5 133–4 / LB IX 485F–486A. These *Errores*, referred to here as in Augustijn, are fifteen responses made by Erasmus in his *Divinationes ad notata Bedae* to objections of Noël Béda. Cf *De delectu ciborum scholia* 11, 109 below.

33 this man ... certain public] Omitted in LB

34 The names seem chosen with some humorous intent. They refer to objects of popular devotion who are the patrons respectively of the author and of the addressee of this tract. On Christopher, see similar comments in the context of devotions to the saints in *Naufragium* in *Colloquia* CWE 39 354–6 with n26. See *Manifesta mendacia* CWE 71 125 no 61 replying to 'Taxander' *Apologia in eum librum quem ab anno Erasmus Roterodamus edidit* ... (Antwerp: S. Cocus 1525) sig G vii r (see the introduction xxvi n65).

35 For all these names, see David Hugh Farmer *Oxford Dictionary of Saints* 5th rev ed (Oxford 2011).

36 For parallel expressions of scepticism about some forms of popular devotion, eg to the Virgin's milk, see Erasmus' colloquies *Peregrinatio religionis ergo* in

If something is of such a nature that it seems worthy of worship, it would be enough to celebrate just in churches a holy day that the rich or anyone for whom it is convenient can attend; the poor whose hands feed a numerous family should not be obliged to observe it. And even if these loyalties are perhaps not to be blamed, the bishop in his wisdom does not need to lend them so much importance that each loyalty should have dedicated to it its holy day, its rituals, and its particular cult. Since the sole means by which they feed their families is snatched away, [12] what does this do but drive people of slender means to starvation or rather, morals being what they are now, entice them away from honest and pious labour towards idleness and extravagance? What days are worse than holidays for sins of extravagance, drunkenness, lust, gambling, quarrels, fights, and murders? And what upside-down justice we have here! If someone was drunk and clung to a prostitute for the whole holiday, if someone played dice, no one bothered them; but if a man stitched a shoe, he is denounced as a heretic.

[13] I am not saying this because I want lay people to be disrespectful of holy days but because [14] it seems to me the shepherds of the church would do well if they cut out holy days like this altogether, with the exception of Sundays and a few special ones. And on the ones they do retain, let them allow impoverished little folk to provide for their children and family with their labour after the service and the sermon, if it is a matter of necessity, or even to prepare something to distribute to the poor.[37] Nowadays it often happens that, although a fine day occurs after a month of rain, the farmer is obliged to allow his unharvested crop to rot in the fields when he could gather it into his barn in favourable weather; and this because of holy days like these imposed on us, to put it kindly, not by the authority of the ancients but by a certain human zeal. These practices creep in at first with an appearance of respectability, then they flood in more profusely, soon they are confirmed by usage and become a tyranny so that now they

*　*　*　*　*

Colloquia CWE 40 632–6 with nn71, 72, 74, 79, 86; and Ἰχθυοφαγία in Colloquia CWE 40 719 nn325 and 327. For Erasmus' positive treatment of the invocation of the saints, see eg Modus orandi Deum CWE 70 186–8; and of veneration of Mary, see his prayers Paean Virgini Matri and Obsecratio ad Virginem Mariam CWE 69 20–38 and 40–54; for his exculpatory note on veneration of Mary, see Manifesta mendacia 18 CWE 71 120 no 18.

37 Cf Béda Errores 3 ASD IX-5 134 / LB IX 486A; Ep 1039:190–209, De delectu ciborum scholia 13 (72 below), and Adagia II vi 12 for similar comments by Erasmus about the perils related to the excessive number of holidays.

can hardly be removed without disturbance. This is why bishops should not overlook these practices when they first creep in. For in general, human rules, like remedies for illness, must be accommodated to the current state of society and the times. Practices that were introduced formerly for pious reasons, it would have been more pious to discontinue later because of circumstances and because of the changed nature of the times and customs. [15] But this should be done not at all by popular impulse but by a decision of the authorities, so that disturbance is avoided; and public custom should be changed in such a way that unity is not destroyed. To ensure that this does not happen, the bishops must be watchful; they should not become rather obstinately deaf to the just complaints of the people.

Perhaps the same judgment should be made about the marriage of priests.[38] [17] Formerly priests were both very few in number and of the greatest piety. These men, in order to be more free to pursue their pious endeavours, castrated themselves voluntarily. [16] And such was the love of chastity among those ancients that some were reluctant to allow marriage for a Christian if baptism had come upon him when he was unmarried, and even more reluctant to allow remarriage.[39] Now what seemed praiseworthy in bishops and priests has been passed on to deacons and finally to subdeacons. A custom voluntarily accepted has been confirmed by papal authority.[40] Meanwhile, the number of priests has grown, and their piety has diminished. How many swarms of priests do the monasteries maintain, how many do the colleges? And beyond these there is everywhere a countless multitude of priests. And among these how rare are those who live chastely! I am speaking of those who openly keep concubines in their homes in the position of wives. I am not concerned now with the secrets of more hidden lusts; I am speaking only of things that are well known to

* * * * *

38 See *Manifesta mendacia* CWE 71 117 no 4 where Erasmus defends this statement on priestly celibacy.

39 Cf *De delectu ciborum scholia* 16 and the associated notes 111 below.

40 On clerical celibacy, see NCE 3 369–74: clerical celibacy reflecting the life of Christ was recommended for clerics (cf Matt 19:12; 1 Cor 7:7–8, 32–5) and had a history of preference; marriage after ordination was forbidden by legislation in the fifth century, and celibacy for all clerics in major orders (subdeacon, deacon, priest, bishop) was legislated in 1123 at the First Lateran Council, when an enactment was passed (confirmed more explicitly in the Second Lateran Council) imposing penalties (eg enslavement) on the children and on wives (henceforth considered 'concubines'). This ruling does not apply to clergy of the Eastern churches, who may marry before being ordained. Cf *De delectu ciborum scholia* 16 n41, 111 below.

ordinary people too. [18] And although we know this, we are still very lax about admitting to holy orders and very rigid about loosening the requirement of celibacy, although [19] Paul taught the opposite of this: that no one should be hasty[41] in the laying on of hands, and in more than one passage carefully prescribed what sort of people should be priests and what sort should be deacons.[42] On celibacy neither Christ nor the apostles laid down any law in the Scriptures.[43]

At one time the church repudiated night vigils at the shrines of martyrs, a practice accepted among Christians by general custom and for several centuries.[44] Fasting, which used to be prolonged until the evening, it changed to finishing at midday, and it varied many other practices for supervening reasons.[45] Why do we insist so obstinately in this case on a human regulation, especially when so many reasons would persuade us to change it? [20] In the first place, a majority of priests lives in infamy and handles the sacred mysteries with no very quiet conscience. As a result, their effectiveness is largely lost, for their teaching is despised by the people because of their shameful lives. But if marriage were allowed for these men who are not continent, they would both live with a quieter conscience themselves and would preach the word of God to the people with authority; they would take care of the education of their children properly and would not be a disgrace to one another. These remarks do not mean that I am seeking to be a promoter or defender of priests who have recently become husbands without the authority of the pope, but that [21] I remind the leaders of the church to examine carefully whether it may be useful to adapt the old regulation to our present advantage.[46]

Meanwhile I would like bishops also to be reminded not to receive all and sundry so rashly into the priesthood without examination. Likewise, I think the other parties should be reminded to examine themselves

* * * * *

41 *facile*, literally 'easy'; Vulg has *cito* 'quickly' (1 Tim 5:22).
42 1 Tim 3:1–7 (on criteria for bishops) and 5:22; on deacons, 1 Tim 3:8–13; on elders, priests, and bishops, Titus 1:5–6, 7–9
43 Cf Béda *Errores* 11 ASD IX-5 138 / LB IX 488A–D.
44 On celebrations at the tombs of the martyrs and the excesses that attended them, see DACL X-2 2458–62; Augustine Ep 22.3–6 and Ep 29 PL 33 91–2 and 114–20. For the variation of practices within the Christian church, see Augustine Ep 54 PL 33 199–204. Clichtove mentions night vigils (giving rise to unspeakable crimes, which increased under cover of darkness) and their removal by ecclesiastical decree; see *De continentia sacerdotum* 22.8 in Clichtove II 326.
45 DTC 1 2/2 1739
46 Cf Béda *Errores* 12 ASD IX-5 138–9 / LB IX 488D–E.

repeatedly, whether they are suited to performing the office they assume, lest they assume the burden of such profession for the sake of gain or out of laziness, calling down condemnation on themselves and reproach on the church. [22] Moreover, I would still advise those who are already inducted, even if popes should open a window to marriage, not to get themselves entangled in matrimony lightly or rashly; it may be that they would then be tormented by a double repentance, both of the priesthood and of marriage. A great part of continence is to want sincerely to be continent. Nothing is more desirable than that a priest be free of marriage and that he serve his Lord freely and wholly. But if, in spite of all remedies tried, the rebel flesh cannot be overcome, it remains for him to live chastely with one woman, taking a wife as a remedy, not as a pleasure, striving with all his might meanwhile to compensate for the weakness of the flesh, for which the wife is granted, by what is left of the integrity of his life and by his pious exertions.[47] In this way all will understand that the wife was sought for reasons of necessity and not for pleasure. And I do not doubt that there are many bishops who perceive that these matters are as I say. But I fear that here too monetary interest may stand in the way of our following what we see to be the best.[48] If the bishops try to make a change, their officials would probably object loudly because they see greater returns from priests' concubines than they would see from wives.[49] But it is not right that money should matter so much among us that our deliberations in such an important matter should be less sincere because of it.[50] There are many matters like this, but let these two serve as examples.

Now I come back to fasts. [23] For anyone sufficiently steadfast to keep himself sober at all times, there is no absolute need for prescribed fasts, except when God's anger must be placated in some circumstances with this sort of sacrifice. 'But,' you will say, 'it is for the ignorant and the dull witted that fixed days are prescribed.' Let's accept that this is quite tolerable. It is laid down that there must be only one light meal, and the type of food is laid down too. But this is not enough; eternal damnation is threatened for anyone who violates this human custom. For this is how some parish priests declare a fast to their people – perhaps not

* * * * *

47 On a wife as remedy, cf Béda *Errores* 13 ASD IX-5 139–40/LB IX 488E–F.
48 Cf Béda *Errores* 14 ASD IX-5 140/LB IX 488F.
49 The Fifth Lateran Council (1514) prohibited concubinage; violators were often fined. See eg M.A. Kelleher '"Like man and wife": clerics' concubines in the dioceses of Barcelona' *Journal of Medieval History* 28 (2002) 349–60.
50 Cf Béda *Errores* 15 ASD IX-5 140/LB IX 489A.

in accordance with pontifical intention. Not even that is enough. Someone
who tasted pork instead of fish is hauled off for punishment, almost, I
might say, like a parricide. [24] I have already said that heedless subversion deserves heavy punishment in all cases,[51] and I am not discussing this
sort of case. But in another respect this judgment seems to me not only in-
equitable but even absurd. It was a fast that had been prescribed; this was
the chief point of the matter, the question of eating such or such foods was
secondary.[52] Now there are dinners everywhere, and no one goes into the
tragic mode. But if someone has tasted flesh, everyone cries, 'O heaven, O
earth, O seas of Neptune';[53] the status of the church totters, heresies flood
in! To dine you need no dispensation; to feed on flesh or eggs lawfully
a papal brief must be bought. [25] Thus we hold doggedly to something
that seems rather close to Judaism and altogether such that anyone may
rightly wonder that it is so seriously accepted by us Christians, who deplore circumcision and the other rituals of the Jews. We place the greatest
importance on kinds of foods, but we allow what approaches more nearly
the endeavours of gospel piety to fall into disuse. Although for Christians
prayer is a particular sacrifice and its companion and associate is fasting,
because in the Gospels and apostolic writings these two, prayer and fasting, are for the most part joined[54] – for the mind is purged and strengthened by fasting so that prayer may be pure and fervent and lively – yet we
are far more tenacious of our human regulation on abstinence than on fasting. [26] But Christians are burdened with many more frequent fasts too
than ever the Jews were. The Lord Jesus said about the kinds of food, 'That
which goes into the mouth does not defile a man,'[55] and Paul did not disagree with his teacher when he said, 'The kingdom of God is not food and
drink.'[56]

   In any case, in the matter of abstinence how much heavier than theirs
does our burden seem! They were allowed to feed on any of the healthiest
of all kinds of fish, four-footed beasts, and birds. For us, eating any flesh
is forbidden for a good part of the year. And see, I beg you, [27] how
meticulous our forefathers were in either their practice or their rule. At
certain times, with the exception of flesh, nothing is forbidden anywhere:

* * * * *

51 See 66–7 above: 'In addition to this ... disturbing orderly conduct.'
52 Cf Béda *Errores* 5 ASD IX-5 135 / LB IX 486E–F.
53 Terence *Adelphi* 790
54 For the joining of prayer and fasting, see eg Matt 17:20; Mark 9:28; Acts 14:22.
55 Matt 15:11
56 Rom 14:17; cf *Apologia adversus rhapsodias Alberti Pii* CWE 84 191.

it is permissible to feed on entrails and fat; at[57] other times one is allowed to taste only fat and at other times again nothing from a land animal or a bird. And at this point indeed not a few questions arise as to the range of meaning of the word 'flesh.' For the sea has many animals that are not dissimilar to land animals, like seals and dogs. It has amphibians too, like the beaver; indeed one may dispute about snails, tortoises, frogs, and serpents. Again on some days it is permitted to eat eggs and dairy products, on others only dairy products. There are days when it is unlawful even to have touched these; there are days when anything that was alive at any time is forbidden, so that even sponges, which some people believe have sensation, are questionable. [28] There are to be found people who allow themselves nothing but bread and water. Let us concede that these beliefs are not to be despised, but who does not see how lifeless they are compared with the precepts of the Gospel, which should have been the prime concern?[58] Then we should also consider whether it is conformable with the freedom of the Gospel, which Paul defends so vigorously, [29] to make such captious and rigorous demands on everyone.[59]

Now let us consider how true is this too that Paul the apostle wrote: [30] 'For while bodily training is of some value, godliness is of value in every way.'[60] [31] On no days are kitchens more busy than on fish days, nor is provision ever greater or expense heavier. So it comes about that the poor suffer hunger and the rich live even more luxuriously. Who does not prefer sheatfish, which I believe is popularly called 'sturgeon,'[61] or trout or moray to smoked pork or mutton? And in these cases too, foods that are not included in the term 'meats' are those that provide more nourishment than beef or mutton, such as tortoise, snails, and snakes; and they provoke even greater lust. And you may find these qualities even in vegetables and in tree fruits. What is the point of abstaining from mutton if you stretch your belly with herbs, dates, figs and raisins, truffles, artichokes, and onions that inflame the sexual organs with lecherousness more than young chickens do? Spiced dates make the body sprightlier than beef. Not one of these is

* * * * *

57 *alias pingui tantum, allias nihil ex animante terrestri aut volatili gustare licet*] Omitted in LB; the translation 'and at other times again ... bird' follows 1522.

58 Cf Béda *Errores* 6 ASD IX-5 136/LB IX 486F–487B.

59 For Paul's teaching concerning the freedom to eat any food, see 1 Corinthians 8–10, especially 10:23–33.

60 1 Tim 4:8

61 Cf *Adagia* IV i 72 where the fish in question is described as 'among the best of fish.'

forbidden. In these circumstances the result is that those of meagre fortune are heavily oppressed by such rules, while the rich, although they want for very little, are incited to luxuries.

Some one may say, 'This comes about through our own fault.' True. [32] And for that reason perhaps the practice should be abolished where we see that more evil results from it than good. And it seems not much greater advantage is to be had from fasting. For those who are poor or physically weak cannot easily go for a long time without eating. On the other hand the strong load their stomachs with food enough for three days, so that from breakfast on they are good for nothing but sleep. And yet fasting is used especially for this purpose, that the spirit may be less burdened with the weight of the body. I shall not speak here of different states of health, sicknesses, the weakness of age, poverty, and the natural peculiarities of individual bodies, which mean that for some even healthy people going without food for a few hours is lethal, for others fish is like a scorpion or a sea hare[62] or a viper. Moreover, to forbid the consumption of meats in regions that suffer from a scarcity of fish is surely to decree starvation.[63] With such wide differences of place, physique, health, and age, [33] it is quite obvious how many will be burdened by a law supposedly equal for all. There are bodies that are licentious even if they feed on hay; there are those that barely live even if they are nourished on partridge and pheasant. If an edict were to order that on these days the rich should live frugally and should send what they take off their tables to the lowly tables of the poor, then there would be equality, and the law would smack of something from the gospel. Now everywhere the situation is as Paul says, 'And one indeed is hungry and another is drunk.'[64] For the rich a change of foods is a luxury and a remedy for boredom, and they never have greater pleasure than when they abstain from meat. But meanwhile the poor farmer, gnawing a raw turnip or leek, adds this morsel to his black bran bread; in place of the rich man's mead he drinks sour whey or water from a ditch, at the same time barely supporting by the constant sweat of his brow his wife, little children, and the rest of his household. [34] In short, people's customs have declined so much that these rules are a burden only to those for whose sake they were not exactly set up, and they have no application to those for whom they used to be particularly pertinent.

* * * * *

62 A sea hare is described by Pliny as the most poisonous of sea creatures; *Naturalis historia* 9.155, 32.8.
63 Cf Béda *Errores* 7 ASD IX-5 136/LB IX 487C.
64 1 Cor 11:21

Some one may say, 'If anyone is oppressed by these rules, there is a source of relief.' What source is that? 'Let him purchase the right to eat from the Roman pontiff.' Fine words! But not everyone has the leisure, nor has everyone the money at hand, with which to buy this sort of right. And here again it is the case that for the rich, for whom the prohibition on meat was most necessary, for whom fasting was most necessary, the rule is quite loose; its heavy yoke falls only on the poor and the needy. Indeed I am at the moment at a loss on this point too, that the right to relax this sort of rule is left to the Roman pontiff alone, for this is what ordinary people think. In my opinion anyway it would be more suitable to transfer it to parish priests, who have taken the place of the bishops now as far as pastoral work is concerned. Priests can really know each person's situation, health, resources, and character, especially since these rules are not of great importance for their piety.[65] Stewardship of the gospel word is entrusted to them, and so is the power of administering the sacraments of the church and the right of hearing confessions and of granting absolution from even unusual sins. They are allowed also, at the risk of their lives, to attend those sick of the plague or of an otherwise loathsome and abhorrent disease. And yet these same priests are denied the authority to grant some people permission to eat the foods that their weakness requires! If the priest is not at all suitable to grant these little dispensations, the fault lies, of course, with the bishops who entrusted Christ's flock to such a man. If he is suitable to have more serious responsibilities committed to him as well, there must be some obscure and strange reason why these less significant ones are not committed to the same man.

But at this point I seem to hear once again the profit of certain people preparing to murmur objections. If only this corrosion could be scoured completely from the church of Christ, for it everywhere prevents anything from being holy and sincere. [35] It turns rules laid down to instil piety into almost nothing more than nets designed to catch money. What was the purpose of producing so many and such strict rules about the election of bishops, abbots, and other leaders of the church if now, with money changing hands everywhere, an election is corrupted or prevented? They say that the tyrant Dionysius of Syracuse gave a host of laws to his subjects, and when these were published, he deliberately closed his eyes until, with

* * * * *

65 Clichtove indicates that dispensation from fasting for reasons of health or poverty may be obtained from one's own pastor, and forgiveness for private lapses may be sought through private confession: *De ieiunio* 27.6, 33.2 in Clichtove III 572, 606–7.

everyone unconcernedly disregarding what had been enacted, he had a large number of persons vulnerable.[66] In this way laws served for him as nets with which he used to catch plunder. But the vicars of Christ should not with similar purpose burden the people with new rules or misuse decrees of the ancients. [36] The rules of our forebears are certainly necessary, and it also happens frequently that it is expedient for particular reasons to relax the rigour of general law providing that this is not done everywhere – not by corrupt agents, not without any judgment, but very simply. It would make a great difference to the purity of church discipline if no relaxation of the law could be bought with money and if it were entrusted to those who can know the individual to whom a dispensation from the general rule is granted. At the moment practically nothing but a name and money are necessary to obtain this. If the case is just, why is money exacted? If it is not, what does a dispensation do? Indeed in some cases I could perhaps make use of this logical dilemma: if the case is suitable, what need is there of a dispensation? If it is not, of what benefit is the dispensation? The Roman pontiff declares a fast, but in my opinion he does not wish by this law to bind children or the very aged, the weak, the sick – in short, all those who may not fast without serious suffering.[67] In these circumstances, therefore, where a particular and clear case arises, there is no need to relax the law but rather to interpret it. In a doubtful case, whom can you consult more readily than your parish priest or your Ordinary? If you flee from the judgment of him to whom you are known, you demonstrate an insincere conscience. But if some hostility or ignorance or some other circumstance arises so that he may not grant a just dispensation, then recourse to the archbishop or to the pope should be open.

The course of this argument reminds us, excellent prelate, that we should give a little consideration to how closely we are bound by rules of this sort, which are creations of human law, and those that are of themselves popes' prescriptions about fasts, abstinence, and marriage of priests; for I am not arguing about any others. Take a man who refuses to support an aged, sick, needy, father with help and service when he has the means to do so. He is instructed to attend to his parent by his bishop, who teaches him

* * * * *

66 Cf *Institutio principis christiani* CWE 27 265 with n6 (in CWE 28 526) where it is suggested that this may be a reminiscence of the spurious book 2 of Aristotle's *Oeconomica* (2.2.20, 1349a14–1350a6).
67 It was affirmed in old decretals that age, weakness, and need were grounds for exception; the scholastics refined this and extended it to children, the senile, the sick, the poor, travellers, and craftsmen; see DTC 2 2 1743–50.

that 'honour' in the divine Commandment means help,[68] not uncovering your head or giving way on the road. If such a man refuses to obey, he will undoubtedly make himself liable to punishment in hell. Again, take a man who has a dispute with his neighbour, and this neighbour who gave offence has returned to his senses, begs for pardon, is prepared even to make amends for the injury. If the one who was injured refuses to comply with his bishop's instruction to set aside vengeance and to reconcile himself with his neighbour, there can be no doubt that by this disobedience he makes himself liable to punishment in hell. Why is this so? Because what the bishop teaches, he teaches according to the doctrine of the gospel, and he is inculcating Christ's teaching rather than putting forward his own. But let us see whether the same is done in these cases with which we are dealing now. [37] For I shall say whatever I have to say, not as one making statements but as one asking questions of a prelate at once the most virtuous and by far the most learned.

It is clear that most rules of the sort I am discussing now were first introduced as a matter of custom and that the question of who is bound by this custom, in what circumstances, how far, when, how long, is too large a matter to examine here. [38] In the first place, it seems quite probable that a custom does not bind anyone more tightly than the authors of the custom would wish, though exception may always be made where there is cause for offence and disrespect. Is it credible that the people who first voluntarily placed their riches at the feet of the apostles did it with the intention that those who did not do so should be liable to eternal punishment?[69] Or that those who began the practice of abstaining from meat wanted to initiate this custom with the intention that those who did not subsequently do the same should be bound to eternal ruin? No, rather I believe that this was their intention and indeed what they said, that if they saw someone weaker in body, who was challenged by their example and tried to do the same, they would advise him thus: 'Dearest brother, my body is ill disciplined, so I rightly subject my flesh by fasts. Your poor body is weak and obedient enough to the spirit. It is more important to take care of its health than to restrain its wantonness. Therefore care for the health of your poor body with suitable foods taken in moderation and with thanksgiving,[70] so that it can serve the spirit more promptly.' This is how Paul advises his Timothy:

* * * * *

68 Exod 20:12 'Honour your father and your mother'; quoted in Matt 15:4 and Mark 7:10
69 Acts 4:35
70 1 Tim 4:3–4

that he should take a little wine because of the weakness of his stomach and frequent ailments.[71]

Now this is not the place to discuss whether a custom may entail criminal guilt beyond the will of its authors – as, for example, in a case when someone admonishes a defaulter without wanting the remonstrance to burden him with blame, yet the person admonished does not turn away from his shameful act but sins more seriously than before.[72] What we must look at is whether, in matters that are licit in themselves and only become illicit by human decision, it was the purpose of the bishops or the Roman pontiffs, when they approved the accepted custom, to condemn to hell anyone who did not observe it, not out of deliberate contempt but out of weakness or forgetfulness. God is not so stern or irascible as to hurl into hell for any slight fault those whom he redeemed with his own blood.[73] He knows the infirmity[74] of his creature and disregards many things in us rather than cut us off from the body of his Son. But whoever perpetrates a capital crime, from being a member of Christ, becomes a member of the devil; from an heir to heavenly life he becomes an heir to hell. [39] Moreover, since bishops stand in the place of him who seeks to save all and lose no one[75] – they who have a father's feelings for their flock, who finally are themselves men liable to infirmities and needful in many respects of the mercy of God – how is it consistent that through their purely human regulations they would have intended to bind their brothers and sons to eternal torments? – especially since they are aware even from their own hearts that the minds of men are prone to sin and and are frequently apt to be provoked by the prohibition itself to take pleasure in sinning.

Secular princes, who wield the sword and openly curb unrestrained liberty in the general population by fear and torture, nevertheless, even if they could, would not want the laws they put in place to be of such rigour that the law breaker instantly incurs capital punishment. And these men can kill only the body. So should bishops, whose duty is to save men by the sword of the divine word, expect, in the matter of food and drink to which Christ gave us the right,[76] that the one who disregards their regulation

* * * * *

71 Cf 1 Tim 5:23.
72 Cf Matt 18:15–18.
73 Cf Acts 20:28; Rom 8:32; Eph 1:7.
74 Cf Rom 8:26.
75 Luke 15: three parables illustrating the inclusiveness of God's love; and John 17:6–20
76 Cf 1 Cor 9:4.

should go body and soul to hell? – especially since it is in their power not to set this snare and not to lead people into this danger. Now the bonds of evangelical charity are stronger than family bonds, those of the spirit stronger than the flesh, those of God stronger than nature. But what father was ever so cruel towards his children that if he had forbidden them to drink wine so that they would not ever contract a fever by drinking too much, he would expect his prohibition to have such force that if they disobeyed, they would suffer capital punishment? – especially since they could drink wine without harm if they drank moderately. At least he would refrain from his command if he knew his children were liable to such a danger and would prefer them to run the risk of fever rather than of capital punishment.

Moreover, I do not think anyone would deny that greater weight must be given to laws instituted by God than to those established by men. The laws of the Old Testament, however, set in place by God, did not render everyone liable to mortal guilt in those times. On the contrary, if we believe theologians of great repute, some laws did not make people liable to any blame; such was the case, I think, if someone touched a carcass. And will the steward, not the author, of a more merciful testament expect that he should, by any of his regulations, make his people liable to the penalty of eternal fire? Let me come to the authority of the apostles, to whom the whole Christian world by common consent has always attributed so much. I would certainly not dare to affirm that, whatever they taught, these men taught with this intent: that they wanted any transgressor to be liable to hell. In many passages Paul prohibits avarice, lust, anger, dissension, envy, adding specifically that we know those who do such things will not possess the kingdom of God.[77] And yet theologians admit that not all anger is a mortal sin, nor perhaps all envy.[78] Again the same Apostle pronounced seriously that women should not speak in church and that their sex should not claim authority rather arrogantly over their husbands.[79] And yet I do not think Paul taught this with the intention that if some woman through feminine weakness had said something in church from a desire to learn, she should be immediately in danger of hell. [40] I put these ideas forward in such a way that each should still be able to form his own judgment. In the end perhaps, even in gospel precepts it is possible to discover some that

* * * * *

77 Cf Gal 5:19–21.
78 Cf Thomas Aquinas *Summa theologiae* II-II 158 1 and 36 2, though Aquinas is there speaking only of *invidia* 'envy.'
79 1 Cor 14:34–5; 1 Tim 2:11–12

do not immediately render anyone guilty of mortal sin.[80] We see that the founders of religious orders plainly declare of their regulations, which they necessarily add to the gospel teachings for the sake of concord and equality in their communal living, that they do not want to condemn anyone thereby even to venial guilt.[81] This makes me marvel all the more at certain people of the same sort who would sooner suffer a brother to die or be tortured by an illness worse than death than allow the eating of meat.[82]

I shall not repeat here what certain not unknown theologians have asserted: that [41] no mortal prelate can lay a subject under sentence of mortal sin by his rule unless what he teaches derives from divine law. Personally I do not either deny or approve this principle at the moment. I shall only ask in passing whether all such regulations make one liable to eternal punishment or only some of them. If all, the Christian's yoke is indeed heavy, since there exist so many pontifical regulations. But if only some, I should like to know by what element they would distinguish those that do and those that do not. Is it when the phrase 'We teach and order' is added? But such regulations come out every year in Rome. 'A husband should not give a wife any gift worth more than twelve ducats': let's take this as an example.[83] My question is: if someone, without any evil intent, were to give a gift of thirteen ducats, would he sin mortally? You will answer, I think, 'Probably not.' But in these and other even less serious matters, besides the heavy guilt, the penalty of excommunication is always added to the sentence handed down.[84] And there are theologians who say that no one can be excommunicated except for an offence that is a mortal sin in the eyes of God.[85] But I will leave aside for the moment this dispute about whether a bishop or a pope can condemn those subject to them to capital punishment in any matter.

* * * * *

80 Cf *De vita spirituali animae* lectio 5 in Gerson III 182–3 and 192–4, although Erasmus paraphrases freely. It was this passage that Latomus targeted covertly in the attack nominally directed at Oecolampadius in his *De ecclesia et humanae legis obligatione*. See the introduction xxvi above; and Rummel *Critics* II 12.

81 Cf *De vita spirituali animae* lectio 6 in Gerson III 197–8.

82 Cf *De non esu carnium* in Gerson III 80–3; see *De delectu ciborum scholia* no 41 with n124, 124 below; cf *De vita spirituali animae* lectio 4 corollary 4 in Gerson III 160–1.

83 Unknown, perhaps a hypothetical example

84 Automatic excommunication incurred as soon as a crime is committed; canon 1314 in *Code of Canon Law Annotated* ed E. Caparros, M Thériault, and J. Thorn (Montreal 1993) 821.

85 *De vita spirituali animae* lectio 4 corollary 12 and lectio 6 in Gerson III 167, 192

This I will ask: 'Is it probable that it is the pope's desire, even if he could, to burden his flock in this way?' Paul expresses anger that anyone should judge his brother on matters of food and drink;[86] so should I thrust my brother down to hell because of food and drink? Now let's leave open for the moment what may be the desire of popes on other matters. Certainly in the matter of fasting it is clear that Paul did not wish to bind everyone by his instruction. Then why do we act as unfair judges towards our neighbour and interpret the pontiff's law otherwise than he intended? Nor is it right to say that he wanted to bind anyone to fast or to eat fish if the person who would be doing this did so at great cost to his health or life. And he does not lay under obligation infants, the very aged, the sick, the impoverished, or, in the end, all those who for any other reason cannot tolerate fasting – still less [an obligation] concerning the eating of meat.[87] If these people eat, it seems they do so in any case in accordance with the intention of the one who established the law. You will say, 'But then the window is open to evil people who will eat on this pretext when they do not have good reason.' I would consider this a risk if it were a question of homicide or some serious evil. In this case I would think it more tolerable if six hundred ate meat without necessity than that one person should be in danger of his life because of such a superstition. Accordingly, I like the custom the Italians have of selling veal, kid, and lamb publicly in the markets even in Lent, though by a select few, so there is no shortage for the sick or those who have difficulty in going without meat. Nor does anyone take down the name of the one who buys or eats, even if there is no obvious sign of sickness, for there are reasons that you could not pick up from the face, and it is a matter of Christian charity to place the more favourable interpretation on what may be done quite legitimately.

Drunkenness, denigration, obscene speech are real evidence of the reprobate according to the gospel standard. Since indeed these are real evils, when they come out of the mouth, they proclaim the corruption of their source – the heart – whence this pestilence is exhaled. And yet we take slight offence at these or even applaud them. We detest the man who eats meat as if he failed to be a Christian, though the Gospel forbids us to judge anyone on things that are not evil in themselves, and Paul does not want anyone to be judged on matters of food and drink.[88] Therefore, the

* * * * *

86 Col 2:16
87 See 81 n69 above.
88 Cf Matt 15:1–20; Mark 7:1–23; Rom 14:2–3; Col 2:16.

person who consumes meat for good reason does not even sin against the Law, since he commits nothing contrary to the intention of the one who established the rule. The person who consumes meat without needing to, if he does sin, sins only in respect of human law. [42] On the other hand, the man who condemns his brother, who denigrates, impeaches, and traduces him, that man sins both against gospel doctrine and against the precept of the apostle Paul.[89] In my opinion he offends worse than if he consumed meat for ten whole years. Those who eat meat are called Lutherans and heretics. Now this is not gnawing at the flesh of calves but at the flesh of one's brother.[90] I ask you, which is the more wicked? And yet no one is upset at actions the authority of the gospel forbids or what Paul the apostle forbids. At actions that human custom has introduced in addition to gospel doctrine we shudder with horror, as if all Christianity were about to collapse once and for all.

But here a double worry sometimes hinders us: on the one hand, it seems to be a matter of order, on the other, a stumbling block for one's neighbour. I acknowledge that great importance must be attributed to order, so much so that it is preferable to suffer a certain tyranny than to throw human affairs into confusion by upsetting order. Even Paul bids us to avoid a Christian who walks ἄτακτος, that is, 'in a disorderly manner';[91] and likewise he teaches us to abstain not only from evil but 'from every form of evil' so as not to be a stumbling block to anyone.[92] [43] But, so that order may prevail and through order peace, it is necessary that authority should be exercised by leaders and that the people should obey them just as they obey God's vicars. I acknowledge that these things are absolutely true. And the apostle Peter condemns those who are slaves to their own desires and despise authorities,[93] that is, prominent men endowed with public power, since at this point the discussion is about magistrates and, if I am

* * * * *

89 Cf Matt 7:1–2; Luke 6:37; Rom 2:1–4, 14:3–4; Col 2:16.

90 Cf Béda Errores 8 ASD IX-5 136–7/LB IX 487E.

91 In his annotation on 2 Thess 3:7 (non inquieti fuimus) Erasmus explains the literal and metaphorical interpretations of ἀτάκτως (2 Thess 3:6) and its cognates; see LB VI 919F–920D; CWE 43 471 n7.

92 1 Thess 5:22

93 Cf 2 Pet 2:10. 'Authorities' (Erasmus gloriae); however, he retains the (1527) Vulgate singular dominationem for Greek κυριότητος in his translation of the NT, expanding the following clause to state 'they do not fear to attack with insults those who excel in glory' (gloria praecellentes non verentur conviciis incessere). On 2:11, a troubled passage, see Metzger A Textual Commentary on the Greek New Testament 2nd ed (Stuttgart 1994) 633.

not mistaken, about pagan princes too.[94] How much more important it is that the authority of the popes should be sacred and inviolate! If they are good, they should be obeyed as friends of God; if bad, but still teach what is right, the doctrine they hand down should be obeyed. If neither they nor their teachings are good, I still think they are to be tolerated to some extent to avoid the outbreak of a worse plague when public order is disturbed. This is the advice I would give to Christian folk. Moreover, if their impiety should increase to the point where it is intolerable to both gods and men, may Christ protect us from that – Christ, who knew how to braid whips to drive out of his temple those he did not want dealing there.[95] For just as, for good reason, the election of popes is delegated from the people to a few, so it does not seem proper to recall instances in which the common people drove out their bishops for some misdeed. In fact, we read that Brictius was expelled by a popular uprising on suspicion of sexual misconduct with a washerwoman.[96]

Anyway, Paul teaches wives that they should in all matters please and revere their husbands as their lords; and he warns that husbands, in turn, should use their authority over their wives gently and with respect, should think of them as companions and equals in Christ, common heirs of the heavenly kingdom, a second part of themselves, and should accommodate themselves judiciously to their weakness.[97] In the same way, church leaders must be warned that they should not misuse their authority over the people or turn the simple obedience of the people into a tyranny of their own. They are sheep, but Christ's sheep rather than the bishops'.

They are sheep, but for these sheep the chief shepherd poured out his precious blood. They are sheep, but so dear to their Lord that just one who is lost is sought with anxious care and when found at last is carried back to his fold on his shoulders.[98] They are sheep, but thinking sheep and to this extent the equals of the bishops; sometimes they are even wiser than certain bishops. And finally it is from these sheep that shepherds are made. The people are not created for the sake of the bishops, but the bishops for the sake of the people. Whence, even if the bishop is eminent when compared

* * * * *

94 Cf Matt 22:21 with its reference to Caesar.
95 Cf Matt 21:12–13.
96 For Brictius (Britius, ie St Brice, the successor of St Martin of Tours), see *Butler's Lives of the Saints* rev and ed Herbert Thurston sj and Donald Attwater (Aberdeen 1956) IV 328.
97 Eph 5:22–33; Col 3:18–19; see also 1 Pet 3:1–7.
98 Luke 15:3–6

to individuals from the common people and is worthy of double honour, as Paul says,[99] yet there should be more account taken of the people as a whole than of one bishop. And if anyone should go on to say, 'The office is still more important,' his remark would not be exactly inconsistent with Christ's words. For in the Gospel the Lord Jesus asks, 'Which appears to be the greater, the one who serves or the one who sits at table?' 'Is it not,' he says, 'the one who sits at table?'[100] But these are a people covenanted to the Son, who recline in the honourable places at the gospel table. The nobility of the church are the servants who attend and move around to see that nothing is lacking for anyone at this feast. And whatever they see is appropriate for each, they provide from the rich store of the bridegroom, Christ. But if Christ, who without question was greatest by any comparison, calls himself a servant and carries his service to the point of washing feet, what must the pontiffs do, who in St Jerome's opinion are fathers, not lords,[101] to whom is entrusted not authority but the ministration of God's mysteries,[102] who can slip themselves and are ignorant of much? Therefore, let the bishop rule the people, but as a father over his children, as a husband over a beloved spouse. And let him not think that he is allowed to do what he likes to his flock, of which he is to give an account to the chief and true shepherd.[103] And let him remember this: that authority should be preserved not only by severe command, by sternness, by threats and punishment – not even tyrants usually preserve their authority adequately by these means – but much more by holiness of life, modesty, gentleness, holy teaching, fatherly advice, and friendly exhortations. In punishing the man who lived with his father's wife, Paul availed himself of his authority as an apostle;[104] [41] but how many times does he stoop to persuade, to plead, to beg, to exhort, to entreat, and to adjure!

Constant purity of life is a particular quality that must be respected. [44] The populace views with unbelievable favour a gospel spirit that despises wealth, honours, pleasures, is eager to earn the good will of all and ready to risk even life for the flock entrusted to it. There is great admiration for the heart that is filled with the Scriptures, the tongue that is no less holy than eloquent, which draws from a well-supplied storehouse things

* * * * *

99 1 Tim 5:17
100 Luke 22:27
101 Cf Jerome Ep 52.7.3 PL 22 533.
102 1 Cor 4:1
103 Cf 1 Pet 5:1–4.
104 1 Cor 5:1–5

new and old.[105] It is with these qualities that the authority of bishops is best equipped and defended, and much more justly and firmly than with the words 'We order, we decree, we determine, we instruct, we wish and command.' These qualities make people do better of their own accord than is demanded, and people are more deeply moved by fatherly encouragement than by any royal threats. Do we not see, whenever there arises someone with some reputation for holiness and giving some appearance of being a gospel teacher, how eagerly the people hang on his lips, how sincerely they favour him? Why? If the people saw a fatherly disposition such as Paul or Peter had, what would they not do? The disciples received Paul as no less than Jesus Christ, ready even to pluck out their own eyes and give them to him if he had asked.[106] So these are the means by which order, authority, peace, and harmony are best established, when both parties contend in their turn to do service. Otherwise, whenever the people are oppressed by force and are physically quiet but mutter and curse in their hearts, peace is a tyranny.

And let there be no instant outcry that it detracts from the authority of prelates if we take account of both the freedom and the tranquillity of the public. In the first place, it matters to the authority of those in charge that the people should have the best possible feelings about them. But it seems they will hardly have good feelings if they believe the purpose of those in charge is to entangle their folk in as many nets of regulations as possible, leaving themselves to rule according to their own inclination. The only one who thinks well of the pontiff is the one who deems that he wants his flock to be as free as possible in Christ and unencumbered by scruples and sophistries. Nor does a person diminish the authority of the ruler if he will not allow him to do anything contrary to what is just and good, against the laws of the state, against the customs and privileges of the citizens, against the oath by which he assumed sovereignty. On the contrary, the person who attributes to a monarch what is worthy of tyrants rather than of a legitimate prince takes away all his authority. Therefore, if a king does not demand that his edict should constrain anyone to pecuniary or corporal punishment, unless the law[107] is equitable, just, reasonable, properly promulgated, and approved by the tacit assent of the people, and finally, if he does not demand that every regulation should carry a capital penalty, does a person not seem

* * * * *

105 Matt 13:52
106 Gal 4:14–15
107 *lex* 'law' is a correction interpolated by Augustijn and explained at ASD IX-1
      41 651n.

to credit bishops with a plainly tyrannical intention if one supposes that they have this purpose: that they want to put their flock in danger of hell with whatever regulations they may make? But the laws of princes often threaten, and they really deter by means of a rather harsh penalty more than they punish, such as the law reported in the Twelve Tables about cutting up the body of the person in debt to several creditors and unable to pay.[108] And indeed with the thunderbolt of Jupiter striking down malefactors, and with the fictions of the terrible punishments inflicted by Rhadamanthys and the avenging Furies,[109] the ancients deterred from crime the ignorant majority, incapable of moral reasoning. We may allow a measure of this sort of pretence to secular rulers, but I do not think it should be accepted in bishops who profess the doctrine of gospel truth. But he who issues instructions casts a net; he who exhorts calls people to better things without taking away their liberty.

Someone will say that exhortation is weak: because people are unmanageable, what is needed is a ruling. To me the opposite seems true. Often fatherly exhortation achieves more than tyrannical demand. It may be that exhortation is vain if we do not make trial of it with wives and children every day and if Jeroboam did not show that it is true by his own misfortune. The savage and tyrannical counsel of the young men turned out badly for him.[110] [45] If the people really look on the priest and the bishop with respect, exhortation will not be ineffective. But if an openly impious life, unclean habits, gross ignorance, insatiable greed, and barbarous cruelty have turned the minds of ordinary people away entirely, what will be gained by instructions? Those who do not obey will sin all the more seriously on account of their obstinacy. One who obeys out of fear will deserve nothing, or certainly very little, because someone who complies with a precept under compulsion does not comply with it, and perhaps hypocrisy will double the fault. It rests with us chiefly, therefore, to ensure that exhortation, however mild and calm, should carry weight with the populace. So those who have regard for the authority of leaders act properly, but those who want it to be maintained by sheer threats and intimidations have poor

* * * * *

108 Cf Ἰχθυοφαγία in *Colloquia* CWE 40 696:32–6 with n141; and *Adagia* I x 24 with n1; Gellius 20.1.48–9; Quintilian 3.6.84.
109 Rhadamanthys, son of Zeus and Europa, was one of the judges of the dead. The Furies or Erinyes were underworld powers of retribution who carried out the curses of a father or mother. See OCD.
110 See 1 Kings 12:1–14:28 where Rehoboam is the one who acted according to the advice of his contemporaries.

regard for it. But at the same time it is fair that we should have regard for the freedom of the flock also, as much as equity requires. For it too has its own authority, nor is that authority exactly small. Does not custom restrict and annul law, to the extent that a law may not deserve the name of law if it did not have the tacit consent of those using it? What was it that annulled so many regulations of the recent Lateran Council, initiated under Julius II and completed under Leo x?[111] Was it not the tacit suffrage of the people that cancelled what had been decreed without any casting of votes? This is indisputably the voice of the people, which is said to be the very voice of God;[112] this is the authority of the free multitude, which it is fair to take into account whenever this does not go astray from the rule of piety. Accordingly, the person whose counsel is guided by consideration of both sides is the one who deliberates rightly.[113]

Now let us cast a quick glance at the importance of the worry about being a stumbling block. Our Prince Jesus Christ in one place attributed considerable importance to avoiding scandal; in another place he disregarded the Pharisees when they took offence. He willed to be born of a married woman, he was circumcised, he observed rituals prescribed by law, he fasted, so that he could be accused of nothing that might have the plausible appearance of impiety or disregard for the Law.[114] But he never stopped proclaiming his Father, he never stopped teaching his heavenly philosophy, he never stopped doing good to all, he did not fear to heal a man on the sabbath, though the Pharisees were galled by these acts.[115] He was a stumbling block even to Herod, whom he despised and was despised in turn by him.[116] And when he was warned in another place of how the

* * * * *

111 The Fifth Lateran Council, 1512–17. See the article in NCE 8 409–10, which concludes that there was little zeal in making the enactments effective and that the church 'was soon confronted with protestations far more perilous.'

112 See Hans Walther *Proverbia sententiaeque latinitatis medii aevi* (Göttingen 1967–c1986) V 919 no 34182: *Vox populi vox Dei.*

113 On the advantages of preferring an exhortation over a rigid requirement, see Erasmus' defence of this passage in his *Apologia adversus rhapsodias Alberti Pii* CWE 84 189.

114 Matt 1:20–4; Luke 2:21; Matt 5:17; see Matt 4:2 for Christ's fast in the wilderness; at 1 Cor 8:8–13 Paul insists that the Christian avoid giving scandal at table; see Erasmus' paraphrase on that passage in CWE 43 115–8 with n25. See also *Ratio* LB V 113C, where Erasmus says that Christ is believed to have fasted 'in the manner of the Jews so that his disciples would not be slandered on that account.'

115 Matt 12:9–14

116 Luke 23:9–11

Pharisees took offence, what did he answer? He said, 'Let them alone; they are blind leaders of the blind.'[117]

Following his example, the apostles too conceded many things to the weakness of the Jews, so that nothing might hinder the progress of the gospel. But they do not yield everywhere to everyone's displeasure. For they could not be compelled by any outcries of the Jews to the point of urging pagans to be circumcised. This alone was granted for a time to the unconquerable obstinacy of the Jews, that gentiles are commanded to refrain from unchastity, from blood, from what is strangled, and from meat that had been sacrificed to idols.[118] Paul shaves his hair, takes part in a barefoot procession, is purified in the temple in order to pacify the minds of certain people meditating dissension.[119] But he does this protesting everywhere he can. He admits that it is permissible to consume any sort of food, but it sometimes happens that it is not expedient to act according to your own rule.[120] He offers the freedom of the gospel, but charity measures all things by the benefit of one's neighbour and often willingly gives up its own right[121] – not everywhere or permanently, but contending for the moment with all its might against the weakness of those who are unwittingly offended, until they too progress to the strength of the gospel and are no longer offended by things that in themselves are neither good nor bad. In matters of food Paul sometimes became a Jew to the Jews in order to win the Jews and likewise a gentile to the gentiles in order to win them.[122] But it would be absurd for someone to become a Jew to the Jews now, abstaining from food that is forbidden to them, so that he would not alienate Jews. No, rather Paul reproaches Peter because, when the doctrine of Christ was already so widely spread that well-informed and instructed Jews might fairly reject their superstitious weakness, still to avoid offending Jews he withdrew from a feast.[123] In avoiding one stumbling block, he fell over another more serious one.

This was, as it were, the infancy of the gospel. The religion of the Law handed down by their ancestors and confirmed by long practice was so firmly imprinted in the Jews that this disposition had to be excused and

* * * * *

117 Matt 15:14
118 Acts 15:1–29
119 See 68 n19 above.
120 Rom 14:13–23; 1 Cor 8:7–13, 10:27–30
121 1 Cor 10:29 and 24
122 1 Cor 9:20 and 21
123 Gal 2:11–14

tolerated for a while, because it arose from an honourable cause and could
not suddenly be plucked out of men's souls. Then this offence entailed a
serious danger. The Jewish people held tenaciously to their ancestral custom and were being alienated from the gospel. The gentiles were so averse
to the burden of the Law that many would sooner have borne withdrawal
from Christ than allow themselves a Judaizing act. And since nothing is
more deplorable than idolatry, anyone who ate food sacrificed to idols at
that time gave plausible grounds to suspect that he agreed with the superstition of those with whom he was eating. And yet here Paul declares that
the Law was already out of date.[124] He declares that 'an idol has no real
existence' and sacrifice to idols is nothing.[125] He reproaches the man who
knowingly offends his brother by what he eats; but he reproaches the man
who judges another's conscience in matters of food or drink, who speaks ill
of his brother on account of food for which he gives thanks to a beneficent
God who created everything for men's use.[126] He mocks the foolish wisdom of those who said, as if they were teaching something important, 'Do
not touch. Do not taste. Do not handle.'[127] Just as, according to Paul, Jewish rules of abstinence began to be disregarded when the gospel was published widely enough, so, in a parallel case, it seemed that food sacrificed
to idols was to be disregarded when it became sufficiently well known that
Christians could consume with a clear conscience any food necessary for
the body, giving thanks to the one who provided everything in this world
for his worshippers, since he is the Lord of all, who intended that to the
pure nothing should be impure.[128]

[46] Likewise, if some proper cause of scandal ceases to exist, and if
'the kingdom of God does not mean food and drink,'[129] and if abstinence
from food tempts many to excess and pleasures but is an unmerciful burden to the poor, we should consider whether we ought to contend so fiercely
over regulations like these. This was a matter for consideration in the circumstances of a time when the gospel was newborn. Some concession was
made to attitudes remaining from an earlier life. And the concession was

* * * * *

124 'Out of date' (*antiquatam*); on Erasmus' use of this word elsewhere, see eg his
    paraphrases CWE 43 41 with n60 (on 1 Cor 1:29), 217 with n12 (on 2 Cor 3:11),
    317 with n31 (on Eph 2:15), and 414 with n43 (on Col 2:14).
125 1 Cor 8:4
126 1 Cor 10:28–30, referring to Ps 24:1, 50:12
127 Col 2:21
128 Titus 1:15
129 Rom 14:17

made for the moment out of charity, not as of right. It was not granted on
every matter, nor was it permanent or without protest. [47] But what cause
for offence is there now in practices the gospel does not forbid?[130] No, rather
the Apostle's Letters condemn their censors when, as he says, [48] they forbid foods that God created to be eaten and forbid marriage.[131] How far are
the limits of scandal to be extended? Paul abstains from what is sacrificed
to idols, but after being warned that it was offered in sacrifice. Yet he eats
any food 'without raising any question on the ground of conscience.'[132] So
in this way, with slight inconvenience, offence is avoided. For anyone who
abstains because of circumstances from sacrificial meats has available other
meats that he may eat. He abstains from beef sacrificed to Neptune and
consumes partridge or chicken that are not sacrificed to any god; and he
does not do even this except as it suits him. He abstains from pork and
consumes *beccafico*;[133] he abstains from eels and consumes sturgeon. [49] At
this time, since the eating of all meats is prohibited for many days,[134] do
you think it fair that I should put my health and my life at risk because of
the weakness and superstition of this man or that, although all Christians
ought to know by now that they should not judge their neighbour on such
matters?

But if Christian charity apparently requires us to indulge the weakness
of the ignorant or the superstitious like this – so that for this reason we want
someone who is strong to be put in danger of his health or life – why do we
not do the same in those matters that cause a real and obvious scandal? [50]
There are leaders of the church who, though they have a superabundance
of ecclesiastical riches, even equal to the wealth of kings, still do not teach
the people and they live openly impious lives. They are an offence to the
laity. In this case, no concession is made to the people's sense of wrong,
but strength is demanded of the weak to the point that they are bidden to
believe, for fear of being heretics, that everything done by these leaders
– whether they absolve or condemn, whether they bless or curse, whether
they grant indulgences or withhold them – is just as valid as if done by an
apostle, Paul, Andrew, or James. Yet this scandal was born from a practice

* * * * *

130 LB has a question mark here; omitted in Augustijn.
131 Cf 1 Tim 4:3, Béda *Errores* 9 ASD IX-5 137/LB IX 487E–F, and *Declarationes ad
    censuras Lutetiae vulgatas* III propositio 3 CWE 82 41–2.
132 1 Cor 10:25 and 27
133 A small bird esteemed as a delicacy especially in the autumn when it grows
    fat on grapes and figs
134 That is, during Lent.

that was in itself bad, and however troublesome it may be to avoid it at the source, it should be avoided because it is an offence in the eyes of God, even if there were no cause of offence to men. In addition, though any criticism may seem the worst possible evil, we still disregard the wrong done to the weak in this case and boldly please ourselves. In just those cases where the censors need defence against the appearance of acting contrary to gospel doctrine, the word 'scandal' has such power that, for the sake of a foolish superstition, we are willing to put in danger a brother for whom food is essential. Is this not to transgress God's precepts for the sake of human traditions?[135]

I know, distinguished prelate, that your piety has been leading you for a long time to say, 'Where does all this tend? Am I to condemn abstinence approved by the usage of the church?' To speak plainly, [51] I would want all practices of this nature, or at least the demand for practices like them, to be immediately abolished, provided that endeavours of true piety may be increased by the same extent as rituals are shortened and that what is subtracted from our Jewishness may be added to our Christianity. [52] Even if the ignorant majority cannot really be kept to their duty without this sort of petty observances, I would not want Christian freedom to be burdened with a large number of them. I would not want consciences to be so constrained that they believe they would be guilty of a capital crime if they eat (unless it were done with a perverse and insolent attitude). I would not want such weight to be given, through some absurd judgment, to practices that are of hardly any importance in themselves when those that are essential to gospel piety are neglected. But still, after these practices have put down roots and the general custom is firmly planted, I would not want them to be mutinously despised but either gradually abolished or removed by a decision of the majority – but removed in such a way that in the process people are attracted to better practices.[136]

But here anyone may raise this objection to me: 'If rituals like these are of little profit, at least they do no harm. Up until now they have supported piety, because they both remind us of true piety and in addition are teachers for the weak, in the same way as the law of Moses was for the Jews.[137] We can see how weak even Christians are; the prohibition on eating meat reminds and teaches us that all extravagance, and what generally follows from extravagance, must be avoided. The prescribed fasting reminds us and

* * * * *

135 Matt 15:6
136 Cf Béda *Errores* 4 ASD IX-5 134–5 / LB IX 486CE (the whole of this paragraph).
137 Cf Gal 3:23–4; and Erasmus' paraphrase on those verses CWE 42 113–14.

teaches us that we must refrain from all vices, for only that sort of fasting is pleasing to God.' If this reasoning appeals, let us be circumcised at the same time, since circumcision both reduces the thrills of passion during coitus and reminds us that the heart must be circumcised from all base emotions. Let us slaughter sacrificial victims: the practice tells us the soul's brutish emotions must be mastered. In truth, it is enough for us to be reminded by such images that these practices were religiously observed in former times by the Jews. But if piety encounters no danger from rituals, why does Paul fight with such fierceness at every point against the rituals of Mosaic law?[138] They overwhelm gospel freedom if they are used excessively. Trust in them, such as the common people generally have, is a plague on true piety. To criticize one's brother on these grounds is a poison for gospel religion. Paul could surely see these things, since he waged a zealous war against the attempted intrusion of Judaism. No, rather if I had time I could show that rituals flood us with plagues that have very serious consequences for Christianity.

I do not approve of the obstinacy of people who have eaten meat blatantly and contemptuously, as if mocking the generally accepted custom. But I condemn them only to the extent that I think they should be instructed and warned and, if the case warrants it, even reproved, not reported to magistrates as if guilty of parricide.[139] And the matter should be disregarded rather than whipped up, so that a greater fire is not thereby ignited from this brief spark and no greater hatred of the clergy, already inflamed more than enough. I am uneasy about anything that tends to revolt. And yet if no one opposes rituals of this sort as they become ever more dominant, gospel freedom will clearly be destroyed. But there is no one who can more suitably stand up against them than the leaders of the church. [54] It was in this way that the custom gradually crept in that made Friday a fish day; then, when this was successful, Saturday was taken too; now even Wednesday is in danger.[140] And for the sake of this sort of petty ritual we see so many

* * * * *

138 Erasmus answers criticism of this passage in *Apologia adversus rhapsodias Alberti Pii* CWE 84 212 item 3.
139 Cf ibidem.
140 Cf Béda *Errores* 10 ASD IX-5 138/LB IX 487F–488A. Clichtove notes that in the early days of the church Wednesday and Friday were weekly fast days; *De ieiunio* 28.6 in Clichtove III 576. See also *Decretum Gratiani* cap 13 dist 3, *De consecratione* (Friedberg I 1356). The observation of Wednesday as a fast day was, at the time of Erasmus, an act of supererogation. Erasmus notes that Baechem refrained from meat on Wednesday, eating only fish; see *Apologia de loco 'Omnes quidem'* 60 above; and Ep 1162:120 with n17.

people suffer, incur danger, and even die, many who are stupidly satisfied with themselves, believing they are Christians although they are Jews,[141] and because of their faith in these practices they neglect those that constitute true piety. But gospel charity tells us to help the afflicted. Gospel freedom ought not to be distracted from serious occupations by an excessive number of such innovations. [55] And let me explain that I speak about practices of this sort in general not in order to defend the arrogant and the contemptuous but in order that, having carefully examined the circumstances of the case, you may in your wisdom judge that neither more nor less is being done than the case itself requires.

Now let me plead my own case in a few words. It is not that I was ever a stumbling block to any good person; what I have done I would not have feared to do if Christ himself were present at the table. I was, in fact, in a state that anyone would sooner have judged worthy of pity rather than reproach; I hope, nevertheless, that I am not guilty of causing anyone among those who are unaware of the real facts to use my example as a pretext for their licence and my need as a defence for their boldness. In the first place, I have never encouraged anyone to consume meat without necessity. No, I have taught rather that general custom should be observed. My own attitude to meats is that if one might preserve life and health with chickpeas and lupin, I would not want either fish or meat. Moreover, although because of my poor physical health and a certain inborn dislike of fish I am usually in danger almost every Lent, I have still never complied with doctors who frequently recommend the safeguard of meat. There was one exception, in Italy, when a doctor threatened that I would die in a few days if I did not yield. But I yielded for a few days to the extent that I ate gravy mixed with egg yolks, but still abstaining from meats, which my stomach would not accept even if the appetite were there – such was my weakness. At present I make an exception for a few days in Lent, and that on doctor's orders and not without a papal dispensation. For several years now I have been provided for this purpose with a diploma, which I have never used up until now in so far as it refers to meats.[142] Now imagine that I did this without a doctor's order; what doctor knows this poor body better than I? Imagine that I did it without the certificate; does not need excuse me better than

* * * * *

141 Cf *Apologia adversus rhapsodias Alberti Pii* CWE 84 183.
142 For references to a papal dispensation from laws of fasting and abstinence issued to Erasmus by Leo x, see Ep 1079:6–8 with n1 (March 1520); and for one by Clement vii from the law of abstinence in Lent, see Ep 1542 from Cardinal Campeggi, February 1525.

any certificate? Consider first my old age, the almost continuous ill health
of this poor body, consider the exertion of travel, the labours of study in
which I am constantly engaged beyond both my physical and my mental
resources. In addition to these factors, for almost twenty days phlegm, or
rather not phlegm but pure pestilence, weakened me to the point of death.
The same thing has recurred from time to time and has affected me even
more seriously and for a longer time. Shortly before Lent I had an attack of
kidney stones with an extraordinary effect on my whole body. This sickness
is most painful and an immediate danger – pregnant women in labour are
not in greater danger to their lives – and it recurred almost every other day
with me, so that one day with wretched fertility I would be conceiving, the
next I would be in labour, and the third I would be giving birth. In these
circumstances what reasonable man would not say that I was killing myself
if I abstained from meat? Let those who wish to imitate Erasmus imitate
him in his entirety, and it will be excused. Now what is to be said to the
healthy, the lazy, and the drunks who eat so as to produce mockery, not,
following the example of Erasmus, to meet their need?

There remains one worry about scandal. Christian charity urges us, I
grant, to take account, as far as we may, of being a stumbling block for the
weak. I hearken to Paul who was prepared even to refrain forever from
eating meat rather than to consume it and offend his neighbour.[143] But that
same Paul, as I have said before, reproaches those who pass judgment on a
brother by reason of his food or drink and at the same time mentions those
most obnoxious individuals who would prohibit the consumption of foods
that God had provided for mortal use.[144] He asks, 'Why do you judge the
servant of another? It is before his own master that he stands or falls.'[145] And
'Why am I judged by another man's conscience because of that for which
I give thanks?'[146] 'The one who eats should not despise the one who does
not eat; the one who does not eat should not pass judgment on the one who
does.'[147] And so in Paul's estimation the weaker person is the one who does
not eat, and the greater sinner is the one who thinks he is the better, whose
duty it was to concede more. And yet charity, which accommodates itself to
all things,[148] yields for a while to the weakness of an individual who may

* * * * *

143 Cf 1 Cor 8:13.
144 Cf Rom 14:3; 1 Cor 10:26, 30.
145 Rom 14:4
146 1 Cor 10:29–30
147 Rom 14:3
148 Cf 1 Cor 10:24 and 13:7.

have given offence for a reasonable cause, if he cannot be corrected. But not in everything! For there is a situation in which the weak person must be advised and instructed, in which he must be reproached, in which he must be spurned. Otherwise, feeding the sickness of the weak with constant indulgence is the most direct way to the destruction of all gospel piety. But Paul is dealing there with weakness that is nearly invincible, because it has been so deeply rooted in men's minds by the tradition of their elders and by long-held custom that it cannot be pulled up suddenly. So the Jews could not tolerate the annulment of the Law under which they had been born and brought up, and in the religious observance of which they had grown old. So if a convert from among the gentiles had seen a Christian at table in a banquet where meat sacrificed to idols was served, he could not avoid suspecting that the Christian was consenting to the superstition of those with whom he was engaged in an unholy feast. And yet Paul declares emphatically at the same time that an idol has no real existence and that it is right to eat whatever is supplied in the meat market.[149] He declares that rituals of the Law were instituted as a temporary measure and become obsolete in the face of the vitality of the gospel.[150] Finally he opposed Peter to his face because he still did not dare to disregard a silly cause of offence to the Jews.[151] So here Paul speaks of another sort of offence, which had its source in a deep-rooted custom of a former life. [56] We create and invent for ourselves matter for offences of this sort, though we see how great a plague for true piety is born of them in ordinary life. Paul is indulgent to the weak in the hope that they will become strong. We are all obsessed with these offences, paying no attention to the practices that alone make us truly pious.

Anyway, to come back to my own case, however the question of offences is taken, no one will find me wanting here either, I think, in the charity that seeks to indulge my neighbour's weakness. I have used the papal certificate as a sort of remedy for such offences, and I do not see what other use it can properly be to me. Finally, I have used meats when there were as far as possible no witnesses; in fact I have often abstained entirely, at manifest risk of my life, against the advice of a doctor. What else can I do, except just die, to satisfy the superstitious weakness, not to say the wilful arrogance, of certain slanderers who stop at nothing? I think anyone who

* * * * *

149 1 Cor 8:4, 10:25
150 'Become obsolete' (*antiquari*). Cf Gal 3:23–5; and 93 n124 above; Col 2:16–17; also *Apologia adversus rhapsodias Alberti Pii* CWE 84 213 / LB IX 1153F.
151 Gal 2:11–14

demands this is ungodly, and I myself a murderer if I were to comply. It is the duty of Christian charity to interpret in a kindly manner whatever may be done with a good intention. And it was reasonable for those with Christian learning not to ignore the fact that fasting and fish were not prescribed for the sick but for those in danger of excessive indulgence in meat. But if anyone is still so subject to superstition, he may be counselled by one who eats meat with these words: 'Brother, don't let my example offend you at all; I am obliged to do what I do. Would that I were more fortunate. I praise your strength; do not, on your part, speak ill of my weakness.' He will have satisfied his conscience, I think, well enough.

But to conclude, just as I think we must censure strictly those who violate a general custom with their rebellious arrogance, especially a custom that does not conflict with true piety, [57] so it seems to me parish priests and preachers will do well if, with the authorization of their superiors, they declare a fast to the people in this way: 'It was needful indeed that the whole life of Christians, through continual sobriety, should be something of a fast, not only from food but much more from every excess, from all the pleasures of this world, from the desires of the flesh that war against the spirit.[152] But church authority and the custom of our ancestors encourage those of you who are able, in view of bodily health, age, or weight of daily occupations, to prepare your soul for a holy day by fasting. But let your fasting be Christian fasting, if you wish it to be acceptable to Jesus Christ; let it be whole and complete. Abstinence from food is the smallest part of fasting. Fasting in which peace and concord are broken is unwelcome to God. Let those who fast give thanks to the Lord for the strength of the body, because it is made more ready for divine things by abstaining from food. Let those who do not fast give thanks to the Lord who in his goodness supplies a varied abundance of foods to restore the weakness of our bodies. Let those who fast not congratulate themselves for this reason as if they do something great, unless they do greater things in addition. Let those who do not fast apply themselves so much more to pious occupations that, by these other occupations, they compensate and make amends for what they cannot perform through bodily weakness. Let the one who does not abstain avoid upsetting public custom and giving offence to the weak as much as he conveniently can. Let the one who abstains beware that, contrary to gospel and apostolic doctrine, he does not judge his neighbour on a matter that of itself is two sided and can be done rightly or otherwise. It is a lesser sin

* * * * *

152 Cf Gal 5:17.

if someone dines all his life without ever being in need than if someone
disparages his neighbour for his eating and drinking and attacks and gnaws
at him when, according to divine teaching, he should love him no less than
himself.[153] Since such counsels are extremely relevant to this matter, they
should be impressed on people repeatedly. Indeed, for the sake of those
of weak and timid conscience, I should like this too to be set out clearly:
what regulations are binding on whom, not binding on whom, or how far
are they binding or not binding? And I do not think that, for those that
can be loosened by man, it is useful to set limits that in my opinion are
far too narrow. In these cases let fatherly charity be mild and indulgent.
For the rest let the authority of the bishops inveigh against malice, against
disparagement, against murders and wars and all the other inevitable and
real plagues of Christian piety.[154]

It has seemed proper to write these words to you, most distinguished
and upright prelate, not in order to teach one most learned or to bring
my case to your highness, who is aware both of my work in studies undertaken for the public good and of this heart of mine (whose desire is for anything but food and drink), of my bodily weakness, which old age makes
even worse, and my present too abiding, too pressing illness, but in order,
through you, to satisfy or heal others if any have perhaps been offended
by my action or enticed into licentiousness by my example. If I have discussed these matters rather freely, there was no other cause but that I was
very well aware of your exceptional wisdom and kindness. Since you[155] ornament the nobility of your family by your very moral integrity, your uncommon learning, and finally your exceptional wisdom and all other gifts
worthy of a bishop, I was not afraid that anything spoken too freely about
the office of prelates might be seized on as suspicious. Farewell, your lord-
ship, most holy prelate.

Basel, on the day after Easter 1522[156]

* * * * *

153 'And gnaws at him' (*ac mordet*); a favourite image of Erasmus. See CWE 43 219
      n27 and 378 n3. For the law of love, see eg Lev 19:18; Matt 19:19 and 22:39.
154 Erasmus repeats the call for gentle exhortation rather than harsh rigidity in
      the requirement of fasting in his *Apologia adversus rhapsodias Alberti Pii* CWE 84
      189.
155 *dotibus episcopo dignis decores*] 1532 and ASD, basis of the present translation;
      cogitarem ... dotibus episcopo dignis decoris in 1522 and 1540, adopted by LB
156 21 April 1522

NOTES ON THE LETTER
ABOUT ABSTINENCE

In epistolam de delectu ciborum scholia

NOTES ON THE LETTER
ABOUT ABSTINENCE[1]

Since the pamphlet on abstinence was pelted with reproofs by many people who thought it defies ecclesiastical regulations encouraging temperance and mortification[2] of the flesh through prescribed fasts and abstinence, and that it entices Christians to lust and pleasures, it seemed right to publish it again, fortified with some very brief comments that I believe have a double value. First, they will ward off the denigrator, and second, they will warn waverers against rushing into something where there is no cause for offence. This procedure will serve both purposes equally, except in so far as the man who contrives slander against his neighbour sins worse than the one who takes bodily refreshment twice a day, eating any food he likes and giving thanks as he does so.[3]

I particularly want the reader to be forewarned that what is said here against the arrogance of some individuals does not refer in any way to the magistracy of this community, much less to the bishop and his officials. For the council was not yet giving approval at that time to such practices, nor indeed does it give approval now, I believe; the bishop, a man of integrity and piety, even brought prosecutions as far as he could.[4]

* * * * *

1 In these notes references to the corresponding passages in the *De esu carnium* are allocated the number given in the text [#], and this marker will be found at the appropriate point in the translation of the *De esu carnium*. It seems from Erasmus' quotation of the words *quorundam iudicium* in scholium 29 (ASD IX-1 29 with apparatus criticus line 278) that he was using the manuscript revised for the second edition of 1532 when writing these notes. In this case he has guarded himself by narrowing the scope of his criticism to the 'judgment of certain people.'
2 Latin *maceratio*. The classical meaning is 'soaking' (in a liquid, to make soft or to wear away the soft parts); cf Tertullian *De ieiuniis* 3. The more usual term is *mortificatio*.
3 Cf Rom 14:6; 1 Tim 4:3; and *De esu carnium* 93 n128 above.
4 'At that time,' ie ten years before, in 1522. Bishop Christof von Utenheim died in 1527.

It was in 1522, if I am not mistaken, during Lent, that certain people ate eggs and were so far unconcerned to keep the fact secret that they threw the shells or fragments of the eggs out of the windows into the public street. Besides this, on Palm Sunday, a number of comrades with the same ideas gathered in some house near the town belonging to one Sigismund, who was eminent in the surgical art but particularly regarded for his skill in cutting stones out of the bladder.[5] For he restored many people to life and, as I heard, was never unsuccessful, so sure was his hand. He was worthy to be granted his life on this count alone. For this gathering came to the worst possible end for him some time later when by chance he was caught by the emperor's provosts. After he was tortured twice in the most frightful way with red-hot tongs, part of his flesh was torn away from his back, then in a slow execution his four limbs with the shoulders and hips were cut off; after this his throat was cut and his tongue pulled out through the wound, his heart was removed and the trunk cast in the fire. Doubtless the example made of him was more severe than deserved, for it was thought large numbers could be cured by the harshness of the punishment inflicted on one man. But it was rumoured that he was half mad, a defect that is commonly associated with exceptional skills. Sometimes he talked very sensibly, at other times you would say his mind had gone. This man produced roast pork on Palm Sunday for a number of guests in the house I have mentioned, and they were not willing to keep even that secret.

Although the bishop denounced this deed and named a lot of people, there were not lacking some who defended their presumption by saying that Erasmus sometimes ate meat too. And this was not entirely untrue. On a few occasions during that Lent, I had taken some pullets, but in private and only when driven to it by the greatest necessity. I was repeatedly tormented by kidney stone, and I suffered such trouble from it in my studies that someone made of adamant could scarcely be equal to it. Finally, I even had a pontifical certificate that allowed me to do this without a bad conscience.[6] I was in no danger indeed from the bishop, who was always very devoted to me as long as he lived; but it was nevertheless proper to inform him so that he would have a reply for those who misused my need to excuse their own indiscretion.

At that time there was no thought of publishing what I had written, since indeed I had written for an individual and more freely for that reason. Besides, when the bishop had repeatedly indicated that he wanted this text

* * * * *

5 The incident at the house of Sigismund Steinschnider, which provoked the original *De esu carnium*. See Epp 1353, 1496; and CEBR III 283–4.
6 See *De esu carnium* 97 n142 above.

to be sent to the printers, I was not a little astonished and was on the point
of advising against it. But when I learned that my original copy, which I
had passed to the bishop, had been copied and was kept by many people
and must inevitably be made public by someone, I looked it over again
carefully, and with the approval of a certain very learned man to whom
both the bishop and I had delegated the job,[7] I sent it to the printers, never
in the least expecting that it would be assailed by those for whom I had
written it. I was more afraid of those whose arrogance I condemn there
rather freely and bitterly, and I was not entirely wrong in that thought
either. Because of that text I have some very hostile enemies instead of
friends, to the point where they have cut my reputation to pieces, not only
with slanders full of bitterness but with written libels. This doubtless is
fortune's game in human affairs, that where you hoped for great praise
you get the worst sort of thanks. From these remarks I think it is clear that
my intention was pious and religious, however the die has fallen in the
event.

Someone will object loudly here: 'You could have been more severe
in your attack on those who violate church regulations.' Perhaps I could
have, but I had to bear in mind the times in which I was writing and the
community. In addition, I preferred to encompass a double purpose, so that
I would not only restrain arrogance but also give a warning against the
superstition of certain people who place excessive importance on this sort
of external ritual.

So much for my preface; now I shall come to my comments.

First scholion[8]

1/ It is now clear, I think, why I recalled the Calydonian boar and a domestic
pig at the very beginning of the letter.[9]

2/ I say that the matter is not a capital one[10] because it is not deserving of
the death penalty, although many people get as angry about the types of
food as if someone had put their grandmother to the sword. And if anyone
argues that a crime worthy of hell is said to be a capital crime, then eating
this or that is not in itself a crime. For if you remove the regulation, there

* * * * *

7 Ludwig Baer. See Ep 1581 to Béda, 15 June 1525; and CEBR I 84–6.
8 This is the only heading; from here on the scholia have a simple number.
9 *De esu carnium* 64 above [1]
10 *De esu carnium* 64 above [2]

would be no guilt; and if the regulation stands, I do not think that the act of eating is necessarily deserving of hell if there is no evil intention.

3/ Where now are those who shout that I condemn fasting and abstinence from foods, when I preach here at some length the value of fasting,[11] and not only fasting but even explicitly abstinence, when I say, 'Just as the withdrawal of food diminishes the wantonness of the body, so there are certain foods that nourish the body so that it may live, but without making it wanton.'[12]

4/ In the third section, to counter anyone who quibbled that fasting was utterly Jewish, I show that after Christ was taken up into heaven the apostles and disciples particularly embraced fasting and prayer and after that abstinence from the more sumptuous foods, but of their own accord and without regard for human prescription. It is thus evident that custom preceded regulation.[13]

5/ Digressing from my commendation of custom, I express approval of the watchfulness of the popes who set up rules to restrain the decline of Christian charity and the rising flood of licentiousness. So far am I from condemning such rules entirely.[14]

6/ Then I am by no means lenient in rebuking those who show defiance in rejecting rules put forward by the most sacred authorities and extremely conducive to increasing piety,[15] since anyone who shows defiance in flouting public custom even in the smallest matters is deserving of punishment. With these words[16] I affirm the authority of the popes, even if they make petty rules with very slight effect on piety, for disturbance of the community's peace and scorn of officials' authority are great evils.

7/ I do not grant entire freedom from rituals to those who are more devout; I say that someone 'perhaps will be forgiven' if, being concerned with more important things, 'he seems less scrupulous in observing ...

* * * * *

11 *De esu carnium* 65 above [3]
12 *De esu carnium* 65 above [3]
13 *De esu carnium* 66 above [4]
14 *De esu carnium* 66 above [5]
15 *De esu carnium* 66–7 above [6]
16 *De esu carnium* 67 above [6]

rituals.'[17] I call 'less scrupulous' someone who is not solicitous and meticulous to excess, as many are.

8/ It is not official regulations of the church that I condemn here but private ones made by certain bishops and deans who take pleasure in imposing something of their own on the people, such as prayers or chants or days of observance for reasons that are not mandatory. Nor do I censure all of them, but I say, 'of certain ecclesiastical leaders],'[18] and I am making a distinction because 'certain ones' are not opposed to such measures introduced by individuals. Pious people too, as we know, complain about the excessive regulations of popes and the thunderbolt of anathema that they brandish too frequently, but without detracting from their legitimate authority. Among these are the abbot Bernard and Jean Gerson.[19] I call 'Jewish' the widespread regulations introduced about external observances. Once again, I am not complaining about regulations as a whole but about the excessive number of them.

9/ In one passage Jerome adduces this one reason, nor is there any doubt but that this was the principal one. For singing psalms and praying is something each person can do in his own house, and holding meetings too.[20] The instruction about hearing mass is more recent.

10/ Certain people have picked out this passage in a vexatious manner, as if I condemn ecclesiastical chants, though I say immediately afterwards that I do not condemn them.[21] What then am I complaining about? For these things [chants], [other] things that charity demands as a matter of

* * * * *

17 *De esu carnium* 69 above **[7]**. Erasmus responds to what Clichtove identifies as the fifth objection of his adversaries; *De ieiunio et abstinentia* 26 in Clichtove III f 179r.

18 *De esu carnium* 70 above **[8]**

19 For Bernard of Clairvaux, Augustijn suggests *De consideratione* I IV 5, I VI 7, III I 5–II 12; ie 'Five Books on Consideration: Advice to a Pope' trans John D. Anderson and Elizabeth T. Kennan in *The Works of Bernard of Clairvaux* Cistercian Fathers Series 37 (Kalamazoo 1976) 31–2, 35–6, 84–93. For Gerson, cf *De vita spirituali animae* in Gerson III 129.

20 *De esu carnium* 70 n28 above **[9]**. Erasmus is probably thinking of Jerome *Commentariorum in epistolam beati Pauli ad Galatas libri tres* 2 (on Gal 4:10–11) PL 26 339. The second sentence is a response to Alberto Pio; cf *Apologia adversus rhapsodias Alberti Pii* CWE 81 215. Augustijn suggests for the hearing of mass: *Decretum Gratiani* pars 3 cap 64 and 65 dist 1 (Friedberg I 1312).

21 *De esu carnium* 70 above **[10]**; *Apologia adversus rhapsodias Alberti Pii* CWE 81 215

necessity are sometimes neglected. Nor am I speaking there of Sundays but of the superfluous holidays set by bishops. Again, I do not simply say that it is more pious to provide nourishment for children than to listen to chants that are not understood but that 'sometimes it would have been more pious,' obviously when wife or children are in danger of starvation. In such circumstance I think it would be right if even the Easter holy day were violated – if indeed that is to violate it.

11/ This passage seemed to some to be close to blasphemy although I immediately add, 'Let me give these cases as examples only, for I preferred to use fictitious examples rather than offend anyone.'[22] Since I declare them to be fictitious, why are they brought up against me as if they were real? More infamous cases than these could perhaps be cited, such as when a law is brought in to net money from the sale of benefices.[23] But it is not enough that the motives for promulgating new regulations should be free of dishonesty; they should also be serious or necessary.[24] Otherwise teaching, warning, rebuke, and exhortation are enough. The Roman pontiff who increased the periods of fasting from three to four because there are four seasons did not have a dishonest motive,[25] but whether it was serious enough I leave others to judge. On the same reasoning, he could have appointed twelve periods because there are twelve months in the year! Besides, I am not talking there about any actual days of observance but about superfluous ones; the course of the argument proves that. And should anyone laugh at this sort of justification, my response is that they rather are the laughable ones because they take the censorial rod to other people's books although they cannot discern the premise of the argument, its purpose, and its motive but are prone to drawing tangential and irrelevant conclusions.

12/ Some have attacked this passage too as if it blames the church for inciting people to idleness and excess by creating holidays.[26] In this they are

* * * * *

22 *De esu carnium* 71 above [11] with n32; Béda *Errores* 2 ASD IX-5 133–4/LB IX 485F–486A

23 Béda *Errores* 2 ibidem; 'Taxander' *Apologia in eum librum quem ab anno Erasmus Roterodamus edidit* ... (Antwerp: S. Cocus 1525) (see the introduction xxv–xxvi nn60, 62, 65). Cf Augustijn 69 120–3n.

24 *Decretum Gratiani* pars 1 cap 2 dist 4 and cap 2 dist 29 (Friedberg I 5 and 106). Gratian does not use the word *graves*, translated here as 'serious'; Erasmus may be paraphrasing any one or all of [*lex*] *honesta, iusta,* or *possibilis*.

25 Calixtus I in *Decretum Gratiani* cap 1 dist 76 (Friedberg I 267); PL 130 29.

26 *De esu carnium* 72 above [12]. According to Augustijn (71 136–7n) this is a response to Taxander.

twice deluded. First, they do not notice that at that point I am dealing with holidays introduced out of private interests, not instituted by general church authority. Second, when I add 'morals being what they are now,' I am not condemning holidays but the failings of people who use good things badly.

13/ You can see how averse I am to any sort of agitation.[27] Even these holidays introduced for unsuitable reasons I would not have rejected by ill-considered lay action but abrogated by a decision of the bishops, so that the people do not become accustomed to disregarding the authority of the bishops. I deal with the same point more precisely in number 15.

14/ This passage seemed too severe to some, but I do not assert anything. I say, 'It seems to me the shepherds of the church would do well ...' I allot to the bishops their proper authority, and I add the condition that it should be necessary: I say, 'If it is a matter of necessity.'[28] If they said that this is an outrage to obedience, I ask what outrage would there be if it is done with the bishops' permission? They will say there is no need for such surpassing charity towards one's neighbour that an act of worship should take second place to it.[29] It follows that Christ was mistaken in teaching us it was right to pull an ass out of a well or to untie a beast of burden and lead it to water on the sabbath.[30] For these are views that the Lord casts against the Pharisees, and he would not have cast them if such actions were against the Law. No one defends an act as right by citing another's sin. Praying and meditating can be done already at home too, and even while working. An act of worship can be put off for a while when a neighbour's need brooks no delay. Finally, someone who has attended mass and the sermon has not been without a chance to lift up his thoughts to God; he spends on the needs of his dependants the hours that others spend on drinking and games. Perhaps they will chirp up here, as they always do, with Bernard's dictum that anything we offer is not pleasing to the Holy Spirit when we have omitted what is due.[31] So attendance at mass and listening to chants are owed to the Holy Spirit, and rescuing children and wife when they are

* * * * *

27 *De esu carnium* 72 above [13]; Béda *Errores* 3 ASD IX-5 134/LB IX 486A
28 *De esu carnium* 72 above [14]; Béda *Errores* 3 ibidem
29 Pio f 111v
30 Luke 14:5 and 13:15
31 Found only in Béda *Annotationes in Iacobum Fabrum ... et in Desiderium Erasmum Roterodamum liber unus* (Paris: Jodocus Badius 1526) f 211r, not in Bernard of Clairvaux.

in danger of starvation are not? The Spirit is charity. The more something accords with charity, the more it is owed to the Holy Spirit.

15/ In every case, as you see, I preserve the authority of officials and provide against popular disturbance when it comes to withdrawing these regulations,[32] which, though they may have been rightly introduced, can appropriately be withdrawn because of the changed condition of the times. If someone says such regulations were introduced by the inspiration of the Spirit, I am not obliged to believe immediately that all the regulations of all the bishops were produced by a particular inspiration of the Spirit. But let me concede that. What the Spirit intended to be enacted by reason of the times, because that was appropriate for the church, that same thing the Spirit intends to be withdrawn for the church's advantage. But theologians have recourse too often to the name of the church and the Holy Spirit when they are in difficulties with a case; it would be more appropriate to have recourse to the Scriptures.

16/ They will say this point does not apply except against heretics. If I had meant to talk about heretics, I would not have said 'reluctant' and 'more reluctant.'[33] The heretics pronounce a simple condemnation: the Manichaeans of marriage, Tertullian of second marriage.[34] But Jerome is orthodox when he says that marriage is not thought to be good except for a weaker man and asks how can it be good when it is an impediment to undefiled prayer.[35] Gregory is orthodox too when he excludes from the church the husband who has had intercourse with his wife during the night, since he is of the opinion that that pleasure is not without fault.[36] So too the early canons that exclude from holy orders a baptized man who sought to return to the married state or who, albeit in error, married a corrupt woman;[37] and the canons that forbid priests to assist at the weddings of those who marry twice, since the twice-married man is in need of penance, to the extent that it is not appropriate for a priest to even pray with these people.[38] This is dealt with in

* * * * *

32 *De esu carnium* 73 above [15]
33 *De esu carnium* 73 above [16]
34 Augustine *De moribus Manichaeorum* 18 65–6 PL 32 1372–3; Tertullian *De exhortatione castitatis* CSEL 70 125 and *De monogamia* CSEL 76 44; but see the comment of Augustijn 71 175n.
35 Jerome *Adversus Iovinianum* 1.7 PL 23 229A–230B
36 Gregory Ep 64 PL 77 1196B–1198A
37 *Canones apostolorum* (c AD 380) XVII and XVIII in Mirbt/Aland 148 no 329
38 Synod of Neocaesarea (c AD 314), canon 7 in Mansi 2 541 and 542

the first canon of the Synod of Laodicea, which prescribes for such people several days of fasting and prayers and temporary abstention from communion, even if they have contracted marriage openly and legitimately.[39] However, what Paul teaches of the bishop – that he should be the husband of one wife[40] – Innocent the First extended to all clerics,[41] though nowadays the lower order of clerics may marry ten times. Also, since these authorities forbid intercourse with the wife on several days of the year,[42] do they not allow marriage reluctantly? They do allow it, in fact, but they do so unwillingly, when they cannot persuade men to accept what they judge to be the best course.

17/ Where now are those who cry that I condemn the decree of the Roman church on the celibacy of priests? I say that the practice arose from extreme love of chastity and that the decree of the pontiffs was added, giving the approval of their authority to a pious practice.[43]

18/ This is to be read conjointly. I do not simply complain that they are unwilling to loosen the requirement of celibacy but that, although they are so rigid about this, no care is taken in accepting anyone into sacred orders.[44] As when someone criticizes ordinary people for taking care of their bodies while neglecting their souls, he does not condemn the care of the body but condemns the one without the other. Nor do I intend these remarks to be a condemnation of the decree on celibacy but to show that this is a human law that can be withdrawn, at least as far as candidates are concerned.

19/ A rule is set up by someone who gives instructions.[45] But it is clear that virginity and continence were not matters of instruction at that time but only of advice.[46] This freedom has now been taken away from some

* * * * *

39 Council of Laodicea (c AD 360–70), canon 1 in Mansi 2 563 and 564
40 1 Tim 3:2; Titus 1:6
41 Innocent I (AD 401–17) Ep 3 6.10 PL 20 493A–B, Mirbt/Aland 183 no 398; cf *De esu carnium* 73 n40 above.
42 *Decretum Gratiani* pars 1 cap 13 dist 31 (Friedberg I 114–15)
43 *De esu carnium* 73 above [17]
44 *De esu carnium* 74 above [18]
45 Béda *Errores* 11 ASD IX-5 138/LB IX 488A–D. Pio f 217r says Christ probably demanded celibacy of his apostles. See *Apologia adversus rhapsodias Alberti Pii* CWE 84 319.
46 *De esu carnium* 74 above [19]; apparently an allusion to 'Taxander' *Apologia in eum librum quem ab anno Erasmus Roterodamus edidit* ... (Antwerp: S. Cocus 1525) sig B vii r 29; *Manifesta mendacia* CWE 71 120 no 19 and 167 n35.

by the obligation of a vow. Two questions arise from this: whether the obligation can be relaxed and whether it should be relaxed. It is clear that the pontiff or a bishop can declare that a vow taken under compulsion or undertaken rashly is not a vow. And there is no lack of distinguished doctors who declare that there is no vow that should not yield to the laws of charity.

20/ There are some who say that a sacred decree cannot be changed unless it is changed to something that in itself is better. Those who compare human laws to the remedies of doctors therefore are mistaken.[47] It would be better to spend the night singing sacred hymns than to sleep.[48] It would be better and more meritorious for those who are fasting to spend the whole day in sacred occupations and to take a sober meal for the body's sake after sunset than to lunch until you have had enough and more at midday and then to have another refreshment, that is, half a meal, in the evening.[49] If these decrees have been changed by bishops because of the weakness of men or because of the perverseness of those who have misused good ordinances, what prevents us from doing the same with this decree? They raise the objection of the vow. My statement can be understood as referring to ordinands.[50] I believe in fact that it is in the power of the church to annul this vow for serious causes. Certainly it is possible not to require the vow of those about to be ordained.

21/ Do I not plainly disapprove here of the arrogance of certain men who marry without any authority and who not only encourage others to do the same but constrain them, as if it were impious not to have wives? What impudence they have then to cry that what we see done is done at my instigation! Again I assert nothing; I only 'remind the leaders of the church to examine carefully whether it is useful.'[51]

* * * * *

47 Erasmus here points to Clichtove's objection 15, which cites Nicolaus de Tude-schis (Panormitanus, abbot of Palermo 1386–1445): 'Whence the church should act like a good doctor: if experience shows that the medicine hinders rather than benefits, he should do away with it'; *De continentia sacerdotum* 27.3 in Clichtove II 113v. For a similar comparison with medicine, see also *De ieiunio et abstinentia* 27.2 in Clichtove III 181r.

48 Cf *De esu carnium* 70 n29 above.

49 Clichtove criticizes Erasmus by name on this point at *De continentia sacerdotum* 30.5 in Clichtove II 121r.

50 *De esu carnium* 74 above [20]

51 *De esu carnium* 74 above [21]; Béda *Errores* 12 ASD IX-5 138–9/LB IX 488D–E

22/ You can see that in the first place I do not suggest allowing marriage without the authorization of the popes. In the second place, even if it is allowed by them, I advise that they should 'not get themselves entangled in matrimony lightly' but rather that they should do everything to live chastely. In addition, I admit that it is most 'desirable ... that a priest be free of marriage and that he serve his Lord ... wholly.' I add that a great part of continence consists in good will, and I criticize those who take wives not because they are driven to it by carnal impulse but because they are driven either by levity or in contempt of the decree. Are these the words, I ask, of someone who puts marriage before continence?[52] And not content with these words, I add that those who have married with papal permission should 'compensate for their weakness by what is left of the integrity of [their] life and by [their] pious exertions.'[53]

23/ If fasts have been appointed for the mortification of the flesh and the uplifting of the spirit, what need is there to compel anyone to do on certain days what he himself does of his own accord all the time? I am still excluding the giving of offence and contempt; and I do not simply deny that it is necessary but say, 'There is no absolute need.' For if everyone were like this, the church would never have prescribed fasts, except perhaps in special circumstances to placate the anger of the Divinity.[54]

24/ Do I not declare plainly here that I do not defend those who with heedless subversion violate the decrees about fasting and abstinence? The 'heedless' ones are those who do so without serious cause; the 'subversive' are those who do so openly and stubbornly. But I do condemn 'the absurd judgment of certain people' who, the more trivial something is, the more violently they blame it.[55]

25/ What I call Judaism is not the Jewish heterodoxy of our own times but the fussy observation of external rituals. And I do not condemn popes who have accepted dietary distinctions; I am speaking of the judgment of common people who disregard what is important and are superstitious about what is secondary. I say 'Christians' not 'bishops'; and I do not say

* * * * *

52 *De continentia* 31.1–6 in Clichtove II 123r; *Dilutio* CWE 83 136–7
53 *De esu carnium* 75 above [22]
54 *De esu carnium* 75 above [23]
55 *De esu carnium* 76 above [24]

'accepted' but 'so seriously accepted,' criticizing their excessive concern over everything else.[56]

26/ Certain people are offended by the word 'burdened.'[57] They say, '[Christians] are not "burdened"[58] but "uplifted."' But Peter in the Acts of the Apostles calls the prescriptions of the Law in similar matters an unbearable burden,[59] although not all of them, even those laid down by God, entailed the penalty of hell. And is it not a burden that so many fasts, so many distinctions of meats, eggs, dairy foods, offal, and fats are proclaimed with the threat of eternal damnation? This is how parish priests declared them loudly,[60] but the theologians winked at the error; and now too they come out finally with the *arcanum* that pontifical indulgences are of no avail to the dead except in the manner of a vote,[61] nor is anyone certain that his soul has been freed by them from the fire of purgatory, especially as Christ alone can grant full dispensation of guilt and punishment. But these are things that should have been preached forty years ago when they saw such a huge amount of money being collected from every region in all those marketplaces, when they saw purveyors and commissioners directing God's angels to carry up to heaven the soul for which cash was paid. Many ignorant people are burdened and taken advantage of in another way too when they, whom it was never the wish of the popes or the intention of the law to put under obligation, believe they are obliged to fast. Finally, in more than one place Jean Gerson, discussing similar decrees, uses the words 'burdened' and 'loaded' and complains that the easy yoke of Christ is made heavy by such human

* * * * *

56 *De esu carnium* 76 above **[25]**; I have not discovered who misquoted Erasmus in this particular way.

57 *De esu carnium* 76 above **[26]**

58 Erasmus' word is *onerare*; the Sorbonne (*Determinatio ... super quam plurimis assertionibus D. Erasmi Roterodami* [Paris: J. Bade 1531]) used *gravare* 'burden'; see *Declarationes ad censuras Lutetiae vulgatas* CWE 82 179. See also *De ieiunio et abstinentia* 26.5–6, 32.1–3 in Clichtove III 180r–v, 189r–190r; Pio 106r–v; cf CWE 84 212–13.

59 Acts 15:10, where Peter, referring to circumcision and the 'law of Moses,' asks 'certain believers who belonged to the party of the Pharisees ... "Why do you make trial of God by putting a yoke (*iugum*) upon the neck of the disciples?"'

60 *De esu carnium* 75 above **[23]**

61 The Sorbonne (see n58 above) said *vivorum iuvantur suffragiis* 'They are aided by the votes of the living'; *Declarationes ad censuras Lutetiae vulgatas* CWE 82 82–4.

prescriptions,[62] admitting that it is extremely difficult for someone finding his way among so many snares not to be caught somewhere[63] and that the progress of charity is impeded by such excessive human regulations.

There occurs to me at this point the comment of a certain theologian striving to excuse the host of such regulations. He says, because more things are demanded of Christians, more regulations became necessary. It would be truer to say 'greater' rather than 'more,' but leaving aside semantic dispute, why are more things demanded? 'Because a richer grace is conferred.' How? 'When faith is increased, charity is increased.'[64] I agree these are the two essential members. But are more vehicles necessary because these members have grown, and should the man whose muscles have grown in strength have his progress loaded with chains?

These same people say that Jewish rules about food are diametrically opposed to Christian prescriptions; the Jews abstained from things impure by nature, we seek practices conducive to temperance.[65] But it is not likely that truly pious Jews judged that those foods were so impure by nature that they corrupted the moral sense of the person who ate them; they abstained from them because they were forbidden by God. 'But many Jews were strengthened by that means.' I agree. And not a few Christians are strengthened in the same way. For if the distinctions of diet are accepted as a means of moderating gluttony, it becomes a moral teaching, and all such teachings should have been brought over to our use – though circumcision too is thought to have been considered a means of moderating lasciviousness in intercourse. But the church has always sought to distance itself from all appearance of Judaism. Hence, although there is some difference between the laws of Moses and our decrees on fasting and types of food, there is nevertheless great similarity, and they are far from being diametrically opposed. So much for the unpopularity of the word [burdened].

27/ Here the disjunctive particle[66] means that there is no restriction in the rule of our forefathers. And when I say 'forefathers,' I mean the bishops

* * * * *

62 *De vita spirituali animae* in Gerson III 129, 161, 163, 166, 194, 196, 201. Cf *De esu carnium* 85 n86 above.

63 *De vita spirituali animae* in Gerson III 129, 196

64 *De ieiunio et abstinentia* 26.5–6, 32.1–3 in Clichtove III 180r–v, 189r–190v); Pio 106r–v. Cf *Apologia adversus rhapsodias Alberti Pii* CWE 84 215.

65 'Diametrically opposed' (*ex diametro . . . distat*); cf *De ieiunio et abstinentia* 31.6 in Clichtove III 189r. On the Hebrews' requirement of abstaining from unhealthy foods, see *De ieiunio et abstinentia* 32.1 in Clichtove III 189v.

66 *De esu carnium* 76 above [27]; the disjunctive particle is 'either . . . or.'

rather than the authority of the church as a whole. Indeed the following remarks for the most part refer to the particular custom of this or that people.

28/ Finally, I do not simply condemn these things in themselves, whatever their source may be, but I say they are lifeless if they are compared with what Christ taught; and I deplore the fact that we are, I might say, superstitious about the former and lazy and bored about the latter.[67] Some teach now that the strength of the church lies in three things: in the mass, in fasts, and in the continence of priests. These are indeed noble, but the strength of the church consists for me mostly in faith, hope, and charity, and in those things that Christ taught so vividly in Matthew chapter 5.[68]

29/ You can see, I do not condemn the fact that these demands are made but that they are 'such captious' demands,[69] though we are lenient about the things that matter more. They will say that other vices are not public. Indeed! Who punishes the drunkard on holy days? The pursuer of a harlot? The player of dice? They reply it does not follow that if they fail to punish this or that crime, they should be slow about others too. I do not suggest this anywhere. But what is wrong with censuring the absurd judgment of certain people?[70] For if they judged correctly, they would not rail extravagantly against petty faults and wink at serious ones. Someone who has tasted an egg is dragged off to prison and forced to defend himself against a charge of heresy; someone who spends the whole of the Lord's day in drunkenness, whoring, and dicing has the reputation of being a fine fellow.

30/ They say that decrees about fasting and dietary distinctions are not condemned by this statement of Paul.[71] That is not what I teach either, but I gather from these words of Paul that we should attach much less importance to such outward matters than to inward piety, though ordinary Christians turn this upside down.

* * * * *

67 *De esu carnium* 78 above [33]
68 Ie the famous 'sermon on the mount.'
69 *De esu carnium* 77 above [29]
70 *De esu carnium* 76 above [24]
71 *De esu carnium* 77 above [30]. The reference is to 1 Tim 4:8; *Declarationes ad censuras Lutetiae vulgatas* cwe 82 178–80; *De ieiunio et abstinentia* 33.6 in Clichtove III 192v.

31/ The following words do not refer to flouting decrees but to the vices of men who turn good laws into bad practices.[72] For although the church forbids certain foods because they arouse the body greatly, Christians should abstain from all foods that have the same effect even if they are not explicitly named in the law. But this is not observed, nor does anyone remind the general public of it.

32/ Again I do not make an assertion; I say, 'Perhaps it should be abolished,'[73] assuming the role of advisor and leaving judgment to the leaders of the church. Their answer is that the law itemizes those that are in common use.[74] But nothing is more common in Italy than snails and tortoises and snakes too; nothing is more commonly eaten in our country than dates and figs and almond milk variously flavoured. I say nothing here of honeywine, spiced wine, exotic wines, and beer brewed from honey, which they call mead.[75] These foods are such as to provoke the one who is not hungry to eat or the one who is not thirsty to drink. It was also necessary to remember among the difficulties that in countries with a hot climate people's bodies do not tolerate well a diet of meat, that they are fed with a more frugal nourishment and are less incommoded by abstention, in Egypt, for example, or Greece and a large part of Italy. And yet it is from those regions that prescriptions like these have come to us.

33/ Here again we have the word 'burdened,' by which certain ears are offended.[76] But it is not the decree that is blamed for this burden but the interpretation of people who believe that laws like these are to be applied equally to all in such unequal circumstances, though this was not the intention of those who formulated the decree. Since they expressly excepted many from the burden of the law,[77] they also desired that those who have any similar reasons should also be excepted, just so that no one should impose a burden on himself. Jean Gerson was of this opinion

* * * * *

72 *De esu carnium* 77 above [31]
73 *De esu carnium* 78 above [32]
74 Clichtove responds to what he identifies as the nineteenth objection of the adversaries: an irrational opposition to some kinds of foods; *De ieiunio et abstinentia* 35.1–3 in Clichtove III 195r–v.
75 Erasmus' Latin for 'honey-wine' is *mulsum*, for 'mead' *medo*; the latter is attested in Isidore of Seville (Latham).
76 *De esu carnium* 78 above [33]; cf scholium 26, 115–16 above.
77 *De esu carnium* 78 above [33]; Augustijn 37 524–31n

too.[78] Moreover, that is what they state that I meant by these words: 'Many will be burdened by a law supposedly equal for all.' If someone says 'supposedly,'[79] he is not criticizing the thing but the opinion. At this point some answer that the decree is not so rigid that it may not be loosened if there are good reasons for it, as, for example, in areas where there is not a good supply of oil, it is allowed to use butter or cheese.[80] Nevertheless, during my stay in Louvain I saw that the bishop allowed those who wanted to eat dairy foods to do so during Lent because of the oil that at that time was rumoured to be spoiled; but the parish priests, when ordered to do so, were reluctant to announce this to the people and could hardly be compelled, even by the threat of anathema, to make it known.

Now those who argue that there is absolutely no element of Judaic superstition in these questions, that no food is considered unclean, and that only foods that contribute less to corpulence are prescribed,[81] I would have them explain why on certain days any sort of dry cheese is forbidden. Is it because it is too nutritious and aphrodisiac? They reply that its source is an animal. So here it seems there is a criticism of the type of food, not just a pursuit of moderation. And those who break pots and scour knives, who in short either throw away or cleanse everything that has had contact with meat – are they entirely free of Judaic superstition? I admit this has nothing to do with the decree, but those who are most fastidious about these matters give extraordinary rein to their passions in serious offences: they insult, they slander, they are vengeful, deceitful, thieving; and these people abhor a knife or a pot that smells of meat!

34/ It becomes clearer that I criticize, in fact, the habits of people, not the decrees, a little later when I say, 'In short, people's customs have declined so much that these rules are a burden only to those for whose sake they were not exactly set up, etc.'[82]

* * * * *

78 *De non esu carnium* in Gerson III 82–3. Cf the colloquy Ἰχθυοφαγία 'A Fish Diet' CWE 40 712 and 751 n258.
79 Latin *ut putant*, literally 'as they think'
80 Clichtove mentions this substitution for oil as an example of flexibility; *De ieiunio et abstinentia* 31.5 in Clichtove III 189r.
81 Clichtove III 188r–189r; Pio XXIII *libri* ff 89r–v; *Apologia adversus rhapsodias Alberti Pii* CWE 84 190.
82 *De esu carnium* 78 above [34]. The sentence is completed with: '... and they have no application to those for whom they used to be particularly pertinent.'

35/ Here I explain in simpler language that the decrees are indeed just and that they were instituted to support piety, but that profit is involved, as they are now nets for catching money.[83] If only I could be justly accused of lack of substance on this point!

36/ Here I am so far from condemning papal decrees that I explicitly admit they were necessary, nor do I condemn relaxation of them here either;[84] but neither I nor anyone of sound mind can approve the sort that are made everywhere today.

37/ At this point, when I am about to discuss to what extent human decrees are binding, I affirm that I make no assertions but am simply asking questions and do so under the guidance of a judge who is a learned and virtuous bishop.[85] And they cannot plead here that this matter is such that it is not lawful to investigate it.[86] It was devised by most holy men, and most learned as well, to whom it seemed that a human decree binds no one to a penalty unless contempt or a monstrous scandal were involved.[87] They deny that it is lawful to abrogate completely those rules that were correctly established and confirmed by lasting usage.[88] I would agree, except that we have seen so many rules abrogated that were decreed even with the authority of synods.

Does someone ask which are these rules that were established correctly but rendered obsolete by human practices? Among the Apostolic Canons, *distinctio* 88 c, 'The bishop and the priest,' we find, and I quote: 'If any bishop, priest, or deacon accepts secular responsibilities, let him be deposed.'[89] There, among secular responsibilities, is mentioned executorship of wills;[90] and suretyship is mentioned in the Apostolic

* * * * *

83 *De esu carnium* 79 above [35]
84 *De esu carnium* 80 above [36]
85 *De esu carnium* 81 above [37]
86 Clichtove III 131r
87 Augustijn suggests Erasmus is probably thinking of Bernard of Clairvaux *De praecepto et dispensatione* 8.18, 9.19–21; ie 'On Precept and Dispensation' in *The Works of Saint Bernard of Clairvaux* Cistercian Fathers Series 1 (Spenser, Mass 1970) 118–22.
88 See *De continentia sacerdotum* 28 in Clichtove II 115r–116r. He argues against the seventh objection of the adversaries at *De ieiunio et abstinentia* 27.1–2 in Clichtove III 180v–181r.
89 *Canones apostolorum* VI (v) in Mirbt/Aland 417 no 329; *Decretum Gratiani* pars 1 cap 4 dist 88 (Friedberg I 307)
90 *Decretum Gratiani* pars 1 cap 5 dist 88 (Friedberg I 307)

Canons.[91] But what is more commonly accepted now than that priests should be stewards of noble men and women? And whom do princes use as administrators more often than priests? I say nothing here of the lay authority held and sought by bishops, abbots, provosts, and deacons.[92] And it is said that they are ornaments of the church, so far are we from deposing them. Yet this decree is not one made by ordinary men but by the apostle Paul: 'No soldier in God's service, etc.'[93] What is more commonly disregarded than what is found in the same canons in [the title] *De consecratione distinctione* 1 C: 'All the faithful, as faithful, who come to church to hear the Scriptures and who do not stay for prayer or take Holy Communion, shall be excluded from Communion.'[94] The things that the *Gloss* puts in here about superstition and due time are trivial.[95] In former time the Sacred Scriptures, the Psalm, the Epistle, and the Gospel were read first, then prayers were said – the main one being the Lord's Prayer – then Communion was taken. Even those not yet baptized were admitted to the reading of the Scriptures and the sermon; they were kept away from holy prayers and Communion.[96] But Communion was the last part of the mass. What has happened to the fragment of the Carthaginian decree that forbids reading anything in churches apart from canonical Scriptures, as instructed in canon 24?[97] Yet the Synod of Laodicea has the same instruction.[98] The Synod of Chalcedon,

* * * * *

91 *Canones apostolorum* xx (xix) in Mirbt / Aland 148 no 329

92 Cf *Adagia* iii iii 1 *Sileni Alcibiadis.*

93 2 Tim 2:4; Erasmus seems to be translating here *nemo militans Deo* [sic] *inplicat se negotiis saecularibus* 'No man, being a soldier to God, entangleth himself with secular businesses.'

94 *Decretum Gratiani* pars 3 cap 62 dist 1

95 To *non perseverant* 'do not stay' the *Glossa ordinaria* adds: 'ex consuetudine vel superstitione. Et est sic nam in vanum currit qui non perseverat usque in finem cursus' (out of habit or superstition, and it is so, for he runs in vain who does not stay to the end of the course); and to *percipiunt* 'take' the *Glossa* adds *tempore deputato* 'at the prescribed time'; *Decretum diui Gratiani ... vna cum variis scribentium glossis & expositionibus* (Paris 1612) 2076. See also Augustijn 79 390–1n.

96 Augustijn (79 393–5n) explains here that the open part of the service ended with the prayer that followed the reading and the associated sermon. In early times catechumens were required to leave before this prayer and the following celebration of the mass. In later times they were allowed to be present for this prayer.

97 Synod of Carthage (AD 397), canon 47 in Mansi 3 891. Erasmus has the numbering of the so-called *Codex canonum ecclesiae africanae* canon 24 (Mansi 3 723 and 724).

98 Council of Laodicea (cf 112 n39 above), canons 59 and 60 in Mansi 2 573 and 574

chapter 7 has the same intention.[99] What has happened now to the observance of this most sacred decree? What has happened to the decree of the Council of Chalcedon that prescribed that if anyone obtained ordination by means of money, both the one received into ordination and the one who was corrupted by the money should be deposed from their office?[100] What has happened to all those frightful decrees that threatened fiery anathema to those who practice simony, who violate the exemptions of churches, who seize their goods or impede the freedom of their elections?[101] What has happened to the decree that orders a bishop given to dice or drunkenness to be condemned, that is, to be struck with anathema unless he desists?[102] What happened to the decree of the Synod of Neocaesarea ruling that no one under the age of thirty should be made a priest, however suitable he may be in other ways?[103] What has happened now to the anathema that the Synod of Gangra hurls at children who leave their parents, even if they are pagans, under the pretext of religion, although nowadays it is considered the greatest piety to become a nun or a monk, even if it means going against the wishes of parents and abandoning them?[104] What has happened to the decree of the Council of Laodicea, smiting with anathema those who worship angels on the grounds that such people commit idolatry.[105] What has happened to the decree of the African Synod forbidding the bishop of Rome to be called 'the prince of priests or the highest priest or anything of that nature, but only bishop of the first see.' But this is quoted in the *Liber decretorum, distinctio* 99 c, 'Bishop of the first see.'[106] What has happened to the decree prohibiting priests and deacons from being present at spectacles,[107] when at Rome cardinals and the pope himself customarily give displays

* * * * *

99 An error. The sentence may belong above, between 'Apostolic Canons' and 'But what is more commonly accepted.'

100 Council of Chalcedon, canon 2. Cf *Acta conciliorum oecumenicorum* ed E. Schwartz II 1 par 2 (Berlin and Leipzig 1933) 158:11–19.

101 Cf DTC 14/2 2141–6, 7/1 1218–62; cf W.M. Plöchl *Geschichte des Kirchenrechts* 5 vols (Vienna and Munich 1960) I 186–90, 365–70 and ibidem (Vienna and Munich 1962) II 206–19.

102 *Decretum Gratiani* pars 1 cap 1 dist 35 (Friedberg I 131)

103 *Decretum Gratiani* pars 1 cap 4 dist 78 (Friedberg I 275–6)

104 *Decretum Gratiani* pars 1 cap 1 dist 30 (Friedberg I 107). The decree does not say 'even if they are pagans' but *maxime fideles* 'most especially believers.'

105 Council of Laodicea, canon 35 in Mansi 2 columns 569 and 570

106 *Decretum Gratiani* pars 1 cap 3 dist 99 (Friedberg I 350–1)

107 Council of Laodicea, canon 54 in Mansi 2 573 and 574; also *Concilium trullanum* or *Synodus quinisexta* (691–2) canon 24 in Mansi 11 953 and 954

of fighting bulls that are not so very different from pairs of gladiators.[108]
What has happened to the decree of Pope Gelasius that the sacrament of
baptism should not be given to anyone except on Easter Day or Pentecost
unless they are ill and likely to die?[109] What has happened to the regulation threatening with rejection priests who sing in church?[110] What has
happened to the regulation forbidding anyone to move to another church
for reasons of ambition?[111] What has happened to the regulations prohibiting the plurality of benefices?[112] What has happened to those mentioned
by Jean Gerson in his treatise on *Declaratio defectuum virorum ecclesiasticorum*?[113] What has happened to the law concerning fasting on Friday and
the sabbath?[114] What about the law prescribed for priests on fasting for the
whole of advent;[115] what about the ban on eating meat for the whole week
before Lent?[116] But I go on clumsily enumerating what is numberless. Although we see these and endless others either fallen into disuse or rejected,
we think the church is about to collapse if the distinction between foods is
removed.

38/ Note that I make exception here too where there is cause for offence
and disrespect.[117]

39/ These remarks are those of one who argues and inquires, as I have
stated before.[118] And in this discussion the question is not whether popes
have the right to makes statutes or the right to impose obligations but to
what extent they can constrain their flock. Now, there is a large difference
between the supreme pontiff and the bishops, between bishops and abbots,

* * * * *

108 Augustijn suggests this may be a personal memory; cf Ep 3032:417–33.
109 Cf Gelasius I *Epistola* 9 decr 10 PL 59 52A.
110 Gregory Ep 44 PL 77 1335A–B; *Decretum Gratiani* cap 2 dist 92 (Friedberg I
    317–8): *cantandi officium sibi diacones non usurpent*, ie Gratian speaks of deacons,
    not priests.
111 *Decretum Gratiani* pars 2 cap 37 c 7 q 1 (Friedberg I 580–1)
112 *Decretum Gratiani* pars 2 cap 1 and 2 c 21 q 1 (Friedberg I 852–3)
113 The *Declaratio defectuum virorum ecclesiasticorum* 'The Shortage of Clerics' is not
    by Gerson but part of the *Concilium pacis* of Heinrich von Langenstein. Cf
    Gerson I 47.
114 *Decretum Gratiani* pars 3 cap 13 dist 3 (Friedberg I 1355–6)
115 Cf *Decretales Gregorii* IX lib 3 tit 46 cap 2 (Friedberg II 650–1). Erasmus is
    mistaken in saying 'for priests'; this applies to the next regulation.
116 Cf *Decretum Gratiani* pars 1 cap 6 dist 4 (Friedberg I 6).
117 *De esu carnium* 81 above [38]
118 Scholium 37 (120 above) and *De esu carnium* 82 above [39]

between the statutes of a pope alone and the decrees of synods; and again
a provincial synod is different from an ecumenical one, a recent one from
an ancient one.

40/ You can see, dear reader, how many times I ward off the risk of making
assertions, how many times I leave the judgment to others.[119] And yet certain men are not ashamed to cry immediately, 'Erasmus proposes, Erasmus
desires.'[120]

41/ This opinion is stated by Jean Gerson in his book *De vita spirituali animae*, but I neither deny nor approve it at this point.[121] In no wise do I
deny the right to make a law to those endowed with legitimate power,
providing it is useful, fair, and attended by the other circumstances that
are required in a law;[122] I am only asking about the type of obligation.
For if it does not derive either from the will of the lawmaker or from
the intention of those who initiated the custom, those who declare that
they do not want anyone to be made liable to any guilt by their regulations, only to an external penalty, are not acting correctly.[123] But less correct are those who persuade their subjects that all human regulations whatsoever render one liable to sin worthy of hell and who call down on the
violator of any regulations whatsoever eternal punishment,[124] although, as
some teach, it is for God to judge how seriously or leniently he wishes
to take the transgression of a human regulation.[125] But what he wishes

* * * * *

119 *De esu carnium* 83 above [40]
120 Cf *Declarationes ad censuras Lutetiae vulgatas* CWE 82 276–7 (*censet*), 278–9 (*vult*),
317 (*censet*) – all censures of colloquies.
121 *De esu carnium* 84 above [41]; *De vita spirituali animae* in Gerson III 160–1 (*Corol-
larium quartum*)
122 *Decretum Gratiani* pars 1 cap 2 dist 4 (Friedberg I 5)
123 Probably Panormitanus, whom Clichtove quotes: 'And would that it were the
same in all positive decrees, that they should impose liability only to a penalty
and not to guilt'; Clichtove III 113v. On Panormitanus, see 113 n47 above; he
was also quoted in Erasmus' disputes with Lee. See *Apologia qua respondet
invectivis Lei* CWE 72 375, 388, and 391.
124 Cf *Declarationes ad censuras Lutetiae vulgatas* CWE 28 325–6. Clichtove discusses
the authority of ecclesiastical leaders to impose unending penalties; *De ieiunio
et abstinentia* 3 in Clichtove III 133v–140r, especially 133v.
125 According to Augustijn (83 448–9n), this is the opinion of Jacobus Latomus
(Jacques Masson) *De ecclesia et humanae legis obligatione* in *Opera* (Louvain:
Gravius 1550) f Dr–v. For Latomus, see CEBR II 304–6; Rummel *Critics* I 63–93;
De Jongh 173–80.

is unknown to us, and the transgressor will be uncertain whether he has sinned mortally or venially. For if the measure of the guilt is calculated according to a reckoning of the matter and the other circumstances,[126] it may be very difficult to assess the importance of the latter. And yet it will be worth the trouble to know. For this opinion seems to me to be closer to the truth.

But meanwhile the question is whether discrimination of foods in itself is matter enough to make one liable to an offence. For this seems to be the opinion of those who teach that we are by the terms of this decree itself straight away liable to the penalty of hell. This opinion is, in my judgment, indeed rather harsh, especially since canonical Scripture gives hardly any grounds for this decree and since in those cases where the teaching of Scripture is strict, the transgressor does not always incur the penalty of hell. Divine law threatens death to children who do not obey their parents;[127] and yet, if a father orders his son to clean his nails and the son fails to do this, I do not believe he is condemned to hell. Abstinence is not of such great importance to anyone nor is it necessary for salvation. For there are other ways of moderating the nourishment of the indulgent. And those who fight most fiercely for this decree admit that not everyone who violates it commits a mortal sin but only the man who eats heedlessly, obstinately, or with serious offence to his brother.[128] Since I say the same more than once in this very pamphlet, what point is there in attacking my opinion with so many battering rams? The Synod of Gangra pronounces anathema on those who annul fasts prescribed and maintained by the church, but it adds: 'without a bodily need.' Nor is this all; it adds: 'arrogantly,' that is, obstinately.[129] But that decree seems strictly to speak of those who have made profession of continence because it is extremely difficult to protect one's modesty among the debauched. They say that an anathema is not inflicted except for a capital crime.[130] Let us grant that what we are arguing about is known everywhere: anathema is not inflicted for breaking a fast but for deliberately and obstinately breaking

* * * * *

126 Probably *De vita spirituali animae* in Gerson III 166, 189.
127 Deut 21:18–21
128 *De ieiunio et abstinentia* 22.3 in Clichtove III 170r; *Declarationes ad censuras Lutetiae vulgatas* CWE 82 34
129 Synod of Gangra (c 343?), canon 19 in Mansi 2 1103 and 1104. Erasmus' *superbiendo, hoc est contumaciter* 'arrogantly, that is, unrepentantly' translates the Greek ὑπερηφανέσοιτο; the Latin text of canon 19 has the similar *insolenter*.
130 *De ieiunio et abstinentia* 6.2 in Clichtove III 138v

a fast. But I do not know what to think of so many anathemas of the Fathers.[131]

Now I see there are some who are well aware that we are not made liable to the punishment of hell by any and every human teaching. 'But,' they say, 'it is not useful to make an opening for those disposed to vices. That fear, even if it is unwarranted, is useful for constraining licentiousness.'[132] Does God need our dishonesty to save the human race? 'Many would neglect their prayers at the canonical times,[133] if they knew that they could be omitted without incurring mortal guilt. The same would happen to attendance at mass on holy days, to fasts, and to the differentiation of foods.' But how much worry is introduced meanwhile into weak or fearful minds! How many, omitting something in these duties or putting in one thing for another, actually commit mortal sin by this very act because they are persuaded that what they do is a capital crime. And yet we find that it is the purpose of most leaders to persuade their subjects that all human decrees, of bishops, abbots, priors, fathers, or mothers, carry a liability to punishment in hell.[134] What is this, if it is not to extinguish the freedom of the spirit? When stipendiary bishops give the first tonsure, they order the recipient to say the office of the Virgin Mother every day.[135] But the majority of men violate this order and bear a branded conscience. Personally, I would think Luther's teaching is much more rightly embraced than such a persuasion.

But if a decree makes a subject liable to guilt, whether the author intends it or not, and has no power to determine how far it renders liable, perhaps the same can be said of exhortation and admonition, if someone encourages us to do what increases piety and good living. I am not talking now about counsel or about the sort of exhortation that is found in matters of divine teaching – as Paul and Peter sometimes use the words 'exhort' and 'beseech' about things that cannot be neglected without heinous wickedness[136] – but about the exhortation that is aimed at those things

* * * * *

131 Erasmus' puzzlement is explained by the fact that since anathema was more severe than excommunication, ancient synods imposed the most severe penalty for venial sins too.
132 *De ieiunio et abstinentia* 4.5, 5.5, 22.3 in Clichtove III 136r, 137r, 169v–170v
133 Latin *preces horarias*
134 According to Augustijn (83 486–8n), this is not argued by any opponent of Erasmus.
135 For the office of the Virgin, but not this detail, see *The Oxford Dictionary of the Christian Church* (Oxford and New York 2005) 1047–8. See also Erasmus' *Modus orandi Deum* CWE 70 224.
136 Cf *De esu carnium* 88 above [41]; 1 Pet 2:11, 5:1, 5:12.

that could be done without blame if a human decree were not involved. Some adduce the verse 'Who hears you, hears me ...' and 'Obey your leaders ...'[137] But this idea, if it were not restricted, would lead to tyranny. Again, others gather from it that the Lord ordered us to pray and did not prescribe a particular time or prayers, so what leaders add here is divine law.[138] This 'prayer' too needs to be restricted, for what is prescribed can be excessive, and perhaps less suitable prayers may be prescribed. Such is the case if the bishop decrees fasts on Sundays or alternate days for a whole year, or if he allows nothing but bread and water.

42/ I am not making an assertion here either;[139] however, I am not speaking about the trivial and the human but about the malicious disparagement that is a sort of homicide and a kind of stealthy robbery. For 'the mouth of the slanderer that lies kills' what is in itself the 'soul' of the one whom he betrays.[140] He who takes away the good name of his neighbour takes away the most precious of all his possessions.

43/ See how everywhere I clear away disorderly uproar, and what I want is that the leaders of the church should keep their authority in good repair.[141] I also think one should submit to even bad leaders if they prescribe heavy burdens, though not ungodly ones. This makes me wonder all the more why this letter should have offended certain theologians so much. It should have offended more those whom theologians consider heretical.

44/ With this passage I in turn remind bishops respectfully of their duty,[142] after I have declared that their authority is so great that I would want even those who make bad, that is, troublesome, regulations to be tolerated. Which term here breathes sedition or rebellion?

45/ There are those who cry out here that the whole discipline of the church would collapse if the decree does not make one liable to the penalty of hell and that no one at all would fast if the obligation threatening eternal torment

* * * * *

137 Luke 10:16; Heb 13:17
138 *De ieiunio et abstinentia* 8.7 in Clichtove III 143v
139 *De esu carnium* 86 above [42]
140 Wisd of Sol 1:11 *os autem quod mentitur occidit animam* 'The mouth that belieth killeth the soul.'
141 *De esu carnium* 86 above [43]
142 *De esu carnium* 88 above [44]

is taken away.[143] People who say this seem to me to have a poor opinion of human character. And they do not bear in mind that fasting and prayer never flourished more in the church than when there was no such human regulation, especially one making such threats. But these same people argue that practice in such observances arose from the decree, not the reverse.[144] This is entirely improbable, especially as concerns the distinction of foods and many similar matters. Where a custom thrives, what need is there of a law? For a law is put up as a restraint when a good custom declines. But why does a custom give way to a decree if it happens to come later in time?

46/ You can see, dear reader, how I assert nothing and that I say, 'We should consider whether . . .' and after conditional clauses, 'if . . . if.'[145] Nor do I bring into the discussion the question of whether decrees about fasting and distinctions of foods are to be rejected or disregarded but whether we 'ought to contend so fiercely' over them. Do we not contend nowadays more bitterly about eating eggs and meat than about incest and adultery?

47/ This passage gives extreme offence to certain people.[146] But I am not excusing those who, contrary to the decree of our forefathers, deliberately eat meat; I criticize those who take such serious offence over a matter that in itself is not wicked, when on things that the Lord forbade we are not at all disturbed.

48/ They deny that papal decrees on differentiation of foods are condemned by these words of the Apostle.[147] This is not what I think either, otherwise I would be fighting with myself. But the argument is correct in so far as I teach that the matter is not one of divine but of human prohibition. I do not deny that those who, albeit of their own accord, abstained from wine and lived on vegetables and herbs were Christians. But I do not believe Paul would have allowed anyone at that time to proclaim the laws about eggs, dairy foods, meats, fat, and offal, which are proclaimed now, either because there was no need or because the practice seemed close to Jewish

* * * * *

143 *De esu carnium* 90 above [45]; Clichtove III 131v
144 *De ieiunio et abstinentia* 1.6, 28.2–4 in Clichtove III 131r, 182v–183v
145 *De esu carnium* 93 above [46]
146 *De esu carnium* 94 above [47]. Cf also *Declarationes ad censuras Lutetiae vulgatas* CWE 82 41–4; Béda *Errores* 8 ASD IX-5 136–7/LB IX 487E.
147 *De esu carnium* 94 above [48]; 1 Tim 4:3. Cf *Declarationes ad censuras Lutetiae vulgatas* CWE 82 41–3; *De ieiunio et abstinentia* 29, 30 in Clichtove III 184r–187r.

abstention. Just how greatly averse Christians were, in fact, to any appearance of Judaism, not only in Paul's time but even four hundred years later, is shown by the *Adversus Iudaeos orationes* of John Chrysostom[148] and by the decree of the Synod of Ancyra that ordains that if a priest or deacon is seen to abstain from meat, he should, as one suspect of heresy, be invited to taste some; and if he refuses or cannot bear to eat even vegetables cooked with meat, he should be deprived of the honour of his office.[149] So I am doing nothing more here than comparing one stumbling block with another; and I explain that people protested against offences in those days when the causes of offence were more serious and more just, and that now people even foster the superstition of certain men who condemn their neighbour because of what he eats, when they do not know his reason in taking food, whether it be from necessity and with permission or in defiance.

49/ From this[150] it is perfectly obvious that I am not complaining about those who are pained by the arrogance of people who are obstinate in eating but about those who detest a neighbour eating of necessity as much as if he committed murder. I know that spiritually refined men do not do this, but still the world is everywhere full of superstitious people from whom the opportunity must be removed.

50/ Here I seem to some to imply that the ordinances and prescriptions of popes who live wicked lives are invalid.[151] But the fact is very different. What am I complaining of then? I am complaining of this: that in matters of such importance no account is made of offence taken, or rather given, for reasons that, if not entirely justifiable in law, are certainly serious, while in matters of much less importance so much concern is lavished on the scandalizing, or more exactly the superstition, of the weak.

51/ This passage seems to be the most troublesome of all, when in fact there is nothing that should rightly offend anyone.[152] For those who declare loudly that this wish of mine is wicked have persuaded themselves that

* * * * *

148 *Adversus Iudaeos orationes* PG 48 843–942. Erasmus' translation of five of these speeches is in LB VIII 1–58.
149 Council of Ancyra (c AD 314–19), canon 14 in Mansi 2 517 and 518
150 *De esu carnium* 94 above [49]
151 *De esu carnium* 94 above [50]. According to Augustijn (85 567–8nn), no such statement is to be found in any opponent of Erasmus.
152 *De esu carnium* 95 above [51]

the whole discipline of the church consists in such petty rituals and that it would collapse once they were removed.[153] My desire is not to eliminate fasts or simplicity of foods and other practices like that, which I want to flourish as much as possible in the church, but to eliminate bishops' regulations, or at least the rigid exaction of such things – though I am dealing here mainly with abstinence. No one is cited by the bishop if he has his dinner; but if he eats mutton during Lent, he is dragged off to prison and is in danger of heresy. This is what I call exaction. Nor do I want this except on the condition that the freedom granted in matters that of themselves do not make one either pious or wicked should turn not into a licence for debauchery but into a more zealous concern for true inward piety. And again, what I call Judaism is not the cursed disbelief of that people, as some misrepresent it, but their meticulous observance of external practices.

52/ But since I knew there are people who think decrees of this sort are absolutely necessary for the ignorant and coarse majority, I moderate my desire and wish first that there should be fewer regulations. Then I should not like them to be put forward in such a way that people think they have been immediately cut off from God's grace if they have thoughtlessly omitted something of the sort. Finally, I should not like these regulations to have such power attributed to them that practices that more directly regard gospel piety should be disregarded rather than they.[154] Then, if it seems any of them should be withdrawn for reasons previously mentioned, I still counsel avoidance of all mutiny and tumult. But I do not want even this to be done unless it is by the authority of our predecessors or by overlooking it, which constitutes a tacit relaxation. For example, there is a decree that prohibits anyone who is not entrusted with the cure of souls from giving absolution.[155] But in certain areas priest confesses to priest without regard to this requirement, and since the bishop overlooks this, he is reckoned to assent to it. Likewise, when everybody everywhere eats

* * * * *

153 *Declarationes ad censuras Lutetiae vulgatas* CWE 82 317–18, where the Sorbonne censures the colloquy Ἰχθυοφαγία 'A Fish Diet' CWE 40 687:15–23.
154 *De esu carnium* 95 above [52]
155 *Decretum Gratiani* pars 2 cap 19 c 16 q 1 (Friedberg I 765–6) and cap 3 dist 6 (Friedberg I 1244). Augustijn (87 596–7n) explains that the Fourth Lateran Council (1215) had allowed confession to a priest other than one's own parish priest, provided that he had 'cure of souls' and therefore also power of absolution.

anything and neither pope nor bishops protest, it may seem that there is a tacit relaxation of the decree. If custom has such power that fasting on the sixth and seventh day could become obsolete, even if it is not a universal custom but one of a region or state, fasting could seem obsolete everywhere. Many people take dinner, and bishops do not object unless there is a fault in the kind of food. In England lay people dine on alternate days in Lent, and no one takes offence. And if someone cuts out bits from this passage and uses them maliciously, will he not stir up serious commotion! 'Erasmus wants to eliminate papal decrees on fasting and abstinence from meat and everything else like that. What a wicked desire!' But it would be a good desire if you add what I added: 'He [Erasmus] wants to give them the least possible importance. But he adds: "... rather than neglecting, because of these things, matters that are essential to piety." He does say they are "of hardly any importance," but he adds "in themselves" and "neglecting the most important."' Is this teaching Lutheranism? Rather, if the 'evangelicals' – as they expect to be called – had obeyed these counsels, I believe this storm would not have been generated in the world. If I had given the advice that Christians should abstain from drunkenness, gluttony,[156] and dice, they would have said it was pious advice. But those sins are 'pointing to judgment'[157] and, to use Paul's word, 'self-condemned.'[158] Under the pretext of religion we find concealed here religion's worst plague, and a warning seems either wicked or superfluous.

53/ I call 'rituals' outward observances that are not very different from those of the Jews but not, for that reason, to be simply condemned. To certain people I seem here to condemn rituals.[159] First, I am not speaking of all rituals, nor do I simply condemn those of which I do speak; but I point to the danger that threatens from them. This is threefold: first, that, if such prescriptions were excessive, they may overwhelm the strength of a Christian spirit; second, putting our faith in these practices and being self-satisfied, we may turn out to be pharisaical instead of pious; finally, we

* * * * *

156 Latin *crapula*, which in classical Latin means also intoxication. Since Erasmus seems to distinguish it from *ebrietas* 'drunkenness,' it may be supposed that he uses it in a sense that is first recorded in the twelfth century (Latham).

157 1 Tim 5:24; Latin *praecedentia ad iudicium*; DV 'Some men's sins are manifest, going before to judgment.' I have translated as RSV 'The sins of some men are conspicuous, pointing to judgment.'

158 Titus 3:11

159 Cf Pio ff 103v, 104r; and Béda *Errores* 10 ASD IX-5 138/LB IX 487F–488A; *Apologia adversus rhapsodias Alberti Pii* CWE 84 209–13.

may despise our brother because of them when we ourselves are guilty of more serious evils.

54/ Here certain people howl that I deplore the fact that we abstain from meat on Fridays in honour of the Lord's passion, but they misrepresent me; I condemn what followed, not the beginning.[160] If we give so much credit to custom that for this sort of reason it is made illegal to eat meat, then because our Lord was crucified on a Friday,[161] slept in the sepulchre on the sabbath [Saturday], was betrayed on Wednesday, and so on for the other days, there will be no day on which it will be legal to dine or use meat. On Thursday he ascended into heaven and removed his presence in the flesh from his disciples; devotion demands that we too deprive ourselves of meat. On Wednesday the Word made flesh was betrayed: it is right that nothing made of meat should be sold in the market. Similar things can probably be said of all the other days. There is no day on which the Lord did not perform some act worthy of worship. But the practice, which at first was an act of private piety, turned into a public custom, the custom into a law with an obligation, the obligation into an object of contempt, and the contempt into wickedness. Or in another way, awe was transformed into superstition, superstition into temerity, temerity into abuse, abuse into discord, and discord into the ruin of religion. They will say these evils were not born of the decrees themselves or the rituals but from the vice of men.[162] I do not deny that at all for my part. But because of the reason I have described, it would perhaps be useful to insist more sparingly on this sort of thing and spend more effort on teaching Christians what affects more immediately gospel piety.

The right-minded person indeed is he who says to himself, 'It is Friday; today the Lord hung on the cross for me. I in turn, for his sake, will abstain from the pleasures of meat, but by his grace I shall mortify my worldly affections. Today our Lord prayed for those who crucified him and insulted him; I, for my part in gratitude to him, will pardon my enemies and will exact no reparation from them. It is Thursday; today the Lord gave his body and blood to his disciples.[163] I shall try to deserve to be of

* * * * *

160 *De esu carnium* 96 above [54]; and the article cited in *De esu carnium* n8.
161 Cf Pio ff 84v, 89r; *Decretum Gratiani* pars 3 cap 13 and 16 dist 3 (Friedberg I 1355–7). See also Augustijn 87 626–30; and *Apologia adversus rhapsodias Alberti Pii* CWE 84 189.
162 Cf scholium 31, 118 above; *De ieiunio et abstinentia* 27.5 Clichtove III 182r.
163 In the Last Supper

the number of his disciples, and I shall not suffer the needy, who are his members, to lack food and drink from me. Today too the Lord ascended into heaven; there I shall place my hope so that, having nothing earthly, I may follow him there. It is the sabbath [Saturday]; today the Lord rested in the sepulchre; let me suppress my base desires and rest with him in hope of the resurrection to come. It is the Lord's day; today Christ rose again to eternal life; may he grant that I rise again with him to newness of life[164] and never slip back into my former vices.' Or 'Today the Lord sent the Holy Spirit; I shall cleanse the house of my soul, in case I deserve to receive such a guest.' One may meditate in this manner about the other days, but I do not want to be more prolix. If the public were taught these ideas carefully by people who were sincere about what they said, either I am mistaken or we would see another sort of Christians.

In former times monks gained for themselves a wonderful reputation for holiness by their vigils, their practice of sleeping on the ground, wearing sackcloth, eating vegetables, drinking water, and prolonging fasts to seven or ten days, to the point that, as a history tells us, worms bred in their teeth.[165] But these same men, when called to the office of bishop where censure had to be pronounced on reprobates and where the force of the spirit of the gospel was supposed to be pre-eminent, they were so irritated that none were more frenzied than they. Chrysostom relates this in his work *De sacerdotio*.[166]

55/ I declare so many times that I do not defend those who obstinately and blatantly violate this sort of decree,[167] and yet I am said to be the teacher of these practices that I explicitly condemn.[168]

56/ Here I do not condemn decrees either but the superstition of those who take offence, without reason or without moderation, and so break up Christian unity, judging and disparaging their neighbour.[169] It happened to me one day that I was returning with friends from an evening walk; our route took us through a cemetery in the centre of which stood a crucifix.

* * * * *

164 Cf Rom 6:4.
165 Cassiodorus Epiphanius *Historia ecclesiastica tripartita* 8.1.104 CSEL 71 472. Cassiodorus talks not of monks but of a number of early church elders.
166 Chrysostom *De sacerdotio* 6.7–8 PG 48 683–5
167 *De esu carnium* 97 above [55]
168 According to Augustijn (89 669n), not found
169 *De esu carnium* 99 above [56]

Occupied with the conversation as I passed, I did not uncover my head. A certain theologian noticed this and to the large number of people present declared that I was a Lutheran, on the grounds that I believed images should not be worshipped, though at that moment I was not thinking of images at all. He did not forgive me for not uncovering my head to a wooden statue, and he forgave himself for openly maintaining a huge prostitute in his house, at the expense of the church and by bleeding the poor. I tell the bare facts without naming place or person so that no one can be exposed.[170] This is the nature of almost all who measure holiness by rituals. Jean Gerson, a man in other respects so pious that he comes in some places close to superstition, laments the fact that many punish the omission of a ritual more severely than a blasphemy.[171]

57/ How stupid are these people who have attacked this passage,[172] as if I wanted parish priests to turn episcopal decrees into exhortations, without paying attention to the fact that I have added, 'with the authorization of their superiors.' If that is present, what reason is there for them to howl? What have I said that is not devout? Alas, there are far too many who are too brutish to know how to say these things in a Christian manner, and they prefer to shout, 'You have to fast or go to hell!' I think such people would prefer everyone to be turned into asses, because it is easier to command them than to govern men.

Let me add this out of all that is left unsaid: if priests lived soberly and fasted frequently, taught the people assiduously and fervently the benefit that is derived from fasting combined with attention to piety, and encouraged them to do this with fatherly advice, many more would be fasting willingly today than they do at the moment when forced to by law. And many fewer would dine with a good conscience than dine now with a bad one. Again there would be much more restraint at those breakfasts too where at present most people stretch their stomachs so much that they could not eat dinner even if they would. And finally, our fasting would not swell the treasury but would help the needs of the poor.

The End

* * * * *

170 Erasmus recounts the same incident, but as if another person was the victim, in *De concordia* CWE 65 205. It is not known who the theologian was.
171 *Sermo de vita clericorum* in Gerson v 458 (*Quintum vae*)
172 *De esu carnium* 100 above [57]

A RESPONSE BY DESIDERIUS ERASMUS TO THE *DISCUSSIONS* OF A CERTAIN 'YOUTH WHO WOULD TEACH HIS ELDERS'

Desiderii Erasmi responsio ad Collationes
cuiusdam iuvenis gerontodidascali

SVPER OMNIA VINCIT VERITAS.

μεγάλη ἡ ἀλήθεια καὶ ἰσχυροτέρα παρὰ πάντα·

Ὁ ἄρχων τοῦ κόσμου κέκρηται

CONCVLCABIS LEONEM ET DRACONEM.

This woodcut is found on the last leaf of the copy of Titelman's *Collationes* held in the Universiteitsbibliotheek Amsterdam (Ned. Inc. 163 f 312b; Nijhoff-Kronenberg no 2036) but does not appear in the copy used here (a microfilm from the Vatican Library) or in that held by the Bodleian Library (Vet. B1.e.45).

Christ holds in his left arm six lambs and in his right hand a sceptre surmounted by a dove; between his feet is an orb surmounted by a cross. Above are the words *Super omnia vincit veritas* 'Above all things truth is victorious' (1 Esd 3:12) and Μεγαλὴ ἡ ἀλήθεια καὶ ἰσχυροτέρα παρὰ πάντα 'Truth is great and stronger than all things' (1 Esd 4:35); on the left, Ἐδόθη μοι πᾶσα ἐξουσία ἐν οὐρανῷ καὶ ἐπι γῆς 'All power is given to me in heaven and in earth' (Matt 28:18); on the right, *In brachio suo congregabit agnos et in sinu suo levabit eos* 'He shall gather together the lambs with his arm and take them up in his bosom' (Isa 40:11); underneath, Ὁ ἄρχων τοῦ κόσμου κέκρηται [sic for κέκριται] 'The Prince of the world is judged' (John 16:11) and *Conculcabis leonem et draconem* 'Thou shalt trample under foot the lion and the dragon' (Ps 90 [91 AV]:13). I am grateful to Dr J. Trapman for help in finding this copy of the illustration.

ERASMUS OF ROTTERDAM TO THE READER

I had decided not to make any response at all to the *Collationes* of this young 'teacher of his elders.'[1] There were quite a few reasons for this, and all my more judicious friends were of the same mind; but when, after reading further in the work, I found clear proof that this person is in many places performing someone else's play[2] and that much poison was furtively sprinkled on my friends with these *Collationes*, I changed my mind to the extent that I would make a cursory answer – not to all of them, for some things do not concern me at all, and some things, which I believe are his own, are so feeble that they do not deserve any sort of response.

Now the Psalms with which he begins and ends these *Collationes*,[3] the title, and the language itself for the most part suggest not only great modesty but even a certain Christian charity and eminent piety. But if he did not want it to seem false, he should have taken care to maintain this consistently throughout the work. In fact, there is too much in it that breathes boastfulness, craftiness, ill will, and quarrelsomeness. This youth, barely out of school, with but a thin smattering of letters, as his material itself proclaims, calls his work *Collationes*, though it would be truer to say that he sounds more like a judge of the Areopagus or Orbilius the flogger.[4] He

* * * * *

1 Greek γεροντοδιδασκάλος; see the introduction n94.
2 Erasmus is probably insinuating that the concealed influence was Jacobus Latomus (Jacques Masson); see also nn2, 7, 75, and 82 on Rom 5:12, 200 and 204 below. Latomus had attacked Erasmus indirectly on the subject of the necessity of classical languages for theologians (Ep 934 introduction) and on the refutation of Luther's doctrines (Ep 1674 n12). These attacks were all surreptitious, but Erasmus' suspicions were probably justified. Latomus had supported Titelmans during his childhood, had been one of his teachers, and was dean of the faculty of theology at Louvain at this time. Some similarity of views is therefore not surprising. Sartori (133) also detects the probability of some influence of Latomus in the composition of the *Collationes*. Titelmans declared in his *Epistola apologetica* that the *Collationes* were entirely his own work (Rummel *Critics* II 14 and 20). For Latomus' role in connection with the *De esu carnium*, see the introduction xxvi n66 above; and for his general relationship with Erasmus, De Jongh 173–80; De Vocht 324–48; Rummel *Critics* I 63–93; CEBR II 304–6.
3 Titelmans' prologue (*Prologus apologeticus pro veteri et ecclesiastica Novi Testamenti latina interpretatione* a2v–e4r) is preceded by the *Sanctus* and opens with the words *Notus olim in Iudaea*, an allusion to Psalm 75 (76 AV). The other psalms, at the end of each 'discussion,' are not biblical psalms but presumably Titelmans' own compositions.
4 'Judge of the Areopagus,' that is, a judge of the supreme court of Athens. The expression was proverbial (*Adagia* I ix 41) and is described by Erasmus as being used *de tristi severoque* 'of a severe and strait-laced person,' as well

thinks he has shown a handsome measure of modesty because he repeats certain phrases frequently: 'dearest Desiderius,' 'greatest friend,' 'in all sin-. cerity of heart before God,' 'so it seems,' 'so it appears,' 'my own insignificance.'⁵ But this same fellow immediately forgets himself, bursts into profuse quarrelling at the slightest pretext, and scourges 'Desiderius dearest in Christ,' accusing him of being impudent enough to 'stick out his tongue' at heaven because somewhere he disagrees with Nicolas of Lyra.⁶ He accuses Desiderius of treachery because he disarms the church of the Scriptures and arms heretics by deceitfully debasing the correct meaning of Scripture.⁷

And as if these were not reproaches, he immediately threatens reproaches; sometimes he nips at me with tricks that go beyond propriety, and like a scorpion his embrace implants a sting. Does he think I do not know what the Victor trampling on the lion and the dragon means?⁸ Often he employs extraordinarily arrogant language in his unseemly raving and certainly does not understand what he is saying. With extraordinary

* * * * *

as of an incorruptible judge. Cf also *Ciceronianus* cwe 28 354 and *Apologia ad Fabrum* cwe 83 14. Horace describes his elementary teacher Orbilius as a 'flogger' (*Epistles* 2.1.70–1); he is also recorded by Suetonius (*De grammaticis* 9).

5 Cf for example the final reproach, which is sugared with *Erasme amicissime, optime Desyderi*, and *Desyderi amicissime* (twice) (*Collationes* 304r–6v).

6 See *Collationes* 306r; and *Responsio* at Rom 16:25, 258 below. See also the *Annotationes* of 1516 (LB VI 655A / Reeve II 436). When it suits his purpose, Erasmus quotes Nicolas in support of himself; see the *Apologia de 'In principio erat sermo'* (1520a and b). For a general account of Nicolas of Lyra (1270–1349), a Franciscan, see NCE 10 453–4.

7 *Collationes* prologus c4r–v

8 Ep 2205 to Johann von Botzheim, 13 August 1529, preceding by only six days that containing a draft of much of this preface (see the introduction xxxiii n91). In this letter (Ep 2205:208–36) Erasmus expresses his contempt for the 'tasteless' (*insulsus*) sort of interpretation that extracts silly meanings from scriptural texts, and which he says seems to be admired particularly by the Franciscans, especially when they are drunk: 'It even seemed a good idea to them to express such a neat thought, please God, in a picture.' The picture, reproduced here (137 above), expresses their thought about *Conculcabis leonem et draconem* 'Thou shalt trample under foot the lion and the dragon' (Ps 90 [91 AV]:13). Erasmus reports that the Paris Franciscan Petrus de Cornibus (Pierre de Cornes) had identified the lion as Luther and the dragon as himself, and observes that they could equally well mean the four mendicant orders. The image was in fact well known, coming from a psalm prescribed by the rule of St Benedict to be sung every day at compline, and signified generally the crushing of enemies of the church. Willibald Pirckheimer, in a letter to Ulrich von Hutten, 26 June 1517 (Pirckheimer *Opera omnia* [Frankfurt 1610; repr Hildesheim 1969] 24–5), applied it ironically to the supporters of Reuchlin and other enemies of Jacob of Hoogstraten.

arrogance he instructs Lorenzo Valla[9] and all the rest of us about the correct meaning of Latin and Greek, explaining Greek words and writing them in Latin script although he is speaking to us. Often he teaches Lefèvre[10] lessons he has extracted from my *Annotationes*,[11] and yes, sometimes he teaches me what he has learned from my writings. But his fairness is such that, although Lorenzo and Lefèvre have often treated the Translator[12] more severely than I, it is with me that he quarrels on every occasion. Even when he has nothing to say in defence of the Translator, he treats them in a friendly manner. He even calls Lefèvre his friend, so that anyone who did not know the fellow would think he was some person of great age and learning who is endowed with supreme authority and high standing and is speaking to pupils, or at least to colleagues. Even if he were their equal, it would still somehow be the modest thing to do, to defer a little to age. But at Louvain, a famous university as everyone knows, he gives public lectures on Holy Scripture before all comers. If only he could do that to good purpose! But what sort of modesty is it to insist on this office at every point when he is lecturing in his own home university and when the appointment is temporary and such that even great men equipped with many other qualifications usually complain that they were enticed into a function beyond their

* * * * *

9 Valla's *In latinam Novi Testamenti interpretationem adnotationes* were edited by Erasmus in 1502. The *Adnotationes in epistolam Pauli ad Romanos* are in Valla I 855–61.

10 Titelmans is attacking Jacques Lefèvre d'Etaples' *Commentarii in S. Pauli epistolas* (1512). See CEBR II 315–18. Lefèvre and Erasmus were generally linked in the minds of contemporaries as leaders of the humanist philological approach to biblical studies. Erasmus had been criticized for using the work of both Valla and Lefèvre by Maarten van Dorp; see his reply to van Dorp, Ep 337:881–906 (Rummel *Annotations* 14–15). In the famous dispute with Lefèvre, which Titelmans is not aware of or ignores, Erasmus, in his *Novum instrumentum* of 1516, had criticized the former's *Commentaries* for an interpretation of Heb 2:7. Lefèvre replied in 1516 in the second edition of his *Commentaries* (dated 1515), and Erasmus issued his *Apologia ad Fabrum* in August 1517 (ASD IX-3 / CWE 83). A note in the *Annotationes*, referring to a phrase in Rom 1:12, which dates from 1516 and was never modified (LB VI 558D–E n12 / CWE 56 28–9), shows that Erasmus maintained his respect and friendship for Lefèvre even in the darkest period of this dispute, which had effectively come to an end in 1522. See the introductions of ASD IX-3 and CWE 83.

11 *Annotationes in Novum Testamentum*, first published as the *Novum instrumentum* in 1516, then progressively enlarged in 1519, 1522, 1527, and 1535. For the text of the *Annotationes* in all these editions, see Reeve I and II.

12 Following the practice of CWE 56 (xv), I have capitalized 'Translator' when referring to the translator responsible for the Vulgate.

powers, rather than use this title to give themselves airs? It would have been a sign of true modesty if he had honestly admitted to whom he was indebted for what he teaches us; nor is my nose so insensitive that I cannot smell it. What could be further from modesty than a case of Aesop's little crow?[13]

But it is no wonder if fame inspires passions in a youth. What is a wonder is that seraphic persons[14] should push forward their colleague onto this stage so that they can win this much praise for their order. Indeed they play several sorts of similar tricks to get my works out of the hands of scholars. This fellow had already replaced my *Paraphrases* with his *Elucidations*.[15] These he did not condescend to dedicate to any mortal, as is Erasmus' custom, but offered them to God alone, to whom he credits whatever he writes or says and with whom he certainly holds intimate conversations.[16] If beneath all this there is deceit, what could be more dangerous? I see many implications, but God is the judge of hearts. So much for the title; now for the rest.

In the long-winded preface he attached to his work, he fumes a great deal against those who execrate the old Translator, 'spit upon him,' 'hiss at him,' 'kick him out,' and 'trample him.'[17] He even scourges us by name at the beginning of his 'discussion'[18] because the Translator is so badly treated

* * * * *

13 *Aesopica cornicula* in B.E. Perry *Aesopica* ... (New York 1980) 101 (Κολοιὸς καὶ ὄρνεα); Babrius 72; Phaedrus *Fables* 1.3; *Adagia* III vi 91. Κολοιὸς is usually *graculus* in Latin, that is, 'jackdaw,' but Horace alludes to the fable and calls the bird *cornicula* 'little crow' (*Epistles* 1.3.19); see the note in Augustus S. Wilkins *The Epistles of Horace* (London 1965) 111. Erasmus is alluding to his assumption that Titelmans is wearing borrowed plumage, performing someone else's play. Zúñiga had used the same image to make an accusation of plagiarism against Erasmus (Ep 2172:10–11; Rummel *Annotations* 14).

14 Ie the Franciscans, whose first general, St Bonaventure, was known as the 'seraphic' doctor. See the introduction to the colloquy 'The Seraphic funeral' CWE 40 996 and 1014 n4.

15 *Paraphrasis in Romanos* (1517) CWE 42; *Elucidatio in omnes epistolas apostolicas* (Antwerp: Vorstermann 1528 and 1529)

16 The *Collationes* are dedicated to 'the highest, first, and uncreated truth, which the eternally unborn bore co-eternal with himself.'

17 Titelmans uses some of these words in a general criticism of 'meddlesome novelty seekers' who attack the translation, not the Translator; *Collationes* prologus [a4]r–v.

18 *Collationes* prologus [a4]v. Titelmans names Valla, Lefèvre, and Erasmus and (after praying that the last two may be given grace to enjoy the same peace as the first already enjoys!) adds: 'They have attempted to compose annotations and analyses criticizing the published Latin edition and the old church version

by our work. These words are certainly not applicable to me, nor as yet do I
see that the translation[19] of the ancients has been 'trampled,' since it is read
everywhere in churches and universities. He must be forgetting that I have
given the contents of the Greek manuscripts, without prejudice to what is
read in public.

He reckons it is a gross insult if someone charges the Translator with a
solecism,[20] although he admits that there are solecisms even in the apostles'
writings; but if the Translator reproduces them, he does not think a solecism
has been committed. However, he does not seem to understand or certainly
not to consider that the language in which the apostles proclaimed the gospel
teaching was not that of the learned but the everyday speech of ordinary
people, cobblers, sailors, weavers, both men and women, even pimps and
procuresses, for the gospel was written for them too. If the Greek language
at that time had been as corrupt as it is today, and if that corrupt Greek
were as widespread as Greek was then, I believe the apostles would have
used that language, just as Christ did not speak pure Hebrew but Syriac,[21]
a language doubtless corrupted by contact with other languages. So too the
Latin Translator – the one who was the first, as I think – adopted the language that was then common to men, children, menial women, and the
lowest levels of society, but which could nevertheless be understood by the
educated because it was in general use. If the Latin of that time had been as
corrupt as it is nowadays among the French, Spanish, and Italians, it is likely
that he would have used the popular language in spite of its degeneracy,
just as today those who preach the Gospel in French or Spanish or Italian are
using a language that, in comparison with Latin, is very debased. So it is no

* * * * *

of the New Testament. In these they have appeared to find fault with, censure,
and reproach many points of that old version and to make changes in many
places contrary to ancient custom, not only in ways that affect the wording
but even in ways that affect the meaning. On top of this, they have been
carried away by the heat of their unrestrained enthusiasm and have sprinkled
sarcasms in not a few places and, to put it plainly, have mocked that translation
and its translator.' He then goes on to blame Lefèvre and Erasmus for stirring
up hatred and contempt for the church's version by producing new versions
based on Greek sources. There are echoes of this passage also at the beginning
of the first *Collatio* f 3r–v.
19 *veterum interpretationem*] 1540 784; *veterem interpretationem* in 1529 a2v, 'the old
translation'
20 *Collationes* prologus [a5]v
21 That is, Aramaic.

wonder if, in the opinion of those who speak correctly, the Translator uses solecisms, since he sought to be understood by the ordinary man rather than by the educated who were particularly resistant to the gospel. Furthermore, this critic does not want to admit there is an error when someone disregards the rules of correct speech for some pious reason.[22] This is an argument I have never heard before. I do not deny that an error may be excused for a pious reason, but anyone who excuses an error is admitting there is one. Moreover, the writings of Augustine, Cyprian, or Ambrose[23] are not without error, especially when they quote Scripture. We too often make mistakes of this sort.

He collects several examples of this in the Vulgate as corrected by Jerome but says nothing about those that differ from what Jerome proposed. 'But,' he says, 'perhaps later Jerome found better manuscripts from which he restored some readings.'[24] But he had said that the earlier correction was inspired by the Spirit. So does the Spirit babble too? But what need was there then of manuscripts if it was a case of supernatural inspiration?

He is fierce in his anger, and not without reason, against those who disdain sacred texts for their lack of allurement and ornament, of long words, of vain and inflated expressions.[25] I condemn such people too; and I have had no other aim than to convey what is found in the Greek manuscripts in a more elegant but simple and clear style.

He praises the Translator extravagantly as an excellent, holy, judicious, and learned man, and proclaims that he was inspired by the Holy Spirit.[26] Perhaps he was. But if anyone presses our eulogist, he cannot settle for us whether the Translator was a Jew, a pagan or a Christian, a heretic or a believer, a cobbler or a soldier, a youth or a veteran, a man or a woman. If we did owe our New Testament to a pagan, it would carry all the more weight with us since the translation would have been made by someone who was a stranger to the gospel. But we need not worry too much about the

* * * * *

22 *Collationes* prologus e2r
23 In this work, as in the *Annotationes*, it is the commentary on Romans by Ambrosiaster that is credited to Ambrose; see CWE 56 xii–xiii.
24 *Collationes* prologus b1r–v
25 Latin *verba sesquipedalia ... ampullae verborum*, an echo of Horace *Ars poetica* 97: *proiicit ampullas et sesquipedalia verba*. The allusion is made by Erasmus, not Titelmans.
26 *Collationes* prologus [a4]r, [a6]v, [c8]v–[d4]r

Translator, for the sources are extant. The church gave its approval without knowing the author. 'But no one can interpret the Scriptures correctly unless inspired by that same Spirit who is the author of the Scriptures.' But the person who translates from one language to another performs one sort of interpretation; the person who expounds the spiritual meaning performs another. There are likewise two forms of inspiration; the inspiration by which Holy Scripture was first produced cannot be attributed with certainty to any but the original authors. But while some sort of inspiration was perhaps necessary in the translation of the Old Testament – just as no one is going to translate correctly the works of the philosophers without difficulty unless he has some knowledge of the subject – in the New Testament the language is so simple that any ordinary person could have produced a version such as this Translator did.

I believe that the inspiration of the Spirit was present in some way to all the recognized Doctors of the church; and yet it is not uncommon for them to slip into errors, even heretical ones. St Jerome translated and interpreted the prophets, yet he frequently admits that he does not quite seize the meaning. So it is possible for someone to translate what he does not fully understand, for translation is a lesser art than exposition. But if, as my critic says,[27] it is unacceptable for the Translator to depart even from the tropes and figures of the original text,[28] then Jerome is guilty of impiety, because he dared to remove almost all the Hebrew tropes despite Augustine's protests. And[29] if the Translator's work comes entirely from the inspiration of the Holy Spirit, Jerome should not have changed even single words. But he was not afraid to do this. I find it amusing that every time something in Jerome is plainly contrary to my opponent's argument, his response is that Jerome is writing rhetorically.

Scripture will not immediately become a human artifact if the Translator uses human powers of the mind to translate what he reads, for the Scripture is in the meaning, not in the words.[30] If it is in the words, then the words keep their integrity only in the original language, not in translation. If he wishes to blame inaccurate copyists for all the awkwardness of

* * * * *

27 Erasmus frequently refers to Titelmans by means of the pronoun *hic* or a simple third person verb. Where 'he' would be unclear or ambiguous, it has been necessary to give him some such designation as 'my critic.'
28 *Collationes* prologus e1v–e2r
29 *et si totum est*] 1529 A4r; *et si est* in 1540 785
30 *Collationes* prologus d2r–v

language, as far as I am concerned he can do so, but I am afraid he will find no one who believes it. So much for his preface.

Perhaps someone else would fault him for having the dead and the living talking together in his *Collationes*. For my part, I can readily overlook the fact that he makes me talk like himself. Moreover, here where a youngster presumes to teach his elders, setting himself up alone as the censor of three older men, often correcting and chastising them severely and confidently, I admit that the Holy Spirit once showed his power in the young Daniel,[31] nor would I be ashamed to learn something worth knowing even from a child. Certain things he approves, some he allows and condones, some he rejects and condemns, rather heatedly. But a young person should have something exceptional to offer if he decides to take the cane to three veterans who, with the possible exception of myself, are men of no ordinary learning. He plays the rather juvenile trick of promising peace if I will try to be a friend of the truth[32] – as if it were impossible for him to be mistaken. Certainly he would have made his book more marketable if he had been more succinct. As it is, by rehearsing what Lorenzo said, what Jacques Lefèvre said, what Desiderius said, and by explaining the same in his own words with preambles[33] and rebukes, with recitals of the readings of Cyprian, Ambrose, Jerome, Augustine, Sedulius,[34] and Hesychius[35] (which proved nothing against me because my argument is concerned with

* * * * *

31 Titelmans refers to Daniel's judgment of the two old men who accused Susanna in order to argue that disagreement between interpreters is cause for suspicion (*Collationes* [b5]v). The story is in Daniel 13 in the Vulgate and in the apocryphal book of Susanna.

32 *Collationes* 135r

33 'With preambles ... by inserting prefaces'; Erasmus uses the same expression (*dum praefatur*) twice, perhaps a sign of haste.

34 Ninth-century *grammaticus* and exegete, usually known as Sedulius Scotus, author of commentaries on the first three Gospels and on the Pauline Epistles in which, like the author of Pseudo-Jerome, he used the commentary of Pelagius (see Souter I 336–9). The commentaries were published in Basel in 1528 (PL 103). See R.B. Palmer 'Sedulius' in NCE 13 46. Titelmans refers to him frequently as Sedulius Hibernensis but, with the exception of one occasion when he mentions him dismissively (Rom 10:16 *quis credidit auditui nostro?*), Erasmus ignores these references.

35 Greek lexicographer, probably of the fifth century, whose work was published in 1514 by Marcus Musurus. The biblical glosses it contains were later shown to be interpolations. Erasmus seems to prefer not to quote him too; see the article on *Eloquia Dei* in Rom 3:2 n2, 169 below.

the Greek and with purity of language), by inserting prefaces and interjec-
tions, by extending one of his *Collationes* with a concluding coda,[36] and by
stirring in much that neither supports the Translator nor stands against me,
he lays a heavy burden on the reader.

* * * * *

36 Latin *coronis*. Cf at Rom 9:5 n5, 231 below. This presumably refers to the
   passage, following the last article and the reproach provoked by Erasmus'
   reference to Lyra, in which Titelmans concludes his work with a sort of homily
   extending the discussion on the grace for which Paul prays at the end of
   Romans 16 (*Collationes* 306v–307r). See also *Adagia* IV vi 20 *Ad coronidem usque*
   'Right to the final coda.'

RESPONSE BY DESIDERIUS ERASMUS
OF ROTTERDAM.
TO THE *DISCUSSIONS* OF A CERTAIN
'YOUTH WHO WOULD TEACH HIS ELDERS'[1]

From the Epistle to the Romans

[ER *qui genitus fuit* 'who was begotten']
[RESP] *qui factus est ei* 'who was made to him.'[2] Valla prefers *genitus* or
natus spacing between sections as CWE 56. [born] rather than *factus*;[3] I repeat
that I neither approve nor disapprove. 'But you approve,' says he,[4] 'because
that is how you translate.' Since either reading is correct, I put the variant
word, partly to let the reader know that it may be read thus and so that
he understands that Christ was not 'made' in just any way but by a birth,
and partly so that I could avoid the clumsiness of the words *factus ex semine
David* [made of the seed of David].[5] For someone can be made without
being born, as Adam was, but no one is born of the flesh without being
made or at least having been made. But it is vain for him to dispute with
me here whether Christ can rightly be said to have been made, since in
my annotation my teaching is the same as his. What prevented me from
contradicting Valla's opinion, however, was that Cicero translated Plato's
sentence, ἕκαστος ἡμῶν οὐχ᾽ αὑτῷ μόνον γέγονεν, as *nemo nostrum sibi natus
est* [None of us was born for himself].[6] Seneca translated more roughly
nemo sibi contigit [No one has found himself].[7] It is apparent from this that
γεγόμενος can correctly be translated as *natus est.*

1 *Desiderii Erasmi Roterodami ad Collationes cuiusdam iuvenis gerontodidascali responsio:* this is the fullest version of the title, as it appears in 1540 786. See the list
   of editions xliii above.
2 Rom 1:3; CWE 56 8–10; *Collationes* 5v–7r (misnumbered '9'). ER indicates Erasmus' biblical translation, as published by Froben in 1527. The wording given
   here of Erasmus' translation does not always correspond exactly to the lemma
   of the annotation as given in CWE 56. RESP indicates the heading of each item
   as it appeared in Erasmus' *Responsio*. Unless otherwise noted, this corresponds
   to Titelmans' cue phrase in his *Collationes* and to the Vulgate text (hereafter VG)
   published alongside Erasmus' translation in 1527. Unless otherwise indicated,

the translation of Titelmans' cue phrase or vg is that found in dv. In this case the lemma *qui factus est ei* is not separated from the text.

3 Valla *Adnotationes* 1 855. *1529* regularly spells the name as 'Vala.' Valla suggested only *genitus*; Erasmus added the variant *natus* in his annotation, not in his translation. See the *Apologia ad annotationes Stunicae* LB IX 324 / ASD IX-2 162.

4 Erasmus frequently attributes responses and objections to Titelmans in the form of direct speech, as well as quoting his *Collationes*. Where this is clearly the case, speech marks are used, but it is to be noted that Erasmus invents dialogue and often paraphrases loosely, rarely quoting word for word.

5 The 'clumsiness' is presumably that the phrase might be understood as meaning that David was the father of Christ or an ancestor in the ordinary human sense, even though Christ was in one sense 'of the line of David.'

6 Cicero *De officiis* 1.22: *non nobis solum nati sumus*. Walter Miller translates: 'We are not born for ourselves alone'; Loeb Classical Library 30 (London 1913). Plato *Letters* 9.358a. R.G. Bury translates: 'No one of us exists for himself alone . . .'; Loeb Classical Library 234 (London 1914).

7 Seneca the Younger *Epistulae morales* 4.3 (32.4). I translate as Erasmus apparently understood the phrase here, though it seems he may have been mistaken in thinking Seneca was translating Plato. Cf *Adagia* IV vi 81: 'Since Cicero translated this saying so clearly, appropriately, and elegantly, I am surprised that Seneca preferred to say *Nemo sibi contigit* "No one has yet found himself." He seems to have wished to render ἐγώετο [ie γέγονεν] in this way. For this is what he writes in *To Lucilius*, book 5, letter 32: "Do you want to know what it is that makes mortals so greedy for the future? No one has yet found himself." He appears to blame parents for the fact that we do not immediately search after what is finest. For he adds: "And so your parents prayed for other things for you, but I pray that you may despise all these things that your parents wanted for you in abundance. Their prayers plunder many others to enrich you."'

[ER *qui genitus fuit* 'who was begotten']
[RESP] *qui factus est ei* 'who was made to him.'[1] I point out that the word *ei* is not in the Greek. 'Perhaps,' says he, 'it was in the old manuscripts.' That is simply guesswork, because there is no extant codex in which it is to be found. 'Valla does not mention it,' he says. If I am in the wrong every time I mention what Valla left out, I am continually in the wrong. Then he informs me at great length that it is correct to say *natus est Abrahae[2] filius* [A son was born to Abraham]. Who denies it? We say it every time we refer to a father. In this case, before this phrase, there were the words *de filio suo* [concerning his Son], and shortly after *qui praedestinatus est filius Dei* [declared to be the Son of God]. However, I do not find fault with the Translator here either, but I say rather that it was his own idea to add the pronoun in order to avoid the incongruity of the expression *factus est ex semine*[3] [who was made from the seed (of David)].

1 Rom 1:3; CWE 56 8–10; *Collationes* 7v–8v. In this case, although the lemma is

the same, it is the pronoun *ei* that is discussed.

2 *Abrahae* is in the dative case, like *ei*.

3 All editions of the *Responsio* have *ut excluderet absurditatem sermonis 'factus est ei ex semine'* (with the pronoun *ei*). The incongruity, or clumsiness as Erasmus calls it in the previous item, would be the mistaken inference that David was the father of Christ. The corresponding annotation says: 'Anyway, the pronoun *ei*, which is added in the manuscripts of the Latins, is not found in any of the Greeks. But since the expression seemed slightly incongruous if he [the Translator] had said *qui factus est ex semine David*, he added *ei* by way of explanation, although the addition of this pronoun is so far from doing anything for the sense that it further obscures it.' It is clear from this either that the sentence here must be rearranged to read 'to add the pronoun – *factus est ei ex semine* – in order to avoid the incongruity of the expression,' or that the inclusion of *ei* at this point is an error. It seems preferable to suppose the latter. See also Bentley 72.

[ER *qui declaratus fuit* 'who was shown']
[RESP] *qui praedestinatus est* 'who was predestinated.'[1] He approves my note but in such a way that he thinks a second note is also appropriate. And yet just before this, he prescribed a rule for us that a translator must not depart from the wording of the original Scripture.[2] In fact, here it is clear that Paul wrote ὁρισθέντος [declared], which cannot be translated as *praedestinatus* [predestined] unless we depart from what the Apostle wrote. To excuse this he contrives two sorts of 'destining' for us, a future action and a present one. A mother 'predestines' her unborn child to the study of letters, and when she hands the same child over to the tutor, she 'destines' him. This is quite absurd, unless you take 'destine' to mean 'send.' I do not deny that some people use the word in this way, but it is not normal usage among those who speak correctly. Indeed it is pointless for him to show at such length that the Son of God is rightly said to be 'predestined' in accordance with his human nature: no one was denying that. But what I pointed out was that, whether you read 'destined' or 'predestined,' *filius Dei* [the Son of God] follows awkwardly. For what was said is *destinatus filius Dei*, as one might say, 'was designated consul,' with *filius Dei* attached after the participle *praedestinatus est*, not before it.[3] But this 'teacher of old men' of ours inverts the order, reading thus: *qui filius Dei praedestinatus est ei secundum carnem* [who as Son of God was predestined to him according to the flesh], and so on, *ex semine David* [out of the seed of David].[4] But just before this we had *de filio suo* [concerning his Son], which it is difficult to follow with *qui filius Dei* [who as Son of God]. Also difficult to fit together are the words *qui filius Dei praedestinatus est Deo*[5] *ex semine David* [who as Son of God was predestined to God out of the seed of David]. More difficult still is what follows: *praedestinatus est ex semine David secundum carnem, in*

virtute spiritus ex resurrectione mortuorum [predestined out of the seed of
David according to the flesh, by the power of the Spirit by resurrection
from the dead]. Add to this that though the word order, which he mixes
up, is difficult for us [in Latin], in Greek it is utterly absurd when the
article is put before the participle and not before *filius Dei*: τοῦ ὁρισθέντος
υἱοῦ Θεοῦ. Finally, as this passage is put forward almost unanimously by
the most authoritative Doctors of the church against the Arians[6] to prove
conclusively that there was a double nature, divine and human, in Christ,
this whole witness is lost if we follow the interpretation of this man.

Anyhow, he gathers from the words of Augustine that this passage
can be understood as he twists it;[7] I could answer that Augustine would
have spoken differently if he had consulted the Greek commentators. But
Augustine does not invert the word order, nor does he apply predestination
to Christ's heavenly role; but he understands that Christ the Son of God as
man was destined in this sense, that he would become head of the church.
Actually, Augustine cannot be better excused on this point than by saying
that he made a human error.

And this is the triumphal passage that he promised so grandly in his
prologue in which he would prove my temerity and would defend the
Translator from false accusations.[8] My note, however, does not censure the
Translator; it only seeks a way out of a difficulty.

1 Rom 1:4; CWE 56 10–15; *Collationes* 8v–11v
2 There appears to be no statement of such a rule in the immediately preceding
   context of the *Collationes*. Erasmus quotes a similar injunction in connection
   with Rom 2:17, 166 below, but he may also be thinking of a passage in the
   prologue (e1r–v) where Titelmans is justifying barbarisms and solecisms: 'It is
   more difficult, in fact, for the translator to avoid incorrect expressions in his
   own language when translating than for the initial writer; for while the latter
   is not bound to anything and is free to write as he would wish, the former
   is bound to the initial script, must adhere to the original reading, and depart
   from it as little as possible. Sometimes, to ensure that the translation does not
   say more or less than the original script has, awkwardness of language has to
   take second place to truth of meaning.'
3 That is, the correct way to read it is: 'was declared to be Son of God,' not 'the
   Son of God was declared.'
4 *Collationes* 10v, although Erasmus does not seem to report the word order
   consistently himself. See the sentence beginning 'More difficult still . . .' where
   he leaves out the word *Deo*.
5 Sic; Erasmus seems to be saying that if you replace the pronoun *ei* with the
   noun for which it stands, *Deo*, the resulting statement is an absurdity.
6 See CWE 56 10 nn8 and 9. Erasmus showed in *1527* how the Arians used
   John 1:15 to support their view that Christ was a creature, but the final sentence of the annotation on this verse ('For he who never began to be God did
   nevertheless begin to be a man'), which was present from *1516*, eliminates the

possibility of an Arian interpretation of this verse.

7 In the annotation on *qui factus est ei* (CWE 56 9) Erasmus had referred to Augustine's *Contra Faustum Manichaeum* 11.4 PL 42 248.

8 *Collationes* prologus [b3]v. The passage is mentioned in Titelmans' discussion of Jerome's translation of Origen's commentaries, but it is not clear why Erasmus should point to it as particularly significant here in Titelmans' argument.

[ER *ex eo quod resurrexit e mortuis Iesus Christus* 'in that Jesus Christ rose from the dead']

[RESP] *ex resurrectione mortuorum* 'from the resurrection of the dead.'[1] My note does not censure the Translator here either. I simply show how many meanings the Greek text offers, without rejecting any of them. But my translation, according to him, restricts this richness of meaning to some extent.[2] There is a fertility in the Scriptures that produces a rich plenitude of meanings for us, the same phrase being adapted now to the head of the church, now to the body, now jointly to both, now to each one of us, now to certain classes of men, now to the heavenly hierarchy. This sort of fertility is, as I observe, lauded by holy Doctors, but they disapprove so strongly of the confusion of meanings generated by ambiguity or obscurity or changing of word order that they strive to their utmost to remove them. Fertility is good, but diversity is a source of trouble. A case is not presented in the best way when the barristers say, 'Suppose this or this or this.' I translated one way because I could not do otherwise, but I gave a note in addition to my translation.

1 Rom 1:4 'by the resurrection [of our Lord Jesus Christ] from the dead'; CWE 56 19–27; *Collationes* 12r–15r

2 *Collationes* 14v. This is a criticism levelled several times at Erasmus by Titelmans; see at Rom 8:18, 15:4, and 15:7, 223 and 252–3 below.

[ER *per quem accepimus gratiam ac muneris apostolici functionem* 'grace and the fulfilment of the office of apostle']

[RESP] *per quem accepimus gratiam et apostolatum* 'by whom we have received grace and apostleship.'[1] *Apostolatus* [apostleship] is indeed a word in common use among Christians, but it is not approved by those who speak correct Latin. *Apostolē*[2] [mission, apostleship] is known in Greek but not heard among us Latin speakers. Therefore, I have translated with *accepimus apostolici muneris functionem* [We have received the task of fulfilling the office of apostle]. However, my critic prefers *apostolicum munus* [the office of apostle] because 'office' is singular, 'tasks' [*functiones*] are multiple. But he should know that in educated usage such words as *functio* do not always signify the action but rather the responsibility. A manager [*procurator*], for example, may have many different tasks in management [*procurationes*], but his management [*procuratio*] remains a single office, as in farming. The office of management remains even with the person who neglects his duty; the steward who fails to distribute rations is still the steward. But even if he accepts that 'function' does mean the activity, is the authority thereby excluded? I think not. But it is the responsibility that is signified rather than the title. Finally, just as Greek κοτή means *sectio* [a cut], so *apostolē* means *legatio* [mission], a verbal noun, just like *functio*.

1 Rom 1:5; CWE 56 18–19; *Collationes* 15r–16r
2 In Latin; a transcription of the Greek ἀποστολή

[ER *super ipsius nomine* 'regarding his name']
[RESP] *pro nomine eius* 'for his name.'[1] Here he prefers the ambiguous phrase of the Translator. But no one has deprived him of it. My annotation says clearly enough that the fertility allowed by ambiguity, which also goes with ignorance, is not desirable. I have rendered what seemed to me the best sense.

1 Rom 1:5; CWE 56 27–9; *Collationes* 16v–18r

[ER *quem colo spiritu meo* 'whom I worship with my spirit']
[RESP] *cui servio in spiritu meo* 'whom I serve in my spirit.'[1] Instead of *cui servio*, I had translated *quem colo*. 'But the Translator,' says he, 'plainly rendered the idea of the reverence due to the one God as *servitus* [servitude].' I don't deny it, but no Latin speaker ever called reverence for God *servitus*, whereas *cultus* is frequently used both by Jerome in the Old Testament and here by the Translator in the New. 'But *colo* [cultivate] has multiple meanings: we cultivate someone whom we respect, whom we frequently attend; we cultivate the farmers' fields, and sky-worshippers have a cult of the heavens.'[2] I agree. But equally the servant serves [*servit*] his lord, the greedy man serves his own advantage, the ambitious man serves glory, the pleasure-seeker serves his belly, the superstitious translator serves the letter, and the cautious man serves the times; and finally Hercules served Omphale. Really the Greek words too are ambiguous: λατρεία, δουλεία, and ὑπερδουλεία[3] do not have only the meanings used for purposes of instruction by Greek theologians, just as *constitutio* means one thing to jurists and another to rhetoricians.[4]

1 Rom 1:9; CWE 56 33–4; *Collationes* 19v–21r
2 This sentence is a loose paraphrase of *Collationes* 20v–21r, as the following *fateor* 'I agree' shows, though LB does not italicize it.
3 The first Greek word is the noun form of the verb λατρεύω, used in the Greek NT and meaning 'hired labour,' as well as 'service of the gods'; the second

and third mean 'slavery, bondage.' In his annotation Erasmus had sought to distinguish λατρεύω as 'to worship' and δουλεύω as 'to serve.'

4 To jurists an imperial regulation, to rhetoricians the issue in dispute

[ER *mentionem vestri faciam* 'I shall make mention of you.']
[RESP] *memoriam vestri faciens* 'making remembrance of you.'[1] He affirms that *memoriam facere* is a correct translation. I admit it, but no speaker of idiomatic Latin ever used the expression. 'But the Translator used it.' Certainly, because people commonly spoke thus at that time, following the Greeks who say, μνείαν ποιοῦμαι, although μνεῖα signifies 'mention' rather than 'recall,' which is rather μνήμη. 'But,' he says, 'we "make mention" of someone whom we are talking about in his absence.' That's right; but my note pointed out that prayer is simply talking with God, in case anyone should think the expression [making mention of you] was rather crude. He pretends not to notice this so that he can fill a page.

1 Rom 1:9 'I make a commemoration of you'; CWE 56 34; *Collationes* 21r–v

[ER *volente Deo* 'God willing']
[RESP] *in voluntate Dei* 'in the will of God.'[1] He informs me, following Origen,[2] that *in voluntate Dei* does not mean the same as *volente Deo*. Origen has many such notes, and they are of little importance. Certainly this one is not of such weight that one may not disagree. As God is often said in the Scriptures to 'wish' what he allows, 'willing' often signifies 'allowing.'

1 Rom 1:10 'by the will of God'; CWE 56 35; *Collationes* 23r–v
2 Origen *Comm in Rom* 1:11 (1–2) PG 14 857/FC 103 80–1

[ER *ut aliquod impartiar vobis donum* 'that I may impart some gift to you']
[RESP] *ut aliquid impartiar vobis gratiae* 'that I may impart some grace to you.'[1] According to him, the word *gratia* has been used in the Latin to mean 'gift.' He approves of this because the Greek is χάρις, and that is what the Doctors of the church say. I admit this is a Christian way of speaking, but it is bad Latin, though that is how ordinary half-Latin, half-Greek people spoke then. 'But,' he says, 'if it is a fault to translate the same word in different ways, you are at fault more than a hundred times.' Variety in translation is not a fault, dear boy, but translating good Greek with bad Latin is an elementary fault, and the affectation of variety where it serves no purpose is inept. But he finds it a matter of great reproach that I should say that the Translator, a man of such importance and inspired by the Spirit, 'plays [*ludere*] with variety of expression.' In case he thinks 'play' refers only to games of chance, we use the word for anything that is not a

matter of compulsion and is done for pleasure. 'To play' is not a derogatory word. And with this Translator the affectation of variety is so marked that if anyone tries to imagine explanations of every case, he would seem to do nothing else but trifle and, in truth, play games.

1 Rom 1:11; CWE 56 35–6; *Collationes* 23v–24v. Erasmus' annotation claimed the Greek had χάρισμα, as in his text, not χάρις; his response to Titelmans seems to accept that it was χάρις as does Titelmans' criticism.

[ER *quo confirmemini, hoc est ut communem capiam consolationem in vobis* 'that you might be strengthened, that is, that I might receive among you a shared comfort']
[RESP] *ad confirmandos vos, id est simul consolari* 'to strengthen you, that is to be comforted together.'[1] According to him, the Greek words τοῦτο ἐστιν [that is] prevent the Translator from translating the second infinitive as such.[2] On the contrary, they make such a translation obligatory, unless it would be correct to say, *litandum est musis, hoc est animum applicare ad litteras* [We should be making an offering to the Muses, that is, to apply the mind to literature], instead of *animus applicandus ad litteras* [applying the mind to literature]. Or *cupidus es illaqueandi nos, hoc est dolo circumvenire* [You are desirous of ensnaring me, that is, to deceive by trickery], instead of *dolo circumveniendi* [of deceiving by trickery]. I had pointed out that for the Greeks συμπαρακληθῆναι 'to be comforted' has 'Paul' as subject, and I had cited particularly Theophylact and Origen.[3] My critic charges me with lying because the Doctors of the church make not just Paul the subject of this verb but both Paul and the Romans. What is this? Did I deny that both could be the subject? But the pronoun ὑμᾶς [you] prevents 'Paul' from being the subject of the second verb unless another pronoun is understood; so I do this to make it refer to Paul as well. How did I lie then, dear boy? In fact, this shared comfort is not expressed by the root of the verb but by the prefix σύμ-.[4] But the very words of my note that he quotes show that I think the same as those he puts up against me. I state that the Greek scholia[5] make 'Paul' the subject of the second verb. Is he ignorant of the force of the following preposition *in*?[6] But shortly after [we have] 'that Paul, however, was to receive mutual comfort.'[7] Does he not know what 'mutual' means? But this fellow quarrels with me as if it were I who wanted to make either the Romans alone or Paul alone the subject of συμπαρακληθῆναι, though the sense itself prevents either one alone being the subject. Then he argues that the Translator was right to leave the infinitive so that the subject could be either the Romans or Paul, when it has been shown that it can only be both. But this is how he proceeds, as if the subject were just one or the other and the infinitive had been translated by some other form. However, this

is absurd. Whether you make the subject first person, as in 'so that I may receive shared consolation among you,' or second person, as in 'so that you may receive consolation with me,' both parties are the recipients of consolation. Clear as this is, he is still wailing at the end: 'See,' he says, 'how the Translator, though exact and faithful, is reproached,' and so on. If I were to try and rebut every case like this, what profit would there be to the reader?

1 Rom 1:11–12 'to strengthen you: that is to say, that I may be comforted together in you'; CWE 56 36–8; *Collationes* 24v–25v

2 The Greek sentence has two infinitives. In his annotation Erasmus followed Valla (I 855) in saying that the two verbs should be translated with parallel constructions, not, as in the Vulgate, the first with a gerundive, the second with an infinitive. In the English and Latin examples below the constructions are also mutually exclusive, but not in the same way.

3 Theophylact *Expos in Rom* 1:12 PG 124 348B; Origen *Comm in Rom* 1.12 PG 14 857B–858A/FC 103 81–2. See also CWE 56 38 nn3 and 7, where it is pointed out that Erasmus' translation did in fact make Paul the subject.

4 Ie from the preposition σύν 'with'

5 A collection of short exegetical comments by the Eastern Fathers from the end of the patristic period; see CWE 56 13 n1.

6 The following phrase in both the Vulgate and in Erasmus' translation is *in vobis*, rendered by the translators of CWE 56 as 'among you.'

7 Rom 1:28

[ER *pactorum haudquaquam tenaces* 'never keeping promises']
[RESP] *incompositos* 'without fidelity.'[1] Here he tries to persuade me that *incompositi* in Latin means people for whom social intercourse with others, as is natural among all men, is difficult. He should give an example of an accepted Latin author who has used the word in this sense. I was aware that Doctors of the church do so. But this word *incompositi* has led some of them to understand it as meaning 'of unseemly[2] dress and behaviour,' though the Greeks call such people ἀσχήμων 'unseemly' not ἀσύνθετος 'faithless.' But here he has contrived a wonderful argument against the witness of Theophylact.[3] He says, 'A corrupted definition in Theophylact has deceived Erasmus. *Incompositos* should have been read as meaning "without covenants," that is, not standing by agreements and contracts, to put it plainly, faithless and changeable, so that this meaning fits those who are ἀσπόνδος "without fidelity."'[4] Yet that is the very definition in the Greek text of Theophylact. But granted that I concede what he affirms, Theophylact did not leave the second word [ἀστόργος 'without natural affection'] unexplained but included both in the same commentary as saying almost the same thing; having explained the first, he put the second with it as if it were clear. Chrysostom,[5] whom Theophylact follows, does the same. His

word order is different from ours.⁶ He links ἀσύνθετος, ἀσπόνδος, ἀστόργος, ἀνελεήμων 'unmerciful' in such a way as to make ἀσυνθέτος refer to the social bond that is common to all men, ἀσπόνδος to civic agreements, ἀστόργος to our feelings for those close to us, and ἀνελεήμων to the pity that the misfortune of the afflicted demands of us. These qualities were implanted in everyone by nature so that men can live together in peace – impossible without respect for contracts and agreements – so that they can love and honour wife, children, parents and relatives, fatherland and friends, and be grieved by the misfortunes of the wretched. Yet they had given themselves over so far to culpable inclinations⁷ that they were deaf to every natural disposition. 'But,' says he, 'the Doctors of the church took [the Greek] as meaning *incompositi*.'⁸ I accept that; but since they knew Greek and the usage of ordinary people, they understood what this word meant, uncouth though it is to educated speakers who call *incompositus* what is disordered, confused, or improper. Such is the note that he thrusts before me with so many tangled words, very nearly carried away in his jubilation.

1   Rom 1:31; CWE 56 64–6; *Collationes* 45r–47v. This response led to a considerable addition in 1535 to the second of these annotations.
2   *inhonesto*] 1540 788; *honesto* in 1529 4r
3   Theophylact *Expos in Rom* 1:31 PG 124 361B
4   *Collationes* 45v. The verse reads in Greek: ἀσυνέτους, ἀσυνθέτους, ἀστόργους, ἀσπόνδους, ἀνελεήμονας 'Foolish, dissolute, without affection, without fidelity, without mercy.' Titelmans appears to think Theophylact omitted the word between ἀσυνθέτους and ἀσπόνδους, ie ἀστόργους.
5   Chrysostom *Hom in Rom* 5.1 PG 60 422 and 428. A modified version of the rest of this paragraph was included in the *Annotationes* of 1535.
6   Ie from that printed in all editions of Erasmus' Greek text; see CWE 56 65 and n8 there.
7   Cf Rom 1:28 *traditi fuerant in reprobum sensum*; DV 'God delivered them up to a reprobate sense'; RSV 'God gave them up to a base mind.'
8   *Collationes* 47r–v

[ER *qui cum Dei iustitiam noverint* 'who though they know the righteousness of God']
[RESP] *qui cum iustitiam Dei cognovissent* 'who though they had known the justice of God.'¹ At this point my critic has the extraordinary nerve to lash me with a prolonged dispute, evidently having found an excellent ground for rebuke. He takes the gravest offence, in fact, because I wondered whether the Translator had changed the reading of the Greek and added something by way of explanation, which it is clear he did elsewhere. And if he did the same here, why was it a crime, o teacher of old men? 'But,' says he, 'these added words change the meaning.'² But my note shows that if you add a question mark, the meaning remains the same. And if

to add some word or other is to corrupt Scripture, it was something often done by this Translator, 'divinely inspired and worshipful,' as my opponent frequently proclaims, though it is not certain whether he was Christian or pagan, heretic or orthodox. But really there's nothing to worry about; he has seen a rather old codex of Brother Amandus,[3] which I believe came from the college of the canons of Corsendonck, for that is where Amandus copied the New Testament from. However, there is nothing more unreliable than that codex, and there are many such Greek manuscripts current that have been corrected to agree with the Latin reading. To castigate me on that basis is to apply an unmarked ruler to an unmarked stone.[4] But he says I have noted the Greek commentaries suggest a different reading. Indeed, but I do not say that it was they who added *non intellexerunt* (which is what we are arguing about); only that the order of two words has been inverted: συνευδοκοῦσιν and πράσσουσιν. He makes a great hue-and-cry saying, since the early editions did not have these words and probably the Translator changed the reading of the Greek – in a number of passages he certainly makes use of the freedom to paraphrase – that I added in the fourth edition what it was better to suppress, although there is nothing about these matters in the fourth edition. He himself says they are not in the second and third,[5] so if he is speaking the truth, they are not to be found anywhere – for I have looked in the first and it has nothing. But perhaps he thought what he had was the fourth when it was the third, for the fourth came out in 1527. To err is human. But let others judge what to call a youth who is so intemperate when he errs, who is so voluble in his wrangling. He admits the Translator proceeds in some places like a paraphraser whenever there is something to be gained; I show rather that he sometimes does it when there is nothing to be gained.[6] And here he declares that it was a serious matter to add something without resorting to an inquiry. But however you may excuse the Latin edition, the Greek is by far the simpler and the more suitable.

1   Rom 1:32; CWE 56 66–9; *Collationes* 48v–55r: 'Who, having known the justice of God.' The dispute is concerned with the two words that follow: *non intellexerunt*. See the annotation at CWE 56 67, where Erasmus explains that these words do not correspond to anything in the Greek, that he suspects they were added by the Translator, and that by adding a question mark to them, he does not change their meaning. See also n4 below.

2   See the annotation at CWE 56 67; and *Collationes* 50v.

3   Titelmans claims the disputed words were in Amandus' manuscript in the original Greek text and in the original hand (*Collationes* 49r). Amandus of Zierikzee was a member of the Franciscan Observants at Louvain from 1506 until his death sometime before 1534. Some of his works were edited by Titelmans. See CEBR I 39. Corsendonck was an Augustinian college near Turnhout; Rummel *Annotations* 38–9; see also Allen Ep 1044 34n.

4 Cf *Adagia* 1 v 88 *Amussis alba* 'An unmarked rule.' Erasmus there quotes an
   expanded form of the proverb, 'A white line against a white stone,' taken
   from Zenobius (4.89) or the *Suda* (Λ 325): 'used for those who have no judgment, or for stupid people, or for people who base proof or exposition of
   doubtful things on doubtful facts' (CWE 31 461). The form given here is more
   exactly like Plato's use in the *Charmides* 154b: 'a white rule against a white
   stone.'
5 *Collationes* 49v
6 *Collationes* 50r

From chapter two of the Epistle to the Romans

[ER *nam hoc ipso quod iudicas alterum* 'now by the very fact that you
judge another']
[RESP] *in quo enim alterum iudicas* 'for wherein thou judgest another.'[1]
He approves of my version but says no one has accepted this meaning.
And whence, pray, does he infer that? 'From translations of Origen and
Theophylact.'[2] As if it were anything new for translators to translate literally
rather than idiomatically. 'But Augustine and Cyprian have *in quo*.'[3] It makes
no difference as long as they mean the same as I translate. 'But,' says he,
'they mean something else.' What is the proof? 'Because they are mindful
that the people addressed have done the same things that they condemned
in others.' Perhaps they did not get this meaning from the words *in quo* but
from what follows: 'For you do the very things you judge.' Since it would
be desirable to make this point clear with the same elegance as the Greek,
Augustine, who did not compare the Latin words exactly with the Greek
and had little skill in Greek, will not carry much weight. Although it is
not allowable to move away from the Translator's meaning as this fellow
understands it, Jerome dared to do so, for his reading is *in quo iudicio* [in
which judgment].[4] And if the Greek text has both meanings, my version
has at least this convenience, that it removes the inconsistency of number
between *in quo* and then *eadem enim* [for ... the same things], not to mention
the fact that the same thing is said twice.[5]

   For *longanimitas* [long-suffering], a word made from the Greek but not
Latin usage,[6] I have translated *lenitas* [mildness]. My critic thinks *longanimitas* is the correct translation; I do not deny it, but it is scarcely Latin. 'But
lenitas suggests the same as the preceding words χρηστότης [goodness] and
ἀνοχή [forbearance]. *Longanimitas* suggests the same too, and there is nothing
new in Paul reinforcing the meaning for his readers by using synonyms.
So what is Erasmus' fault if he has replaced a barely Latin word with an
idiomatic one? For myself, I could wish that *longanimitas* had been accepted
in Latin.

1 Rom 2:1; CWE 56 72; *Collationes* 58r–59r

2 *Collationes* 58v. Origen has no commentary on Rom 2:1. Theophylact *Expos in Rom* 2.1 PG 124 362D–365A. See CWE 56 72–3 n3.

3 *Collationes* 58v–59r; Augustine *Contra Cresconium grammaticum Donatistum* 3.27 PL 43 512; Cyprian *Ad Quirinum* 3.21 PL 4 750A

4 *Collationes* 59r, citing Jerome *Commentaria in Ezechielem* 2.7.27 PL 25 76B

5 *in quo* is singular; *eadem enim* is plural. VG *In quo enim alterum iudicas teipsum condemnas. Eadem enim agis quae iudicas* 'For wherein thou judgest another, thou condemnest thyself. For thou dost the same things which thou judgest.'

6 Reinforcing his point about elegance, Erasmus has moved on to Rom 2:4 (*Collationes* 59v–60v). *Longanimitas* is listed in Lewis and Short as used only in the Vulgate and by Cassiodorus. The Greek word is μακροθυμία. The word is not discussed in the *Annotationes*.

[ER *ad poenitentiam te invitat* 'invites you to repentance']
[RESP] *ad poenitentiam te adducit* 'induces you to repentance.'[1] Here he informs me of what ἄγω [I lead] means in Greek and tries to persuade me that it would be correct to say *adduxit me ad coenam* [He induced me to the feast] for *conatus est me adducere* [He tried to induce me] or *invitavit me ad coenam* [He invited me to the feast]. 'But the Translator is excusable if he rendered the Greek word rather unidiomatically.' That is not what he did; the Greek does not say 'induces you' [*adducit*] but 'leads' [*ducit*]. How would the Translator have translated if he had found ἐπαγωγή? Would it be 'introduction' or would 'inducement' be better? How would he render ἀγωγή? 'Direction' or 'education,' especially of liberal education? How would he render συνάγω? 'Lead together' or 'unite' rather? He says, 'God does not always call us to repentance gently.' I agree, but if you bear in mind that he is no less beneficent when he sends unhappiness than when he sends adversity, he is clearly 'inviting' us either way. But what purpose was served here by recalling the fierceness of God when Paul is evoking his beneficence and mildness? We use *trahere* [to draw], meaning *pellicere* [to entice], of gentle actions too. For Chrysostom here interprets ἄγει [he leads] as ἕλκει [he draws].[2] But what was the point of citing fellow Christians who read *adducit*, as if we did not know this or as if it counted against us? The case should be examined on the basis of good Latin. Moreover, since it is clear that 'lead,' meaning 'entice,' fits the sense better here, I wonder why the Translator wanted to avoid the Apostle's word. For there is the same difference between *ducere* and *adducere* as between *trahere* [draw] and *pertrahere* [draw into, entice], and between *pellere* [impel] and *perpellere* [force]. And so those who are allured by hope are said 'to be led' [*duci*], not 'induced' [*adduci*]; and everyone is 'drawn' [*trahit*] by pleasure, but not everyone is 'drawn into' [*pertrahit*] sin. We say correctly, 'I cannot be induced [*adduci*] to believe that,' but it is incorrect if we say, 'I cannot be led' [*duci*]. Sometimes the simple forms may be used in place of the compounds, but certainly not

the reverse. So he would be more correct to excuse the Translator by saying
that he spoke to ordinary folk in the ordinary way.

1 Rom 2:4 'leadeth thee to penance'; CWE 56 74; *Collationes* 61r–62r
2 Chrysostom *Hom in Rom* 5.2 PG 60 424

[ER *colligis tibiipsi iram* 'You are gathering up wrath for yourself.']
[RESP] *thesaurizas tibi iram* 'Thou treasurest up to thyself wrath.'[1] I preferred *recondis* [store away] or *colligis* [gather]. My critic thinks since *the-
saurus* is a common word in Latin, *thesaurizare* should not be unacceptable
either. No, *thesaurizare* is neither a Greek word nor a Latin one; θησαυρίζειν
is Greek, *thesaurisso* is a word invented according to Latin practice but not
used by any Latin speakers. If an analogy is acceptable, it is as if, because
we commonly use *ecclesia*, we might say *ecclesiazare*. There is nothing indeed
of any good use in these annotations!

1 Rom 2:5; CWE 56 75; *Collationes* 62r–64v

[ER *his quidem qui perseverantes in benefaciendo* 'to those who, persevering
in well doing']
[RESP] *his quidem qui secundum patientiam boni operis* 'to them indeed,
who according to patience in good work.'[1] Here strangely my critic separates 'eternal life' from 'glory and honour,' as if it is possible to seek after
eternal life but not glory and honour, although just as the eternal life of believers is God himself, so also is their glory and immortality – for we are
not speaking of mortal glory. In pious language God is said to be eternal
life, and so in the same way of speaking he is said to be glory and honour;
and quite rightly my critic says all these are not God, for the gift of immortality of soul and body is a favour granted by God, not God himself. Now
what is immortality if not eternal life? The separation he makes is probable if you supply the word *sunt* [are]; but this is exactly what is implied in
my note where he attacks me.[2] Nor does the article τοῖς [to those], which
I think was added by scribes, make much difference. 'Why then did you
not take it out?'[3] Because I do not usually change what the Greek manuscripts say unless some exemplar persuades me to. But I point to Rufinus
precisely because he changes the earlier accusatives to nominatives,[4] different from what the Greeks have. However, the Translator added the verb
sunt in the second part; he did not add it here, though he would certainly
have added it if he had understood as that man [Rufinus] imagines. And
yet the sense that the Greeks follow is more acute. The Romans sought after
glory and the title of immortality among men in this world; Paul shows that
true immortality is prepared for those who[5] persevere here in good works,

not for those who raise triumphal arches or hold triumphs over conquered peoples.

1 Rom 2:7; CWE 56 76–9; *Collationes* 64v–70r. It is not this phrase that Erasmus discusses here but the following words: ER *his quidem qui perseverantes in bene-faciendo, gloriam et honorem et immortalitatem quaerunt, vitam aeternam* 'to those who, persevering in well doing, seek glory and honour and immortality, eternal life'; VG *his quidem secundum patientiam boni operis gloriam et honorem et incorruptionem quaerentibus vitam aeternam* 'to them indeed who according to patience in good works seek glory and honour and incorruption, eternal life.' For the Greek text of the whole passage (Rom 2:6–9) and translations of the Vulgate and of Erasmus' version, see CWE 56 76 and 78 n1.

2 Erasmus says in his annotation, 'The sense [of the Greek] is: 'to those who here seek that glory and honour and immortality, persevering in the good works through which those things are procured, he will give eternal life, which is the very thing they have sought' (CWE 56 76). He is suggesting, 'Glory and honour and immortality – these are [*sunt*] eternal life.'

3 *Collationes* 68v

4 Ie suggesting the insertion of *sunt*; see CWE 56 77. The reference is to Rufinus' *De principiis*, which is a translation of Origen's Περὶ ἀρχῶν (3.1.6. PG 11 258C). See CWE 56 78 n14 and 94–5 with n11. According to Erasmus, the text of Rufinus reads: *iis quidem qui secundum patientiam boni operis, gloria et incorruptio, qui quaerunt vitam aeternam* 'to those indeed who according to their endurance in good work – who seek eternal life – [there are] glory and incorruption' (LB VI 570 n14). The passage was added to the *Annotationes* in 1527.

5 *qui hic perseverant*] 1529 7r; *qui perseverant* in 1540 790

[ER *et immortalitatem* 'and immortality']

[RESP] *et incorruptionem* 'and incorruption.'[1] I doubted whether *incorruptio* is a Latin word. My critic says it is accepted by the learned Fathers, and I use it often in my writings whenever I prefer to speak in church language rather than classical Latin. He informs me that φθορά is the word for *corruptio*, so ἀφθαρσία is correctly rendered as *incorruptio*; I agree, if Latin speakers recognized the word. He admits the Translator sometimes renders ἄφθαρτος as *immortalis*. There is no reason, therefore, for him to be cross with me because I dare to do the same. But I myself repeatedly translate with *incorruptibilitas*; true, but only when obliged to. For *mortalitas* and *immortalitas* would not be suitable for φθορά and ἀφθαρσία in every context. It is not surprising if I preferred to translate with 'incorruptibility,'[2] since this is an immediate consequence of immortality. However, one can be ἀθάνατος [immortal, deathless] without being ἄφθαρτος [uncorrupted]. The bodies of unbelievers will be deathless but not uncorrupted, since they will be subject to torment, as will their souls. But whenever the Scriptures speak of 'immortality,' they mean the life that is free of all evils. However, this word *incorruptibilitas* is correct word formation rather than good usage.

1   Rom 2:7; part of the passage discussed in the annotation on *his quidem secundum patientiam boni operis*, immediately above; *Collationes* 70r–71r
2   *incorruptibilitas*] In *1516*; *immortalitas* from *1519*

[ER *qui veritati quidem non obtemperant* 'who do not indeed obey the truth']
[RESP] *qui non acquiescunt veritati* 'who do not give assent to the truth.'[1] I merely note that the pleasure produced by the words in opposition is hardly conveyed by the Latin;[2] I do not reproach the Translator, who cannot often, or certainly cannot easily, do it. Nor was there any need to explain that pious men value clarity of meaning more than charm of words, although such charm is common in Paul's language, not forced indeed but not despised either.

1   Rom 2:8 'who obey not the truth'; CWE 56 79; *Collationes* 71r–v
2   Erasmus is referring to the antithesis produced in the Greek by the participles ἀπειθοῦσι 'to those not obeying' and πειθομένοις 'to those obeying.' Cf CWE 56 79 n2. His own translation repeats the word *obtemperant*.

[ER *afflictio et anxietas* 'suffering and distress']
[RESP] *tribulatio et angustia* 'tribulation and anguish.'[1] I preferred *anxietas* rather than *angustia* as a translation of στενοχωρία here. 'But Origen talks in philosophical terms about the "anguish" of heart of unbelievers and the "freedom"[2] of believers.'[3] He speaks as a philosopher, yes, but briefly, as he often does. And I will say the comment is appropriate whenever Paul boasts of his anguish and his stripes, as in 2 Corinthians 6, and the anguish he suffered for Christ's sake in chapter 12 of the same Epistle.[4] Also when Susanna says, 'Anguish is upon me on every side,'[5] I shall allow that a reference to Origen is appropriate. If the 'affliction' or 'anxiety' of a man with a bad conscience can properly be said to be 'anguish,' then one who is so affected can properly be said to be 'anguished.' Nor was I unaware that the Doctors of the church use these terms, but I preferred the more idiomatic Latin. To those who know nothing but Latin, *angustia* means something different from what it means to Paul when he speaks of 'anguish.' However, wherever there is *anxietas*, there is something of *angustia*, for grief constrains the mind, just as joy expands it. But elsewhere [he says] I translate στενοχωρεῖσθε as *angusti estis* [you are anguished] for *angustiamini* [you are constrained]. What is strange about that if it is more appropriate there? The same Greek word does not have the same meaning in every context.

1   Rom 2:9; part of the passage discussed in the annotation on *his quidem secundum patientiam boni operis* above; *Collationes* 71v–72r

2 *angustia* and *latitudo*; the Latin words reproduce the Greek, opposing the ideas
   of narrowness and broadness.
3 Origen *Comm in Rom* 2.6 (6) PG 14 885 / FC 103 121–2
4 2 Cor 6:4–5, 12:10
5 Dan 13:22 VG

[ER *non enim est personarum respectus apud Deum* 'There is no regard for
persons with God.']
[RESP] *non est personarum acceptio apud Deum* 'There is no acceptance
of persons with God.'[1] I said that the expressions *personarum acceptio, personam accipere* [to accept a person] and *personarum acceptor* [acceptor of per-
sons], translating προσωποληψία, πρόσωπον λαμβάνειν, προσωπολήπτης, are
scarcely good Latin. I prefer *personarum respectus* [respect of persons], *personam respicere* [to respect a person], and *qui personae respectum habet* [who
has respect of a person]. My critic says this is not the main meaning. I
am not concerned with the Greek word, which I believe is the common
one, but with the meaning. The meaning, as I believe, is 'discrimination between one person and another.' But Lefèvre and I, as he says, translated
in the Epistle to the Galatians *Deus personam non accipit* [God accepteth no
man's person].[2] 'If *personam accipere* is Latin,' [he says,] 'then *acceptio* is
Latin too.' I am not so fussy that I do not occasionally leave some word
that was rarely accepted in Latin, and it could be that this slipped through,
it could be that I did not trouble myself about something that was more
or less tolerable, for if you accept one person you reject another. Nor, if
accipit personam is Latin, does it follow straight away that *acceptor* and *acceptio* are Latin. There is nothing wrong with the first expression except
in the association of the words, but I think *acceptor* and *acceptio* are not
to be found anywhere in established authors – just as *bibit* is good Latin,
but *bibitor* and *bibitio* never are. Analogy does not always result in good
Latin.

1 Rom 2:11 'There is no respect of persons with God'; CWE 56 80–1; *Collationes*
   72r–73r
2 Gal 2:6. Erasmus' translation has *personam hominis Deus non accipit*; VG *Deus
   enim personam hominis non accipit* 'For there is no respect of persons with God.'

[ER] *qui legem factis exprimunt, iusti habebuntur* 'Those who clearly reflect
the Law in their deeds will be held to be just.']
[RESP] *factores legis iustificabuntur* 'The doers of the Law shall be justified.'[1] I suggested that *factores legis* is not pure Latin usage for 'those who
keep the Law.' 'But,' says he, 'this is the word used by the holy Scriptures.'
Who denies it? 'Anyone understands what *factor legis* is,' he says. I agree,
but what else would it mean but 'lawmaker' to one who was accustomed

to this sort of phrase, who knew only Latin? In the same way as the Father
is said to be the maker [ποιητής] of heaven and earth. 'But,' says he, 'even
hypocrites reflect the Law in their deeds.' Hypocrites too do what the Law
has prescribed in the same way. 'But,' he says, '*exprimunt* means "vain
display."' I never saw it used to mean 'vain display,' but the son who is
like his father clearly reflects [*exprimit*] the father, and speech is a clear
reflection [*exprimit*] of the mind. But let's accept that one who 'devises'
[*fingit*] something 'expresses' [*exprimere*] it; you will still find *facere* used for
fingere much more often. I could have said, 'Who observe [*observant*] the
Law,' but I wanted to render the feeling of *factor*.

1   Rom 2:13; CWE 56 81; *Collationes* 73r–v

[ER *cogitationibus ... accusantibus, aut etiam* 'thoughts ... accusing, or
also']
[RESP] *cogitationum accusantium, aut etiam etc* 'thoughts ... accusing, or
also.'[1] Here this youth scourges Erasmus with extraordinary arrogance because I threw accusations of dozing and making mistakes at a Translator
who is dead and looks with the principal angels on the face of God, more
especially as he wrote with the inspiration of the Holy Spirit, though none
of these things can be shown to be true by this censor. The church accepted
the translation; it did not know the man, nor did it approve or disapprove
of him; for it is possible that the unknown author of this translation was
a pagan. And yet on these grounds my critic has woven a long-winded
and stern rebuke; you would say it was some ferocious schoolmaster rebuking a pupil and 'punishing my impudence,' as Plato has it,[2] but with
greater impudence. He praises the moderation of Valla and Lefèvre, as if
elsewhere they had not treated the Translator more harshly than I and as
if I had not defended him on some occasions against them. He is particularly offended by the inference I draw, because I said, 'Here it is plain how
much he is to be trusted in other places.'[3] 'So the whole translation,' says
he, 'is a human production.'[4] What is the harm in that, since the apostles
wrote in Greek? It is a question here only of an error in language ascribed
to him by Valla,[5] whose moderation this man applauds. Which is more abusive, to point out an error or to point out looseness? He does not always
err just because he erred here, but what he offers should not always be
held to be good Latin; nor should the reader be offended if at any point
he is said to speak incorrectly, since he speaks to common folk. My words,
which this man interprets harshly, imply nothing else. 'It is a serious insult,' he says, 'dozing and slackness!' I agree with respect to the rendering of the meaning, but as far as the language is concerned, looseness has
some merit; for Gregory even boasts that he did not heed Donatus' rules

when he was dealing with Holy Scripture.[6] My critic adds another inference: 'If anyone makes an error,' he says, 'he is not inspired by the Holy
Spirit and the evangelists were not inspired by the Holy Spirit.' As if the
standing of the evangelists and the apostles were the same as that of this
completely unknown Translator! Nor is there any harm in saying that the
Spirit governed the minds of the apostles in so far as it was present in their
meanings; but in their expression it left them to their own human ability,
because the common speech they possessed was appropriate for the gospel,
which was not to be proclaimed in words of human wisdom. The fact that
in the fourth edition I added a few words that softened the harshness of
my reproach he attributes to a bad conscience.[7] Not at all! I said this to
counter those who misrepresent everything, from whom nothing is safe.
My critic has persuaded himself that this Translator was a man of unimag-
inable holiness, who has most nobly served the church, and is reigning in
heaven. I confess plainly that I do not know what sort of man he was, nor
do I say anything reproachful about him – only about his language. 'But,'
you say, 'you should spare the dead.' Who ever had such regard for the
dead that in enquiring after truth he has not dared to disagree with them
or shown their opinion to be false? So what reason was there here for him
to threaten that my reproaches should be thrown back at me, this youth
who wants to seem so moderate? But all is well! He has spotted a way
out of the problem if the two genitives are attached to the word 'consciousness.' I mean 'consciousness of their thoughts, accusing or defending.'[8] That
is what the *Glossa ordinaria* suggested,[9] I admit, but quite shamelessly. For
against it there stands the pronoun αὐτῶν [their], there stands the conjunction καὶ [and], there stands μεταξύ [meanwhile]. And then, setting aside the
Gloss ordinaria, to this comment he adds, as is quite probable, that the genitive is used in the Greek manner for the ablative. But putting the genitive for the ablative in the Greek manner is nothing if not an error, especially if you translate one in Latin and leave the others as they are. There
was another way of excusing the Translator whenever he speaks incorrectly,
for he wrote for ordinary people in ordinary language. My critic will say,
'Why then do you not excuse him in that way?' Because that had not yet
occurred to me, as it had not occurred to Valla or to Lefèvre. If it had occurred to me, I would gladly have used that explanation. I do not consider
it a contrived reason, nor do I detest the Translator. And if my critic attributes this error of language to the Holy Spirit, how do the holy Doctors dare to use a different expression? 'But,' says he, 'they nevertheless
repeat this phrase in the same way, though perhaps overlooking the awkwardness of the expression, or, more probably, scribes emended those few
passages for this edition.' See what a serious charge our youth has found,

so that he can virtually spit upon his elder. But while he is ready to wrangle as much as possible with Erasmus, he is more moderate against Valla and Lefèvre, although for the most part they dealt more harshly with the Translator than I.

1   Rom 2:15; CWE 56 82–3; *Collationes* 73v–77v. The problem here is that two Greek constructions with the genitive absolute were not translated by exactly parallel constructions with the ablative absolute in the Latin. See CWE 56 83 n1 for the Vulgate and Erasmian texts of the whole phrase. Cf *Soloecismi* LB VI *5v.

2   *Hippias maior* 298a

3   *hic patet, quantum illi sit in aliis tribuendum.* Erasmus paraphrases his annotation: *satis argumento potest esse, quantum illi fidendum sit in aliis.*

4   *Collationes* 74r and 75v

5   *Adnotationes* in Valla 1 856 2

6   Donatus, a grammarian of the fourth century whose pupils included the future St Jerome, wrote two *Artes* that were standard school texts throughout the Middle Ages. The *Ars minor* explained the eight parts of speech; this is probably an allusion to the *Ars maior*, which included sections on good and bad expression.

7   The 'few words' were two sentences added in 1527: 'I am speaking of the propriety of language, not of thoughts. It is not necessary to ascribe everything to the Holy Spirit.' The rest of the annotation was added in 1535 in response to Titelmans. See CWE 56 83 nn12 and 13.

8   CWE 56 83 n1 explains that in the Greek these are parallel clauses in the genitive absolute construction; a literal translation should therefore give two equivalent Latin ablative absolute constructions. The Translator, however, kept the Greek genitive absolute construction in the second clause, making the sentence impossible to construe in Latin. The Greek, to which Erasmus refers here, is: γραπτὸν ἐν ταῖς καρδίαις αὐτῶν, καὶ μεταξὺ ἀλλήλων τῶν λογισμῶν κατηγορούντων ἢ καὶ ἀπολογουμένων 'written on their hearts, while their conscience also bears witness and their conflicting thoughts accuse or perhaps excuse them.'

9   *Collationes* 77v; *Biblia latina* VI f a[7]v

[ER *ecce tu Iudaeus cognominaris* 'Behold, you are called a Jew.']
[RESP] *si autem tu Iudaeus cognominaris* 'but if thou art called a Jew.'[1] I said that ἰδὲ, that is, 'behold,' was the truer and older reading.[2] I said 'older' because that is what I found written in the older manuscripts; I said 'truer' because it is simpler and less awkward. He puts up against me Origen and Theophylact, but verses from which nothing can be deduced.[3] But ἰδὲ 'behold,' expressing more vehement reproach, made the sequence of the words less awkward, as I pointed out. According to him, 'No rash changes should be made departing from the reading of the ancient authors, so that we can run after novelties.'[4] What? Have I removed what is in the church's edition? Do I not rather excuse the accepted reading? So this splendid dictum could have been used elsewhere.

1 Rom 2:17; cwe 56 83–4; *Collationes* 77v–78r
2 The other Greek reading is εἰ δέ, that is, *si autem* 'if however.'
3 Origen *Comm in Rom* 2.11 pg 14 894–8/fc 103 135–40; Theophylact *Expos in Rom* 2.17 pg 124 372c. See cwe 56 84 n3.
4 *Collationes* 78r, the last sentence

[ER *non is qui in manifesto Iudaeus* 'not he who is outwardly a Jew']
[RESP] *non enim, qui in manifesto Iudaeus* 'for not [he] who is outwardly a Jew.'[1] Because of a Hebrew idiom, I think, Paul expressed what he meant rather obscurely when speaking Greek. I rendered this more clearly, making explicit those words that were understood.[2] 'But,' he says, 'the Translator's expression is no more obscure than the Greek.' Let's suppose that this is so. Is it not permissible to supply what is omitted, especially in a publication that is prepared with the purpose of understanding the Vulgate more correctly? And yet I did suggest that Greek articles have a brevity of their own, so the expression becomes less clear for us. If the Translator had wanted to render the Greek exactly, he should have said, 'For it is not the one who is so outwardly who is a Jew, nor is it what the flesh outwardly is that is circumcision.'

1 Rom 2:28 'For it is not he is a Jew, who is so outwardly'; cwe 56 89; *Collationes* 78r–v
2 As well as the antecedent pronoun *is*, Erasmus adds *Iudaeus est* to the end of the phrase.

From chapter three

[ER *quid igitur habet in quo praecellat Iudaeus?* 'And so what has the Jew in which he is superior?']
[RESP] *quid ergo amplius est Iudaeo?* 'What more therefore has the Jew?'[1] Although he is saying the same as I, he still argues against me. He proceeds as if *eximium*[2] [exceptional] is not measured against something lesser, though no word expresses the fact more clearly. 'But,' says he, 'it is followed by "has the Jew."' Is it not correct to say, 'What is exceptional about the Jew?' or 'What exceptional thing does the Jew have in comparison with everyone else?' And does *excellit* [excels] not signify a comparison with lesser things? No word could say it more explicitly; no one excels unless there is someone to whom he is superior. Now *amplius* is an ambiguous term; the phrase can be taken as meaning 'What does the Jew have besides, in addition to what has been said?' Anyway, the Greek adjective is positive, not comparative – περισσόν [exceptional], not περισσότερον [more exceptional] – and *amplius* translates πλέον [more] rather than περισσόν.

1 Rom 3:1 'What advantage then hath the Jew?'; cwe 56 90; *Collationes* 78v–79v

2 Translation of the Greek περισσὸν, used by Erasmus in his annotation. See the last sentence of the item.

[ER *illis commissa sunt oracula Dei* 'To them were committed the oracles of God.']
[RESP] *credita sunt illis eloquia Dei* 'The utterances of God were entrusted to them.'[1] He informs me that something is 'committed' without being 'entrusted,' because one who 'entrusts' has confidence, not so one who 'commits.' Not at all; who, unless he is stupid or trying someone out, 'commits' something of consequence to anyone he mistrusts? Is not someone who gives a loan on a trial basis said in Latin to 'give credit' [*credere*] and to be a *creditor*? And where then do jurists get the expression *fidei commissum* [bequest in trust]? A weighty note indeed! And it was not without reason that I preferred *commissa sunt*; the ambiguity has been avoided. If this fellow thinks that is unimportant, Jacques Lefèvre slipped up here. Yet this censor does not seem to notice how Lefèvre had been deceived. For Lefèvre thought that *eloquia* here is a nominative case preceding the verb ἐπιστεύθησαν 'entrusted,' though it is an accusative following the verb. For this is how the Greeks say it: 'He was entrusted a son,' just[2] as Latin speakers say, 'He was taught grammar.'

1 Rom 3:2 'The words of God were committed to them'; CWE 56 90–2; *Collationes* 80r–v
2 'Just as ... grammar'; Erasmus is quoting cases where an accusative follows a passive verb. The example is a delightful sarcasm.

[ER *oracula Dei* 'oracles of God']
[RESP] *eloquia Dei* 'utterances of God.'[1] Λόγια, which [the Translator] renders as *eloquia*, I translated as *oracula Dei* [oracles of God].[2] In the first place, *oracula* is more idiomatic Latin than *eloquia*, at least in this sense; then *oracula* is a loftier word, for *eloquium* is used of human speech too, *oracula* only of God. My critic cries that *oracula* is said of the responses of the gods given by word of mouth. That is so, sometimes. But quite often they were given out in written form. Even so, if he finds it offensive because it is used of 'the gods,'[3] they also say 'the oracles of Apollo,' and it is not wrong for us to say the 'temple of God' just because they used to say the 'temples of the gods.' Nor can the word offend by its novelty, since it is not unusual in the Scriptures, especially in the Old Testament. 'But *oracula* seem to be so called from *os* [mouth].' No, rather from *oratio* [speech]. We speak orally, granted, but writing is also said to be speech. 'Which part of the body, in fact, do we use to form speech? Is it not the mouth?' And yet we are said to speak by means of the written word. Otherwise how can they

be said to be 'oracles' of God since God has no mouth? Finally, since we call a human pronouncement, uttered with authority, an 'oracle,' what is to prevent everything contained in the Scriptures from being called the 'oracles of God,' which make known to us the divine will? 'But,' says he, 'in some places *oracula* would not do for λόγια,' and elsewhere I myself have translated λόγια as *eloquia* – surprising indeed, if for the sake of the meaning another word fits better in another place. What need was there, pray, to fill sheets of paper with such trifles?

1   Rom 3:2 'words of God'; CWE 56 90–2; *Collationes* 81r–v
2   A reference to the lexicographer Hesychius was added to the annotation in 1519 in support of *oracula* (Reeve II 356) and quoted by Titelmans (81r). Erasmus seems to avoid repeating it here and in his prefatory letter (145 n35 above) accuses Titelmans of unnecessary 'recitals of readings' from authorities including Hesychius.
3   In the plural

[ER *fidem Dei faciet irritam* '**shall make the faith of God without effect**']
[RESP] *fidem Dei evacuavit* '**has made void the faith of God.**'[1] Although it is clear that καταργήσει [shall make useless] is future tense and that no one is accusing the Translator here, but that it is likely this was an error made by scribes – because many people pronounce b^2 as *v* and *v* as *b* – this man still defends the reading.[3] If he thinks this is the Translator's doing, what reason was there here for him to depart from the Apostle's word? What a weighty defence!

1   Rom 3:3 'shall their unbelief make the faith of God without effect'; CWE 56 92; *Collationes* 81v–82r
2   σ [sigma] *pro v, v pro* σ] *1529*; σ *pro* ζ [zeta], ζ *pro* σ *in 1540*. Neither reading explains a difference of tenses in the Greek. It seems more likely Erasmus was referring to an error by the Latin copyists and that his *b* (written *b*) was misread in 1529 as sigma, and consequently his *u* as upsilon. The emendation of *1540* (followed by LB) is a further misguided attempt to explain on the basis of the Greek.
3   Titelmans would defend the perfect tense; the modern Vulgate has the future *evacuabit*.

[ER *imo sit Deus verax* '**Rather let God be true.**']
[RESP] *est autem Deus verax* '**But God is true.**'[1] Since it is clear that the reading is γινέσθω [let him be] in all Greek sources and the commentators agree, why does this man prefer *est* [is] rather than *esto* [let him be]? 'This,' says he, 'is how "is" is expressed in the Psalm: "Every man is a liar."'[2] In that passage there is no verb; but suppose there is. Can Scripture on that account not express it differently, especially as the meaning is the same?

What the prophet perceived there, [Paul] wishes to make clear to everyone here. And the testimony he adds from the Psalms has the subjunctive
mood: *ut iustificeris* [that you may be justified].[3] My critic claims this is what
is found in the approved commentators; I agree, but sometimes we find exceptionally *esto*. Accordingly, whenever we find *est*, let us believe either that
the passage is corrupt there or that they are not reproducing Paul's words
but his meaning.

1   Rom 3:4; CWE 56 92; *Collationes* 82r–83r
2   Ps 116 (115 VG):11 *omnis homo mendax*
3   Ps 51:4. Rom 3:4 continues: *sicut scriptum est ut iustificeris in sermonibus tuis
    et vincas cum iudicaris* 'As it is written, "That thou mayest be justified in thy
    words, and mayest overcome when thou art judged."' Erasmus is arguing that
    one should read: 'Suppose God to be true ...' See also CWE 56 93.

[ER *mundum* 'the world']
[RESP] *hunc mundum* 'this world.'[1] I excuse the Translator's version, although he does not do it consistently.[2] But my critic rejects what my note
said – 'as if there is another world' – and informs me 'another world' is
used in allegory. I was afraid, however, that philosophers would suspect I
meant other worlds similar to our own.

1   Rom 3:6; CWE 56 96–7; *Collationes* 83r
2   Erasmus had admitted that the addition of the article in Greek sometimes
    implied that a specific thing is being designated.

[ER *ac non potius (quemadmodum de nobis male loquuntur)* 'but not rather
(as they say in reproach of us)']
[RESP] *et non sicut blasphemamur* 'and not as we are reviled.'[1] He agrees
with me here. But I laughed and took it as a joke that when he proposed
his meaning, he makes me answer as if I translated as best pleased him,
following his advice. But he does the same in the next note and in many
others. Come, we must forgive this young man.

1   Rom 3:8 'and not rather (as we are slandered)'; CWE 56 97; *Collationes* 83r–v

[ER *obnoxius fiat totus mundus Deo* 'All the world may become guilty
before God.']
[RESP] *subditus fiat omnis mundus Deo* 'All the world may be made subject to God.'[1] Instead of *subditus* I translated *obnoxius*, but without condemning *subditus*. 'But,' says he, 'a woman is "subject" to a man without being thereby "guilty."'[2] And admission of the crime causes a man
to give himself up because he has no way of defending himself. I do not
know what ὑπόδικος may mean,[3] but Chrysostom interprets it thus: Ὁ γὰρ

ὑπόδικος κυρίως ἂν ἐκεῖνος λέγοιτο, ὁ μὴ δυνάμενος ἑαυτῷ ἀρκεῖν πρὸς ἀπολογίαν
'Hypodicus means literally one who cannot provide of himself for his own
defence.'[4] And since in the preceding passage [Paul] said neither Jews nor
Gentiles have kept the Law and immediately afterwards mentions sin,[5] of
which we have knowledge[6] when the Law reproves our conscience, this
is consistent with my translating more correctly with *obnoxius* rather than
subditus.

1   Rom 3:19; CWE 56 99; *Collationes* 84v–85v
2   Erasmus' recall here is not even paraphrase of Titelmans, who does not use this
    example; the nearest he comes to it is to say that ὑπόδικος may mean 'subject
    to another,' 'having an obligation to another' (*Collationes* 85r *in fin*).
3   This is the Greek word translated by *obnoxius* or *subditus*.
4   Chrysostom *Hom in Rom* 7.1 PG 60 442
5   Rom 3:9
6   *peccati, cuius cognitio fit*; see Rom 3:20 and CWE 56 99, where Erasmus declares
    a preference for *agnitio peccati* 'acknowledgment of sin.'

[ER *dum comprobatur testimonio legis ac prophetarum* 'being now sanctioned by the witness of the Law and the prophets']
[RESP] *testificata a lege et prophetis* 'being witnessed by the Law and the
prophets.'[1] In Scripture people are said to have witness borne about them
[μαρτυρεῖσθαι] when others testify about them. Among Latin speakers this
is not the case, and I do not know whether *testificare* can be used passively.
Certainly I have not found an example up until now; so with the addition of
a verb even the suspicion of error seemed to be excluded, and the sequence
of tense has been preserved. But my words in no way prevent you from understanding either that the glory of the gospel was foretold by the prophets
or that the Law bears witness of divine justice in that it declared that all are
sinners and are in need of God's glory, for the verb in the present tense is
used in such a way that it refers to all times.

1   Rom 3:21; *Collationes* 85v–86v; Erasmus made no comment on this verse in his
    Annotationes until 1535 when he added an annotation on the first part (CWE 56
    100–1) but not on this phrase.

[ER *destituuntur gloria Dei* 'are bereft of God's glory']
[RESP] *egent gloria Dei* 'do need the glory of God.'[1] In the Greek codices I
find no other reading than 'the glory of God.' Again it is not surprising that
some have mentioned 'grace'[2] since it is God's gratuitous kindness towards
us that takes away the glory of our works and throws the light on his own
glory. And for this reason we should not read in the text what is added by
the commentators.[3]

1   Rom 3:23; CWE 56 100; *Collationes* 86v–88r

2   It is not clear of whom Erasmus was thinking here, though it must be certain
    commentators, as his last sentence seems to confirm. The word *gratia* does not
    appear as a variant in the Vulgate at this point. See CWE 56 100 n4.
3   Titelmans, who agrees with both Lefèvre and Erasmus that the correct read-
    ing is *gloria*, not *gratia*, nevertheless takes two and a half pages to con-
    firm it and refers here to Sedulius, the *Glossa ordinaria*, and Nicolas of Lyra
    (87v).

[ER *destituuntur gloria* 'are bereft of glory']
[RESP] *egent gloria* 'do need the glory of God.'[1] My critic is not satisfied
that I translated with *destituantur*[2] instead of *egent*, 'because,' he says, '*des-
titui* is said of those for whom there is no hope.' True, if you add *peni-
tus* [utterly], as he does. But people who speak correctly say 'bereft of
strength' of those who lack the strength to achieve what they want. However, the Greek is ὑστεροῦνται, and I have tried to make clear the particular
significance[3] of the Apostle's term, which is equivalent to saying, 'They are
behind,' and someone 'is behind,' 'is left behind' if he does not succeed.
For Paul is arguing here that neither the Jews nor the gentiles could, of their
own strength and without grace, achieve the justice and mercy that shine
forth in God's glory. Since this word [*destituere*] is more appropriate for
the meaning and expresses better the particular significance of the Greek
term, I preferred it to *egere*, seeing that even after the Gospel has been proclaimed, all are in need of [*egent*] God's grace. *Carere* [to lack] was more
appropriate than *egere*, for even someone who has may still need more. But
it is frivolous of him to tell us that the only ones 'bereft' are those who
are utterly rejected from grace, since God sometimes deprives [*destituat*]
true believers temporarily of his grace so that they may acknowledge their
weakness.

1   Rom 3:23; CWE 56 100; *Collationes* 88r–v
2   *destituantur*] 1529 12r, 1540 794, LB (subjunctive); *destituuntur* ER, Erasmus' an-
    notation, and *Collationes* (indicative). Since *egent*, the verb it replaces, is indica-
    tive, it seems likely this is simply a mistake that has gone uncorrected.
3   Latin *emphasis*, a word with which Titelmans makes great play at many points
    in his *Collationes*. Cf CWE 56 8 n3; Chomarat II 806–15.

[ER *ad ostensionem iusticiae suae* 'to declare his righteousness']
[RESP] *ad ostentationem iustitiae eius* 'to declare his righteousness.'[1] Instead of *eius* I have translated *suae*.[2] Since my critic is only guessing, without
any authorities, I do not think there is anything to confute.

1   Rom 3:25–6 'to the shewing of his justice'; *Collationes* 89v–90v and VG *ad osten-
    sionem iustitiae eius.* The phrase occurs twice in this passage in slightly differ-
    ent forms. In his *Annotationes* Erasmus makes no comment on it, rendering it

in his translation the first time as *ad ostensionem iustitiae suae* and the second time *ad ostendendam iustitiam suam*.

2   More correct than *eius* when referring to the subject of the principal clause

[ER *interveniente ipsius sanguine* 'through the intervention of his blood']
[RESP] *in sanguine ipsius* 'in his blood.'[1] Since *in sanguine* is hardly good Latin, I have made the meaning clear with a little circumlocution. My critic is not dissatisfied with this.

1   Rom 3:25 (immediately before the preceding item); *Collationes* 90v–91r; again Erasmus made no comment on this in his *Annotationes*.

[ER *ubi ... gloriatio?* 'Where is the boasting?']
[RESP] *ubi est gloria tua?* 'Where is then thy boasting?'[1] I pointed out that *tua* is not added in the Greek, but from translated commentators it cannot be shown conclusively what they read. Now, with omission of the possessive adjective, the phrase is more inclusive. For as it stands, it seems [Paul] is speaking only to the Jews, and in this case the singular possessive is rather awkward. If the possessive is left out, the reproach can be read as addressed to all; besides the remark is weakened by the addition of the possessive. For it is not only the boasting of the Jews that is rebutted but all cause of boasting. 'Where is the boasting?' means 'What reason is there for boasting?' However the article [ἡ] in ἡ καύχησις 'the boasting' does provide some support for the Translator.

1   Rom 3:27 vg *gloriatio*; cwe 56 102–3; *Collationes* 91r *gloriatio*

[ER *qui iustificabit circumcisionem* 'who will justify the circumcised']
[RESP] *qui iustificat circumcisionem* 'who justifies the circumcised.'[1] I am quite satisfied with *iustificat* [present tense] if the Greek codices agree. Since the majority of these have δικαιώσει [future tense], I made the distinction of tenses apparent: in one period many placed their faith in works of the Law or in the teachings of philosophy; in the other it was made clear that justification could not be hoped for except through the grace of the gospel. This future tense does not exclude those who were justified by grace before the Law and under the Law. For at that time it was a matter for judgment, but now it is thrown open to the whole world through the gospel. I do not know what my critic might mean by *plenius* [more fully]; if someone names Jews and pagans, does he not include all men? Perhaps he wanted those already justified to be included; as I said, they are not excluded by the future tense. In any case, given the consensus of the Greek readings, how will those who are already justified be justified?

1   Rom 3:30 'that justifieth circumcision'; cwe 56 103; *Collationes* 91r–92r

From the fourth chapter

[ER *imputatum est ei ad iustitiam* 'It was imputed to him for righteousness.']

[RESP] *reputatum est illi ad iustitiam* 'It was reputed to him unto justice.'[1]
Here Erasmus is scourged again with extraordinary severity because he
threw in the face of that saintly man the Translator his 'childish striving for
variety.' Indeed these words may well be fitting for some Jew or pagan or
some otherwise base man. But if my critic did not make the Translator a
man equal to the angels, there would be no need for these loud reproaches
in which this pillar of moderation indulges himself so strangely. He excuses
Valla for having written a more moderate note on this passage, as if that
man never criticizes the Translator unrestrainedly.[2] But when, after spelling
out several passages, [Valla] says, 'Who can believe that in Greek these are
one and the same word?' is he not showing his distaste clearly enough? Then
my teacher gives us instruction on this matter out of Perotti.[3] But why was
it necessary to resort to this when Valla, whom he admires, gives better information in book 6, chapter 44 on the difference between *imputare, deputare*
and *reputare*?[4] My critic says, '*Imputare* is used only of bad deeds, *reputare* or
deputare of good deeds.'[5] I say rather *reputare* is used of what we turn over
in our minds, especially things past. And *imputare* is used not only of bad
deeds but also of good deeds when they are called to account. However,
Valla doubts whether the verb *imputare* is found in Cicero, but he suggests
it is used without any implication of reproach. The examples that he quotes
from Quintilian have a favourable sense.[6] Only Pliny the Elder, in the preface of his *Historia mundana*, uses it otherwise, humorously: 'And so you
will impute this boldness to yourself and excuse your part in my guilt.'[7]
He said, 'You will impute' for 'You will attribute,' speaking of his fault.
Valla adds this too: '*imputare* is also used of items that form part of an account,' a meaning that *computare* also has, except that Juvenal used *computare* in an absolute sense: 'counting [*computat*] now his years upon his
right hand'[8] – where *supputare* is more usual. But *deputare* is simply 'to esti-
mate' or 'suppose.' Thus Terence: 'My master reckons [*deputat*] my work is
not worth much,' and in his *Phormio*: 'Anything unexpected that happens,
he should count [*deputare*] it all as gain.'[9] In the argument of the *Pseudolus* Plautus used *deputare* as if it were equivalent to *valde putare* [to believe firmly]: 'I think [*puto*] enough has been said already, and so I believe [*deputo*].'[10] Terence in the *Adelphi* used it for *subduco* [reckon up]
or *supputo* [compute]: 'It is in vain that I make these private calculations
[*deputo*].'[11] Now the two examples that Valla quotes from the jurists are
such that it is more likely that the abbreviator scribes[12] changed *reputare*

into *imputare*.[13] For in the passage he quotes from Ulpian, at the first oc-
currence there is *imputare* and in the later one *reputare*. And if the text has
no errors, who is ignorant of the fact that in those times when eloquence
was declining, certain terms were in use that nowadays the learned prefer to avoid. My 'teacher of the old' should have considered these matters
before prescribing for me, like an oracle, the proper use of these words.
'Who ever,' says he, 'heard of virtue being "imputed" [*imputari*]?' Nevertheless, if in the context of marriage a girl's modesty is considered a
dowry, would it not rightly be said to be 'imputed' to her? So too, although Abraham did not have justification by works since the Law had not
then been proclaimed, yet his faith was 'imputed' to him for justification,
God accepting, as it were, his faith in place of works.[14] If this young man
wants to prescribe new rules for speaking Latin, let him prescribe them
for his own pupils, not for me. If only bad things are 'imputed,' how often
has blasphemy been uttered by those who say, 'God allows to be imputed
to himself whatever would be costly to his members.' And in the jurists,
how often are expenses or tasks or provisions or other similar things 'imputed' when there is nothing bad about them? 'But,' says he, 'the Fathers
read *reputatum est* here.' Doubtless they followed the Translator, who spoke
in the manner of common people, not in the manner of those who speak
correctly.

1 Rom 4:3; CWE 56 107–8; *Collationes* 92r–94v
2 In this case Valla (*Adnotationes* 4 in Valla I 856 2) expressed himself as quoted
   hereafter. It was Erasmus who used the words *puerilis affectatio copiae* 'childish
   striving for variety' (LB VI 578C).
3 *Collationes* 94r. Niccolò Perotti (1429–80) produced two popular works: an elementary grammar, *Rudimenta grammaticae*, and an encyclopedic commentary
   on book 1 of Martial's *Epigrams* entitled *Cornucopiae*, both of which were well
   regarded by Erasmus. See CEBR III 68.
4 *Elegantiarum linguae latinae libri sex* in Valla I 223
5 *Collationes* 93r
6 Valla's examples both come from the pseudonymous *Declamationes* XIX *maiores*,
   long attributed to Quintilian.
7 Pliny the Elder *Naturalis historia* preface 4. According to Ermolao Barbaro's
   notes to Pliny's preface, Erasmus may have found this variant of the title in
   any one of the 'old exemplars'; see Ermolao Barbaro *Castigationes plinianae* ed
   G. Pozzi (Padua 1974) I 23 (originally published in Rome, 1493).
8 Juvenal 10.249
9 *Hecyra* 799; *Phormio* 246 (see also 251)
10 *Pseudolus*. In the 1500 edition, which Erasmus is known to have possessed,
   the editor, Giovanni Battista Pio, states that he has found another 'argument,'
   which he has placed before the prologue and which begins: *Studete hodie mihi:*
   bona in scaenam affero ... The line quoted by Erasmus is line 19 (of 25): *satis*
   id dictum puto iam: atque deputo (f H [vi] v). The argument, headed *Prologus*, is

also found in the Filippo de Giunta edition (Florence 1514) f F iii r–v, but not in the edition by Giorgio Merula (Venice 1472), nor in that of M. Sessa and P. de Ravanis (Venice 1518).

11 *Adelphi* 208. The accepted text is now *frustra egomet mecum has rationes puto.*

12 Latin *scribae abbreviatores.* The *abbreviatores* were a class of scribes employed in the curia who produced the shortened form of papal bulls, the 'briefs.'

13 The two passages Valla quotes from Ulpian are *Digest* 27.3.1.4: 'Praeterea si matrem aluit pupilli tutor, putat Labeo imputare eum posse, sed est verius non nisi per quem egenti dedit, imputare eum oportere' (Further Labeo thinks that if the tutor makes provision for the mother of the *pupillus*, this can be charged); and *Digest* 27.3.1.8: 'Sed et si servis cibaria praestiterit, vel libertis scilicet rei pupilli necessariis, dicendum est reputaturum' (If he provided food for slaves or freedmen, that is, for those dependent on the property of the *pupillus*, it is to be held accountable).

14 Paul is referring here to Gen 15:6.

[ER *iis qui non solum genus ducerent a circumcisis* 'to those who not only traced their descent from the circumcised']
[RESP] *non his tantum qui sunt ex circumcisione* 'not to them only, that are of the circumcision.'[1] Here he promises grandly to show that all the authorities I invoked argue against me and support the Vulgate reading. But first he assumes something that is obviously false: that I deny that Abraham is the father of the gentiles. For who would deny what Paul clearly teaches in this passage? Indeed this is what my note shows when I say, 'For [Paul] does not mean that Abraham is the father of both Jews and gentiles but that he is not the father of the Jews unless they follow in his footsteps.' When I said, 'He does not mean,' I meant 'He does not mean by these words what we understand,' but that what preceded and follows explains that meaning. To what purpose then was it necessary to bring in so many authors' testimonies showing that Abraham is the father of all believers, both Jews and gentiles? That is what this whole passage shows. But the particle that I noted does not show this.[2] Theophylact does not agree with this, but it is not clear from his commentary what he read;[3] and it is possible that [Theophylact's] translator did not render it clearly. My annotation points out that in the Greek codex οὐ [not] was omitted through scribal negligence and added by someone else in the space above, but not in the right place. He says, 'It is not likely that Theophylact understood something different from Chrysostom.'[4] I agree, but in details of this sort it is difficult to judge from the Latin translations, something that my critic does all the time, for he does not seem to have read any Greek commentator.[5] He said, rather grandly and not without some irritation, 'About Chrysostom, whom you claim entirely as your own ...' What are you saying, dear boy? Do I make him so entirely mine that if you do not have a Chrysostom, you will not allow that anyone else has either?

What reason was there here for this taunt? No, it is Ambrose and Origen whom I claim here.[6] 'You do not report the words of Chrysostom,' you say. What need was there, since I have two most weighty authorities? Augustine rarely consulted the Greeks, and he had very faulty codices – something which is obvious from many passages. Chrysostom's words are as follows, since he asks for it: 'And of those who are circumcised – not simply "those who are circumcised," he [Paul] also adds, "to those who are merely of the circumcision." For if he is said to be the father of the uncircumcised, not because he was uncircumcised (although he was declared righteous when he was uncircumcised) but because they have emulated his faith, much more certainly is he the progenitor of the circumcised – and not because they have circumcision – if only they have faith.'[7] There he has Chrysostom's words, which he said he wanted to consider.

There remains one small difficulty concerning the conjunction repeated in the following phrase,[8] ἀλλὰ καὶ τοῖς στιχοῦσι [but also walk in the footsteps], which seems to hinder the sense.[9] From Chrysostom it is not clear whether he added it, and it is probable that it was added by scribes. See now how the whole direction of the passage demands this reading. Just before this, [Paul] stated that Abraham was the father of all the gentiles through the faith he had received when he was uncircumcised. He says, 'He received the sign of circumcision, a seal of the justice of the faith that is in uncircumcision, so that he may be the father of all believers through uncircumcision, so that it may be imputed for righteousness to them as well, and so that he may be the father of the circumcised.'[10] Is he not clearly stating here that Abraham, being uncircumcised, was justified by faith and that he is the father of all the uncircumcised who conform to his faith; and that though also justified when circumcised, he is the father of the circumcised by faith, not by circumcision? Indeed, lest anyone should believe that it is sufficient that they should be circumcised, he denies that the Jews are the sons of Abraham unless they resemble him in faith as well as in circumcision. This is why he adds 'to those who not only are of the circumcision, but who follow also in the footsteps of the faith ...'[11] Again, lest anyone should believe that circumcision is necessary after the promulgation of the gospel, he adds, 'This justification by faith is in the uncircumcision of Abraham.' Further, if you follow the Vulgate reading, see how awkwardly the context fits together: 'So that Abraham may be [the father] of the uncircumcised, being[12] justified by faith when he was uncircumcised, and [father] of the circumcised, not only of the circumcised but also of those who follow in the footsteps of the faith of our father Abraham when he was uncircumcised.' What need was there for him to repeat what he had said just before?

1   Rom 4:12; CWE 56 113–6; *Collationes* 97r–99r
2   The Greek negative particle οὐ; cf CWE 56 113.
3   Theophylact *Expos in Rom* 4:12 PG 124 393A–C. See CWE 56 115 n7.
4   Chrysostom *Hom in Rom* 8.3 PG 60 457–8
5   Not fair. Titelmans has certainly read Origen; see, for example, on Rom 4:17, 179 below.
6   Ambrosiaster I 136–7; Origen *Comm in Rom* 4.2 (8) PG 14 969A–B/FC 103 250. Erasmus claims the unquestioned support of these two first, then Chrysostom and Theophylact with some reservations (see CWE 56 113).
7   Given in Greek and Latin; I translate Erasmus' Latin.
8   In the NT
9   That is, the καὶ in ἀλλὰ καὶ 'but also,' corresponding in the Vulgate to *sed et*. See CWE 56 115–6 nn14 and 17.
10 Rom 4:11. Erasmus quotes here according to the Vulgate (but reversing the order of the last two phrases), not from his own translation (cf 1529 14v). VG 'Et signum accepit circumcisionis signaculum iusticiae fidei, quae est in praeputio: ut sit pater omnium credentium per praeputium, ut reputetur et illis ad iusticiam, ut sit pater circumcisionis' (And he received the sign of circumcision, a seal of the justice of the faith, which he had, being uncircumcised; that he might be the father of all them that believe, being uncircumcised, that unto them also it may be reputed to justice). In Erasmus' translation, where the difference of tenses is particularly noticeable: 'Et signum accepit circumcisionis, signaculum iustitiae fidei, quae fuerat in praeputio, ut esset pater omnium credentium per praeputium, ut imputaretur et illis iustitia, Et pater circumcisionis ...' 'He received the sign of circumcision, a seal of the righteousness of the faith, which had been in uncircumcision, so that he would be the father of all believers through uncircumcision, so that it would be imputed for righteousness to them as well, and [so that he would be] the father of the circumcised' (VG 324–5/LB VI 578B–580A). Erasmus has clearly put events in their historical setting instead of the Vulgate's timeless present.
11 Here Erasmus reproduces neither the Vulgate text nor his own, though it is effectively equivalent to his own. He continues the same shift of tenses as in the passage in the preceding annotation. In the Vulgate: *non his tantum qui sunt ex circumcisione sed et his qui sectantur vestigia fidei* 'not to them only, that are of the circumcision, but to them also that follow the steps of the faithful.' In Erasmus' translation: *iis qui non solum genus ducerent a circumcisis, verum etiam ingrederentur vestigiis fidei* 'to those who not only traced their descent from the circumcised, but set out in the footsteps of the faith' (VG 325/LB VI 580A).
12 *qui incircumcisus per fidem iustificatus est*] 1529 15r; *qui circumcisus per fidem iustificatus est* in 1540 796 and LB. This is a paraphrase of the context, but Rom 4:11 would seem to suggest that 1529 is what Erasmus intended.

[ER *non ei quod est ex lege tantum* 'not to that (seed) which is of the Law only']
[RESP] *non ei solum qui ex lege est* 'not to him only who is of the Law.'[1]
It is clear that the pronoun τῷ [to him] can refer to Abraham. But my critic says he cannot conceive who these two Abrahams are that I picture as one.

I shall put it briefly, since he asks to be instructed. There is the Abraham justified by faith when he was uncircumcised, whom the gentiles consider to be their father because of his faith alone. There is the Abraham justified by faith when he was circumcised, who is considered by a twofold right to be father by Jews who trace their descent from him and are circumcised like him and who also imitate him in faith. But in my translation I make the pronoun refer to σπέρματι [seed]. Is there anything strange about that, since I cannot give both meanings (though I approve of both)? 'But no commentator accepts this meaning.' What then? Can I not even point out that the text can be understood in several ways? And if there were surviving works of the ancients that have been lost, perhaps we would find this sense too.

1   Rom 4:16 'not to that [seed] only which is of the Law'; CWE 56 116–7; *Collationes* 99r–100r

[ER *qui vitae restituit mortuos* 'who restores the dead to life']
[RESP] *qui vivificat mortuos* 'who quickeneth the dead.'[1] I do not censure the Translator's version, but instead of *vivificat* I have translated *vitae resti-tuit*, to make a clear allusion to the fact that Abraham had been promised posterity when his body was already worn out, and that it was promised through Isaac, and he was ordered to put to death this only child. Yet he did not hesitate in his faith, knowing for sure that he who had made the promise was all powerful, so that he could recall the dead to life, that is, give to the worn out body of an old man the power to procreate or to bring a dead Isaac back to life. 'But,' says my critic, 'what never lived is not re-stored to life.' I agree; the body of Abraham lived when he was younger, and Isaac lived before he was ordered to be put to death (for to Abra-ham at that time, as he was preparing to immolate his son at the divine command, Isaac was as dead). This is the occasion for Chrysostom, depart-ing a little from the literal sense, to remind us of the resurrection.[2] And the Apostle talks of the resurrection of the dead at the end of this chap-ter. 'But,' says he, 'Origen explains here that the dead are the sinners.'[3] He may be allowed to philosophize in allegories; it is something he does freely, even to the point of strain. My task is to expound those things that are ap-propriate in the context of the present passage. But so be it; let us under-stand that it means all sorts of sinners. Does it not mean those who had been circumcised and later died in sin? And also those have been washed through baptism and slip back into sin and are restored to life through cleansing and penitence? Moreover, as the whole human race was alive in Adam when he was innocent, so it died in him when he sinned; and as Adam was restored to life through Christ, so in Adam all who believe are restored to life.[4] So what reason is there now to say that my circumlocution

does not fit the meaning? How much more properly would this good young man have used his leisure if he had produced something other than these trivia!

1 Rom 4:17; *Collationes* 100v–101v. The phrase is not glossed in the *Annotationes*. See *Paraphrasis in Romanos* CWE 42 30–1.
2 Chrysostom *Hom in Rom* 8.5 PG 60 460
3 Origen *Comm in Rom* 4.5 (10) PG 14 977 / FC 103 263–4
4 Cf 1 Cor 15:22.

[ER and VG] *vocat ea quae non sunt* 'He calls forth those things that are not.'[1] My critic gathers some questionable points from Latin authors or those translated into Latin, nor do I see what is relevant to me here. Augustine reads it in different ways. But since in the Psalms he clearly reads and expounds in a way that supports my translation,[2] it is likely that the other passages are corrupt.

1 Rom 4:17; *Collationes* 101v–102v. Again this phrase is not glossed in the *Annotationes*; but see CWE 56 119–20; and the *Paraphrasis in Romanos* CWE 42 30 with n11. Titelmans is actually disputing Erasmus' rendering of the following phrase, ὡς ὄντα, as *tamquam sint* 'as though they were.' Erasmus points out that the Greek for VG *tamquam ea quae sunt* 'as those which are' would be τὰ ὄντα.
2 Augustine *Enarrationes in psalmos* 104 (103 DV):11 PL 37 1396. See CWE 56 120 n5, where the phrase is associated with God's calling forth a famine in Ps 104 (105 AV):16.

[ER *se fore patrem multarum gentium* 'that he would be the father of many nations']
[RESP] *ut esset pater multarum gentium* 'so that he would be the father of many nations.'[1] I had translated with *credidit se fore patrem multarum gentium*. He is vexed by the preposition εἰς in εἰς τὸ γενέσθαι [in being], but he would not have been vexed if he had recognized the Hebrew idiom, for they commonly add this preposition, contrary to Latin habit: *qui confessus fuerit in me* [he who has acknowledged me];[2] *ero illi in patrem* [I shall be a father to him],[3] etc.

1 Rom 4:18; CWE 56 121; *Collationes* 103v–104r *ut esset*. VG *ut fieret* 'that he might become'; DV 'that he might be made the father of many nations.' Erasmus' annotation suggests that he preferred the accusative and infinitive construction rather than the final clause, because this is a noun phrase, object of the verb *credidit*.
2 Luke 12:8; but both 1527 and the modern Greek have πᾶς ὃς ἂν ὁμολογήσῃ ἐν ἐμοί.
3 Heb 1:5 ἐγὼ ἔσομαι αὐτῷ εἰς πατέρα

[ER *sic erit semen tuum* 'So shall your seed be.']

[RESP] *sic erit semen tuum sicut stellae coeli* 'Your seed shall be as the stars of the sky.'[1] I had pointed out that *sicut stellae coeli* is not in either the Greek codices or the old Latin ones; my critic thinks it has to be added because *sic* refers to another thing that is similar. But he should have remembered that whenever *sic* is understood demonstratively, it does not need anything further, as when someone points to a tortoise and says to a fat man, *sic ambulas* [That's how you walk]. Here I am certainly not censuring the Translator but pointing out an addition by someone else. How happy he is to disagree with me, and how he enjoys 'looking for a knot in a bulrush,'[2] every time declaring that he never speaks except before God in the most sincere charity.

1 Rom 4:18; CWE 56 121–2; *Collationes* 104r. VG *stellae coeli et arena maris* 'the stars of the sky and the sand of the sea.' In DV the phrase is not present. It is an allusion to Gen 15:5. In 1529 16r, 1540 797, and LB this item runs on as if part of the previous one, although in LB the cue phrase is italicized. In Erasmus' annotations it is the subject of a separate note.

2 *Adagia* II iv 76 *Nodum in scyrpo quaeris*

From the fifth chapter to the Romans

[ER *pacem habemus erga Deum* 'We have peace with God.']

[RESP] *pacem habeamus ad Deum* 'Let us have peace with God.'[1] I have translated ἔχομεν [we have (indicative)], as I find in the text. In the *Annotationes* I pointed out that certain commentators read and interpret ἔχωμεν [let us have (subjunctive)].[2] For Greeks who are familiar with reflexive verbs[3] it makes no difference to the meaning. I was not dissatisfied with the indicative, and indeed in my opinion it seems the more correct reading. For since justification is peace with God, what need was there to warn those who have peace with God that they should have peace with God? Nor is there anything in what follows to dissuade us from sinning, but everything declares the joy that is brought to us by faith in Christ Jesus, who was delivered for our sins and rose again for our justification. It is certain that Ambrose read it as indicative.[4] The words of his commentary make this clear: 'Faith, not the Law, makes us have peace with God. For [faith] takes away the sins that made us enemies of God and reconciles us to God; and because the Lord Jesus is the minister of this grace, through him we have made peace with God.' Here we have the clear testimony of one very weighty authority. My critic puts up Origen against me, but he has not understood him.[5] For there we have in this passage the very point that my critic hides, and [Origen] interprets what he reads in these words: 'Through these things that he has perceived – what it is to be justified by faith and not by works – [Paul] very clearly gives an invitation to the peace of God, which passes all understanding and in which consists the fullness of perfection.' That is what Origen says. My 'teacher of old men' has been deceived by the verb *invitare*. As if it meant someone proclaiming the praises of virginity or declaring the happiness of true believers is not inviting people to take up the things he praises! Moreover, [Paul] is not inviting the justified; he is congratulating them while inviting to this worthy state those who are not yet justified, in the same way as someone who congratulates the scholar, because he has laid up so much fame for himself by his writing, thereby invites others to take up studies. He could have deduced that it is to be taken in this way from what follows, again in Origen. He says, 'Although we were enemies of God, we have been reconciled to God.'[6] But he shows the consequence that one who has been reconciled to God no longer thinks those things that are inimical to God. And so there is no need of a verb in the subjunctive to express exhortation; in fact I suspect neither Chrysostom nor Theophylact read ἔχωμεν but ἔχομεν in the indicative.[7] For the codices do not use ω [omega] consistently but sometimes ο [omicron], sometimes ω [omega]; they seem to write either. This is evidence of corruption. What about the fact that the verb ἔχωμεν 'Let us have' is not appropriate for the exhortation that, once justified, we should flee those things that are inimical to God, but rather τηρῶμεν 'Let us keep.' You see, reader, how undeserved is this young man's stern reproach that I translated the Greek badly and contrary to the opinion of both Greek and Latin [writers]. How long a complaint would he weave here if he found me being silly in the same way?

1 Rom 5:1; CWE 56 127–30; *Collationes* 104v–105v. In *Collationes* there is no heading to mark the beginning of items from Romans 5, and the running title remains '*Super IIII. Cap. Epis. Ad Rom.*'

2 Erasmus means Theophylact, Chrysostom, Ambrosiaster, and Origen. See CWE 56 128–9 nn3, 4, 5, 7, 8; and nn4, 5, and 7 below.

3 *verba* αὐτοπαθητικὰ; apparently not in the sense in which modern grammars use the term 'reflexive verbs.' Erasmus seems to be thinking rather of what is now called the 'middle voice.' See CWE 56 129 n6, which reports that in all editions of the *Annotationes* before 1535, and therefore in those that Titelmans would have seen, Erasmus had used the term τὰ αὐτοπροστατικὰ, which seems to have meant 'the imperative mood' or possibly 'reflexive imperative.' This explains his reference to the imperative mood (*imperandi modum*) in the next sentence of the annotation and his question here: 'What need was there to warn [*monere*] those who have peace with God that they should have peace with God?' The change is not picked up by Reeve II 363.

4 Ambrosiaster I 150–1. According to the CSEL edition, all manuscripts have the subjunctive *habeamus*, but as Erasmus understands it and CWE 56 129 n7 remarks 'Ambrosiaster's is the only patristic interpretation that presupposes the indicative as the reading.'

5   Origen *Comm in Rom* 4.8 (1) PG 14 988B. See CWE 56 129 n9.
6   Origen *Comm in Rom* 4.8 (1) PG 14 988C/FC 103 279
7   Chrysostom *Hom in Rom* 9.1 PG 60 467; Theophylact *Expos in Rom* 5:1 PG 124 400B–C

[ER *per quem et contigit nobis ...* 'through whom it also happened that we ...']
[RESP] *per quem habemus*[1] *et accessum* 'through whom we have an access also.'[2] I had translated *per quem et contigit nobis, ut fide perduceremur in gratiam hanc* [through whom it also happened that we were led by faith into this grace]. He approves of the periphrasis (which this fellow always calls 'paraphrase'[3] – I don't know why). I preferred to translate thus to keep the past tense as well, which is the tense of ἐσχήκαμεν and make clear the particular meaning of προσαφωγή [access]. In case the note should be too short, it informs us that in Greek some verbs in the perfect tense have the meaning of an enduring action, not mentioning the fact that he took those examples from[4] this very note of mine. It's a trick he uses repeatedly.

1   *habemus et accessum*] 1529 17r, 1540 798; *et* does not appear in either VG or the *Collationes*.
2   Rom 5:2 'by whom also we have access'; CWE 56 130; *Collationes* 105v
3   Not quite fair; Titelmans uses both terms and generally distinguishes them correctly. 'Always' (*semper*) here may reflect the fact that in this article he uses *paraphrastice* or *paraphrasis* three times.
4   *ex hac ipsa annotatione mea*] 1540; *ex annotatione mea* in 1529, 'from my annotation.' Such additions lead one to suspect that 1540 was made from a copy of 1529 with ms notes by Erasmus. Cf CWE 72 xx.

[ER *sub spe gloriae* 'with the hope of the glory']
[RESP] *in spe gloriae* 'in the hope of the glory.'[1] There is nothing here that stands against me. I do not disapprove of the usual reading, but I have translated into Latin only what the Greek codices have.

1   Rom 5:2; CWE 56 130–1; *Collationes* 105v–106v. The annotation argues that there is no textual evidence or patristic support for *filiorum*, the word following *gloriae* in VG.

[ER *nec id solum* 'and not only this']
[RESP] *non solum autem* 'and not only.'[1] My critic claims that the pronoun can be omitted just as easily in Latin as in Greek. On the contrary, it is put in by Greeks in normal correct speech, never by Latin speakers. 'But,' says he, 'Scripture pays no heed to correct style.' So why does he combat so fiercely the idea that there are grammatical errors in the sacred books?'

1   Rom 5:3 'and not only so'; CWE 56 131; *Collationes* 106v–107r

[ER *porro spes non pudefacit* 'Moreover, hope does not make ashamed.']
[RESP] *spes autem non confundit* 'And hope confoundeth not.'[1] I preferred
to translate οὐ καταισχύμει as *non pudefacit*. He adduces a large number here
who read *confundit*. Why should they not? They have followed the Translator and the practice of ordinary people. How does this affect me? Ambrose knows Latin,[2] but because he uses the words of Scripture as commonly handed down and adjusts his speech to common practice, he often
speaks bad Latin. It annoys the man that the annotation says, 'What Latin
speaker would understand ...?' 'Everyone would understand,' he says. But
not as Latin speakers, my good man, for many Latin speakers understand
Greek words too. And my critic, please God, ties me up in a syllogism.
'If no Latin speaker would say *confundere* for *pudefacere*,' he says, 'then you
are not a Latin speaker, for in Acts 9[3] you have translated with *confundebat Iudaeos*.' This is laughable. As if I did not speak Latin simply because
I leave the word as it was normally read. I have left many words that are
scarcely Latin because they are the received ones and cannot be rendered
more aptly in Latin. But what did you want me to translate there, my most
ingenious young man – *pudefacit*? The word there is not καταισχύμει [shame]
but συνέχυνε,[4] which means precisely *confundebat*. 'But,' says he, '*confundere*
seems to be used here for *pudefacere*.' It seems otherwise to me. *Confundere* means *perturbare* [throw into confusion]. Hence people are said to be
confused when they cannot find understanding or a way out of a situation.
Am I really not a speaker of Latin because that is what it seems to mean
to this youth? 'But in Scripture,' he says, 'it is often used in this way.'
I don't deny it; it may be right according to the old practice of ordinary
people, but never according to the usage of those who spoke correctly. But
if it is enough for him that it is the usage of the Scriptures, let us assert
that it is Latin to say *qui me confusus fuerit coram hominibus* [who will be
thrown into confusion about me before men] instead of *quem mei puduerit*
[who will be ashamed of me] – for the former is what the translated Gospel
says.[5] *Suffundi* [to be embarrassed] is said of those who blush, and mental
confusion or disturbance is a consequence of a deep shame; but *confundi*
does not on this account regularly mean *pudefieri*. Drunkenness results from
drinking wine, yet οἰνοποτεῖν [to drink wine] was not on that account to be
translated as if it were μεθύσκεσθαι [to be drunk]. And even in a matter of
such little importance this pillar of modesty insults me: 'I willingly let pass
your *pudefacit* as more correct, if that is what pleases you, so that you can
change *confundere* to *pudefacere* everywhere; in exchange, allow the Latin
Translator the term *confusio* that he has had up until now.' Those are his
words.[6] Why? Have I eliminated the verb *confundere* from books? And how
can he call the Translator Latin when it is clear he does not speak in Latin

idiom? You see how thoughtlessly these things are said, and yet pages are filled with such trifling ditties after such boastful preliminaries.

1 Rom 5:5; CWE 56 131–3; *Collationes* 107r–108r. The third, fourth, and fifth sentences of the annotation were added in 1535 and repeat the substance of this response (see CWE 56 132 n2).
2 Ambrosiaster I 154–5
3 *act. 8*] 1540 798; *ACT VIII* LB; *Act. 9* in 1529 17v; Acts 9:22
4 See CWE 56 132 n3, where Erasmus mistakenly said the verb in Acts 9:22 was κατέχυνεν (132 n3). He has corrected himself here without noticing the discrepancy or without admitting it.
5 Mark 8:38; Luke 9:26
6 *Collationes* 108r. The final sentence of the article is quoted, for once, verbatim except for the addition of *tibi* 'you' before *placet* 'pleases.'

[ER *iuxta temporis rationem* 'in accordance with the order of the time']
[RESP] *secundum tempus* 'according to the time.'[1] I have shown that the Greek words can have two meanings, without disapproving of either; I translate only one, but in such a way that when the comma is moved, the other meaning also results.[2] Since κατὰ καιρόν in Greek means 'at the opportune time' or 'in accordance with the order of the time' rather than 'according to the time,' I translated with what would allow both meanings. For before the grace of the gospel was made known, the course of time was the cause of men's ignorance; thus in Acts Paul calls that period 'the time of ignorance.'[3] In this way Paul softens his condemnation of the life of unbelievers, putting the blame on the times, as does Peter: 'Turn[4] away from from this wicked generation.'[5] It is not incongruous that Christ is said to have suffered 'in accordance with the order of the time' instead of 'at the opportune time'; nor is it thereby not opportune if God determined it from eternity.

1 Rom 5:6; CWE 56 133–5; *Collationes* 109r–110r
2 In 1516 Erasmus placed a comma in both Latin and Greek texts before and after this phrase; in editions from 1519 to 1527 he removed the preceding comma so that the phrase could be read with 'when we were weak'; in 1535 he restored the comma before *iuxta*. See CWE 56 134 n2.
3 Acts 17:30
4 *convertimini*] 1529 18r and 1540 799; *servemini* ER, 'preserve yourselves'; *salvamini* VG, 'save yourselves'
5 Acts 2:40

[ER *pro bono forsitan aliquis etiam mori sustinet* 'Perhaps for righteousness someone even endures to die.']
[RESP] *pro bono forsitan quis moritur* 'Perhaps for a good man someone dies.'[1] It is marvellous how authoritatively this young man carps at things

he does not understand and teaches things he has not learned. Τολμᾶν in Greek is taken in two senses: 'to dare,' as it refers to an outrage or to a courageous act, sometimes 'to set the mind to' or 'wish.' Here in fact, since it is not so much a question of courage as of will and of setting the mind, I preferred *sustinere* [endure, bear] rather than *audere* [dare]. When we say, 'He cannot bear to resist the desires of his family,' this will be neatly expressed in Greek as οὐ τολμᾶ, but it would be very inappropriate to translate as *non audeat* [he may not dare]. At least my critic should have learned the precise meaning of this verb from the passages in Suetonius that I pointed out.[2] That would have been more modest than finding fault with things he had not understood.

1 Rom 5:7; CWE 56 136. The heading in *1529* (18r) and *1540* (799) is a confusion of the two phrases of verse 7; it does not correspond to the intended text (*pro bono forsitan quis* [*et*] *audeat mori*) or to what Erasmus discusses, the verb *audere*. This is probably because in the *Collationes* (110r–111v) there are two articles headed respectively *Vix enim pro iusto quis moritur* (directed exclusively to Valla) and *Pro bono forsitan quis audeat mori*. The meaning that Erasmus attributes to *pro bono* (the abstract thing, not a person) is made clear in the preceding annotation (CWE 56 135).

2 CWE 56 suggests *Augustus* 66.4, *Vespasian* 13.

[ER *quatenus omnes peccaverunt* **'inasmuch as all have sinned']**
[RESP] *in quo omnes peccaverunt* **'in whom [or, in which] all have sinned.'[1]**
Here I am aware of something that usually happens in theatres: one person has written the play, someone else does the performance.[2] Notwithstanding this is of no consequence to me, I should wish the person who supplied him with these ideas had advised him on all points. Indeed it is both more useful and more enjoyable to dispute with knowledgeable people. The essence of the whole of this excessively prolix complaint, however, is this: there is an original sin for which all mortals are answerable and of which they must be purged by holy bathing, whether they be babes or adults. Concerning this belief there is no dispute between us. He finds fault only in that I have interpreted this passage of Paul as applying to what is called individual sin, even though I did this in such a way that I did not exclude original sin. But he complains that by this interpretation a weapon against the Pelagians[3] and others who denied the existence of original sin is taken away from orthodox believers, and a rift is opened for the Pelagians to slip out of the net in which they are held; and he heaps up numerous factors in the decadence of the times that cause many people to turn aside at whatever slight occasion to ungodly beliefs – a complaint I share with him entirely. If only it were as easy to make remedies as laments.

But when my work was first published, there was nothing by way of comment either in the text or in the annotation of this passage that would exclude a reading assuming original sin. The text reads thus: *in quo omnes peccavimus* [in whom or, in which we have all sinned]. For it shows that this too can be rightly understood, that all men have sinned in Adam in whose loins they were hidden. The annotation has the following: 'Some refer *in quo* [in whom] to Adam, some to the particular sin of each person. I do not think it unreasonable to take ἐφ' ᾧ in the sense of "inasmuch as" or "since," so that the meaning is that through one man sin came into the world. Death, however, was the companion of sin; accordingly death came to all inasmuch as all had sin.' There is nothing here that cannot be understood as applying to original sin, and that edition was, if I am not mistaken, the very first, published in 1516[4] at a time when no one dreamed of the sects by which the church is now shaken. And this passage would not have aroused any tumult if Lee had not stirred one up, perhaps inspired by these same people who are now complaining vehemently.[5] Moreover, those who now adhere to the opinions of Luther are so far from being Pelagians that they accuse scholastic theologians of Pelagian heresy and are so far from denying original sin that they teach that it remains in infants even after baptism. If such danger hung over the church as this man wants to make appear, why did Jan Briart,[6] the leading light in that college both by his experience and by his skill in matters of theology, who at my request read the whole of my *Novum Testamentum*, not give a single word of warning, and particularly since I on my side had solicited this service from him with many prayers and he for his part had promised that he would carry it out in a brotherly spirit? Why at the very least was there no admonition from the man – who, if I am not mistaken, is now bringing up this complaint[7] – back then when he was asked as a friend and in a friendly manner, since I declared myself ready, as I was in truth, to correct anything that might be detrimental to morals or the purity of Catholic doctrine? A tiny admonition at that time could have remedied this evil that my critic now pretends is most horrible. But how can belated complaining provoke anything but evil? Not even Dorp warned me personally, and yet afterwards I noticed he had made some notes in the margins of his manuscript that he could have told me of when I was present, especially as he was asked both as a friend and in a friendly way.[8] So whence does this youth acquire such perception that he sees what they did not see, or such assurance that he dares cruelly to commit to print what they could not bear to warn me of when I was present and asking the questions?

Having said this by way of preliminaries, let me come to the main counts of accusation: the first is that I replaced Paul's 'through one man' [*per unum hominem*] with 'on account of one man' [*propter unum hominem*];

the second, that I replaced the verb 'passed universally to' [*pertransit*]⁹ with 'broke through upon' [*pervasit*]; the third, that for 'in whom all' [*in quo omnes*] I said 'inasmuch as all' [*quatenus omnes*]; the fourth he almost condones, where for '[all] have sinned' [*omnes peccaverunt*] I translated 'we all have sinned' [*omnes peccavimus*].¹⁰ These are the bases of the whole dispute on which he builds such bitter rebukes laced with insults and jokes. But hear now on the other hand how much easier it is to quibble than to view the matter as it is. In the first edition, since I did not have in Basel the manuscripts that I had collated, the one used at that time by the correctors, had δι' ἕνα ἄνθρωπον, and following this they put *propter unum hominem* [on account of one man].¹¹ For I do not myself correct the pages to be typeset; and if I did this job too, it is impossible but that something should escape notice. So, being now alerted by this rebuke, I looked to see what had happened: I examine the first edition, I examine the second, I examine the third and fourth; I find *propter unum*, except that in the second the margin had *per* added in my handwriting – *propter* having been crossed out – and the copyists seem to have missed this, for I usually entrust to them such things as are to be copied into another version. Besides, this censor could very well have found out how I myself read the passage from my annotation,¹² which has the following: 'Just as through [*per*] one man sin entered into the world, so also through [*per*] one man death entered.' And just before that: 'So through [*per*] one man righteousness came into the world,' which I wanted to correspond to the phrase 'Just as through [*per*] one man ... death.'¹³ That these words were not read by my fault finder I can scarcely believe; if he read them and is dissimulating, I am forced to find wanting in him that sincerity of a Christian heart that he preaches to me immediately after.¹⁴ Nor do I see any reason why I should have preferred *propter* to *per*. For as far as the sense is concerned, it is of very little importance which way you read it. What he tells me – that *per* indicates the true cause and *propter* the occasion rather than the true cause¹⁵ – is an ignorant fantasy; and yet from this argument he sets in motion such a melodrama. They occasionally differ in usage; there are times when one can be used for the other, except that *propter* sometimes indicates the final cause and *per* has the sense of the means. Nor does it matter whether you say, 'It was not possible to write because of [*propter*] my occupations' or 'It was not possible to write in consequence of [*per*] my occupations,' and 'In consequence of [*per*] your arrogance we are now detested by many people' or 'We are now detested by many people because of [*propter*] your arrogance.' Come, let him tell me, in what the Psalm says, 'For thy sake [*propter te*] we are killed all the day long,'¹⁶ whether *propter* indicates the true cause or some occasion or other? Consider now, my reader, what sort of modesty it is to adduce such unsupported absurdities in order to rebuke someone with such severity and almost to suggest heresy. As far as I know nothing here has been changed, and if it were, 'through one man' or 'because of one man' makes no difference to the sense; both phrases indicate the efficient cause. This for the first count.

With similar authority he informs me there is a distinction between *pertransire* and *pervadere*,[17] believing there is some remarkable special force in the verb *pertransire*, not to be found in *pervadere*, which expresses the idea that the evil arose from one individual and was spread out to all, when the fact is quite otherwise. In the first place, the verb *transire* [to pass, go through] is ambiguous, for someone who goes by is said to 'pass,' someone who goes over or crosses a mountain or a river 'passes,' someone who digresses to other subjects 'passes.' But I do not remember reading *pertransire* in the accepted authors.[18] What is occasionally said in the Scriptures, to 'go through' [*pertransire*], is not what flows down into all things, but what passes through the inside. This is what is meant when it says, 'A sword shall pass through your own soul.'[19] So too Paul, when he is indicating he will make a journey through Macedonia, says, 'I shall come to you when I pass through Macedonia.'[20] It is true, however, that if things jump over by contact from some people to others, one says *transire* in Latin, as in: 'Many things do harm by bodily transfer.'[21] And perhaps in this case *transire* [pass across] was more appropriate than *pertransire* [pass through], since the Greek word has only one prepositional prefix.[22] But it is good Latin to say, 'Plague or rumour *pervadit* [pervades] an army or a region,' since it spreads through everything. So this word, being better Latin, expresses the meaning no less fittingly. *Dimanare* [flow down] or *derivare* [spread out] would have been entirely suitable, but the verb *pervadere* also expresses the rapidity and violence of the contagion. So all this argument of his about the special force of the word that has been changed is frivolous. Do the morals of parents not pass [*transeunt*] to the children when they are corrupted by their example and turn out bad? This for the second count.

The fourth is not serious, and I did not know it was in my manuscript. But I suspect the fact is that in the manuscript from which I took it in England there was written ἡμάρτομεν [we have sinned] instead of ἥμαρτον [they have sinned], and this was afterwards left there through inattention; one can hardly avoid a slip of this sort with any amount of care. This is not an idle argument, as is confirmed by the fact that I made no mention of it in the annotation and I actually gave the reading 'they have sinned.' I am astonished that not one of the correctors has noticed it so far, since this task was undertaken in the first edition by Johannes Oecolampadius and Nikolaus

Gerbel, and in the fourth edition by Sigismundus, an exceptionally learned man.[23] However, although in other places too the annotations do not correspond to the text, it came about on this occasion because I carried out the task of collation in England and in Brabant, having no intention of adding a new translation, perceiving indeed that this was not so very profitable but likely to inflame a great deal of ill will. But certain friends urged me with excessive insistence and contrary to my inclination that since the edition of the *Annotationes* was already being finished, the text should also be renewed. In this process, since I was fully engaged elsewhere and had neither time available nor inclination, the work was completed with insufficient care. But, though I asked them time and again after they gave the advice to lend some measure of help, those who urged me to this could not be brought to the point of contributing even one little line. Then of course they were unwilling to be mixed up in someone else's work, though they had urged me, resisting and reluctant as I was, to undertake this further stage.[24]

Before I answer to the third count, I thought I might show, by the way, how wrong is this critic of mine. I explained in my answer to Lee why I preferred *pervadere* to *pertransire*.[25] Augustine was deceived by the ambiguity of this word, thinking that *pertransire* [pass through] is a word meaning *praeterire* [pass by].[26] My critic says, 'How could Augustine suppose this when he interprets this passage as referring to original sin, etc?'[27] But if he had read my notes with as much care as he hunts zealously for things to criticize, he would have recognized that in Luke, chapter 2[28] I censured Augustine for having misunderstood 'A sword shall pass through your own soul,' interpreting 'shall pass through' [*pertransibit*] as 'shall pass by' [*praeteribit*], and hence concluding that Mary also had doubted, but less than the disciples.

Now let me come to what is the principal point in this accusation. According to him, no one before myself translated ἐφ' ᾧ as *quatenus*; everyone had translated as *in quo*.[29] So be it, but people accustomed to the commonly spoken language, which imitated Greek, understood *in quo* as *quatenus*, or at least could do so. In other cases Greeks rarely say ἐφ' ᾧ when they mean something is 'in' something else, as the foetus is in the parent, or food is in the stomach; they say more often ἐν ᾧ. In fact the preposition ἐπί[30] is used in various ways in Greek: when it means 'towards' [*ad*] it takes the accusative case, when it signifies authority it takes the genitive case, as 'under this prince' or 'under this judge'; likewise when it stands for 'in' [*in*] or 'upon' [*super*], as in 'on the head' [*in capite*, ἐπὶ κεφαλῆς]. When it signifies proximity, it takes the dative case, as in 'at the approach of death' [ἐπὶ θανάτῳ], 'on the threshold of old age' [ἐπὶ γήραος οὐδῷ];[31] likewise when it signifies circumstance, as in 'on these conditions' [ἐπὶ τούτοις], that is, *hac lege*. Now since even as my adversary he concedes that ἐν ᾧ does not always mean 'in which' [*in quo*] but sometimes stands for ἐφ' ᾧ – yet here he contends that *in quo* is taken to mean that Adam's descendants are understood to have lain hidden within him – let him show me just one passage from the Scriptures in which ἐφ' ᾧ is used in a similar sense. In Hebrews, chapter 7, 'in the loins of his father' is not ἐπὶ τῇ ὀσφύϊ but ἐν τῇ ὀσφύϊ.[32]

But I am afraid that at this point he will again cry that I am supporting the party of the Pelagians.[33] It is not at me that this charge should be levelled but at those who with their stupid and malicious accusations make challenges and claims for this purpose.[34] 'But,' he says, 'Augustine condemned this interpretation in his treatise *Contra Iulianum*.'[35] But perhaps he [Augustine] would not condemn it so vehemently if he had been better skilled in Greek or had consulted Greek sources. And even if we suppose that ἐφ' ᾧ is what was written, is there anything more common for the Hebrews and for Paul than to use 'in' [*in*] for 'through' [*per*]? And are we not said to be corrupted 'through' [*per*] him who gives an example of sin? Nor do I fall under the reproach that Augustine hurls at Julian, because those people contended that this passage must be understood in this way.[36] I only give a warning that it can be understood in this way, but the meaning that Julian condemns I approve, and I do not reject it even in this passage, if that is what anyone prefers. But there is a danger that what this same Augustine writes against Julian is more fitting for you yourself, my very audacious young man. However, it is not on me that this fellow, who never wrote anything except from motives of the purest love, turns this reproach of Augustine so many times, repeats it so many times, hammers it in so many times, and heaps it up, since he himself admits afterwards[37] that the sense that Augustine defends can be understood from my words 'inasmuch as they have sinned,' certainly in our first parent in whom they are also said to have died. But he should have pointed this out before he started raving with so many terrible accusations against a brother a hundred times most dear,[38] and giving way so freely to his irritation. If original sin can be effectively proved from other passages in Scripture, why should we draw swords over this one? But he wants this one to be the most effective.

To me it seems otherwise. The passage in Job is more effective where it is said that a child on the day of its birth is not free of sin. For this is how the ancients quote this passage from the Septuagint,[39] although Augustine had some doubt about this too, whether it could also refer to individual fault, because he detected signs of envy and anger in the infant who looked with resentment on a sibling drinking from the same breast when there was abundant milk for both. Very close to this are the words of David: 'For behold I was conceived in iniquity.'[40] Finally, suppose there were no such scriptural passage: does the church not teach many things, as articles of faith, that cannot be clearly proved from the canonical Scriptures, such as the perpetual virginity of the Blessed Virgin? Is this not one of the dogmas particularly repeated in the schools?[41] Where does one read that it is forbidden to translate Holy Scripture into popular language, since it was first proclaimed in the language of the people and translated into a language of the people comprehensible to weavers, sailors, and ostlers? And yet now because of articles of faith like this men are burned at the stake.

But my critic is indignant if anyone disagrees with Augustine, who says this passage cannot be taken in any other way. If this is true, why do the scholastic theologians disagree, inasmuch as this is the essence of the prolonged and heated dispute in which he is opposed to the Pelagians? Augustine asserts that by the strength of his free will man can neither will to do good nor do good, neither begin it nor complete it, is only capable of evil;[42] [that] there is no merit in man, but God crowns his gifts in us.[43] Augustine insists on this at every point. And yet certain scholastics now teach that God owes eternal life to our works, not only because he promised it, not only because it is fitting [de congruo] but even because it is deserved [de condigno].[44] These are terms that Augustine would have anathematized as blasphemous, which the Pelagians never dared to pronounce. Augustine in his dispute with the Pelagians often asserts that baptism is of no benefit to infants unless they are given the body and blood of the Lord and believes this is demonstrated from these verses of the Evangelist: 'Unless you have eaten the flesh of the Son of Man and have drunk his blood, you will have no life in you.'[45] Zosimus interprets it in the same way,[46] and it is probable that the whole Western church was of this opinion. On this point we not only disagree with him but we even judge that what he believed to be a mighty weapon against the Pelagians is an error worse than heretical; for we teach that infants are saved by baptism alone without the Eucharist, and in the sacrament we do not give the blood of Christ even to adults. Moreover, just as we condemn the opinion of Augustine, so we reject the interpretation of Scripture on which he relies. And yet Augustine is called the Catholic Father, and this great commotion is stirred up against me just because I have pointed out that these two words, ἐφ' ᾧ, can be understood differently – though on the substance he is in complete agreement with Augustine, and I am with Augustine in abominating the Pelagians.

It is not only slanderous but obvious falsehood when he says that this interpretation is peculiar to myself and Pelagius alone. Does he know how this passage was interpreted by the oldest Greek Fathers who lived before

Pelagius? Nothing certain can be proven from Origen, as he is loosely translated. Only the books Περὶ ἀρχῶν [*On First Principles*] were translated by Jerome as they were written by the author, and this translation has been lost;[47] other things were translated in such a way that those that contained any un-Catholic doctrine were either passed over or corrected. My annotation on this very passage also shows just how slanderous, not to say malicious, it was to say that I share this opinion with Pelagius, though I declare my hatred of his opinion at every point. 'But,' he will say, 'you do have an interpretation in common with him.' Not even that is true. He [Pelagius] argues that this is the true sense; I only point out that it is likely that it can be taken as referring to individual sin, when Augustine would have it that the sin of action[48] is excluded by these words *in quo*. But how brazenly he says this interpretation is peculiar to myself and Pelagius, when he will have read in the *Scholia* – whose title claims they are Jerome's and are certainly by some learned man – extracted from the commentaries of scholars:[49] 'Sin came into this world by example' or 'pattern.' Again: 'And thus it has passed to all men, while they thus sin, they also likewise die.' But shortly after that: 'For it passed down to all men who transgressed the natural Law.' Then he adds: '"In which all have sinned," that is, in so far as all have sinned, they sin through the example of Adam.' Is this author not clearly explaining this passage as referring to the sin of action and not evoking original sin by even a word? So how can this man pretend that this opinion is peculiar to myself and Pelagius?

There is no doubt but that this censor has looked carefully at this passage [of Pseudo-Jerome]. For if he is pretending that there is no question of some wicked 'trick'[50] here, where is that sincerity in the sight of God that he proclaims so often? 'But a council, the council of Milev I think,[51] pronounces an anathema on those who interpret this passage otherwise than Augustine interprets it,' and, we should add, as the synod intended: 'and interprets it as Pelagius interprets it.' But not even what my critic relates is entirely true, as is amply clear from the fragments of the councils in which we read the following: 'Whoever denies that newly born infants should be baptized or says that they are baptized in fact for the remission of sins, but that they bear nothing of original sin from Adam ... let him be cursed.' And then there follows: '... for it is not to be understood otherwise.'[52] And I am not bound in this respect by an African regional council, for there were many councils in which it was decreed that those baptized by heretics should be rebaptized. How many anathemas there are in those councils, which Hilary translates for us not very satisfactorily into Latin! In the Council of Sirmium[53] it is said, 'If someone speaking of the Holy Spirit the comforter should say that he is the uncreated God, let him be cursed.' Someone will say, 'By the "uncreated" they mean the Father.' But if ἀγέννητος is said of one who is not born, this term is fitting for the Holy Spirit no less than for the Father; but if ἀγέννητος means one whose existence had no beginning, it is equally fitting for all [three] persons. Finally, since in particular African councils many other decrees were made that the church has either disregarded or corrected, I shall not allow myself to be incommoded by the authority of such councils, unless there is a question of something that is obviously contrary to true belief. I have stated that there is nothing of this nature in this passage and will state it more fully in the future.[54]

Now he opens another subject of debate in which he deploys his triumph. I had mentioned briefly that Chrysostom and Theophylact interpret this passage as referring to anyone's personal sin.[55] Here this very modest young man fells me with blows of his fists and spits in my face, no less, even citing the legal rule that no one may use the defence of having been deceived and tricked.[56] And though the whole book swarms with such remarks, he boasts of his modesty and swears that he has no desire to slander or to utter any insult. He could have said that I had considered this passage with little care. That is very true. For looking more exactly now, I see that Origen too interpreted this passage as referring to individual sin. Origen's words are as follows: 'The Apostle has declared in an unqualified statement that the death resulting from sin has passed universally to all men in so far as all have sinned.[57] Elsewhere too: "All have sinned and fall short of the glory of God,"[58] and if you were to mention even that righteous man Abel, he cannot be excused. For all have sinned . . .'[59] And in case anyone should hold back at this, saying their sin was original sin so as to approve of what Origen said, he [Origen] explains Abel would not have offered sacrifice if he had not sinned. He makes the same claim about Enosh, who, he said, was the first to call upon the Lord because he had earlier despaired, conscious of his own guilt. He makes similar statements about Methuselah and about Noah.[60] However, up to this point a shifty fellow could twist these witnesses to refer to original sin, but what he brings in about the drunkenness of Noah utterly refutes this remark.[61] In addition, what he says about Abraham – that he would not have gone when ordered to leave his country if he had been able to please God there – if he were not pleasing to God for the reason that he was subject to original sin, he would have been no less displeasing abroad than at home. Finally, in case anyone should quibble that these are remarks made by way of digression according to Origen's judgment and not following Paul's opinion, [Origen] concludes his catalogue thus: 'But there is no need to take the immense risk of enumerating each one of the saints, since there is sufficient

answer also in the Apostle's opinion, which says that death passed universally to all men, and [in the opinion] of him who said, "No one is free of
uncleanness even if his life were of a single day."'[62] From this it is clear
that Origen read this passage, which these people argue speaks especially
of original sin, as referring to personal sin. For it makes no difference that
there we read *in eo in quo* for ἐφ' ᾧ, since these are the Translator's words,
not Origen's.

This becomes clearer from the words with which he continues. For he
points out the exactness of the Apostle's language and shows us that Paul did
not say, 'Sin entered into all men,' but it 'entered into the world';[63] and he
said, 'Death spread to all men,' not 'to the world.' The 'world' he interprets
as 'men given to worldly appetites.' This comment, whatever we may think
of it, makes it quite clear that he does not take the passage to refer to original
sin, which, there is no doubt, passed universally to all. However, he notes the
verb 'pass universally' [*pertransire*], because death does indeed enter since it
is imposed upon us, but sin 'passed to' us [*transiit*], certainly by the contagion
of imitation. Again, what [Paul] says about the death from sin that came to
Christ but was driven back and did not 'pass through' to him [*pertransiit*],[64]
is not compatible with original sin. For [original sin] did not come to him,
but when the Lord was tempted, in a sense death from sin came to him.

Ambrose disagrees with Origen here and says, 'All have sinned in
Adam as though in a lump.'[65] But the words that follow, 'For until the Law,
sin was in this world,'[66] which can hardly be taken otherwise than as referring to personal sin, he connects with what went just before, 'All have
sinned in Adam as though in a lump, and all were born under sin,' because
by this expression he seems to be saying that they were born subject to
death because of Adam's sin. Otherwise the words that he associates do not
make coherent sense. 'But here,' they say, 'Paul turns to the other sort of
sin.' But the conjunction *enim* [for] is not at all suitable for such a transition,
and[67] it is found consistently in both Greek and Latin sources. 'For' has introduced the cause whereby sin passed through to all because the Law that
imposed a penalty for sin had not yet been proclaimed and people sinned
with impunity, as it were, in the world, since everyone thought he was allowed to do what he liked. This argument has no relevance to original sin,
and the words that precede do not obviously imply original sin. [Ambrose]
says that all have sinned in Adam as though in a lump, not because infants have really sinned the sin that Adam committed but are in some degree participants in the misfortunes that Adam brought on himself by his
sin. They are exiles from paradise, they are liable to sicknesses and death,
and finally they are born with a propensity to sin, a desire that Paul sometimes calls sin. They are said to be under sin and sinners; so, for example, if

someone having contracted syphilis through immoral intercourse has children whose physical health is poor, his children have not sinned themselves
but have, as it were, sinned in their parent.

As for Theophylact's witness,[68] he is so awkwardly translated and has
so many mistakes in the printing that even now I cannot see clearly enough
what he believes, and the matter was dealt with hastily at that time. I had
the Greek itself, but the pages were so mixed up through the carelessness
of the copyists that often I could not find what I was looking for. I had
Chrysostom in Greek, but badly copied and even with parts missing, so
that I was in some doubt whether it really was Chrysostom. It seemed to
me at the time that I understood from it the meaning that I indicate in my
Annotationes. Since then I have acquired a complete [Chrysostom] of my
own, on examining which I find that Theophylact used almost his words,
except that he sometimes mixes in a word or two. Chrysostom explains the
particle *in quo* thus: 'What is the meaning of "in whom all have sinned"?
When [Adam] fell, even those who had not eaten from the tree became
mortal from him.'[69] He does not say that they sinned in Adam but that
through him they became mortal. In what follows [on verse 13], however,
it seems as if he corrects the first opinion (for he suggests two) with the
second as fitting Paul's thought better. But I rather think the argument he
accepts has not enough weight. This is how he argues: 'Before the Law sin
was not imputed, so how was it then that even before the Law all died?
It is to be understood, therefore, that the sin of Adam held sway.' But
Ambrose refutes this argument, saying that before the Law of Moses it was
the law of nature that was applied. The[70] same [author] explains this word
imputabatur [was applied] quite differently.[71] I do not have Athanasius in
Greek to hand at present.[72] The Dominicans used to excuse themselves,
saying they kept back books in this way so that they should not be taken
away to other cities. I responded that they had allowed it on occasion.
They admitted this, but said, 'On that occasion we lost some volumes.' The
translation, however, to speak honestly, I do not understand well enough
even now, and it could be that, as my critic guesses, I was distracted by
various thoughts and was deceived by these words of Theophylact: 'They
became mortal by their wickedness [*suo crimine*].' *Suo crimine* was added by
Theophylact or perhaps by his translator;[73] the rest agrees with Chrysostom.
But my critic shows that *suo* [their] is a mistake for *illius* [his]. At least it is
clear from this how much danger there is of speaking incorrectly.

So since he understands that I was mistaken on a demonstrable occasion, what is the point of those cries about trickery and about a strange intent to corrupt this passage of Paul? He should have admitted in the beginning what he admits now,[74] that there was no call for such cries of trickery

and shrewdness. But because he did not want to omit them, he deferred his confession to the end. And if the man who now incites this little crow[75] had offered a word of warning about my slip, it would have been picked up in the subsequent editions. Why is it so important if it happens that I fail to see something somewhere in a work of such diversity, when this fellow, decked in feathers not his own, talks nonsense so often, as here where he does not understand Origen!

Thereupon he comes back to his hue and cry about how wicked it is to snatch away the protection of Scripture from orthodox believers.[76] As if the protection of the Scriptures is taken away by the one who does not allow them to be violated! But if I have pointed out several passages in which the Doctors of the church misuse the witness of Scripture against the heretics – and one can point to more if the occasion demands – in noting these one does not shake the authority of the church but confirms it. He will object that such behaviour is a stumbling block. I wrote these things for the learned, not for ordinary people, and the stumbling block must be attributed rather to those who[77] attack with enormous outcries these briefly noted points. But if my critic is justified in crying out against me because I pointed out that this passage can be interpreted as referring to personal sin, let him also cry out against Jerome. Jerome interprets the witness of Ephesians, chapter 2 as referring to something other than original sin and in the end indicates that the Greek text is ambiguous, that φύσει [naturally] sometimes means *prorsus* [certainly] or *omnino* [altogether].[78] Why does he not shout that courage has been given to the Pelagians, that orthodox believers have been disarmed because Augustine turns this witness too against the Pelagians? Why does he not cry out against Origen who interprets this passage as referring to the sin of each individual?[79] Now the protests he heaps up with extraordinary loquacity about the impiety of certain men of our time, whose intention seems to be to introduce either Judaism or paganism to us instead[80] of Christianity – this is more applicable to those who have so unashamedly abused[81] their authority, have oppressed Christ's flock with tyranny, have diverted the Scriptures to human teachings, have offered human regulations in place of divine teachings, have tied up the consciences of the simple in too many entanglements, who have hitherto deceived the innocent with tricks and hypocrisy and deluded them, not to say insulted them as if they were simpletons, and caused them so many evils. Who ever found cause for error in this passage? And if there were some cause, do not many hunt for cases of error in well-meant statements every day?

There remains the sophistry that I suspect he has borrowed from the *Quodlibetica*, for I recognize the author's mind and style no less than his

face.[82] And he is not ashamed to let this little crow thus blazon himself
in other birds' feathers,[83] as if no one has the nose to detect anything. 'A
proposition,' says he, 'consists of axiom and argument and cannot be said
to be true unless each constituent is true. For if either has any falsity, the
whole statement is false.'[84] He posits three types of sin: original, venial, and
mortal. Then three types of death: death of the body, the death of hell, and
the shadow of death.[85] He says:

If you understand 'in that all have sinned' to refer to individual sin, it is widely
agreed that innumerable infants die who have not committed any sin at all. Therefore
since the premise is false, it follows that the whole enthymeme is false, and certainly
the statement that death passed through to all; on the contrary, it was the death of the
body that passed to all. Nor did death pass to all because all are corrupted by their
own misdeeds, but it is through Adam's transgression that they have now become
mortal, whether they sin or do not sin, and hence again the whole proposition is
false. Now if we understand [the passage to mean] mortal sin for which alone the
death in hell is inflicted, there is a double falsity since that death does not come to
all, nor did this sort of sin flow down to all. And so if the passage is understood as
referring to original sin and we understand 'death' as the shadow in which infants
who died without baptism are held, there is no difficulty.

I could make a knot to set against his:[86] if the sin of Adam passed through
to all and that sin was the mortal one for which the death in hell was the
penalty, the whole of this proposition is false according to the reading of
such people, because this sin did not pass to all, nor did any penalty fall
on anyone from it.

   Let us not, however, waste time on such niceties. I take death here
as the separation of the soul from God, which is created in us by the sin
we have committed; this death would have passed to all while they were
deprived of grace and ravaged by their appetites, and the death in hell
would have passed to these same souls if grace had not come to their aid.
For this is now my interpretation: Paul is speaking here not of infants who,
as I believe, were not customarily baptized at that time but of adults, as
he does almost everywhere. This is made likely by the very context of the
discussion. In chapter 3, [the words] 'They have all turned aside, together
they are become unprofitable'[87] cannot be referred to original sin. Likewise
the preceding passages in the first and second chapters where he reproaches
the gentiles for their evil deeds.[88] And it does not refer to anything else
when he concludes against both [Jews and gentiles], 'For all have sinned
and fall short of the glory of God.'[89] Nor does there seem to be anything
that refers to original sin in the fourth chapter, whose conclusion is 'Who

was delivered for our offences and rose again for[90] our justification.'[91] When this conclusion is followed by this statement 'Therefore being justified by faith ...,'[92] it is very clear that this too refers to the sin of action. And what follows shortly – '[Christ] died for the ungodly'[93] – cannot be referred to infants; they are said to be exempt from justice and cannot be said to be unrighteous. And so since up to this point the whole discussion has dealt with personal sins and to this is added, 'Wherefore, as by one man sin [entered into the world],'[94] does it not seem clumsy to have gone over suddenly to another sort of sin? There is nothing here either to force us to read it in the sense of original sin, except this phrase 'in[95] whom all have sinned.' For through one man sin came into the world, he who was the first author of sin and fathered and still fathers children prone to sin.

Now I think the importance of *in quo* is sufficiently explained. I have shown that Origen interprets it as referring to the sin that these people call personal. But what Ambrose intended when he says, 'As Adam sinned in all, so Christ conquered in all,'[96] I leave to others to discern. For if we are said to sin in Adam as he sins in us, the meaning is very obscure. In what follows shortly after this, both the reading and the interpretation are at variance. The first part, 'But sin was not imputed when there was no Law,'[97] seems to be about our own offences. Whichever way the passage is turned early on by Chrysostom, from whom Augustine extracted certain words – calling him 'Bishop John' without adding the place name, because he had already been driven out of his see, although not struck out of the catalogue of bishops[98] – certainly the words that then follow are perfectly fitting for the sin of action.[99] Where then is there anything here that forces us to bend this passage of Scripture to mean original sin? 'But Augustine argues that it is to be understood thus.'[100] What was the point of this as far as the Pelagians were concerned? This is what the Council of Milev taught?[101] Not even that moves them. This passage is not essential for us who[102] consent to the decrees of the church and believe even without Scripture.[103] 'But infants are baptized in vain if they have no sin.' That I have never said. Although what the nature of this sin may be is not so far sufficiently agreed among the scholastics. I believe that there is [sin] in infants, which the sacrament of water washes away through the faith of the church. He says, 'This cannot be deduced from any other source.' This is false. 'It cannot be deduced as effectively.'[104] It seems otherwise to me. But if it is not right here to deviate by as much as a wide straw from Augustine, why do the theologians speak more mildly about the damnation of infants than Augustine, who says in the book *De fide ad Petrum*, 'These, unless they are reborn, are to be consumed by the eternal fires.'[105] This work does not seem to be by Augustine, though many passages are quoted from it in the *Sententiae* and in the decrees of the popes.[106] For while he writes many harsh things about infants, often allots to them annihilation, damnation, ruin, and denies that they are saved, as far as I can rightly remember he never says that they are consumed by the eternal fires. I have said these things not because we should doubt that there is some original sin – far from it – or because this passage cannot include original sin, but because it is not necessary to involve original sin here. Origen affirms at length that the passage is full of obscurity and that Paul touched on certain things that he was unwilling to develop fully.[107] These remarks are sufficient answer for this long and clamorous wrangle.

1   Rom 5:12 'in whom all have sinned'; CWE 56 137–61; *Collationes* 113r–135r. Titelmans' article is headed *Propterea sicut per unum hominem peccatum etc* and raises objections against Erasmus on all the parts of Rom 5:12. The second of Erasmus' two annotations was greatly expanded in *1535* on the basis of this response and the *Responsio ad annotationes Lei*. The texts of the annotations of *1516–27* are translated in CWE 56 151–2 n2.

2   Erasmus suspects the 'writer' is Latomus; see the prefatory letter 138 n2 above.

3   See the introduction xxxiii n95 above.

4   For additions to the text in *1519* and *1527*, see Reeve II 565, appendix A; CWE 56 151–2 nn1 and 2.

5   After considerable procrastination, Lee's *Annotationes* were published in February 1520. See CWE 72; and the introduction xiv above.

6   Formerly dean of the faculty of theology and vice-chancellor of the University of Louvain and a supporter of Erasmus, Briart had on some occasions been the object of the latter's suspicions as an opponent of the *Collegium trilingue* and as responsible for the attacks of Maarten van Dorp and Edward Lee. Before Briart died in 1520, however, Erasmus seems to have acknowledged that his real enemies were others, including Latomus. His question at this time (1529) would therefore suggest that he implies Briart had found nothing objectionable in his *Annotationes*, not that he had not examined them properly. See CEBR I 195–6.

7   Latomus again; see the prefatory letter 138 n2 above.

8   For Maarten van Dorp, who had died in 1525, see CEBR I 398–404; Rummel *Critics* I 3–13 and II 63–4.

9   The prefix *per-* implies completeness or universality of the action, and the verb *pertransire* is sometimes used hereafter to show that original sin passed to all men, which is not usually what is meant by 'pass through.' I have therefore preferred, where it is necessary to make the distinction, to translate it as 'pass universally.' Erasmus has another distinction (see 188 after n14) but equates it with *pervadere* as meaning 'spread through everything.'

10   From *1516* to *1527* Erasmus' version had *quatenus omnes peccavimus*. Titelmans says that he does not understand why Erasmus put the verb in the first person, but that it gives no cause for suspicion (*Collationes* 114v–115r).

11   The preposition διά with the accusative, as here, may correspond to Latin *propter* 'on account of.' With the genitive, as in the Greek followed by Erasmus (and Titelmans), it may correspond to Latin *per* 'through, by means of.'

12 CWE 56 137–9. Erasmus uses *per* in all cases.
13 See the last paragraph of the annotation.
14 *Collationes* 123v–124r
15 *Collationes* 115r
16 Ps 43 (44 AV):22
17 Cf CWE 56 141 and 154–5 n19; *Collationes* 116r–v
18 It is found once in Pliny *Naturalis historia* 37.5.18 §68, otherwise only in the Vulgate and other late Latin texts.
19 Luke 2:35. See CWE 56 154–5 n19.
20 1 Cor 16:5
21 Ovid *Remedia amoris* 616
22 That is, the Greek verb διέρχομαι has only the one prepositional prefix (διά), whereas the Latin *pertransire* has two (*per-* and *trans-*).
23 See the relevant articles in CEBR III 24–7 and II 90–1. Sigismundus is Zikmund Hrubý z Jelení or Gelenius (CEBR II 84–5), who is known to have collaborated on several editions by Erasmus and was named by the latter, in the will executed on 22 January 1527, as one of the editors of the collected works to be published after his death.
24 See the references to Briart, Latomus, and Dorp, 187 above.
25 Ep 1037 (Lee's preface); *Responsio ad annotationes Lei* (1520) CWE 72 270–1, concerning n142. See also CEBR II 311–14.
26 *Quaestiones veteris et novi testamenti* PL 35 2267–8. These are now thought to be by Ambrosiaster, not Augustine; see CWE 56 154–5 n19.
27 *Collationes* 116v
28 Luke 2:35; *Annotationes* LB VI 236D–E; Reeve I 166. Cf n19 above.
29 *Collationes* 117r. Erasmus was also attacked on this subject by Noël Béda. See the *Divinationes ad notata Bedae* LB IX 469A–B and the *Declarationes ad censuras Lutetiae vulgatas* CWE 82 208–10.
30 ἐπί becomes ἐφ' before an aspirated vowel.
31 Homer *Iliad* 22.60, *Odyssey* 15.348
32 Heb 7:10. Here Erasmus has correctly repeated the definite article; cf CWE 56 154 n16.
33 See 191 above and the introduction xxxiii n95.
34 Edward Lee had made this accusation in notes provided to Erasmus between 1516 and 1519 and published in February 1520; see n25 above; and *Responsio ad annotationes Lei* (1520) CWE 72 269–70, concerning n141. In a letter to Georgius Spalatinus (1516), Luther had objected to Erasmus' annotation on this passage (and to those on Rom 9:31–2 and 10:3); this letter was extensively quoted by Spalatinus to Erasmus in Ep 501, 12 December 1516. Luther persisted in accusing him of Pelagianism in *De servo arbitrio* (1525; *D. Martin Luthers Werke* [Weimar 1908] 18 664 and 755), responding to the *De libero arbitrio*, where Erasmus explicitly rejected Pelagius' position (CWE 76 78 and 86) and adopted one closer to St Augustine's (CWE 76 79–80). Erasmus replied in *Hyperaspistes* 1 (1526) CWE 76 268–79 and in *Hyperaspistes* 2 (1527) CWE 77 341, 677, 700, 720–1, again condemning Pelagius' position. Luther did not reply to these. The paraphrase of this verse also evoked the name of Pelagius from Béda; see the *Declarationes ad censuras Lutetiae vulgatas* CWE 82 208–11, with Erasmus' response following, and n29 above.

35 *Contra Iulianum* passim, with particular reference to Rom 5:12 at 1.3.8, 1.7.33 FC
35 9 and 40. For Augustine's anti-Pelagian works, see CWE 56 152–3 nn4 and
5; PL 44; and CSEL 42. Titelmans (*Collationes* 118r) also refers to the *Expositio
super Lucam*.

36 *Collationes* 118r–v

37 *Collationes* 130r

38 Latin *in fratrem centies carissimum*; the literal expression is not in the *Collationes*,
but see the prefatory letter 139 n5 above.

39 Job 14:4–5; quoted again through Origen at 195 n62 below.

40 Ps 50 (51 AV):5 'For I know my iniquity, and my sin is always before me.'
Both of these passages are quoted by Titelmans.

41 The subject had been much discussed since the appearance of Cajetan's *De
conceptu B. Mariae Virginis*, dedicated to Leo X. See NCE 7 378–82.

42 *1529* (22r) and *1540* (802) have a question mark here.

43 Cf for example Augustine *Contra Iulianum* 6.12.39 FC 35 344–5.

44 For these scholastic terms, see Oberman 169–72 and 207–9. Cf also *De libero
arbitrio* CWE 76 28–9 with n106, where the 'certain scholastics' are identified as
followers of Scotus.

45 John 6:53. See CWE 56 159 nn66–9.

46 Pope Zosimus (AD 417–18), successor of Innocent I. See CWE 56 152–3 n5. For
more on disagreements with Augustine, see the annotation at CWE 56 148–50.

47 Only fragments of the original Greek survive, and the only complete version
is the translation of Rufinus.

48 *peccatum actionis*; ie the sin of imitation or individual sin

49 That is the *Hieronymiana*, as Titelmans refers to them, or the scholia of Pseudo-
Jerome, which, unfortunately for both the disputants, were primarily the work
of Pelagius. See Souter II 45 and III 8; see also *Apologia de loco 'Omnes quidem'*
53 n42 above; and CWE 56 142 and 155 n22.

50 Latin *machinamentum*; the word is Titelmans' (*Collationes* 128r).

51 Probably the Council of Milev (AD 416); Mansi 4 355D. This is an objection that
Erasmus attributes in his annotation to his opponents; see CWE 56 148 and 158
n61.

52 The editors of CWE 56 (148 and 158 n62) compare these anathemas to those
translated by Hilary *De synodis* 1.13–16 PL 10 490–4. They are also cited by
Titelmans (*Collationes* 129v).

53 The Synod of Sirmium (AD 351)

54 An undertaking for the expanded *1535* version of the annotation?

55 Latin *de peccato cuiusque proprio*; this term is used by Titelmans (*Collationes* 119r).
Erasmus had mentioned these two names in *1527*, adding 'And yet both views
amount to the same thing.' He now strengthens his assertion that they support
his view of Rom 5:12 as a reference to individual sin. Chrysostom *Hom in Rom*
9.1 PG 60 470 (with reference to Rom 4:25); Theophylact *Expos in Rom* 5:12 PG
124 404B–C.

56 *Collationes* 119r

57 Latin *in eo in quo omnes peccaverunt*, which, as Erasmus points out at the end
of the paragraph, does not authorize Titelmans' reading. Cf *Annotationes* CWE
56 144, where, however, Erasmus uses the passage to argue against those who
would interpret Rom 5:12 to refer to the sin of infants.

58 Rom 3:23
59 Origen *Comm in Rom* 5.1 (20) PG 14 1011B–1012C / FC 103 313–15
60 Gen 4:2 (Abel), 26 (Enosh), 18 (Methuselah), 5–10 (Noah)
61 Gen 9:21
62 Origen *Comm in Rom* 5.1 (21) PG 14 1012C–1013A / FC 103 315. As Erasmus
    remarked earlier (at n39 above), the quotation is an allusion to Job 14:4–5
    according to the Septuagint.
63 I use the words of DV. Erasmus uses two different words for 'entered into':
    intrasse and *introisse*, but there appears to be no significant difference of mean-
    ing in this context. The explanation may be that the Vulgate used the former at
    this point, and Erasmus, in his translation and in the latter case here, follows
    the translator of Origen.
64 As is clear from the following sentence, Erasmus takes this as referring to the
    moment of the temptation of Christ, not to the crucifixion. Death did not 'pass
    through' to Christ as it 'passes universally' to humanity, not because he was
    free of original sin but because he was the exception to the rule of mortal
    weakness.
65 Ambrosiaster I 164–5
66 Rom 5:13
67 *quae constanter habetur*] 1540 804 and LB; *quae constet aut* [sic] *habetur* in 1529
    24v. I follow 1540 and LB; the latter italicizes *enim* after the word *conjunctio*
    'conjunction.' The Greek conjunction is γάρ.
68 Theophylact *Expos in Rom* 5:12 PG 124 404B–C. See the annotation, CWE 56 147
    and 157 n54. Titelmans' objections here (*Collationes* 119r–122r) obliged Erasmus
    in 1535 to expand his hitherto brief allusions (CWE 56 151–2 n2).
69 Given in Greek. The *Annotationes* add *ex illo* 'from him' (CWE 56 146), which
    Erasmus seems to have inadvertently omitted from his translation here. See
    n73 below.
70 *idem, illud imputabatur, longe secus exponit*] 1529 25v; 1540 (804) and LB omit the
    comma after *idem*, and LB fails to put *illud imputabatur* in italics, as it would
    normally with quotations. I translate as I understand 1529.
71 Ambrosiaster I 166–7 (with reference to Rom 5:13)
72 Titelmans does not mention Athanasius at this point.
73 Theophylact *Expos in Rom* 5:12 PG 124 404B–C. The words were in fact added
    by the translator; the correct reading is *ex illo* 'from him,' ie 'from Adam' or as
    Titelmans suggested (*Collationes* 119v–120r) *illius* [*crimine*]. See n70 above and
    CWE 56 157 n54. Erasmus is referring here to the Latin translation of Theo-
    phylact by Christopher Porsena, librarian to Pope Sixtus IV. He had known
    since 1518, having found a Greek manuscript of Theophylact in the library of
    the Dominicans in Basel in that year, that the attribution to Athanasius was
    false and had said so in the annotation of 1519 on Rom 1:4 (*qui praedestina-
    tus est*): 'These words are used by the translator of the work falsely ascribed
    to Athanasius. (As I had earlier suspected, I discovered once I had compared
    the Greek and Latin that this was the work of Theophylact)' Reeve II 337.
    See CWE 56 12, 15 n25, and 157 n54. There is a fuller account in the annota-
    tion on 1 Cor 12:27, most of which was added in 1535 (LB VI 721E–F / Reeve II
    497): '. . . Theophylact, the Latin version of whom was originally put out by
    certain publishers with a completely false attribution to Athanasius. [Rome:

Udalricus Gallus, alias Han, 25 January 1477, f 2r: *In prima Pauli ad Romanos epistola Athanasii prologus*] And it is said this was done not as a result of carelessness by the publishers but by a deliberate trick of Christopher Persona [sic] himself, who translated this work. This is attested by the manuscript that Christopher presented, beautifully ornamented, to Pope Sixtus IV. He had inserted the attribution "Athanasius" in red capitals, although he makes no mention in the preface of either Athanasius or Theophylact. So it seems he deceived the pontiff. This story is told by people who have seen the manuscript conserved in the Pontifical Library.' See also *Apologia ad annotationes Stunicae* ASD IX-2 131 457n.

74   *Collationes* 122r

75   Jacobus Latomus (Jacques Masson); see the prefatory letter 138 and 141 with nn2 and 13 there.

76   *Collationes* 122v–125v

77   *qui*] *1529* 26r; *qua* in *1540* 804 and LB. I translate following *1529*, since a relative clause following *illis* 'to those' seems to be called for.

78   Eph 2:3 *eramus natura filii irae* 'And we were by nature the children of wrath.' Cf CWE 56 150 and 160 n70; Jerome *Commentariorum in epistolam ad Ephesios* PL 26 497–8.

79   Origen *Comm in Rom* 5.1 (12–14) PG 14 1009A–1010C / FC 103 309–11

80   *pro Christianismo*] *1540* 805; *pro Chrysostomo* in *1529* 26r. There is no mention of Judaism in this section of the *Collationes*, but Erasmus is probably thinking here of the exordium (*Collationes* 133r–134v), where Titelmans does speak of atheists and 'seekers of novelties' who respect nothing – a clearly antihumanist outburst.

81   abused ... oppressed ... diverted] *abutebantur ... praemebant ... detorquebant 1540* 805; *abutentes ... prementes ... detorquentes 1529* 26r. The present participles of *1529* subordinate these three actions to the following finite verbs, *praeferebant* 'offered,' etc; the *1540* correction makes them all equal elements of the list.

82   Latomus again? Is Erasmus referring to *quodlibetica*, oral exercises he has listened to at Louvain? Latomus' nephew, also Jacques Masson, included some hitherto unpublished *Quodlibetica* in the posthumous edition of his uncle's *Opera* in 1550; see De Jongh 179–80 with n3.

83   See the prefatory letter 141 n13 above; perhaps also Horace *Epistles* 1.3.19–20.

84   The following alleged statements of Titelmans are only a summary paraphrase, and Erasmus does not use quite the same terminology; but he does not misrepresent him. Cf *Collationes* 130v–133r.

85   Latin *umbra*; it refers to the limbo in which are held infants who have died innocent of any individual sin.

86   That is, make an argument as knotty as his. Cf *Adagia* I ii 5 *Malo nodo malus quaerendus cuneus* 'A hard wedge must be sought for a hard knot.'

87   Rom 3:12

88   Rom 1:18–2:5; 1:18 'against all ungodliness and unrighteousness of men [*hominum*], who hold the truth in unrighteousness'

89   Rom 3:23. The preceding verse has 'upon all them that believe: for there is no difference.'

90   *pro iustificatione nostra*] LB; *p. i. n.* in *1529* 27r and *1540* 805

91   Rom 4:25

92 Rom 5:1
93 Rom 5:6
94 The first phrase of Rom 5:12
95 LB italicizes *in quo omnes peccaverunt. Per unum enim hominem peccatum venit in mundum.* It is not, however, a single quote. The second phrase, not an exact quote, should be: *Propterea sicut per unum hominem peccatum in hunc mundum intravit,* which comes in Rom 5:12 before the first phrase and is separated from it by *et per peccatum mors et ita in omnes homines mors pertransiit.* I have punctuated on the assumption that this second phrase is paraphrased by Erasmus and intended as part of his own sentence. It is not possible to see what was intended from *1529* 27r–v or *1540* 805, which use the same typeface throughout.
96 Ambrosiaster 1 162–3
97 This is the second part of Rom 5:13.
98 Augustine *Contra Iulianum* 1.7.33 and 34 FC 35 39–43; but elsewhere in the same work (1.6.21–6, 1.7.29, and 2.6.17) he does call him *Constantinopolitanus* and in 1.6.26 quotes a passage from Chrysostom's *Homilia ad neophytos* (FC 35 31). Chrysostom became bishop of Constantinople in 398 and was exiled in 404, but still supported by Innocent 1 in Rome. According to P.W. Harkins (NCE 7 1041) the surname Chrysostom does not occur until the sixth century. Cf *Collationes* 118v and 122r–v.
99 Rom 5:14 'Yet death reigned from Adam to Moses even over those whose sins were not like the transgression of Adam who was a type of the one who was to come.'
100 This sentence is not italics in LB but seems to be a purported intervention from Titelmans, followed by the question from Erasmus.
101 *1529* (27v) and *1540* (806) make this a question, though there is no question mark in LB. It is presumably a question attributed to Titelmans.
102 *qui decretis ecclesiae consentienti*] *1529* 27v (sic for *consentientes*?); *1540* (806) has emended to *contenti* 'are content with.'
103 Titelmans also numbers himself among such believers; *Collationes* 126r and 126v–127r.
104 Again this is not italicized in LB but appears, given the following sentence, to be a purported intervention by Titelmans.
105 The work is not by Augustine, as Erasmus suspected, but is now attributed to a St Fulgentius, bishop of Ruspe. For Augustine's view, see *Contra Iulianum* 5.11.44 FC 35 285–6.
106 Erasmus is alluding to the famous theological teaching manual the *Sententiae* of Peter Lombard and to the *Decretum* of Gratian; see Friedberg 1.
107 Origen *Comm in Rom* 5.1 (1–11) PG 14 1004–8 / FC 103 303–9. See also the annotation in CWE 56, especially 42–4.

From the sixth chapter to the Romans

[ER *quicunque baptizati sumus in Christum* 'whoever of us have been baptized into Christ']
[RESP] *quicunque baptizati sumus in Christo* 'whoever of us have been baptized in Christ.'[1] I had pointed out that in Greek this was 'into Christ,' adding that the preposition had two meanings and is correctly translated

as 'in Christ.' My critic proves from Latin writers or writers translated into Latin that the reading is 'in Christ' – which was entirely unnecessary.

1 Rom 6:3 'all we, who are baptized in Christ Jesus'; CWE 56 175–6; *Collationes* 138r–139r

[ER *nam si insititii* 'for if (we have become) engrafted']
[RESP] *si enim complantati* 'for if [we have become] planted together.'[1]
Because I have not found *complantati* [planted together] in Latin authors and since the word was ambiguous (for things planted in the same field are also 'planted together'), then because the expression as a whole seemed rather strained (*complantati similitudini* [planted together in the likeness (of his death)] for *imitatione mortis eius* [in imitation of his death]) and what follows is no less strained (*et resurrectionis erimus* [and we will be of the resurrection]), I expressed the same idea in other words, more clearly as he admits, and, as I believe, even more meaningfully.[2] Firstly, the Greek σύμφυτοι is a noun, not a verb. A graft does not live or die except with the tree to which it is grafted. But, with plants set in the same field, nothing prevents one living and another dying off. I was not unaware of how others may read it. But what he explains about the particular meaning of the word *planta* is even more true in the case of grafted ones. For plants that are not grafted can be said to be 'planted together.' Besides, what is grafted is something which at some time was not part of the tree, an idea that Paul expresses with the verb γεγόναμεν 'we have become.'[3]

1 Rom 6:5 'if we have been planted together'; CWE 56 176; *Collationes* 139r–140r
2 The whole verse in VG is: *Si enim complantati facti sumus similitudini mortis eius, simul et resurrectionis erimus* 'For if we have been planted together in the likeness of his death, we shall be also in the likeness of his resurrection.' ER reads: *Nam si insititii facti sumus illi per similitudinem mortis eius, nimirum et resurrectionis participes erimus* 'For if we have become engrafted to him in imitation of his death, we shall surely also be participants of the resurrection.' The opening phrases of this comment, which need to be read as one rather rambling sentence, are printed as three separate sentences in 1529. 1540 and LB punctuate with colons (equivalent to commas) instead of full stops.
3 Translated by both VG and by ER as *facti sumus*.

[ER *mors illi non amplius dominatur* 'Death no longer rules him.']
[RESP] *mors illi ultra non dominabitur* 'Death shall no more rule him.'[1]
Although I stated that in the Greek sources we regularly find κυριεύει, that is, 'rules,' which is a universal present [tense], my critic informs us from Latin and translated authors that 'shall rule' is the reading.[2] It's a marvellous proof, especially as it is not clear from their commentaries what they read.

1 Rom 6:9 'Death shall no more have dominion over him'; CWE 56 177; *Collationes*
   140r–v
2 Titelmans cites Ambrose, Origen (translated), and Augustine.

[ER *nam quod mortuus fuit, peccato mortuus fuit semel* 'For that (death)
which he died, he died to sin once.']
[RESP] *quod enim mortuus est peccato, mortuus est semel* 'For in that he
died to sin, he died once.'[1] Here although he ·approves all the points I
had made against Valla and Lefèvre, he nevertheless introduces himself as
the single opponent of three σνμμάχοι [allies], as he calls them, who have
the unanimous purpose of carping at the Translator. He could have made
this introduction somewhere else more opportunely, for here I refute the
opinion of both and defend the Translator. The comparison he puts in here
is no less untimely: he concedes pre-eminence of seniority to us; he also
concedes that our reputation for learning is greater than his own; he does
not concede the same in respect of learning itself. Indeed he even grants
that we are experienced in several disciplines; he does not grant it simply
but adds, 'I believe.' And so that he should not seem inferior in this respect
too, he adds, 'before the divine hand brought me forth from my mother's
womb,' as if he had no other midwife than God. Then, after a lot of other
preliminaries about divine help, so that you expect some great objection that
he is going to make to all of us, he has nothing further to say except that
there is nothing to add to what I had noted. I take no offence indeed at these
remarks, but I fear a lot of people may not read them without laughing.

1 Rom 6:10; CWE 56 177–8; *Collationes* 140v–141v (where the comma is between
   est and *peccato*). For the substance of the points Erasmus has to make on this
   text, see his annotation, where he points out that *quod* (Greek ὅ) is a relative
   pronoun ('what, that which'), not a conjunction ('because'). Here he merely
   responds ironically to Titelmans' pretentiousness.

[ER *reputate vos ipsos mortuos esse peccato* 'Consider that you yourselves
are dead to sin.']
[RESP] *existimate vos mortuos esse peccato* 'Judge yourselves dead to sin.'[1]
For λογίζεσθε I preferred *reputate*. He says *existimate* is more meaningful, for
one who yet remains in sin may 'think' [*cogitet*], but they who 'judge' [*exis-
timant*] or 'ponder' [*putant*] 'think' much more.[2] Knowing comes first, then
remembering and turning over in the mind. '*Reputare*,' says he, 'is sometimes taken to mean *existimare*.' What is the proof of that? 'When we say
sometimes a wise man is "esteemed" [*reputari*],' he replies. Who talks like
that? Ordinary people spoke like that formerly, not educated people. Ἀνα-
λογίσεσθαι, according to him, 'corresponds more to the meaning of *reputare*'

– as though the Greek term always corresponds in every way to the Latin one. 'Augustine and Hilary read *existimate*.' I never said they did not. But they read it thus because they followed this Translator, whom I do not reproach because I believe he spoke correctly for his time.

1 Rom 6:11 'So do you also reckon, that you are dead to sin'; CWE 56 179; *Collationes* 141v–142v. For Erasmus' rejection of *existimare* and the distinction with *reputare*, see also the annotations on Rom 4:3 CWE 56 107–8 and 8:18 CWE 56 214–16.

2 These are distinctions made by Titelmans; the following sentence also paraphrases his development. Cf *Collationes* prologus b3v.

[ER *ut obediatis illi per cupiditates eius* 'so that you obey it through its desires']
[RESP] *ut obediatis concupiscentiis eius* 'so that you obey its lusts.'¹ Since the meaning is the same, since what I say is what is found in the Greek, there is nothing here to answer.

1 Rom 6:12 'so as to obey the lusts thereof'; CWE 56 179; *Collationes* 142v–143v

[ER *gratia autem Deo* 'But thanks (be) to God.']
[RESP] *gratias*¹ *autem Deo* 'But [let us give] thanks to God.'² 'The pagans said *gratia diis*,' says he, 'Christians say *Deo gratias*. This is a distinguishing mark between a pagan and a believing Christian.' But since the Greeks also said, χάρις θεοῖς πᾶσι καὶ πάσαις [thanks (singular) to all gods and goddesses], why did Paul prefer the pagan expression to the Christian one?³ 'People said *Deo gratias* in the old days.' What is that to us? But that's all right;⁴ 'Let the pagans have their own [way of saying] "Thanks [*gratia*] to the gods,"' says he. 'Let us sing our thanks [*gratias*] to our one God, and this song is sweet and will always be to true lovers of the church as it endures to the end.' Are these not serious annotations?

1 *gratias*] 1529 and VG; *gratia* in 1540 and LB, which makes the argument incomprehensible
2 Rom 6:17 'But thanks be to God'; CWE 56 180; *Collationes* 143v
3 The Greek is χάρις [nominative singular] δὲ τῷ θεῷ. The argument is about whether one should use the singular *gratia* or the plural *gratias* [*ago*], not about a single or multiple gods.
4 *sed bene habet*] 1540 807; *sed bene ha- habet* in 1529 29r (sic at the end of a line); *sed bene habent* LB

[ER *in eam in quam traducti estis formam doctrinae* 'into that form of doctrine to which you have been brought over']
[RESP] *in eam formam doctrinae, in quam traditi estis* 'into that form of doctrine to which you were entrusted.'¹ I liked *traducti* more than *translati*,²

instead of *traditi*, because a person is entrusted [*traditur*] to a person rather than to a thing, nor does *tradere* mean literally the same as *transferre* [carry over].

1 Rom 6:17 'unto that form of doctrine, into which you have been delivered'; *Collationes* 145r–v. There is no annotation on this point.
2 VG *trado*, compound of *dare*, is a literal translation of Greek παραδίδωμι, compound of δίδωμι 'give.' It is Titelmans who suggests that *trado* includes the meaning of both *traduco* and *transfero* (past participle *translatus*), but Erasmus prefers *traduco*, probably because, in addition to the reason he gives, he believes the change is made with a free will, as his paraphrase shows (CWE 42 39).

[ER *iniquitati, ad aliam atque aliam iniquitatem* 'to iniquity, and from one iniquity to another']
[RESP] *iniquitati ad iniquitatem* 'to iniquity unto iniquity.'[1] In order to express the movement from vices to greater vices, I preferred 'from one iniquity to another.' My critic does not like this. He says, 'Why did you not translate what follows as "from righteousness to righteousness"?' Because vice is multiform, virtue is one; and because Paul does not repeat 'righteousness,' whereas he does repeat 'iniquity.' Is he not ashamed to publish these things in print?

1 Rom 6:19; *Collationes* 145v–146r. There is no annotation on this point.

[ER *manumissi a peccato* 'set free from sin']
[RESP] *liberati autem a peccato* 'but made free from sin.'[1] I had often translated [ἐλευθερωθέντες] with *liberati*, but I found that *liberari* [to be freed] is a verb with many meanings – for the sick are 'freed' of illness, we are 'freed' of danger, which the Greeks express rather as ἀπολύεσθαι [loosened from] or σωθῆναι [saved] – so in order to express Paul's metaphor of slavery and freedom restored, I put *manumissi* [manumitted] for once instead of *liberati* [freed]. However, I used 'manumitted' in an absolute way, just as 'manumission' is used to mean liberty recovered. He says, 'They are freed even by force.' What does it matter how you are freed? No matter how a man is sent away, he is said to be 'manumitted.' The master grants freedom by the laying on of a hand. The praetor's rod has the same function, as does the will of a dead owner without [the laying on of] a hand.[2] And I, when I get away from the vice to which I have long been a slave, can I not be said to be 'manumitted'? The whole discourse here consists of a metaphor of slavery and release from slavery, which is properly called 'manumission.'

1 Rom 6:22; *Collationes* 146r–147v. There is no annotation on this point. Both Latin texts (ER and VG) have *nunc vero* 'but now' before the words quoted; *autem* appears in the cue phrase in the *Collationes*.

2   Erasmus seems to speak of informal emancipation by the laying on of a hand
    and two legal procedures: *manumissio vindicta* and *manumissio testamento*. See
    the *Digest* 40.1–5; or the *Codex Iustiniani* 7.1–2; OCD 'Freedmen.'

[ER *auctoramenta peccati mors* 'The recompense of sin is death.']
[RESP] *stipendia peccati mors* 'The wages of sin is death.'[1] The Translator
had rendered ὀψώνια [wages in kind] as *stipendium*, which is correct. For
my part, in order to represent this properly military word, which is the sort
Paul often likes to use, I have translated with *auctoramenta* instead of *stipendia*,
understanding it exactly as the Translator does. But my critic charges
me with falsity, on the grounds that death is not the security for sin, but sin
rather the security for death,[2] and eternal life is the recompense of righteousness. This he proves from Valla who quotes Seneca as saying, 'There is
no evil without [the expectation of] recompense,'[3] meaning there is no vice
that does not tempt us by some reward. Death, however, does not tempt us
to sin but causes horror. In short, he does not want anything to be called
a recompense except what entices with the appearance of good. If Seneca
turned it to this sense, am I not on the same account allowed to turn it to
another sense? What he had just called *auctoramentum*, Seneca himself soon
after calls *merces* [wages, reward], and *merces* is what Ambrose reads in this
passage instead of *stipendium*.[4] Now does *stipendium* not have a good sense?
And yet Paul used it differently in a bad sense, just as 'fruit, prize, price,
consideration, gain' and 'reward' have a good sense and yet can be shifted
appropriately not only in Latin to a bad sense. Was Terence wrong to say,
'This is considered to be the reward [*honos*] you get for that,'[5] because 'reward' here does not mean anything desirable? Would anyone be wrong to
say, 'For my merits I enjoy this fruit, that I am hated by you all'? Is it not
good Latin to say, 'Infamy has been his gain [*lucrifecisse*]' of someone who
has accepted infamy in place of gain [*lucrum*]? Is the salary not the attrac-
tion of military service?[6] It follows [from the argument that death is not the
recompense of sin] that Paul was wrong to call death the wages of sin. Does
not the hope of reward entice people to doing a job? It follows that Ambrose was wrong when he read *merces* for *stipendium*. The subject here is not
what this soldier of sin expects but what he is paid. 'But,' says he, 'the *auctoramentum* entails an obligation. Hence those who have been released from
the oath of military service are said to be *exauctorati*.' The *stipendium* im-
poses just such an obligation too, and those who are accepted under the oath
are said to be *stipendiarii* or *stipendiati*.[7] And they would be called *exstipendiati* if the usage of Latin writers authorized it as it has authorized *exauctorati*. There is no difference between *stipendium* and *auctoramentum* except
that *stipendia* are given for other offices too, and *auctoramentum* is strictly

a military term. Nor is it any wonder that *auctoramentum*, like *stipendium*, refers to all three things: the giver, the recipient, and the work for which it is given. Here sin, like a commander, repays his soldier with death as a reward for service.

What could be more shameless than this youth who, on the basis of such trivia, casts such insults at me, saying that I translated with the wrong meaning, insisting repeatedly 'wrong, wrong,' though he does not know what he is saying? There is nothing wrong in my translation, but there is intolerable wrong in his reproach and his ill-educated loquacity. 'Death,' says he, 'is not desired' – and yet we read that unbelievers invited death by deeds and words, and we say that those who prepared their own ruin through their own vice have found what they sought because they embraced those things through which they know they will end in ruin. But it is marvellous how this man puts so much exertion into teaching me how to speak properly, when he does not appear to have any experience of the standard authors of the Latin language. I do not want to recall the remaining points that he prattles about, nor is it worth the effort. I do not wonder so much that a youth is carried away by ambition for glory; I wonder more at his colleagues to whose applause and with whose help he publishes these things,[8] to the great disgrace, if I am not mistaken, of the whole order. Which is why after this I shall respond only to a few scattered points.

1 Rom 6:23; CWE 56 182; *Collationes* 147v–151v
2 Titelmans understands *autoramentum* in the sense of a down payment made beforehand as security, whereas Erasmus, like the Translator, means the reward paid afterwards.
3 *Elegantiae* 4.32 in Valla I 133; Seneca the Younger *Epistulae morales* 69 4–5
4 Ambrosiaster I 208–10
5 Terence *Eunuchus* 1023
6 For Erasmus' opinion of soldiers, see his annotation (CWE 56 182), the colloquies *Militaria* 'Military Affairs' and *Militis et Cartusiani* 'The Soldier and the Carthusian' in *Colloquia* CWE 39–40, and the figure of the beetle in *Adagia* III vii 1 *Scarabaeus aquilam quaerit* 'A dung-beetle hunting an eagle.'
7 or *stipendiati*] Not in 1529; added in 1540 in order to match *exstipendiati* in the following sentence
8 See the prefatory letter 138 with n2, 141 with n14 above.

From the seventh chapter to the Romans

[ER *viventi viro alligata est per legem* 'She is bound through the Law to her husband while he lives.']
[RESP] *vivente viro alligata est legi* 'Whilst the husband liveth, she is bound to the Law.'[1] Here, in order to defend the Translator, he wants the dative ζῶντι ἀνδρὶ 'to the husband while he lives' to be translated by an

ablative absolute. But it is the Greek genitive that is usually translated thus, and the dative, like νόμῳ 'to the Law' as it is used here, by an ablative of the instrument, never by an ablative absolute. The other points he mentions are mere jingles.

1   Rom 7:2; CWE 56 184; *Collationes* 152r–v. The annotation in all editions had the cue phrase *vivente viro alligata est lege*, with the last word in the ablative ('by the Law'), whereas the VG text had *legi*, dative ('to the Law,' as in DV), as Titelmans quotes it. In his annotation, where he explains the ablative *lege* as *per legem* 'through the Law,' Erasmus seems to prefer the ablative to the dative, and here he suggests an ablative of the instrument (ie *lege* for νόμῳ), though he has *per legem* in his translation.

[ER *quod si mortuus fuerit vir, liberata est a lege viri* 'But if the husband dies, she is freed from the law of the husband.']
[RESP] *si [autem] mortuus fuerit vir eius. soluta est a lege viri* '[But] if her husband dies, she is released from the law of the husband.'[1] I had pointed out that the word for *viri* [husband] is not repeated in the Greek manuscripts, noting that ἀνδρὸς is, however, added in certain ones. My critic reproaches me for not adding ἀνδρὸς in my [Greek] version, since on the facing page we have 'of the husband' in Latin, and he scourges me for dozing because I did not harmonize the Greek with the Latin. But I believe, my distinguished young man, that the word ἀνδρὸς was added by the Greeks who, after the accord with the Roman See was made, corrected their manuscripts to match Latin versions.[2] 'So,' he will say, 'why have you added it in your translation?' Because the particular meaning of the noun here lies in the article τοῦ, for he is speaking of that law he had mentioned before, that is the rule or law of marriage.

1   Rom 7:2 'But if her husband be dead, she is loosed from the law of her husband'; CWE 56 186–7; *Collationes* 153r. The cue phrase here is correctly cited from Rom 7:2 VG (apart from the period following *eius*, which should be a comma) and the discussion does not suffer from the confusion with Rom 7:3, which seems to have affected the annotations; see CWE 56 186 n2.
2   Erasmus is thinking of the Council of Ferrara-Florence (1438–58). See Jerry H. Bentley 'Erasmus and Jean Le Clerc, and the Principle of the Harder Reading' *Renaissance Quarterly* 31/3 (1978) 309–21, especially 315 n21.

[ER *ut iungeremini alteri* 'that you may be wedded to another']
[RESP] *ut sitis vos alterius* 'that you may be another's.'[1] I had pointed out that *vos* was superfluous for Latin speakers. 'But it is in Paul,' he says, 'εἰς τὸ γενέσθαι ὑμᾶς.' But in Greek γενέσθαι does not indicate the person[2] as *sitis* does in Latin. What a fine annotation!

1   Rom 7:4 'that you may belong to another'; CWE 56 187; *Collationes* 154r–v
2   Because it is an infinitive.

[ER *nunc autem non iam ego* 'Now then it is no longer I.']

[RESP] *nunc autem iam non ego* 'Now then it is no more I.'[1] Here although I
am defending the Translator,[2] he still does not refrain from loud contention,
saying that I could defend the Translator if I applied my mind to this as
much as when I reproached him hitherto. As if it were my intention to
reproach the Translator, or as if it is abuse to point out a fault of expression
in one who wrote not in correct Latin but in the common language for the
general mass of people.

1   Rom 7:17; CWE 56 193; *Collationes* 155r–156r
2   In this case Erasmus was responding to Lefèvre, who thought the Latin should
    be *non etiam ego* 'not even I.'

[ER *imo peccatum. ut appareret peccatum* 'No, rather, sin. In order that it
might appear (that) sin . . .']

[RESP] *sed peccatum ut appareat peccatum* 'But sin, that it may appear
[that] sin . . .'[1] For me the sentence division caused no difficulty in so far
as the Translator changed the Greek participle κατεργαζομένη [working] to
the [finite] verb *operatum est* [worked]; but this is not what the Greek reads,
unless you punctuate as I have indicated.[2] I do not have Theophylact in
Greek to hand. Chrysostom is unclear about the phrase *operatum est* and
anyway is very little concerned to investigate the meaning of the text.[3]
However, I proposed the following meaning: 'So that which is good – that
is, the Law – did it become death for me?' It was not the Law that produced
death, but sin introduced death, so that it is clear that sin is the cause of
death in us by reason of the Law. Why has the Lord allowed this? So that the
sickness cannot be hidden, because the evil is blatantly obvious as long as
sin, having the Law against it, is not cured but further increased. Origen's
interpretation, which turns sin into the devil, is rather forced, but this is
what Ambrose follows.[4] If anyone prefers another reading, let him clear up
the difficulty of the Greek text, which I have indicated. I have pointed out
particularly to the reader the punctuation of the Greek manuscripts.

1   Rom 7:13; CWE 56 189–90; *Collationes* 156r–157r. This item is out of order in all
    editions of the *Responsio* and in the *Collationes*.
2   See CWE 56 190 n1 and the following annotation at CWE 56 190–1. In the
    first of these annotations Erasmus makes the purpose, in both the Greek and
    Latin, to be that sin should appear to be the cause of death, and seems to
    take the Vulgate to mean that the purpose is 'that sin should reveal itself
    to be sin.' This is how Valla read it (I 857), and Erasmus admits the pos-
    sibility in the second annotation: 'but sin (that it might become more evi-
    dent how great an evil it is).' The *Paraphrase* also implies that this reading
    is included: 'Thus it became more evident how abominable a thing sin is
    by whose fault things which are very good fall into the worst state' (CWE
    42 43).

3 Chrysostom *Hom in Rom* 12.6 PG 60 502–3
4 Origen *Comm in Rom* 6.8 (10) PG 14 1083 / FC 104 34; Ambrosiaster I 228–9

[ER *gratias ago Deo per Iesum Christum* 'I give thanks to God through Jesus Christ.']

[RESP] *gratia Dei per Iesum Christum* 'the grace of God by Jesus Christ.'[1]
It is clear that Chrysostom both reads and comments on εὐχαριστῶ [I give thanks], and that Theophylact follows him, although they mention 'grace' sometimes because no one gives thanks except for benefit received;[2] thanks are not given for what is owed. Hence the points my critic brings forward from Origen translated into Latin and from Ambrose and other Latin writers do not argue against me at all, since the noun 'grace' is in the verb.[3] I set out this argument and said that 'will free me' [*liberabit me*] would not be suited to Paul who was free, and I explain at the end in what sense it can be suitable. Ambrose supports me when he speaks thus about St Paul: 'For the man placed in a carnal body would not say that he is snatched from the body itself, but he said "this body," etc.'[4] But if 'the grace of God' is the answer to the verb ῥύσεται [(who) shall save?], Paul, according to Ambrose, did not say that 'he was to be freed' but that 'he was freed.'[5] Anyway, the person who says, 'I give thanks' [εὐχαριστῶ] or 'Thanks be to God' [χάρις Θεῷ] makes it clear that he is free by grace. Nor did Origen read otherwise, as is proved by the fact that he adds, 'From how many evils and from how many deaths Christ has snatched us.'[6] What he [Origen] proposes about the change of *persona*, however, my censor has not understood.[7] The question 'Who [shall save] me?' is assigned by Origen too to the imperfect man, who still has a hard struggle with vices and desires, because he [Origen] does not think it suitable for Paul who has been saved. Further, what follows, 'I thank God,' is a complete sentence, so Origen would have it refer to the Apostle's authority; for one who gives thanks declares himself already freed from the body of death.[8] For the same reason he would not have it that the many things Paul had mentioned before, about the law of death, about the inevitability of sin, about lust, were said in the *persona* of the Apostle. Whence it is clear that this youth has not seen what Origen noted about the change of *persona*. Where now is the objection that this constantly triumphant censor makes against me for the cunning of my words, my tricks and my falsity? How base to scoff at someone else when all the time he himself does not understand either what he says or what he reads.

1 Rom 7:25; CWE 56 195–8; *Collationes* 157r–160v
2 Chrysostom *Hom in Rom* 13.3 PG 60 512; Theophylact *Expos in Rom* 7:25 PG 124 432D

3   Origen *Comm in Rom* 6.9 (11) PG 14 1089C/FC 104 41–2; Ambrosiaster I 244–
    5. Concerning Ambrosiaster at least Titelmans was right; see CWE 56 198 n10.
    'Noun ... verb'; ie χάρις is in εὐχαριστῶ. This appears to be a reference to
    Valla's indication (I 857) that in some manuscripts χάρις τῷ θεῷ was found,
    conveying, according to Erasmus, the same idea.
4   Ambrosiaster I 246–7
5   Ambrosiaster I 244:18 and 245:16
6   Origen *Comm in Rom* 6.9 PG 14 1089/FC 104 42. See also especially CWE 56 197
    n6.
7   Origen *Comm in Rom* 6.9–10 (2–4) PG 14 1090C–1091B/FC 104 36–8. *1529* (32r),
    1540 (809), and LB appear to put a comma in the wrong place: *quod autem adfert
    de mutata persona meus reprehensor, non intellexit.* See the third sentence from
    the end.
8   Reminiscence of Jerome Ep 121.8.21 CSEL 56 36. See CWE 56 196–7 and 198 n15.

From the eighth chapter

[ER *liberum me reddidit a iure peccati et mortis* '... set me free from the
authority of sin and death']
[RESP] *liberavit me a lege peccati et mortis* '... hath delivered me from
the law of sin and death.'[1] *Lex* in Latin sometimes means 'enacted law,'
sometimes 'condition,' as in 'I forgive you on this condition [*hac lege*].' Νόμος
for the Greeks often means 'enacted law,' often 'usage' or 'custom,' which
sometimes gains the force of law. But Paul, following, it seems to me, a
practice of the Hebrew language, sometimes uses 'law' to mean 'enacted
law,' as when he says, 'the law of Moses' or 'the law of nature' but often
means 'power to prescribe,' as when he says, 'by the law of the husband'[2]
and 'the law of sin.' For as a king and lord has power to prescribe what he
wishes for his citizens and servants, so when [Paul] says sin has ruled and
governs, he ascribes to it 'law,' that is, 'power to prescribe.' Wishing to let
the reader know this, I translated here 'from the power of sin,' because 'law'
is not associated so easily with 'death,' which does not prescribe anything,
unless you were to translate 'death' in a rather forced way as 'the devil.' The
other passages give the sense of the noun 'law' quite correctly, but taking
into account this range of meanings they are understood more exactly.

1   Rom 8:2; CWE 56 199–200; *Collationes* 160v–161v
2   Cf Rom 7:2, 211 above.

[ER *at qui spirituales* 'but those who are spiritual']
[RESP] *qui vero secundum spiritum sunt* 'but they that are according to the
spirit.'[1] Although Valla declares that the Translator's variety of expression
is both untimely and unsuitable,[2] my critic nevertheless quarrels with me
because I said the same thing in different words; and he believes that the

Translator, a man to be admired though not known to anyone, has been treated with intolerable contempt because I wrote that he strove needlessly for variety of expression. For it is not a question of meaning but of the appropriateness of the language, nor does he offer an explanation of why the Translator should have changed [his translation of] this Greek word [φρονοῦσι 'care for']. He does in fact collect many examples from Latin authors or authors translated into Latin[3] in which there is no distinction between *sapientia* [rational wisdom], *prudentia* [wisdom of experience], and *sensus* [wisdom of feeling], and which do very little against my case. But what he finds inexcusable is that I myself incur the same fault that I bring against the Translator.[4] For whereas I had translated φρονοῦσι as *curant* [care for], I soon after translated φρόνημα as *affectus* [desire].[5] But I can give reason for my variety; let[6] him give reason for the variety the Translator 'loved' – since he does not like 'affected.' That φρονεῖν sometimes means *curare* is made clear by the derivatives φροντὶς 'care' and φροντίζειν 'care about.' 'But why,' says he, 'do you thereafter translate φρόνημα with *affectus* rather than with *cura*?' Because *affici his quae sunt carnis* [to be affected by things of the flesh] sounds strained in Latin. *Curare* is more natural and more common, and [the noun phrases] *cura carnis* and *cura spiritus* are not only strained but ambiguous; *affectus*, on the contrary, is more natural and more suitable. My critic informs me, following Valla of course,[7] of the difference between *affectio* [disposition] and *affectus*, for *affectus* [plural] are what the Greeks call πάθη [disturbances]. This is precisely the distinction Latin writers make whenever they discuss Greek philosophy. However, there is nothing to stop me saying in Latin '*pius affectus* [pious desire] for God, for the fatherland, for children,' since this feeling is not in the lower part of the soul but in the higher. Accordingly, I liked the word because it was applicable to both parts of the soul, spirit and flesh.[8] I do not see, moreover, what may be learned for sure from the Latin translation of Origen, which is not a reliable translation, for the Greek occasionally cites Latin sources. Augustine, as my critic himself admits, supports me.[9] That Ambrose certainly speaks here in the same way as the Translator is no wonder, since he often does so.[10] And just as for Seneca *sapere* [to be wise] means more than simply *intelligere* [to understand] – for one who is wise loves what he understands[11] – so you will never find *sapientia* used for *affectus*; although according to the Stoics, no one is really wise unless he has a desire [*affectus*] worthy of a wise man, even if certain of them admit of no desires. And people afflicted by the desires of pride and presumption are said to 'think big thoughts' [μέγα φρονεῖν].[12] So those who take 'flesh' to stand for the baser part of the soul – as Chrysostom also indicates by the way[13] – and 'spirit' for the higher do not weaken my argument. For when the will inclines to reason, it loves things eternal; when it lets itself descend to the flesh and bodily things, it loves that which should not be loved. Both dispositions, however, are in that part of the soul called the will. Nor is it always true that the Greek word for wisdom [σοφία] entails the notion of virtue. They often use σοφός of a skilled artist, and Paul talks of the 'wisdom of this world.'[14] In addition, rhetoricians say that no one is a good orator who does not himself both understand and love what is honest, but rhetoric does not on that account mean the same as understanding and love of what is honest. 'But,' says my critic, 'Origen interprets *affectus* of the flesh as carnal understanding of the Law and *affectus* of the spirit as spiritual [understanding of the Law].'[15] He is apt to philosophize[16] freely like this, being a man more than somewhat averse to the letter. Ambrose includes the two, both desire and understanding. It is no surprise that commentators include both in the words they use since the realities are interrelated; for a corrupt desire is born for the most part from corrupt understanding and vice versa. This is why the Jews, having desires for bodily things, embraced only the baser part of the Law and understood what is spiritual in the sense of the flesh. To conclude, I admit that the Greek words φρονεῖν and φρόνημα have two senses. In addition, since Origen connects this passage with the points he has discussed before concerning the law of the mind, the law of members [of the body], the law of sin, and since it is clear that the law of sin and the law of members of the body are concupiscence, they are not consistent if you exclude here the desires of the flesh.

1 Rom 8:5; *Collationes* 162r–165v. There is no annotation on this phrase, which is out of order in *Collationes* and all editions of the *Responsio ad Collationes*. It concerns the Greek words φρονοῦσι 'care for' (VG *qui enim secundum spiritum sunt* 'they that are according to the spirit') in the second part of verse 5, and φρόνημα 'desire' (VG *prudentia* 'wisdom') in verse 6. The words are translated differently here in order to follow Erasmus' distinctions. The recurring controversy on 'variety' (*copia*) is reflected briefly in the following annotations on *quae spiritus sunt, sapiunt* in this verse (CWE 56 203–4), on *quoniam sapientia carnis* in verse 7 (CWE 56 204–5), and on *quid desideret spiritus* in verse 27 (CWE 56 222–3).

2 *Adnotationes* in Valla 1 857 2

3 *latine*] 1540 809; *graece* in 1529 32v

4 Erasmus uses the same verb, *impingo*, for 'incur' and 'bring against' – no doubt with ironic intention.

5 The problem with the translation of the verb φρονέω 'to have understanding, to take heed of' and the nouns φροντὶς 'thought, concern,' φρόνημα 'mind, spirit,' and φρόνησις 'prudence' is the relatively restricted usages of the Latin *curare/cura*, *affectus*, and *sensus*. It is not, Erasmus points out, that these words correspond strictly in their meanings, as Titelmans would have it, to higher or lower mental functions, understanding, or emotion but a matter of style and usage. For the English translator, however, there is also a problem of meaning, because no single English word will serve satisfactorily for each Latin one in

every context. Since the Latin words are under discussion, they have been retained in the body of the sentences with suggested translations in square brackets. See also CWE 56 204–5 nn2 and 4.

6 reddat ille causam varietatis quam amavit Interpres, quando illi non placet, *affectavit*] *1540* 809 (typeface as in LB). *1529* (33r) has no comma before *affectavit* and uses the same typeface throughout. It seems likely that Erasmus, by using the word *amavit* 'loved,' is making fun of Titelmans, who objected to the accusation that the Translator 'affected' an unnecessary variety. Valla and Erasmus open the discussion in the *Collationes* with this accusation, and Erasmus is made to say, as he does in the *Annotationes*, 'It is strange that the Translator strove here [*affectarit*] for an unprofitable variety'; cf CWE 56 203.

7 *Elegantiae* 4.78 in Valla I 147. Erasmus' 'of course' (*scilicet*) is ironic or mischievous. In the *Elegantiae* Valla says there seems to be no distinction of meaning between the two words, though he thinks only *affectio* is used by Cicero, *affectus* by Quintilian and others. He does, however, oppose *affectus* to *ratio*. Titelmans quotes him correctly, except that he puts this point first.

8 That is, spiritual and sensual. See the sentence below: 'So those who take "flesh" to stand for the baser part of the soul ...' For the contrast of flesh and spirit in Erasmus' view of human nature, see John B. Payne *Erasmus: his Theology of the Sacraments* (Richmond, Va 1970) chapter 2 'Anthropology.' For the triple division of the soul into 'flesh,' 'soul,' and 'spirit,' also Pauline but not apparently in question here, see M.A. Screech *Ecstasy and the 'Praise of Folly'* (London 1980) 103–6.

9 Eg *Confessions* 9.6.14 *affectus pietatis* and 9.13.34 *carnalis affectus*

10 Ambrosiaster I 258–9

11 The phrase is not a quotation from Seneca. Erasmus seems to be thinking of the distinction between *sapientia* 'wisdom' or the Greek 'sophia' and *philosophia* 'love of wisdom,' which Seneca the Younger makes in *Epistulae morales* 89.4–7; but here he is using *sapere* in the sense that Seneca gives it in *Epistulae morales* 117, where he says, for example, *qui sapit, sapiens est; qui sapiens est, sapit* (117.8).

12 Homer *Iliad* 11.296, 13.156; Xenophon *Cyropedia* 7.5.62; a satirical example, of course

13 Chrysostom *Hom in Rom* 13.5 PG 60 515

14 Eg 1 Cor 1:20 τὴν σοφίαν τοῦ κόσμου

15 Origen *Comm in Rom* 6.12 (6) PG 14 1096A / FC 104 50

16 *Philosophari* is the word Erasmus commonly uses when speaking of Origen's allegorizing of Scripture.

[ER *Deus proprio filio, misso sub specie carnis peccato obnoxiae* 'God by his own Son, whom he sent under the appearance of flesh subject to sin'] [RESP] *Deus filium suum mittens in similitudinem carnis[1] p[eccati]* 'God sending his Son in the likeness of sinful flesh.'[2] I wonder at how eager this youth is to slander other peoples' work. First he complains that the full meaning has been removed. What full meaning is he dreaming up for me here? This passage has only one meaning, that Christ came in the

likeness of a sinful man, although he was free of all sin. For *caro peccati*
here means nothing if not 'a sinful man.' 'But,' he says, 'someone can come
under an appearance that is false, as Christ comes to us under the appearance of bread, although in that case it is not really bread.' Bravo! In the
same way, Christ comes under the false appearance of a sinful man and
in that time is baptized, suffers hunger, is condemned, and dies. 'You do
not,' says he, 'express the true nature of the likeness with the word *species*.'
On the contrary, ὁμοίωμα, which is used here, often means a false likeness,
not a true one, as in chapter 1 of this Epistle: 'in[3] the likeness of an image
of corruptible man.' And statues are not in reality men. But the idea that
the Eutychians, who deny that Christ was a man, will put forward – that
Christ came 'under the appearance [*sub specie*] of sinful flesh' but not also
'in the likeness [*in similitudine*] of sinful flesh' – is pure madness.[4] How can
it happen that they can deny Christ was true man, even if they were deceived by the word 'likeness'? When Mercury is said to have shown himself
to Battus 'under the appearance [*in specie*] of a man,' an undoubtedly false
image, can it not be said that he showed himself 'by appearing [*specie*] as
a man'?[5] And the son who bears the 'likeness' of his father – does he not
also have his 'appearance'? A false likeness is both false and true. And the
same may be said of an appearance. 'But,' you say, '"appearance" means
something that appears other than the true.' So it fits even better in this
passage where the truth of sinful flesh is denied. He says that the Euty-
chian heretics are excluded by this passage. This is false; on the contrary,
the Eutychians defend themselves with this passage. But these [heretics] are
excluded by the explanation of the ancients who demonstrate that this passage does not deny the likeness of human nature but the likeness of man
subject to sin. And they would have said the same whether they had read
in specie or *sub specie*. What could be more ignorant than this quibbling?
And where is that 'fullness of meaning' that he complains is diminished,
where is there anything taken away from what Catholics declare? What
a disdainful censor, what trivial ditties he babbles! And he even commits
them to print.

1   *carnis p*] 1529 33v and 1540 810; *carnis etc.* LB. The *p* after *carnis* in 1529 and
    1540 is the initial of the next word, *peccati*, which is found in *Collationes* and
    is part of the text discussed here.
2   Rom 8:3; CWE 56 201–2; *Collationes* 165v–166v. Out of order; see Rom 8:5, 217
    n1 above.
3   *in similitudine*] 1529 34r and 1540 810 (ablative); *in similitudinem* VG (accusative);
    Rom 1:23 '[changed] . . . into the likeness'
4   See 'Eutyches' and 'Eutychianism' in NCE 5 642–3. Eutyches of Constantinople
    was considered the father of Monophytism, which holds that after the hypo-
    static union (union of the divine and human natures) in Christ there was only

one nature, not two. He was definitively condemned at the Council of Chalcedon in 451. Erasmus is perhaps reflecting the opinion of Pope Leo I who described him as unlearned, unqualified, and imprudent.

5 Ovid *Metamorphoses* 2.687–707

[ER *affectus carnis inimicitia est adversus Deum* 'The desire of the flesh is hostility towards God.']
[RESP] *sapientia carnis inimica est Deo* 'The wisdom of the flesh is hostile to God.'[1] The Greek manuscripts are in complete agreement here, reading ἔχθρα 'hostility,' not ἐχθρὰ 'hostile,' which is both more meaningful and stronger, just as 'This man is my plague' is stronger than 'He is a pestilent fellow to me.' Moreover, it matches Hebrew usage. In addition, if you read *inimica* [hostile], it does not fit exactly with what follows: εἰς τὸν Θεὸν ['into' plus accusative; that is, 'towards God']; it was enough to say τῷ Θεῷ [dative].[2] Finally, an abstract noun is better matched with an abstract noun: 'wisdom' and 'hostility.' Moreover, since the meaning is the same, how does he prove from Latin authors or those translated into Latin what they may have read?

1 Rom 8:7 'The wisdom of the flesh is an enemy to God'; CWE 56 205–6; *Collationes* 166v–167r
2 Latin grammar also requires a dative with the adjective *inimicus* 'hostile' (*inimica Deo*).

[ER *spiritum adoptionis* 'spirit of adoption']
[RESP] *spiritum adoptionis filiorum Dei* 'the spirit of adoption of the sons of God.'[1] Although I am not reproaching the Translator here but rather excusing him, and although my censor informs me, from my own annotation, that according to the jurists even grandsons can be adopted, my remark that *adoptio filiorum* is not a normal expression in Latin for what the Translator means 'was,' says he, 'rather impudent; this I recognize clearly as an obvious cavil,' and so on.[2] Would this remark not seem exceedingly impudent from such a person, even if I were in fact caught in error? Now since he understands neither what I am saying nor what he himself is saying, what sort of evidence of modesty is this? 'The expression *adoptare filium*,' says he, 'is like *creare consulem* or *imperatorem* [appoint as consul or commander].' But he should offer at least one example of this construction. But granting that one says in Latin *adoptavit sibi filium* [he adopted a son for himself], who used *adoptio filiorum* instead of what was actually *adoptio in ius filiorum* [adoption into the rights of sons]? For the jurists' expression is: *sibi filium per adoptionem* or *arrogationem facit* [He makes a son for himself through adoption or arrogation] and *licet in locum neptis adoptare* [One may adopt into the position of granddaughter].[3] A father is said to give his

son or his grandson for adoption. He who adopts adopts a son or grandson, but someone else's. And just as someone else's son can be adopted into
the position of grandson, so a grandson can be adopted into the position of
son. This is the language of the jurists whom he wishes to appear to have
read. So great-grandsons. Our very modest young man should have learned
this before announcing so haughtily 'an obvious cavil.' To avoid this difficulty of expression, I translated, with Augustine, *spiritum adoptionis*.[4] 'It
is not the full meaning,' says he. On the contrary, it is full and complete.
For 'adoption' standing by itself is understood as adoption most lovingly
bestowed, and the words that follow[5] show that the Apostle is thinking of
those adopted into the position of sons. If it were I he had caught in an
error like this, when would he ever stop his reproaches?

1 Rom 8:15 'the spirit of adoption of sons'; CWE 56 209–11; *Collationes* 168v–170v
2 *Collationes* 170r
3 *Digest* 1.7.2
4 Augustine *De correptione et gratia* 47 PL 40 945
5 Rom 8:15 'When we cry Abba! Father!'

[ER *idem spiritus testatur* 'The Spirit witnesses the same.']
[RESP] *ipse enim spiritus testimonium reddit* 'For the Spirit himself giveth
testimony.'[1] Since the Greek is συμμαρτυρεῖ and I wanted to make explicit
the significance of the prefix συν- [together], my words are such as suppose two testimonies. My critic shows, from the mysteries of theology, that
there was a single testimony, not two. He would have it that the prefix is
superfluous. If several witnesses give the same evidence, the testimony is
single because they say the same thing, but in Latin the testimonies will be
said to be more than one because they are given by different people. The
testimony of our spirit is weak unless it is accompanied by the testimony
of the [Holy] Spirit, and the commentators point to this sense of the prefix when they say that the Spirit of God 'con-firms' our spirit: something is
'con-firmed' when strength is added to it. But what is there to prevent us
talking of the mutual testimony of spirits, just as we speak of the mutual
love of God and man, though the love we render to God originates from
him? Furthermore, even in the wicked and the imperfect there is some love
for God, but it is feeble unless strengthened by God's grace.

1 Rom 8:16; CWE 56 212–13; *Collationes* 170v–172r

[ER *siquidem simul cum eo patimur* 'if indeed we suffer together with
him']
[RESP] *si tamen compatimur* 'if only we suffer.'[1] Chrysostom informs us
that εἴπερ is often used to indicate confirmation, not doubt.[2] But *siquidem*,
as I have translated, includes both meanings: either inference and doubt or

confirmation. Why does my critic not praise me for preserving the possible extent of meaning and take issue with the Translator for restricting the Apostle's twofold word to one sense? Nor does εἴπερ have the sense of 'if only' in Greek.

1 Rom 8:17 'yet so, if we suffer with him'; CWE 56 213–14; *Collationes* 172r–173v
2 Chrysostom *Hom in Rom* 13.8 PG 60 518. See the explanation of εἴπερ in the annotation on Rom 8:9 CWE 56 206.

[ER *nam reputo, non esse pares* 'For I consider they are not equal.']
[RESP] *existimo enim quod non sunt condignae* 'For I suppose they are not of comparable worth.'[1] I render λογίζομαι as *perpendo* [weigh carefully].[2] My critic informs me that the Greek word in the strictest sense means *existimo*, but he cannot offer a single passage from the authors where it has this sense; he simply instructs me that it is so. But if λογίζεσθαι does not mean 'to turn over in the mind' [*in animo volvere*], the Translator made a mistake when, in Philippians, chapter 4, he translated ταῦτα λογίζεσθε as *haec cogitate* [think on these things].[3] 'But even an unbeliever can "turn over in his mind."' An unbeliever can 'suppose' [*existimat*] likewise. Satan 'supposes' likewise, nay, rather he 'believes' [*credit*]. Paul, writing to the Philippians, is not writing to unbelievers but to pious people whom he wants to keep turning over in their minds what they have heard and believed, lest[4] they should be lost. But if Paul were speaking of a 'persuasion' of faith, he would certainly have used the weak word *existimo* [suppose], which means no more than *opinor* [conjecture]. There is such a thing as a 'certain opinion,' but the word has a double meaning. Here in fact, since Paul made mention of imitation of the suffering of Christ so that he could strengthen them against ills to come by his own example, he adds it by way of a reason, comparing the measure of the sufferings and the greatness of the reward; and he points out that the ills seem slight if we reflect that for temporary ills we shall receive eternal joys.

1 Rom 8:18 'For I reckon that the sufferings of this time are not worthy to be compared'; CWE 56 214–16; *Collationes* 173r–174r
2 In fact, Erasmus' translation has *reputo*, and he does not seem to have changed this at any time; but the two verbs are given as alternatives in the annotation: *id est, perpendo, sive reputo*.
3 Phil 4:8
4 *excida[n]t* 1529 35v (plural; the macron is clear; page misnumbered 53); *excidat* in 1540 811 and LB (singular). It seems likely that Erasmus intended the subject to be 'they,' the Philippians, rather than 'what they have heard' (*id quod audierunt*), as 1540 and LB seem to understand.

[ER *quae revelabitur erga nos* 'that shall be revealed for us']
[RESP] *quae revelabitur in nobis* 'that shall be revealed in us.'[1] Εἰς ὑμᾶς.[2]

I have admitted that the Greek preposition has two meanings, excusing
the Translator by saying so, but I indicate the other meaning and translate
erga nos. 'The glory of God,' says he, 'is revealed rather for unbelievers.'
No, rather 'against unbelievers.' What is done 'for' you is done 'for your
benefit.' Why did he not consult his Valla here?[3] And that glory, by which
believers will be blessed, will not be revealed to unbelievers, although they
are destined to see the one whom they have offended. I do not argue that
the other meaning is wrong.[4]

1   Rom 8:18; CWE 56 216; *Collationes* 174r–v
2   εἰς ὑμᾶς] 1529 36r, 1540 811, and LB, 'in you'; εἰς ἡμᾶς in Erasmus' Greek text
    LB VI 603A and *Collationes* (the correct reading), 'in us'
3   There appears to be no discussion of this use of *erga* and *in* in the *Elegantiae*,
    nor of this phrase in Valla's *Adnotationes*. This seems to be another mischievous
    or exasperated question motivated by Titelmans' deference to Valla; cf Rom
    8:5, 218 n7 above.
4   In the annotation Erasmus added in 1535 that *in nobis* 'also has a pious sense'

[ER *etenim sollicita creaturae exspectatio* 'for indeed the eager expectation
of the creation']
[RESP] *nam exspectatio creaturae* 'for the expectation of the creation.'[1] On
the authority of the Greek scholia I translated ἀποκαραδοκία as *sollicita exspectatio*, and this is how Chrysostom and Theophylact interpret it.[2] 'But some,'
says he, 'translated it as "remote" [*longinquus*], others as "assiduous" [*fre-
quens*].'[3] I agree, but they were Latin speakers.

1   Rom 8:19 'for the expectation of the creature'; CWE 56 216–17; *Collationes* 174v–
    175v
2   Chrysostom *Hom in Rom* 14.4 PG 60 529; Theophylact *Expos in Rom* 8:19 PG 124
    445C–D. For the Greek scholia, see Rom 1:11, 155 n5 above.
3   *Collationes* 175r. In 1535, inspired by Titelmans' remark, Erasmus added to his
    annotation references to Ambrose (ie Ambrosiaster I 278–9) and Hilary.

[ER *omnis creatura congemiscit* 'The whole creation groans together.']
[RESP] *omnis creatura ingemiscit* 'The whole creation groans.'[1] The pre-
fixes of συστενάζει [groans together] and συνωδίνει [is in labour together][2]
show that the creation groans together with us. Since the Greek sources are
uniformly in agreement, and since the meaning is appropriate, why was
it important to review how the Latins or those translated into Latin read
it? He approves the Translator's version, and I do not disapprove of it, except in that the force of the prefix is not apparent; this I have striven to
express.

1   Rom 8:22 'Every creature groaneth'; CWE 56 218–19; *Collationes* 175v–176r
2   The next word in the verse

[ER *spiritus auxiliatur infirmitatibus nostris* 'The Spirit gives aid to our infirmities.']

[RESP] *spiritus adiuvat infirmitatem nostram* 'The Spirit helps our infirmity.'[1] Since it is clear that we find in the Greek 'infirmities' [plural], I am in no way at fault when I show this and translate it. What the Latins or Latin translations say has no relevance for me. Yet I do not condemn the Translator's rendering, for in Chrysostom I later noticed the singular, but in the genitive case.[2] But [the prefix] συν- requires the dative,[3] so that we understand the Spirit is there to help like a hand outstretched to our struggling spirit – unless we understand that there is another helper in addition to the Spirit.

1 Rom 8:26 'The Spirit also helpeth our infirmity'; CWE 56 221–2; *Collationes* 176v–177r
2 Chrysostom *Hom in Rom* 14.7 PG 60 532
3 The verb translated as *auxiliatur* or *adiuvat* is συναντιλαμβάνεται.

[ER *at ille qui scrutatur corda, novit quis sit sensus spiritus* 'But the one who searches the hearts (of men) knows what is the mind of the Spirit.']

[RESP] *qui autem scrutatur corda, scit quid desideret spiritus* 'He, however, who searches the hearts [of men] knows what the Spirit desires.'[1] I translated τὸ φρόνημα as *affectus* [desire] or *sensus;*[2] but in case anyone should think that *sensus* is not used for *affectus* in Latin, I cite in my annotation the phrase of Terence: *ego illum sensum pulchre calleo* [I know his mind pretty well].[3] Here with much irritation he tells us that *affectus* [desire] is of the flesh and is not suitable for the spirit.[4] So henceforth a pious desire towards God will not be called an *affectus*, and although Christ had pity on the crowd, it will not be said to have been an *affectus*. He disputes many things too about the sly, good-for-nothing, fleshly, and impudent *affectus* of the slave in Terence (whereas at that point the slave is talking about the *sensus* [mind] of the old man), as if we do not speak of God using the same words as when we speak of the vilest of men. A pimp begets a son from an immoral relationship, and God the Father begets the Son; a lovesick adolescent loves a prostitute, and God loves his Son. O, what profound annotations these are, for which he called Valla, Lefèvre, and myself together![5] This fellow probably wants to give instruction to us whom he pretends he is addressing, though there are so many childish, so many ignorant, so many ridiculous things here. He spells out Greek words in Roman script and explains them, talking to us as if we cannot read Greek. He could have taken on some other pupils for this sort of nonsense.

1 Rom 8:27 'And he that searcheth the hearts, knoweth what the Spirit desireth'; CWE 56 222–3; *Collationes* 177r

2   For this problem, see Rom 8:5, 217 n5 above.
3   Terence *Adelphi* 533
4   Erasmus later set out this argument again at some length in Ep 2260 to Pieter Gillis, 28 January 1530, complaining about the silliness of Titelmans' attacks.
5   Latin *annotationes ad quas convocavit*; ie in the meetings imagined in the *Collationes*

[ER *quos autem iustificavit, hos et glorificavit* 'These whom he justified he also glorified.']
[RESP] *quos autem iustificavit, illos et magnificavit* 'Those whom he justified he also magnified.'[1] We find δοξάζω for *honorifico* [honour], *clarifico* [make famous], *illustro* [make illustrious], and *glorifico* [glorify] – nowhere *magnifico* [exalt] among Latin speakers. Nevertheless, it is true that one who is glorified is exalted.

1   Rom 8:30 'Whom he justified, them he also glorified'; CWE 56 228–9; *Collationes* 178v

[ER *quis intentabit crimina adversus electos Dei?* 'Who will bring charges against the elect of God?']
[RESP] *quis accusabit adversus electos Dei?* 'Who will make accusation against the elect of God?'[1] Here I had to laugh at the duplicity of this youth. Although Lefèvre, inexcusably, both reproaches the Translator and twists the Apostle's words incongruously, yet my critic deals with him gently,[2] informing him in his own name of what I have detailed in my annotation, just as shortly afterwards he has borrowed from my annotation all the points of which he informs me. No doubt because I had said that in church [those words, *Christus est qui mortuus est*] are read as an affirmative statement and that this way of pronouncing it [interrogatively] had a blasphemous meaning, he admits this is true according to Augustine's distinction.[3] But I add that remark after mentioning Augustine's distinction, and my critic understands [that I meant] 'of those who say it like that' [that is, interrogatively].[4] I have never once heard pious men asking about that distinction. But how few perceive that the verb [is] is understood: 'It is Christ, [Christ] who died . . .'[5] – because unless it is understood, the blasphemous meaning remains. Here after long and bitter wrangling, after being so mild towards Lefèvre who was really at fault, he informs me of another more convenient reading from Origen[6] – which he has learned from my annotation. There's a proof of modesty! I am not censuring either the Fathers or the church, but I am warning those who read in church. He says, 'I perceived this meaning when I was a boy.' I do not know whether this is true; perhaps he was already inspired at that time by the Spirit, which he claims for himself in the Psalm that he places as the preface to his *Elucidationes*.[7] Few pay attention

to it, many do not understand, or if they do understand they know that it is incorrectly spoken or that some things have to be supplied: 'is' and the fact that before that we have 'who will make accusation, who will condemn?' I myself have followed Origen's reading, which appealed to me then, but yet at the same time this repetition of what precedes is somewhat rough in so far as the expression is concerned,[8] for the sense is extraordinarily fitting. 'The translator was right to omit *est*,' says he, 'because it is not there in Paul.' On the contrary, you inordinate wrangler, it is there in the [definite] article: Χριστὸς, ὁ ἀποθανών, that is, 'It is Christ, the one who died.' For the same reason he is wrong to say that this expression is no more difficult than the Greek.[9] But this fellow is in the habit of making all his pronouncements as if speaking an oracle,[10] though he is so badly informed in the disciplines that are necessary for this business. He says, 'The Translator was not at fault,' as if I had accused him.

1 Rom 8:33 'Who shall accuse against the elect of God?'; CWE 56 230–3; *Collationes* 179v–183r

2 The first two pages of Titelmans' article are in fact a quite severe response to Lefèvre. It includes the quotation from Augustine and a first allusion to what he claims as his own preferred reading.

3 'No doubt ... meaning' refers to phrases in the first four editions of the *Annotationes* but omitted in 1535; see CWE 56 232 n4; Reeve II 388. *Iuxta distinctionem Augustini*; Augustine had clearly said the first phrase of the verse is a question; see LB VI 607D; Reeve II 389; Augustine *De doctrina christiana* 3.3.6. The distinction Erasmus is discussing here, however, is not the slight difference (*differentiola*) between two types of question (*percontatio* and *interrogatio*) initially made by Augustine but that between the interrogative and affirmative pronunciations of the second phrase of this verse ('It is God that justifieth') and verse 34 ('It is Christ that died'). Augustine would read this phrase also as a question, and it is this that Titelmans discusses. In fact, Erasmus is complaining, as he does so often, that Titelmans agrees with him in this (though still claiming there is a disagreement) and in following Origen, who reads the second phrase of the verse as an affirmation (see n6 below).

4 I have followed the text of 1529 37r; the Latin phrase *et ita pronunciantium intelligit* is difficult to read, as the editor of 1540 812 (and following him LB) evidently thought when he made a drastic emendation (see below). The relevant passage in 1529 reads: 'Verum quoniam dixeram in templis recitari pronunciative, eamque pronunciationem habere sensum blasphemum: Id fatetur esse verum, iuxta distinctionem Augustini. At ego post indicatam Augustini distinctionem hoc dictum subiicio, et ita pronunciantium intelligit. Nec ego semel audivi pios viros querentes de hac distinctione.' However, the later editors do not seem to have realized that Erasmus is primarily concerned here with responding to Titelmans, who claims that Erasmus' statement makes heretics of all those who have ever read the passage up until now in church (*Collationes* 180v–181r). The phrase *et ita pronunciantium intelligit* must in fact be understood as having Titelmans as subject, the words *ita pronunciantium* being his

understanding of what Erasmus had said. *1540* (812) emended the passage, reversing the order of the second and third phrases and changing *intelligit* to *intelligentiam*: 'At ego post indicatam Augustini distinctionem, et ita pronuntiantium intelligentiam, subiicio hoc dictum: Nec ego semel audivi pios viros querentes de hac distinctione' (the last sentence is in italics in LB) 'But I, after indicating Augustine's distinction and his understanding of those who pronounce it this way, add this remark: "Nor have I once heard pious men complaining about this distinction."' The *dictum*, which Erasmus is made by the emendator to quote as if from his annotation, does not in fact appear there.

5 Ie Erasmus wants *Christus est, qui mortuus est* 'It is Christ who died' (as in his translation) enunciated affirmatively as the response to the question in the previous verse.

6 Origen *Comm in Rom* 7.10 PG 14 1130A–B / FC 104 95

7 Titelmans' psalm offers his first work to God and attributes to him all the inspiration for it. The passage in which he claims the inspiration of the Holy Spirit for himself reads, in translation: 'You have established them [the Scriptures] in the expedient form of words and in obscurity of meaning, so that by these two means [erudition and faith] you might drive the proud and the unworthy idle away. / But to the humble you, who listen to the humble, do not deny entry; you give them the key by which they may gain entry to those Scriptures. / Your Holy Spirit itself is the key to understanding your Scriptures, since it is also itself the pen. / It was the pen of those who wrote them and it is the same pen of those who read them' (Antwerp: Io. Steelsium 1540) a2r–v. Erasmus would have seen the first edition of 1528.

8 The repetition Erasmus appears to be thinking of here is perhaps that which would be involved in actually supplying the phrases that he takes to be understood and implied by Origen's reading.

9 *Collationes* 183r

10 Latin *velut ex tripode pronunciare*; cf *Adagia* I vii 90 *Ex tripode*.

[ER *quemadmodum scriptum est: propter te morti tradimur (tota die)* 'As it is written, "On account of you we are (daily) handed over to death."']
[RESP] *sicut scriptum, quia propter te mortificamur [tota die]* 'Just as it is written that on account of you we are [daily] put to death.'[1] I had pointed out that sometimes in Greek ὅτι does not signify a cause but an affirmation, and at that time ordinary people spoke as the Greeks usually did. Nowadays, if someone wants to speak correct Latin, the conjunction [*quia*] should be omitted. Here once again he quarrels senselessly with me, bringing forward good Latin clerics who use the expression thus. I admit this, since they are dealing with Scripture; and those using the expression at that time were understood by the people. But when they are explaining their own ideas in their own words, I ask you, would they speak in this way: 'It is written in the Gospel, "Since [*quoniam*] the Son of Man goes, as it is written of him ..."'? You will hardly ever find this. And if it is found,

who now, knowing no other language than Latin, will understand from
these words 'It is written because [*quia*] we are put to death' anything other
than 'For this reason this is written that [*quod*] we are put to death.'² He
praises Lefèvre for having retained *quia*. It is not surprising, since that man
seeks the maximum rhetorical effect with his words and not infrequently
commits solecisms. But if I am not allowed to comment on the correctness
of the language when it departs from the usage of the ancients, why does he
not dispute it every time I do it? 'Leave the Translator his ὅτι,' says he. Do
you understand, most impudent youth, what you are saying? I did not say
ὅτι was to be erased but that it was not to be translated. It is not superfluous
in Greek; it is superfluous in Latin. And this is that eminent master who
teaches me to speak with care.

1   Rom 8:36 quoting Ps 43 (44 AV):22 'As it is written: For thy sake we are
    put to death all the day long'; *Collationes* 183r–184r. There is no annotation
    corresponding to this phrase, but see CWE 56 235–6. *1529* (37v) and *1540* (813)
    omit the word *est* after *scriptum*, though it is found in VG and in the *Collationes*.
2   Erasmus is suggesting here that the Greek clause introduced by ὅτι, an indi-
    rect statement, should be rendered in classical Latin by a direct statement; a
    clause introduced by *quia* or *quoniam* would be a causal clause. In the Vulgate,
    however, a direct statement is frequently construed as a subordinate clause
    introduced by *quoniam*, *quia*, or *quod*.

From chapter nine to the Romans

[ER *attestante mihi simul (conscientia mea)* '(my conscience) as well wit-
nessing for me']
[RESP] *testimonium*¹ *mihi perhibente [conscientia mea]* '[my conscience]
bearing me witness.'² Since [the Greek] is συμμαρτυρούσης, in order to express the force of the prefix I added *simul*, so that the witness of the conscience is joined to the witness of the voice. He says no one commented on
this. It is not surprising, since the meaning is the same.

1   *testimonium mihi perhibente conscientia mea*] *Collationes* and VG; *perhibent* in *1529*
    38r, *1540* 813, and LB
2   Rom 9:1; CWE 56 239; *Collationes* 188v–189r

[ER *et cultus* 'and the worship']
[RESP] *et obsequium* 'and the subservience.'¹ Λατρεία [worship] was never
translated by anyone who spoke correct Latin as *obsequium*. Horace renders it
as *cultura*.² For *obsequium* is used properly when we comply with the customs
and wishes of others, and it is often used in a bad sense. However, *cultus*
is properly said of those who offer a sacrifice. But who was not aware that
the early church used *obsequium* for *cultus*?³ The difference that he makes
between *cultum* and *obsequium* is pure dreaming. He could have excused

the Translator with some other pretext, because in those times the common run of folk would have used *obsequium* for 'worship.'

1 Rom 9:4 'and the service [of God]'; CWE 56 241–2; *Collationes* 190r–v
2 Horace *Epistles* 1.18.86 (as 'courting, flattering'), 1.1.40 (as 'care, cultivation')
3 Titelmans quotes Augustine and Cyprian as confirming that Paul uses *obsequium* in this sense here.

[ER *qui est in omnibus Deus (laudandus)* 'who is in all things God to be praised']
[RESP] *qui est super omnia benedictus Deus* 'who is above all things blessed God.'[1] Although I have given answers so many times about this passage to Lee, to Stunica, and to my Spanish detractors,[2] yet my critic renews the whole dispute for me so that he can fill up his pages. For it is obvious that his principal concern was to make his volume fat. To start with, indeed he addresses me more agreeably: 'dearest Desiderius,' 'most welcome Desiderius,' but the whole lecture is full of the harshest abuses. I open breaches through which the enemy can escape; I wrest away the church's sword with which he was about to slay the enemy; no more thanks are due to me than to a traitor of the state; I introduce malicious, crafty, artful devices; I advance invented, trivial, shrewd pretexts, which have cleansed me no more than a pig rolled into a muddy hog pool.[3] What does he not say? He raves until he can say no more, and yet I am 'most beloved in the Lord, in the sight of God and all the saints.' But no point is so minute that he does not magnify it, make it into a fallacy, you would say. It is a huge crisis for the church because I pointed out that in Cyprian the word *Deus* is not added, though my critic himself indicates a similar passage in Hilary.[4] He preferred to exaggerate the crisis rather than be seen to have been ignorant of this. He gets angry because I said that it seems to have been omitted through the carelessness of scribes; I should have affirmed it, I should have corrected the passage. To affirm what you cannot prove is temerity, and to change a passage in the works of the ancients without the support of any exemplar is hardly scrupulous. And in this respect certain people allow and have allowed themselves too much, even in the canonical Scriptures. Anyway, what was the danger if the name of God was left out? Is there anything 'above all,' apart from God? What treachery towards the church does this fellow fancy I commit if I indicate the meaning of what Paul said in Greek? How much more serious a danger to the church threatens when Scotus, with the slenderest of arguments, attacks the most firmly accepted doctrines of the church and weakens them with unsound reasoning? Those doctrines are propounded to confirm the faith; I, if I make the briefest of comments, betray the church to the heretics. If someone puts forward annotations about the reading, should he not first give a warning about these

things? But this is the interpretation of the Doctors of the church, and I embrace this sense. If they believe that heretics cannot escape this passage if I had not opened breaches, the fact itself contradicts it. As for the added coda, I take back[5] what I said, on the basis of the consensus of the manuscripts. As for this passage, the case speaks for itself, Paul's words allow no more obvious sense than this: 'God, who is above all things, be blessed forever.' To this prayer is added the chant 'Amen.' 'But,' he will say, 'this should not have been revealed.' Why? Is Catholic truth to be defended by tricks? And if it should not have been revealed, why do these people agitate and ensure that no one can be unaware of it? Again, if they have no reproach here but the triviality [of it], why do they argue that it cannot be understood otherwise – although there is nothing here to endanger ecclesiastical doctrine, since it is amply proved both by the evidence of Scripture and the authority of the church. It follows that this whole complaint is full of pretence and magnified so as to stir up hatred of me. If it is true that this passage does not effectively refute the Arians, why is it important to assert that it is not true? The true believer does not have the sword struck out of his hand by one who advises him to take up a spear instead of a walking stick if he wants to destroy an enemy, nor are breaches opened for the enemy by one who advises the generals to block up the breaches through which enemies can either break in or escape.[6] Again, if he alleges against me three thousand doctors who interpret this passage in a similar way, what does that do to repress the heretics who consider the Scripture not just ambiguous but more probably giving a meaning that allows them to escape repression? Why does the church still stand firm, why is the authority of the orthodox Fathers still valued, though theologians have rejected many of their opinions and interpretations of the Scriptures, and condemned them as heretical? Why did they not fear some stumbling block there? Here such a frightful brawl is stirred up because one passage was pointed out. And if there is something of a stumbling block, it is rather to be attributed to those who make a commotion attacking these points that I have raised briefly for the learned. What benefit would it have been to the church if I shouted that Paul's words had only one sense, although they have three and none of them impious? He wanted me to assert that *Deus* was omitted in Cyprian through the fault of scribes, yet he himself does not dare to affirm that I have a correct idea of the Divinity of Christ, though I have produced so many testimonies from my writings. 'If indeed the heart agrees with the writings,' he says. There's a proof of frankness! He thinks tricks like this are not understood. But let me not linger any longer in this wrangle. I have long since corrected my statement in the annotation that the word *Deus* is not added in Chrysostom,[7] and I have indicated the reason for my slip. I would perhaps have changed a few other things if this censor had come at the right time. Although he knew this was done, he still, after a lengthy reproach, asked me to do it as if he did not know it was done. I shall not add *Deus* either in Cyprian or in Hilary unless an exemplar is found in which I can see it. About the added coda, although I myself immediately rejected this, it can be omitted since I see how very suspicious men are.

1 Rom 9:5 'who is over all things, God blessed for ever'; CWE 56 242–52; *Collationes* 191r–198r. The dispute is about whether this passage proves or allows for the divinity of Christ. See CWE 56 246 n1 for the radical revision of the annotation in 1535 and the context of the cue phrase.

2 *Responsio ad annotationes Lei* 2 (1520) CWE 72 273; *Apologia adversus Stunicae Blasphemiae* (1522) LB IX 362F–363B; *Apologia adversus monachos* (1528) LB IX 1043F–1045B. For Edward Lee, see CEBR II 311–14, and for Diego López Zúñiga, CEBR II 348–9.

3 *Collationes* 194r

4 Cyprian *Ad Quirinum* 2.6 PL 4 702A; Hilary *Tractatus super psalmos* 122.7 PL 9 671B; *Collationes* 197r. Although Erasmus edited Hilary in 1523 (Basel: Froben) and omitted the word there, it was apparently Titelmans who inspired the reference in the 1535 version of the annotation. See CWE 56 249 nn20 and 21.

5 *de coronide adiecta reiicio*; as he explains immediately, Erasmus is referring to the words *in saecula: amen* 'forever. Amen,' which he had thought to be an unwarranted addition. In his annotation from 1519 to 1527 he had said: 'However, in some places, clauses of this kind are found to be added, for example at the conclusion of a reading; just as it is customary for us to add "You, O Lord, glory to the Father, glory to you Lord," so among the Greeks, at the end of the Lord's Prayer, there is added as a conclusion "Yours is the kingdom and the power and the glory forever and ever. Amen"' Reeve II appendix B/CWE 56 251. This was removed in 1535. For *coronis*, see also the prefatory letter 146 n36 above.

6 1529 (39r), 1540 (814), and LB have a question mark here.

7 Chrysostom *Hom in Rom* 16.1 PG 60 550. See the two versions (1527 and 1535) of the annotation CWE 56 242–52, especially 250 (beginning of the second paragraph) and n18 in both cases. Cf Reeve II 391.

[ER *ex uno conceperat Isaac* 'from one (father), Isaac, had conceived.']
[RESP] *ex uno concubitu habens Isaac* 'having from the one intercourse with Isaac.'[1] Here, although Jacques Lefèvre, as well as criticizing the Translator's version, even censures him for using immodest language contrary to Paul's custom, and although Valla is the originator of the opinion to which I subscribe in part, yet my critic turns the whole dispute onto me and is kinder to them, so that it may seem likely that he is not at all motivated by personal feelings in his writing but by heartfelt honesty. He adduces for me a large number who have translated *ex uno concubitu*. This is true, but they are Latin writers or writers translated into Latin; in the Greek of Chrysostom I find nothing of the sort.[2] (I do not have Theophylact in Greek

to hand at the moment.) 'But,' says he, 'the translation is right if, instead of κοίτην (feminine accusative) [marriage bed] we read κοίτου (masculine genitive) from κοῖτος [bed, sleep.]'³ But since this reading is nowhere found among the Greeks, did he want me to change Scripture, which is consistent? This great man himself does not dare to do this. But unless this is done, all these magnificent arguments of his have been set out in vain. He is angry that I have counted this passage among those that are corrupted,⁴ although he himself cannot solve the difficulty without changing the Greek reading; but, just as if he had made a valid point, he concludes by repeating the attack, even acting as if he were victorious and accusing me of impudence for having dared to say this. If he thinks this meaning, 'She had conceived from the one intercourse,' is the right one and the Greek text does not allow it, there must be a corruption either in the Greek sources or in the Latin. Here, in order not to abandon the meaning, which I do not accept, he tries to change what the Apostle said. My critic says, 'Whoever used the phrase "to have a bed" for "to conceive"?'⁵ Latins do not use this expression, but it is likely that the Hebrews did; and if instead of κοίτην [the Apostle] had said κύησιν,⁶ he would still have been speaking in the Greek idiom. But again, who ever said ἔχουσα, that is, 'having' for 'pregnant'? For this is how he must read it if he is to defend his meaning. No commentators, not Ambrose in explaining this passage, not Origen, not Theophylact, not Chrysostom, not the scholiast Jerome talk about 'intercourse one time' but interpret it as meaning 'from one father.'⁷ He had undertaken to defend the Translator, so why does he get angry with me because I said the passage is corrupt? For I suspect the Translator wrote *concubitum habens* [having intercourse]. I blame the copyists, not the Translator. It is my critic who acts shamelessly, trying to alter what the Apostle wrote. As he says, he has more faith in these holy Doctors than in me; but he has to agree with me unless he corrects either Paul's Greek words or the common edition. But he prefers to twist and turn any way rather than abandon his 'intercourse one time.'

1 Rom 9:10; CWE 56 255–60; *Collationes* 199v–202v. The complete phrase in ER is: *sed et Rebecca ex uno conceperat Isaac patre nostro* 'But Rebecca also had conceived from one – Isaac, our father'; VG *sed et Rebecca ex uno concubitu habens Isaac patris nostri* 'but when Rebecca also had conceived at once of Isaac our father.'
2 Chrysostom *Hom in Rom* 16.5 PG 60 555
3 *Collationes* 201v
4 *Collationes* 200r; *Loca depravata* *[7]r
5 *Collationes* 202r
6 From κύω or κυέω 'to be pregnant.' This argument is the major part of the rewritten annotation in 1535; see CWE 56 256–7.
7 Ambrosiaster 1 310–11 (but see CWE 56 259 nn19 and 22); Origen *Comm in Rom* 7.15 PG 14 1142/FC 104 111–13. For Theophylact, see CWE 56 259 n25;

Chrysostom (see n2 above); Pseudo-Jerome or *Hieronymiana* in Souter II 74 and III 18.

[ER *miserebor cuiuscumque misereor* 'I will have mercy on whomever I have mercy.']

[RESP] *miserebor cui misertus sum* 'I will have mercy on whom I have had mercy.'[1] Here he becomes peevish because I pointed out in a few words that there was an unfortunate affectation of variety. Why, just before this, did he not vent his spleen on Lefèvre who criticized the Translator rather offensively because, contrary to Paul's habit, he had uttered an expression unfit for chaste ears?[2] What harm is done to the Translator's dignity if he has sometimes taken unwarranted pleasure in variety? But he cannot explain here why the Translator used the same word in the first part [of the verse] but not in the second part.[3] Yet though he has no reason, though he cannot answer the objection, he still casts against me a fierce reproach worthy of a judge of the Areopagus[4] and produces this petty annotation. No opportunity is so slight that it cannot serve as an occasion for him to wrangle with his 'dearest Desiderius.'

1 Rom 9:15 'I will have mercy on whom I will have mercy'; CWE 56 260–1; *Collationes* 202v–203r. For the importance of this verse and Erasmus' insistence on the freedom of the will, see John B. Payne 'Erasmus and Lefèvre d'Etaples as interpreters of Paul' *Archiv für Reformationsgeschichte / Archive for Reformation History* 65 (1974) 54–82.
2 In the previous article on Rom 9:10; *Collationes* 199v
3 The second part of the verse was translated in VG as *et misericordiam praestabo cui miserebor* 'And I will show mercy to whom I will show mercy' and in ER as *et commiserabor quemcumque commiseror* 'And I shall pity whomsoever I shall pity.' See CWE 56 260–1 n2.
4 See the prefatory letter 138 n4 above.

[ER *atqui O homo tu quis es qui ex adverso respondes Deo?* 'But who are you, O man, who reply against God?']

[RESP] *O homo tu*[1] *quis es, qui respondeas Deo* 'O man, who are you that you should reply to God.'[2] Since the Greek is ἀνταποκρινόμενος [replying in opposition], he says that both translations are correct, *qui respondeas* [subjunctive] or *qui respondes* [indicative]. But to those qualified in Greek it is clear that this is wrong. It is even more wrong to say that *qui respondeas* is a more correct reading. What he brings forward against this from Latin writers or those translated into Latin proves nothing, although there is nothing in their interpretation either that tells us we should read *qui respondeas*.[3]

1 *tu quis es*] 1529 40v and *Collationes* (interrogative rather than relative, as one would expect); *tu qui es* in 1540 815, LB, and VG

2 Rom 9:20; CWE 56 262–4; *Collationes* 203v–204v
3 *1529* 40v and *1540* 815 have a question mark here. The writers in question are Chrysostom, Theophylact, Ambrosiaster, and Augustine. See CWE 56 264 n10, which points out that the latter's comments indicate that he did read 'that you should reply,' ie with the subjunctive.

[ER *vasa irae apparata in interitum* 'vessels of wrath made for destruction']
[RESP] *vasa irae apta in interitum* 'vessels of wrath fitted for destruction.'[1]
Here he maintains that *apta* is a correct translation, like *praeparata* [made ready], if the participle καταρτισμένα [fitted, prepared] is taken in its literal sense. But this is found nowhere, nor does Paul mean this, nor does *apta in interitum* suit any better than *praeparata*.

1 Rom 9:22; CWE 56 267; *Collationes* 206r–v. DV translates *apta* with the verbal 'fitted,' CWE with the adjectival 'fit,' which corresponds better to the context where Paul is speaking of those who may have been predestined from creation to destruction. The distinction is clearer if Erasmus' *apparata* is translated 'made for,' as in RSV.

From the tenth chapter to the Romans

[ER *quod studium Dei habent* 'that they have a zeal for God']
[RESP] *quod aemulationem quidem Dei habent* 'that they have indeed an emulation of God.'[1] *Zelus* means various things to the Greeks as does [the verb] ζηλόω: referring at one time to admiration, at another to jealousy, at another to zeal to imitate, at another to ardent love, at another to some other base appetite. So it is not surprising that it is rendered by different words; though explaining the same word, one cannot always translate it in the same way.

1 Rom 10:2 'that they have a zeal of God'; CWE 56 276–7; *Collationes* 208r–209r

[ER *Moses enim scribit de iustitia quae est ex lege* 'For Moses writes concerning the righteousness which is from the Law.']
[RESP] *Moyses enim scripsit, quoniam iustitiam quae ex lege est* 'for Moses wrote since (the one who does) the righteousness which is from the Law.'[1]
I had noted this passage as being among those obviously corrupted, blaming the copyists, not the Translator.[2] Hence there is contestation again, as if I harmed the authority of the Translator. Which therefore does he prefer: to correct the Greek manuscripts in which there is nothing difficult at this point or to admit that this passage is incorrectly rendered by the Translator?[3] He says it is to be blamed on the copyists. Though that is what I do, he still quarrels with me.

1   Rom 10:5 'for Moses wrote, that the justice which is of the law, [the man that shall do it] ...'; CWE 56 278–80; *Collationes* 209v–210r. For the full texts of this passage, see CWE 56 279–80 n4. For Moses, see Lev 18:5.
2   *Loca depravata* 7r
3   *1529* (41r) has a question mark; *1540* (815) and LB have not.

[ER *hoc est Christum ex alto deducere* 'that is, to bring Christ down from on high']
[RESP] *id est Christum deducere* 'that is, to bring Christ down.'[1] He notes I remarked that in Greek *deducere* [ie καταγαγεῖν] means literally 'to bring down from on high,' and I add that the Translator translated with *revocare* [to call back] in order to remove a previously rather obscure expression. Here he accuses me of lying, by saying that the Translator did not translate καταγαγεῖν thus but ἀναγαγεῖν. But my censor has not understood the point of my annotation. Although there is in both verbs the idea of 'bringing,' *deducere* is in fact ambiguous; for *deducere* is said of a person who for duty's sake accompanies someone and of a person who brings down from above. The Translator does not put *ducere* for the second verb but *revocare*, that is, 'to bring back up.' So he avoided the ambiguity in the first verb too. My critic, I believe, will plead that I spoke obscurely.[2]

1   Rom 10:7; CWE 56 281–3; *Collationes* 211r–v
2   The annotation concerned both Rom 10:6 and 7. VG had *deducere* for καταγαγεῖν in the first and *revocare* for ἀναγαγεῖν in the second. Erasmus had *deducere* and *reducere*, but his annotation before 1535 suggested that *revocare* translated καταγαγεῖν. See CWE 56 282 n2; Reeve II 400.

[ER *omnis qui fidit illi non pudefiet* 'Everyone who trusts in him will not be made ashamed.']
[RESP] *omnis qui credit in illum non confundetur* 'Whosoever believeth in him shall not be confounded.'[1] I know what Cyprian and the many who followed him say about the distinction between *credo illi* [trust in him], *credo in illum* [believe in him], and *credo illum* [believe him].[2] Certainly this construction [*credo in illum*] derives simply from the Hebrew idiom, just as in the Gospel we read *confitebor in illo* [I shall confess in him] for *confitebor illum* [I shall confess him].[3] But what he adds – that on the day of judgment there will be many who trust in Christ [*Christo fidentes*] who will go to the eternal fire – is false in my belief since the Psalm declares that those who trust [*confidunt*] in the Lord are blessed.[4] The devils believe; they do not trust. Since, therefore, I knew that *credere in illum* is not Latin,[5] nor does the distinction they propose hold, I could not express better the idea of trust in God than with the word *fidere*.

1   Rom 10:11; CWE 56 280–1; *Collationes* 211v–212r

2   Not found in Cyprian. Titelmans remarks on the distinction but does not
    name Cyprian. He refers instead to Ambrose's commentary (ie Ambrosiaster
    I 348–9).
3   Matt 10:32; Luke 12:8
4   Ps 2:12
5   Erasmus means, as usual, not classical Latin. Lewis and Short sv *credo* de-
    scribe it as ecclesiastical Latin. For scholastic usage, see Oberman 229 n119 and
    464–5.

[ER *at non omnes obedierunt evangelio* '**But not all have obeyed the gospel.**']
[RESP] *sed non omnes obediunt evangelio* '**But not all obey the gospel.**'[1]
Here he would have defended the Translator better if he had pointed out
that ὑπήκουσαν belongs to the category of verbs that signify a continuing
action, or rather state, in the past tense.

1   Rom 10:16; CWE 56 285; *Collationes* 212r–v

[ER *quis credidit sermonibus nostris?* '**Who has believed our words?**']
[RESP] *quis credidit auditui nostro?* '**Who has believed our hearing?**'[1] Here
again he makes a great to-do of the fact that I placed this phrase, *quis credidit
auditui nostro*, on my list of inexcusable solecisms,[2] although he himself
admits elsewhere that solecisms are found even in apostolic writings. Why
is it then that he becomes so agitated whenever I impute an error to the
Translator? But he denies that this is an error. How so? 'Because ἀκοή means
literally *auditus*.' No; whenever it is used as a noun, *auditus* means to Latin
speakers the sense of hearing. And if ἀκοή means no more than *auditus*,
why did the Translator render the expression in Mark,[3] chapter 3, καὶ ἀκοὰς
πολέμων, as *rumores bellorum* [rumours of wars] rather than *auditus bellorum*
[hearings of wars]?[4] But this exceedingly modest young man declares that
he would prove what I said was true was certainly false, that there was no
solecism here, and that Latin speakers do speak thus. In order to prove this
he subsequently adduces Ambrose, Jerome the scholiast, Origen translated,
Sedulius the Irishman, Jerome, and so on.[5] When he has amplified these
rhetorically and brought forward against me such great pillars of the church,
he asks me again, 'Were these Latin speakers, or were they not?' If I should
answer that they were not, everyone will cover their ears and stone me.
If I should say they were, there cannot be a solecism, for they are Latins
who speak. What is it to me that he should adduce three hundred of this
sort, much more Latin than these? I did not say they were not Latins, I
said that no one who spoke Latin used this construction. When Jerome says
this, he is using the Translator's words, not his own. Otherwise, speaking
for themselves and in their own way, when do they say, 'I know you will

not trust my hearing' instead of 'my words'? Even Cicero, who is more Latin than they, is capable of speaking incorrect Latin. Who is denying that Ambrose and Jerome speak Latin elsewhere? Now, if we call Latins those who speak correctly and whose authority allows us to excuse a solecism, no one will include Ambrose, Cyprian, Augustine, or Jerome among the Latins. They made many concessions to the ears of their times, and this is not necessary nowadays. And Roman eloquence was already growing old in their time. Tertullian often affects solecisms and is far from being counted among those who speak correctly. What in fact is this despised authority of ancient writers, which he exaggerates with his words against me? Does their authority really totter if they do not change the simple language of the Scriptures? They should rather be given this credit that, though they were eloquent, yet they did not despise the simplicity of church language. Finally, if he thinks so great a crime has been committed in my declaration that the Translator's rendering was scarcely Latin, how is it that he himself is not afraid to ascribe solecisms to the apostles and the evangelists. When he does this, he does not think the authority of the Scriptures wavers. If only he had put forward just one passage from approved authors to excuse the solecism, rather than rave against me with so many insults. But he calls it a friendly admonition when in fact it is a wrangling as vulgar as it is contemptuous. He commands that this should be erased from the list.[6] What shall I replace it with then? That the language is good Latin? If I do that, everyone with a knowledge of Latin will say that I am lying most shamelessly, and they will say it with perfect justice. He gets exceedingly angry about that list. Why is he not indignant rather at those who drove me with their seditious clamour to publish the list? For the first edition had no list. Let him excuse just one solecism, and then let him wrangle. What could be more impudent than this youth who does not understand what I say or mind what he is saying, yet teaches us so haughtily what he has not learned? And he calls these nonsense rhymes 'friendly *Discussions* [*collationes*] in sweetness of spirit.'[7]

1   Rom 10:16; CWE 56 285–7; *Collationes* 212v–214v. Erasmus takes this quotation from Isaiah (53:1) to mean 'Who has believed the things heard from us?'
2   *Soloecismi* 5v
3   *Mar. iii*] *1529* 41r (sic for *xiii*?); *Mar. 3* in *1540* 816; *Marc.* III LB IX; *Matthaei tertio* LB VI 619F. It is in fact Mark 13:7 or Matt 24:6.
4   No question mark in *1529* 42r and *1540* 816
5   Ambrosiaster I 354–5. Jerome the scholiast, that is, Pseudo-Jerome or the work now known to be principally by Pelagius; see *In quo omnes peccaverunt* Rom 5:12, 202 n49 above; Souter II 83. Origen *Comm in Rom* 8.6 PG 14 1171A (as translated by Rufinus; see CWE 56 95 n11)/FC 104 149. For Sedulius, see the prefatory letter 145 n34 above. Jerome *Commentariorum in Isaiam prophetam liber* XIV (not XV as stated by Titelmans) 53.1 PL 24 505B–C.

6   Ie the *Soloecismi*
7   In the concluding reproach, *Collationes* 306r

[ER *ego ad aemulationem provocabo vos* 'I will provoke you to jealousy.']
[RESP] *ego ad aemulationem vos*[1] *adducam* 'I will move you to jealousy.'[2]
Although nothing in the published text offends him here, he nibbles at my
annotation because it speaks of anger, grief, and jealousy. This is clearly the
case, and this is how the Greeks interpret it: the Jews are both jealous and indignant that the blessing of the gospel is distributed to the gentiles. Did not
baptized Jews once murmur against Peter because [the disciples] preached
the gospel to gentiles and because they admitted the wives of Greeks to
the ministry?[3] But he charges that I have translated $\dot{\epsilon}\nu$[4] οὐκ ἔθνει as *in gente
quae non est gens* [in a nation that is not a nation], to make clear the nature
of the thought. A 'non-nation' is what Paul calls the idolaters despised by
the Jews and considered almost dogs by them, just as elsewhere he says the
most contemptible things 'are nonexistent.' My critic says, 'The expression
is self-contradictory: "to be a nation and not a nation."' True, unless you
recognize the figure; and if you do not, there is the same contradiction. For
since Paul is speaking of Greeks or other peoples, he is undoubtedly speaking of a 'nation.' 'Shortly after,' says my critic, 'you do something different;
you translate "a foolish nation," not "to a nation that is a foolish nation."'
In this case there was no need for the figure; the language is literal and
clear, an explanation of the earlier phrase. O, what subtle annotations!

1   *vos addam*] LB IX 1006B
2   Rom 10:19 'I will provoke you to jealousy'; CWE 56 288; *Collationes* 214v–216r.
    This response, however, is mostly concerned with the phrase that follows
    immediately, *in non gentem* 'those who are not a nation,' which is part of the
    cue phrase in *Collationes* and a separate note (18) in *Annotationes*. See n3 below.
    The whole of Rom 10:19 is a quotation of Deut 32:21.
3   Acts 11:2–3, 17:4 and 12
4   Sic in 1529 43r, 1540 816, and LB. Titelmans gives the correct Greek, $\dot{\epsilon}\pi$' οὐκ
    ἔθνει. In his annotation, Erasmus translates $\dot{\epsilon}\pi$' οὐκ ἔθνει as *in non gente* (abla-
    tive), explaining that the Greek is a dative. In ER he had $\dot{\epsilon}\pi$' οὐκ ἔθνει, trans-
    lated in 1516 as *in non gente*, in 1519 and 1527 as *per gentem quae non est gens*
    'through a nation that is not a nation.' VG *in non gentem* 'by that which is not
    a nation.'

From the eleventh chapter to the Romans

[ER *non repulit Deus populum suum, quem ante agnoverat* 'God has not
rejected his people whom he had acknowledged before.']
[RESP] *non repulit Deus plebem suam [quam praescivit]* 'God has not rejected his people [whom he foreknew].'[1] Here I follow a new meaning,

because this seemed to me simpler and better suited to what precedes and follows. 'But,' he says, 'you are bringing in something different from what everyone understands.' I admit it, but there is no conflict. For the fact that he acknowledged them and embraced them was surely part of his eternal intention.

1 Rom 11:2 'God hath not cast away his people, which he foreknew'; CWE 56 291–2; *Collationes* 216r–217r. Titelmans' objection and Erasmus' response concern the verb *praescivit*, which provided the cue phrase for the annotation and which Erasmus would extend to include all peoples, while Titelmans would restrict it to the children of Abraham.

[ER *reliquiae secundum electionem gratiae fuerunt* 'There has been a remnant according to the election of grace.']
[RESP] *reliquiae secundum electionem gratiae Dei salvae factae sunt* 'The remnant according to the election of the grace of God has become saved.'[1] My critic thinks the word *salvae* should be added, following the argument that the translator of Origen recalls something about those who are to be saved and those who are not to be saved.[2] It is not surprising since [Paul] is speaking here of the remnant of those who believe. Anything that is quoted elsewhere has little bearing on the matter, since scribes habitually correct this sort of witness according to the Vulgate text.

1 Rom 11:5 'There is a remnant saved according to the election of grace'; CWE 56 293–4; *Collationes* 219r–220v
2 Origen *Comm in Rom* 8:7 (4) PG 14 1177B–C / FC 104 157. The translator is Rufinus.

[ER *quandoquidem gratia, iam non est gratia* 'inasmuch as grace is no longer grace']
[RESP] *alioqui*[1] *gratia non est gratia* 'otherwise grace is not grace.'[2] With Lefèvre, who declares the Latin translation is corrupt, he has no dispute; with myself, when I defend the Translator, he seeks a quarrel, reproaching me for the fact that, while I prefer the Latin reading to the Greek [here], I do not do the same in many other places. But that is what I was prepared to do and what I do whenever it seems the likely solution. He goes on to say that Greek sources should be corrected from the Latin rather than the Latin from the Greek. If he had said, 'each from the other,' it would have been acceptable. But as for removing from the Greek whatever I judged to be superfluous, as he wanted me to do, I had not undertaken the task of emending Greek texts, unless there were some passage with an obvious mistake committed by copyists. He says in addition that the Aldine and Spanish editions are paramount.[3] Why he should think this has to be pointed out I

do not fully understand, unless perhaps he was seeking to make Froben's books less marketable.

1 *alioquin gratia iam non est gratia*] VG and *Collationes; iam* omitted in 1529 43v and 1540 817
2 Rom 11:6 'otherwise grace is no more grace'; CWE 56 295–6 (but see n1); *Collationes* 220v–222r
3 *Collationes* 221r: *Aldina aeditio et Hispaniensis, quae nunc accuratissimae habentur* 'the Aldine edition and the Spanish, which are now considered to be the most accurate.' Erasmus used the Aldine Greek in the 1522 edition of his NT; the 'Spanish edition' refers to the NT volume of the Complutensian polyglot Bible, which appeared in 1520. See CWE 56 296 nn9 and 10.

[ER *dedit eis Deus spiritum compunctionis* 'God gave them the spirit of remorse.']
[RESP] *dedit illis Deus spiritum compunctionis* 'God gave them the spirit of remorse.'[1] Here, although Jacques Lefèvre changes the meaning beyond all probability and without any authority, translating κατανύξεως as *repugnans* [one who contradicts] instead of *compunctio* [remorse], he still does not dispute with him.[2]

1 Rom 11:8 'God hath given them the spirit of insensibility'; CWE 56 297; *Collationes* 222r–v. For Erasmus' understanding of κατανύξεως 'the sting of a grief that goads us on,' see CWE 56 297 n1. It was perhaps inspired also by Rom 11:14 'in order to make my fellow Jews jealous, and thus save some of them.'
2 Not true. Titelmans' objection is quite clearly addressed to Lefèvre, though part of it is also addressed to Erasmus and admits Lefèvre is partly right.

[ER *num ideo impegerunt ut conciderent* 'Have they slipped in order that they should utterly fall?']
[RESP] *numquid sic offenderunt ut caderent* 'Have they so stumbled that they should fall?'[1] It is clear that in the Greek sources we have ἵνα [in order to]. Here he ought to have given an example in which ἵνα means οὕτως [in such a way that]. Latin authors or those translated into Latin provide no certainty.

1 Rom 11:11; CWE 56 298–301; *Collationes* 222v–223v

[ER *sed per lapsum illorum salus* 'but through their fall salvation']
[RESP] *sed illorum delicto salus* 'but by their offence salvation.'[1] *Delictum* is used of a minor fault, committed not out of malice but rather out of ignorance or thoughtlessness. 'But παράπτωμα has the same meaning.'[2] But how can it be appropriate for [Paul] to call the disbelief of the Jews and their stubborn rejection of the gospel a *delictum*? Besides, they fell as if cut from the olive tree,[3] so that by their fall the gentiles should be raised up.

1 Rom 11:11; CWE 56 301; *Collationes* 223v–224r
2 LB does not italicize this sentence, but it is an objection made by Titelmans and loosely paraphrased by Erasmus.
3 An allusion to the passage in verses Rom 11:17–24; see also the next item.

[ER *tu vero cum esses oleaster* 'but since you were a wild olive shoot']
[RESP] *tu autem cum oleaster esses* 'however since you were a wild olive shoot.'[1] Instead of *insertus in illis* [inserted in them], I had translated *insitus illis* [grafted on them]. My critic says it is absurd to say the gentiles 'were grafted on broken branches,' and so it is necessary to have the preposition *in illis*, that is, *pro illis* [in their place]. This comment raises too great a difficulty: whoever said *in illis* for *pro illis*? However, it is correct that the gentiles are grafted on to the wild olive where branches have been cut out; a broken branch has two parts, one that falls off and another that remains on the tree. The part from which something has fallen is also said to be 'a broken branch'; it is on these branches that the gentiles have been grafted.

1 Rom 11:17 'and thou, being a wild olive'; CWE 56 306; *Collationes* 228r–v. The dispute here is actually about the phrase that follows: ER *insitus fuisti illis*; VG *insertus es in illis*.

[ER *vide ne qua fiat ut nec tibi parcat* 'Take care lest it should somehow happen that he should not spare you either.']
[RESP] *ne forte nec tibi parcat* 'lest perhaps he also spare not thee.'[1] Making *ne* refer to the verb *timeo* [fear] in the preceding verse is very strained; as for his idea that a good translation of πῶς [somehow] is *quomodo*,[2] I have made it *ne qua*, which is more idiomatic than *ne quomodo*.

1 Rom 11:21; CWE 56 307; *Collationes* 229r–v
2 This is Titelmans' suggestion for the Vulgate's *forte*, which Erasmus agrees is out of place here (see the annotation).

[ER *per illorum incredulitatem* 'through their unbelief']
[RESP] *propter incredulitatem illorum* 'on account of their unbelief.'[1] I had translated *per incredulitatem illorum*. He prefers *propter*, because *propter* signifies the occasion and *per* the cause. I have shown that this distinction is trivial.[2] He says 'There is no preposition here.' I agree, but this is an instrumental dative,[3] which can only be translated either by an ablative or by an accusative with the preposition *per*.

1 Rom 11:30 'through their unbelief'; CWE 56 312; *Collationes* 231r–v
2 Cf the discussion on Rom 5:12, 188 above.
3 Greek τῇ τούτων ἀπειθείᾳ 'by their unbelief'

[ER *increduli facti sunt, ex eo quod vos misericordiam estis adepti* 'They have become unbelievers from this, that you have gained mercy.']

[RESP] *non crediderunt in vestram misericordiam* 'They have not believed in your mercy.'[1] I translated a similar Greek dative τῷ ὑμετέρῳ ἐλέει [through the mercy shown to you] in a similar way: *ex eo quod misericordiam estis consequuti.*[2] Here he denies that the salvation of the gentiles was the occasion for the fall of the Jews, but was rather the opposite. No! Each was the occasion of the other. The unbelief of the Jews made way for the gentiles; the Jews, considering the gentiles unworthy to be received into the grace that they believed was promised to themselves, fell away or abstained from the gospel.

    1 Rom 11:31 'These [also now] have not believed, for your mercy'; CWE 56 312–6; *Collationes* 231v–232v

    2 The discrepancy with the text of ER above is explained by the fact that Erasmus used *consequantur* 'They may gain' in the following phrase of this verse. He also used *consequuti* in the 1519 text of his annotation, which was considerably enlarged in 1535.

From the twelfth chapter to the Romans

[ER *ut praebeatis corpora vestra* 'that you furnish your bodies']

[RESP] *ut exhibeatis corpora vestra* 'that you present your bodies.'[1] I have preferred *ut praebeatis corpora vestra.* Here he quotes a usage from the Latin translation of Theophylact. I admit there is very slight difference between *praebere* and *exhibere*, though you cannot always use one for the other. [We use] *exhibere* when things once promised are in fact made good; *exhiberi* is also used when things kept aside until they are needed are produced, as when a judge orders promissory notes to be presented; but in that case it would not be correct for you to say *praeberi* or *praestari*. [We use] *praebere* of something that is supplied for use, or put at someone's disposal. Thus we 'provide expenses' [*praebemus sumptum*], and a king 'provides auxiliaries' [*praebet auxilia*] to a friend for war. *Praestare* [is used] strictly of what is performed on trust, as in *praestatur promissum* [what was promised is carried out], and here it does coincide with the verb *exhibere*. So here it is more appropriate to use *praebere* than *exhibere*. Strictly we do not 'present' [*exhibere*] the armies we draw up, but we 'furnish' [*suppeditamus*] arms, money, machines, or even men for use in war.

    1 Rom 12:1; CWE 56 320–1; *Collationes* 240v–241r

[ER *rationalem cultum vestrum* 'your reasonable worship']

[RESP] *rationabile obsequium vestrum* 'your reasonable service.'[1] Here again, as if he has found a splendid battlefield, he omits nothing in an

attempt to heap hatred on me and all but has a victory parade over me. But
if you look at the matter more closely, it will be clear how vainly he inflates
his pride here and raises his crest. First, he relies on worthless grounds, informing us that *rationale* is said of something that possesses reason and *rationabile* of something that accords with reason. But the Greeks call what is
equitable and conformable to reason εὔλογον, not λογικὸν,[2] although λογικὸν
is used not only of what is conformable to reason but also of anything related to reasoning or speaking. *Rationabile* and *rationale* differ either very
little or not at all, just as *aequale* and *aequabile* [equal] or *exitiale* and *exitia-
bile* [destructive] differ only in sound. You can see, dear reader, that these
grounds for lengthy dispute, or rather wrangling, are immediately under-
mined. From authors translated into Latin there is nothing to be learned
with any certainty on this point. It is clear from the interpretation of all
commentators that in this verse the dead animals that the Jews sacrificed
are excluded by [the words] 'living sacrifice,' and [the word] λογικὸν excludes the corporal sacrifices of irrational animals, or certainly of bodies
alone. For this sacrifice is not entire unless the spirit sacrifices itself too, embracing spiritual things instead of the appetites of the flesh. It is quite clear
too that the phrase *rationale obsequium vestrum* is joined here in apposition
to the words *hostiam viventem, sanctam, Deo placentem* [a living sacrifice, holy
and acceptable to God], nor is there any doubt but that he uses 'sacrifice'
to mean man's living body. But man's living body is the abode of reason
and the part of the man endowed with reason. If man can rightly be said
to be a 'living sacrifice,' why can he not be said to be 'rational worship'?
'But worship is an action.' So are θυσία 'sacrificing' and *sacrificium*, and yet
they are correctly used for the thing sacrificed, just as *immolatio* too is used
of the thing immolated. *Agricolatio* [agriculture] is the activity, and yet Paul
calls the Corinthians *Dei agricultura* [the field of the Lord];[3] and we call a
man by whom we are defended *munimentum nostrum* [our defence]. And
again the Apostle calls his people his 'joy and crown' and his 'boast.'[4] So
there is no reason why this figure of speech should shock. Nor is it absurd
that man should be said to be a sacrifice since Paul says that he sacrifices
himself for his brothers. Perhaps my critic will say [the Apostle] does not
call himself an offering. On the contrary, Chrysostom explains σπουδὴν δὲ
ἑαυτὸν ἐκάλει as 'he called himself a sacrifice' or 'an offering.'[5] In the same
way a theft is an action, but it is also taken for the thing [stolen]. Now let us
see how splendidly he fulfils his promise to explain this with the greatest
clarity. I had quoted [the letter of] Jerome to Pammachius.[6] My critic has
looked at the passage and found these words: 'Haec moneo, frater caris-
sime, pietate qua te diligo, ut non solum pecuniam, sed teipsum ófferas
hostiam, vivam, sanctam, placentem Deo, rationabile obsequium tuum, et
imiteris filium hominis, qui non venit ministrari, sed ministrare' [I give you

this advice, dearest brother, by the piety for which I love you, that you offer not only money but yourself, a living, holy sacrifice, acceptable to God, (which is) your reasonable service, and that you imitate the Son of Man who came not to be served but to serve]. He says there is nothing in these words to support me.[7] But it does support me: Paul refers to bodies, and [Jerome] interprets this as 'you offer yourself,' that is, the whole person; and he does not separate 'your reasonable service' from what precedes, nor can it be separated. Does my annotation not say the same, that you should understand the person himself is sacrificed? Again, when he [Jerome] mentions Christ, does he not state clearly enough that just as Christ sacrificed himself, so we too, following his example, must present ourselves as a sacrifice to Christ? I make no answer here to the Origen,[8] which is freely translated with much added and much omitted, except that it is incongruous that someone threw in here the fact that 'reasonable service' is said of service for which an explanation can be given. Were the sacrifices of the Jews not conformable with reason? Can no explanation of them be given? But according to their lights, this is said to be reasonable. [I make no answer] to the Theophylact either;[9] I do not have the Greek to hand. In his expositions Chrysostom always opposes λογικός 'rational' to the corporeal sacrifice. This is what he says: Ταῦτα γὰρ ποιῶν ἀναφέρεις λογικὴν λατρείαν, τοῦτ᾽ ἔστιν οὐδὲν ἔχουσαν σωματικόν, οὐδὲν παχὺ, οὐδὲν αἰσθητόν, that is, 'When you do these things, you offer a reasonable sacrifice' or 'worship, having nothing corporeal nor base nor sensible.'[10] It is quite clear from this that he does not distinguish reasonable worship from the living sacrifice. But let's concede here that *latria* is taken to mean not the sacrifice itself but the performance of the sacrifice, for this is what Origen implies when, having recalled many sinful affections in taming each of which we immolate our bodies, he goes on: 'But the reasonable worship of God is all these things.'[11] This is also supported by the Greek pronoun τὴν [which],[12] so that anyone would rightly translate 'that you should present your bodies a living sacrifice, holy, acceptable to God, which is your reasonable worship.' And he calls it reasonable because it is of the mind, not only of the body, adding that the sacrifice is not entire unless the mind too brings forth pious desires and good deeds instead of evil works. Certainly there is nothing here that points to moderation of vigils, fasts, or similar things. On the contrary, he informs us: Οὐδὲ γὰρ εἶπε ποιήσατε τὰ σώματα ὑμῶν θυσίαν, ἀλλὰ παραστήσατε, ὡς ἄν εἰ ἔλεγον, μηδὲν κοινὸν πρὸς αὐτὰ ἔχετε, that is, 'For he did not say, "Make your bodies a sacrifice," but "present," [*exhibete* for παραστήσατε] as if he had said, "Have nothing in common with them."'[13] For when the sacrifice is placed on the altar, the whole is delivered to God. Not one of the ancients interprets this as having anything to do with moderating bodily deprivation or even suggests it.[14] Nor is the species understood here as the genus but is said to be different. The Apostle says that worship, not corporeal but of the mind, is this: to offer our bodies to God when the appetites of the flesh have been overcome. And these people interpret this as meaning that we should be moderate in our physical disciplines! So he is wrong to excuse the Scholiast[15] and Thomas, whom he wants to seem harmed by me because I disagree with them; as if I do not do that in other places, or as if I am the only one to disagree with Thomas, and as if the seraphic[16] Scotus does not do it often. Perhaps Thomas was deceived because ordinary French people call 'reasonable' what is fair and conforms to reason, though this usage is not found among Latins. Here my critic will say, 'In this you have certainly erred, because you have said that rational man is worship.' Where do I say that? In the text there is nothing of the sort. In the *Annotationes* I suggest only that in this passage man himself is understood as a rational sacrifice, that is, not a dumb or irrational animal. 'But the reason sacrifices; the body does not sacrifice unless bodily appetites are overcome.'[17] But these appetites are in the mind. So it is the mind that sacrifices and is sacrificed. For when man offers himself entire to God, as if placing a victim on the altar, then the Holy Lamb, coming from heaven lays hold of the victim and removes what is of the flesh. Chrysostom scatters into [his commentary on] this passage many points like this, which are a long way from the question of moderating bodily disciplines. But I disagree only with this opinion [about moderating bodily disciplines]. And yet what refrain is more commonly chanted now among theologians – when they are giving advice about abstaining from excessive physical discipline – than 'Let your service be reasonable, that is, moderate'? The cause of the mistake was the French language, or perhaps even the Italian. If he cannot defend that [language], why is he so offended? Origen is not reluctant to depart from the literal meaning, and Ambrose follows him for the most part;[18] I am not willing to be coerced by their authority, and no more by that of Theophylact, whom we have in translation anyway.

Now let me ask you to imagine that λατρεία is taken actively for the act of sacrifice itself; if on that account the sacrifice is said to be rational, as Peter calls milk 'spiritual' when speaking of the milk of the mind[19] – because [the sacrifice] is made by the spirit, not by the body, and it is made in the body of man – is it not correct to say that the man who sacrifices himself to God is called the victim? In the same way the third interpretation that my critic adduces here is clearly forced, relying on the fact that 'rational' is said of what accords with reason. I say the same of the fourth, which he wants to attribute to 'reasonable worship,' that is, well ordered and conforming to its purpose. The words that Thomas attributes to Jerome, I believe, are nowhere to be found in his writings. Moreover, as far as the meaning of the text is concerned, the true one seems to me to be that we should make τὴν explicit: '*which* is your rational worship,' and take 'rational' to mean 'spiritual' so that with this word we can at one and the same time exclude the temple, the sacrifices, the rites, and the victims of the Jews.

1 Rom 12:1; CWE 56 321–3; *Collationes* 241r–248v
2 This is the word in the original Greek text.
3 1 Cor 3:9 VG *agricultura*; ER *agricolatio*
4 Phil 4:1 *gaudium et coronam*; 2 Cor 8:24 *gloriationem*; ER *nostrae de vobis gloriationis*; VG *nostrae gloriae pro vobis*
5 σπουδὴ 'libation'; Chrysostom *Hom in Rom* 20.1 PG 60 596; see CWE 56 323 n14.
6 Jerome Ep 66.12 CSEL 54 662:14 / PL 22 646 12; the last clause of the quotation is from Matt 20:28.
7 *Collationes* 242r–v
8 Origen *Comm in Rom* 9.1 (5) PG 14 1204 497C / FC 104 193. Erasmus means of course Origen as quoted by Titelmans.
9 Theophylact *Expos in Rom* 12.1 PG 124 497C. Erasmus does make a brief comment in his annotation.
10 See n5 above.
11 See n8 above.
12 Paul's text is τὴν λογικὴν λατρείαν ὑμῶν.
13 Origen *Comm in Rom* 9.1 (3) PG 14 1203B–C / FC 104 192
14 This dispute contributed to some rewriting of the annotation in *1535*; see CWE 56 322–3 n5.
15 Pseudo-Jerome again; see Rom 5:12, 202 n49 above.
16 Ie, the Franciscan, like Titelmans. See the prefatory letter 141 n14 above.
17 Implied objection by Titelmans, though the punctuation does not indicate it
18 Ambrosiaster 1 392–3
19 1 Pet 2:2

[ER *cuilibet versanti inter vos* 'to whomever it may be who dwells among you']
[RESP] *omnibus qui sunt inter vos* 'to all that are among you.'[1] Παντὶ τῷ ὄντι ἐν ὑμῖν I have translated as *cuilibet versanti inter vos* [to whomever it may be who dwells among you]. He prefers *exsistenti* [who lives]. But if I had said this, I would have been speaking bad Latin. He comes close to condemning Origen's comment himself.[2]

1 Rom 12:3; CWE 56 327; *Collationes* 252r–v
2 Origen *Comm in Rom* 9.2 (2) PG 14 1208A / FC 104 198. Erasmus takes the participle ὄντι to mean 'living' in the simple sense of 'dwelling.' Titelmans, however, points out that Origen asserts that Paul means 'living in God' (having been converted) and uses *existenti* to cover this possibility, but then goes on to suggest that this interpretation, which may have been a genuine divine inspiration on Origen's part, may seem inappropriate, forced, or even absurd (*non germana, extorta, absurda*) to those endowed with lesser grace.

[ER *sed tamen habentes dona* 'but nevertheless having gifts']
[RESP] *habentes etiam*[1] *donationes* 'even having gifts.'[2] Here again my censor creates a wrangle: he considers it a 'bitter irony'[3] that I said the Translator seeks to achieve variety when there is no need – something that is
nevertheless remarkably easy to see in the translation. My words are as follows: 'how he seeks to achieve variety when there is no need.' Is there anything bitter in this? Is there any irony? I think 'seek to achieve' is synony-
mous for him with 'kill,' and 'variety' must be the name of the Translator's
mother. What was the point here of wrangling, since he can give no reason
why he would prefer to translate with *donationes* rather than *dona*, nor is it
correct to teach that it is good Latin to use *donationes* for *dona* at this point.

1   *etiam*] 1529 47r and 1540 819; *autem* VG and *Collationes*
2   Rom 12:6 'having different gifts'; CWE 56 330; *Collationes* 253v–254r. This note
    concerns the second of two annotations that were separate, as in CWE, in all
    early editions, though LB VI conflates them. See the first annotation in CWE 56
    330 with n6.
3   *Collationes* 253v

[ER *iuxta portionem fidei* 'according to the portion of faith']
[RESP] *secundum rationem fidei* 'in accordance with the rule of faith.'[1]
He prefers the Translator's *ratio* to Origen's *competens mensura* [appropriate
measure],[2] as if 'measure' cannot be applied to a quality, especially in figu-
rative speech, or as if the word 'measure' is not often used of things that are
not countable. My translation, *iuxta portionem* for *ratio*, does not satisfy him,
'unless perhaps,' says he, '*portio* means the same as *proportio*.' On the contrary, scholars doubt very much whether *proportio* is found as a single word
in Latin writers. So we do not really have a word [by which] to translate
ἀναλογία.[3] *Pro portione* [in proportion] is common among scholars. Certainly
Chrysostom interprets ἀναλογία [proportion] here as μέτρον [measure].[4]

1   Rom 12:6; CWE 56 331; *Collationes* 254r–v
2   This is Erasmus' translation of Origen's word ἀναλογία; Origen *Comm in Rom*
    9.3 (2) PG 14 1213A–B / FC 104 205.
3   In fact Quintilian (1.6.3 and 9) proposes *proportio* as a translation of the Greek
    analogia.
4   Chrysostom *Hom in Rom* 20.3 PG 60 599. In 1527 (Reeve II 412) Erasmus had
    pointed out that Paul himself speaks of the two words in the same way.

[ER *per fraternam charitatem ad mutuo vos diligendos propensi* 'through
fraternal charity eager to love each other']
[RESP] *caritatem fraternitatis invicem diligentes* 'loving in turn the charity
of brotherhood.'[1] He suspects the text is corrupt and that *caritate* has been
changed into *caritatem* by the copyists. This is taken from my annotation, as
he informs me, agreeable man that he is. Is there no end to his thirst for

glory? Anyway, granting this, *caritas fraternitatis* [love of the brotherhood] is still not a good way to say *caritas fraterna* [brotherly love]. The scholiast Pseudo-Jerome says, 'Love one another as if you were born of the same mother.'² Φιλόστοργος is expressed well enough by Tertullian who translates *invicem affectuosi* [affectionate towards one another], but this is hardly good Latin.³ Φιλόστοργος is used strictly of those who are committed with tender affection especially to their own relatives.

1 Rom 12:10 'loving one another with the charity of brotherhood'; CWE 56 332–3; *Collationes* 254v
2 Souter II 97
3 Tertullian *Adversus Marcionem* 5.14.11 CCSL 1 707. Φιλόστοργος, translated as 'honour,' is in the next phrase of the verse and should be in the next comment but is displaced to the one following that.

[ER *tempori servientes* 'serving the time']
[RESP] *Domino servientes* 'serving the Lord.'¹ I had pointed out in my annotation that Origen and Ambrose mention the two readings.² He tells me this about my own statement, for it is to me he is speaking in his dialogue.³ Everything else is pure guessing.

1 Rom 12:11; CWE 56 334–6; *Collationes* 254v–256r. Out of order in both *Collationes* and *Responsio*; cited as an example of undesirable modern emendation in Titelman's prologue (b6r).
2 Origen *Comm in Rom* 9.10 PG 14 1220A/FC 104 213; Ambrosiaster I 404–5. See also CWE 56 335 nn6 and 7.
3 True. This article consists of two replies to remarks of Erasmus.

[ER *honore alius alium praevenientes* 'in honour anticipating one another']
[RESP] *honore invicem praevenientes* 'in honour mutually anticipating.'¹ If you understand *honor* as *subsidium* [aid], it does not matter whether you read *praevenientes* or *praecedentes* [preceding] or *praecurrentes* [hastening before] or *antevertentes* [placing oneself before]. If, however, you take *honor* actively, as 'reverence' shown by one who defers, as Chrysostom interprets it,² the meaning will again be the same. And he who is first in honour is quicker in bestowing honour. If you take it passively,³ whether you read it as *praevenientes* or as *praecedentes* or anything like that, the meaning is inappropriate. So there is no reason for him to praise me because I replaced *praecedentes* with *praevenientes* in the fourth edition.⁴ But there remains a slight problem concerning the accusative case of ἀλλήλους [one another], since προηγεῖσθαι, because of the prefix, requires the genitive case. Hence it would perhaps be more correct to translate with *praeferentes* [preferring], for ἡγοῦμαι means *existimo* [I judge] and προηγοῦμαι *pluris facio* [I judge more highly]. So that we should not only rejoice to be first in bestowing

honour but should put anyone before us and count them more worthy of honour.

1 Rom 12:10 'with honour preventing one another'; CWE 56 333–4; *Collationes* 256r–257r. This note and the preceding one appear in the wrong order in *1529* (48r) and*1540* (820), as well as in LB.
2 Chrysostom *Hom in Rom* 21.3 PG 60 605
3 Ie as 'dignity, office'
4 Ie in *1527*; cf *Collationes* 257r: *id magis laudo*.

[ER and RESP] *necessitantibus sanctorum communicantes* 'sharing in the needs of the saints.'[1] Almost everything he tells me here he took from my annotation.

1 Rom 12:13 'communicating to the necessities of the saints'; CWE 56 336–7; *Collationes* 257r–258v

[ER *bene loquamini de iis qui vos insectantur* 'Speak well of those who assail you.']
[RESP] *benedicite persequentibus vos* 'Bless them that persecute you.'[1] Since I had written 'annotations,' and since there was no intention at the time to add the text, it happens in some places that they do not correspond very well. This is what happened here. Moreover, I do not know if *benedicere*, meaning *bene precari*[2] [invoke good upon], is found in Latin writers; one who invokes good upon another does speak well of him.

1 Rom 12:14; CWE 56 337–8; *Collationes* 258v–259v
2 *bene precari* was suggested by the translator of Origen *Comm in Rom* 9.14 PG 14 1221/FC 104 215. See CWE 56 337 with n2.

From the thirteenth chapter

[ER *omnis anima potestatibus supereminentibus* '[Let] every soul [be subject] to the powers that stand over [us].']
[RESP] *omnis anima potestatibus sublimioribus* '[Let] every soul [be subject] to higher powers.'[1] He shows that the prefix ὑπερ- gives the force of a comparative, as if *praecellere* does not have the same force from the prefix *prae-*.[2] But Paul wants us to obey officials precisely because they are pre-eminent in their public authority. Now my critic seems to suggest that we should obey not every official but only the higher ones, that is, kings or governors, but not praetors or tribunes.[3]

1 Rom 13:1; CWE 56 346; *Collationes* 261r–v. In an addition to the annotation in *1535* Erasmus admitted the meaning suggested by Titelmans is possible.

2   The Greek ὑπερέχοντι is translated as praecellens by both VG and ER in 1 Pet 2:13.

3   'Praetor' here refers to the judges in Roman law courts of the imperial period. The tribunes were deprived of their original powers under Caesar and Augustus, and the position remained only as a step to a senatorial career for plebeians. See OCD 'praetor' and 'tribuni plebis.'

[ER and RESP] *Dei enim minister est tibi* 'For he is God's minister to thee.'[1] Although Lefèvre declares the Translator has been dreaming here and translated badly into Latin, yet my critic does not get angry with him as he usually does with me, demonstrating clearly enough how honestly he conducts the business.

1   Rom 13:4; CWE 56 350; *Collationes* 262v–263v

[ER *in hoc sermone summatim comprehenditur* 'It is summarily embraced in this saying.']
[RESP] *in hoc verbo instauratur* 'It is restored in this word.'[1] Here *instauratur* can be taken as meaning *renovatur* [is renewed]. The New Law, as it were, renews the Old, reducing it to a summary.[2] For the force of this prefix *re-* is in the Greek word used by the Apostle.[3]

1   Rom 13:9 'It is comprised in this word'; CWE 56 354–5; *Collationes* 264r–265r
2   An acknowledgment of Titelmans' defence of *instauratur* in the face of Valla's dissatisfaction.
3   The word is ἀνακεφαλαιόω; DV and RSV 'summed up.'

[ER *quod tempestivum sit nos iam a somno expergisci* 'that it is high time for us to rise now from sleep']
[RESP] *hora est iam nos de somno surgere* 'It is now the hour for us to rise from sleep.'[1] Here he informs me with many witnesses that ἐγείρεσθαι can be translated as *surgere*. But nobody was ignorant of that, for indeed even a tower ἐγείρεται [rises] while it is being built. And in John, the Lord, declaring that he would raise up the temple of his body again in three days, says ἐγερῶ, translated as *excitabo* [I will raise it up].[2] But in this respect *expergisci* does not mean any different either. For what we have in Genesis 41, ἠγέρθη δὲ Φαραώ, is translated *expergefactus autem Pharao* [And Pharaoh awoke].[3] To say, as he does, that many are awoken who do not rise is frivolous. Many, after they have risen, go back to bed too. But anyone who is aroused is aroused so that he may get up. It seems the verb *expergisci* is derived from *pererigo* [make erect]. I changed *hora* to *tempus*, because I doubted whether *hora* was used in this sense in Latin.[4]

1   Rom 13:11; CWE 56 357–8; *Collationes* 265v–267r

2 John 2:19
3 Gen 41:4. *Expergefactus* is the past participle of *expergefio*; in the annotation this
   is quoted as *experrectus* from *expergiscor*. The meaning is the same, but see CWE
   56 358 n6.
4 The Latin *hora*, here translating the Greek ὥρα, is used in poetry to mean 'time'
   or 'season,' as well as 'hour,' but Erasmus is perhaps thinking of 'opportune
   moment' (καιρός), which he translates with *tempus* in the previous phrase (as
   does VG). Cf Rom 5:6 *secundum tempus*, 185 above.

From the fourteenth chapter

[ER *alius quidem credit vescendum esse quibuslibet* 'One indeed believes
he should eat any kind of food he likes.']
[RESP] *alius enim credit se manducare omnia* 'For one believes that he
consumes all kinds of foods.'[1] Since *omnia* [all things] for *quaevis* [anything
whatever] is rare in the orators, though it is found in the poets, I preferred
to translate thus: *vescendum esse quibuslibet*, and I add [in the annotation],
'For what one person would be able to eat "all" things?' Here he wrangles
saying, 'Who could not pick out things to sneer at and taunt sarcastically
even from the writings of the greatest?' At whom am I carping here, my
very hasty young man? I am not carping at the Translator in my annotation
or at the Apostle, whom you defend of course. I merely pointed out the
ambiguity of the word *omnia* and the rather rare usage. And here he argues
at length that the Apostle is caught in the same raillery. But he could have
learned from my annotation that πάντα is commonly used in Greek to mean
quaelibet [any kind of], so it can include the distributive sense by means of
the conjunction 'or,' not by means of 'and.' He could have found another
subject to wrangle over: the verb *manducare* [to chew] for *edere* [to eat],
which I believe was very common usage in the Translator's time, for in
Suetonius' *Octavian*[2] it is used just like that. Nowadays scholars prefer to
avoid it.

1 Rom 14:2 'For one believeth that he may eat all things'; CWE 56 368; *Collationes*
   269v–270v
2 Suetonius *Divus Augustus* 76

[ER *alius autem qui infirmus est oleribus vescitur* 'But another who is weak
eats vegetables.']
[RESP] *qui autem infirmus est, olus manducet* 'But he who is weak, let him
consume vegetable food.'[1] Since the Greek sources are in complete agreement in reading ἐσθίει [eats – indicative], I am surprised that he defends
manducet [let him eat (subjunctive)], for this was probably a mistake made
by the negligence of the copyists. The points he adduces out of Ambrose,

Jerome, and others do nothing against my case, for they adapt Paul's words to their own sense.[2]

1 Rom 14:2 'But he that is weak, let him eat herbs'; CWE 56 368–70; *Collationes* 271r–v
2 Ambrosiaster I 432–3; Jerome *Commentarius in Ecclesiasten* 2:5 PL 23 1078C; but see CWE 56 370 n11.

From chapter fifteen

[ER *nam quaecunque praescripta sunt* 'for whatever things have been described before']
[RESP] *quaecunque enim scripta sunt* 'for whatever things have been written.'[1] When Paul instructs us that we should bear with the weakness of our brothers, he adduces the example of Christ and adds the witness of the prophet from the Psalms: 'The insults of those who insult thee have fallen on me.'[2] Lest this prophecy should seem to have been made only of Christ and not to apply to us, he adds, 'For whatever things have been written have been written for our instruction.' Both of my interpretations fit this sense: things written previously and things described before are to be imitated.[3] For the prophet predicted this before Christ was made manifest, and it was set out as an example for us. 'But,' says he, '*quaecunque* includes everything that is written.' True, everything of that sort. But to say the Scriptures contain the crimes of unbelievers, which are not to be imitated, is plainly sophistication, for those things too are relevant as examples, not to be imitated but so that we should be warned about what is to be imitated. The crossing of the Red Sea too and other miracles and rituals are set forth as examples for us to be understood allegorically.[4]

1 Rom 15:4; CWE 56 390–4; *Collationes* 279r–281v
2 Ps 68:10 (69:9 AV); for the rest, Erasmus is referring to Rom 15:1–3.
3 Here again Erasmus is responding to the criticism that his reading restricts the possible understanding of Paul; see the second article on Rom 1:4 *ex resurrectione mortuorum*, 151 n2 above.
4 Exod 14:21–8, cited in *Collationes* 281r.

[ER *in gloriam Dei* 'unto the glory of God']
[RESP] *in honorem Dei* 'unto the honour of God.'[1] Since I said in the annotation, 'The Translator indulges in an affectation of variety,' he fabricates a long wrangle, and although I note this so many times in the Translator, still at every place he renews his clamour. But it would have been enough if he had gratified his indignation fully just once. To indulge in variety is not a shameful thing, but to wrangle with your 'dearest brother' at every possible occasion is a sin. It is a fact that τιμή in Greek means *honor* and δόξα is

gloria. Now *honor* is often used in the Scriptures for *subsidium* [help]; *glo-* *ria* never is. Since this is so, let this censor explain why the Translator here preferred to say *honor* rather than *gloria.* If he cannot give any explanation, why does he wrangle so, as if I had brought an accusation of falsehood against the Translator? I am not making any complaint about the meaning. If, moreover, he approves the interpretation of certain people concerning glory in times to come, has the Translator not restricted Paul's statement to a single meaning? This is a subject he has often disputed with me.[2]

1   Rom 15:7; CWE 56 395–7; *Collationes* 282v–285r. Again, this note motivated a
     long addition to the corresponding annotation.
2   Cf, for example, in the previous article, *Collationes* 281r.

[ER and RESP] *ad confirmandas promissiones patrum* **'for confirming the promises of the fathers.'**1 Here he wants both infinitives to refer to the preceding verb, λέγω [I say]. But *dico glorificare* [I say to glorify] is awkward for *iubeo glorificare* [I order to glorify] or *debere glorificare* [ought to glorify]. However, I do not disapprove of what he suggests here if the difference remains clear. Ambrose certainly distinguishes these two things [mercy and promises], as do Chrysostom, Theophylact, and Thomas, expounding *glorificare* as *debere glorificare*, as if the infinitive δοξάσαι were to be taken as an imperative verb: *glorificate.*[2]

1   Rom 15:8 'to confirm the promises made unto the fathers'; CWE 56 397–9; *Colla-
     tiones* 284v–285r. The discussion in the annotation concerns the syntax of both
     Rom 15:8 and 9, but here only the phrase: VG *gentes autem super misericordiam
     honorare Deum* 'The gentiles, however, honour God over mercy'; or ER *ut gentes
     pro misericordia glorificent Deum* 'that the gentiles might glorify God because
     of mercy.'
2   Ambrosiaster I 456–7, quoted by Titelmans; Chrysostom *Hom in Rom* 28.1 PG 60
     649–50 in fact says nothing about the syntax (see CWE 56 398 n4); Theophylact
     Expos in Rom 15:9 PG 124 537C–D; Thomas Aquinas *Super epistulam ad Romanos
     lectura* 15:1 in *S. Thomae Aquinatis super epistolas S. Pauli lectura* ed P. Raphaelis
     Cai (Turin and Rome 1953) I 217 n1156. Aquinas, of course, expounds the
     Vulgate *honorare*, not Erasmus' *glorificare*.

[ER *pro misericordia* **'because of mercy'**]
[RESP] *super misericordia* **'concerning mercy.'**1 Here Valla expresses surprise that the same preposition is rendered differently.[2] Lefèvre declares it is more correct not to vary it.[3] Yet my critic has no dispute with them. 'But they do not say "affect" or "indulge in variety."'[4] Someone who makes changes for no reason, is he not affecting variety? Someone who alters the Latin term on a whim, is he not indulging in and amusing himself with variety? But his orders were that he should dispute with Erasmus, in order

to gratify his colleagues. They do the same in the next passage and still he defends his Translator modestly.

1 Rom 15:9 'for his mercy'; *Collationes* 285r–v. There is no annotation on this point.
2 *Adnotationes* in Valla I 860 2. CWE 56 398 n1 gives the full Latin text and translation of Rom 15:8 and 9. The two Greek phrases are ὑπὲρ ἀληθείας and ὑπὲρ ἐλέους, rendered in VG as *propter veritatem* and *super misericordia* (sic; Vulg *misericordiam*) and by ER as *pro veritate* and *pro misericordia*.
3 Jacques Lefèvre *Commentariorum in epistolas beatiss. Pauli apostoli liber primus* 102v 126 in *Pauli epistolae* XIV ... *cum commentariis* Faksimilie Neudruck der Ausg. Paris 1512 (Stuttgart: Frommann Holzboog 1978).
4 Titelmans does not repeat his accusations on this matter at this point; Erasmus is still smarting from earlier occurrences (see the introduction xxxv above).

[ER *valentes etiam invicem alius alium admonere* 'capable even yourselves of admonishing one another']
[RESP] *ita ut possitis alterutrum monere* 'so that you are able to admonish one another.'[1] In writing the *Annotationes*, I was using manuscripts that had ἄλλους [others]; later, although I learned from other manuscripts that there was some variation in the text, I left the meaning that the Translator rendered. In his text Chrysostom has ἀλλήλους [one another]; in his commentary he reads ἄλλους,[2] and I believe the former was the true and original reading, even if I did use the latter. Moreover, if the Translator rendered ἀλλήλους as *alterutrum*, there is no better way of excusing his solecism[3] than by saying that the ordinary run of people spoke like that in those times, trying to render the single Greek word by a single [Latin] one.

1 Rom 15:14; CWE 56 402–3; *Collationes* 286v–287r
2 ἄλλους] In *1516* only; see CWE 56 403 n7. Chrysostom *Hom in Rom* 29.1 PG 60 653; but see the annotation and CWE 56 403 n5.
3 Ie *alteruter* means 'each of two,' not 'each of several.'

[ER *administrans evangelium Dei* 'ministering the gospel of God']
[RESP] *sanctificans evangelium Dei* 'sanctifying the gospel of God.'[1] Since *sanctificans* does not seem to render the particular meaning of the Greek term ἱερουργοῦντα, I translated with *administrans*. 'You do not give the full meaning,' says he. But what follows supplements it: 'so that the offering of the gentiles might become acceptable.'[2] What I say is elementary; he carefully points out to me from my own annotation the force of the Greek participle and the meaning of this passage, and makes me appear to agree with him, as if he were teaching me.[3]

1 Rom 15:16; CWE 56 404–5; *Collationes* 288r–v
2 See the last sentence of the annotation and CWE 56 405 n10.

3 *quasi me docuerit*] 1540 822; *quasi me docuerim* in 1529 50v, 'as if I were teaching
   myself.' The reading of 1540 seems more likely than that of 1529.

[ER *praepeditus sum saepe* 'I have often been prevented.']
[RESP] *impediebar plurimum* 'I was hindered very much.'[1] Τὰ πολλὰ: Chrysostom clearly interprets τὰ πολλὰ as πολλάκις [many times], inferring that
[Paul] had tried often and had often been prevented from acting.[2] My annotation links *praepeditus* with the Apostle's work.[3] My critic prefers to link
it with disapproval by the Spirit, following what we read in Acts, and I
do not contradict this.[4] However, the following words support my argument: *Nunc autem ulterius locum non habens in his regionibus* [Now, however,
not having occasion for anything further in these regions], for this indicates that it was the business of teaching the gospel that stood in his way,
preventing him from coming.

1 Rom 15:22; CWE 56 410–11; *Collationes* 291r–292r
2 Chrysostom *Hom in Rom* 29.3 PG 60 657
3 CWE 56 411:4–5: 'For [Paul] tried very often, and work always stood in his
   way to hold him back.' Erasmus may be thinking, for example, of Acts 19:21.
4 Acts 16:6–7 'Having been forbidden by the Holy Spirit to speak the word
   in Asia ... they attempted to go into Bithynia, but the Spirit of Jesus did not
   allow them.' Erasmus added this argument to his annotation in 1535. Titelmans
   had given his interpretation of the matter in his criticism of Rom 1:13, where
   Erasmus had *praepeditus fuerim* for *prohibitus sum*. Erasmus did not respond at
   that point in 1529 but added the same explanation to that annotation as well
   in 1535.

[ER *quandocunque iter instituero in Hispaniam* 'whenever I undertake the
journey to Spain']
[RESP] *cum in Hispaniam proficisci coepero* 'when I shall begin to set out
for Spain.'[1] Chrysostom does not add these words ἐλεύσομαι πρὸς ὑμᾶς 'I
shall come to you.'[2]

1 Rom 15:24 'when I shall begin to take my journey into Spain'; CWE 56 412;
   Collationes 292r–v
2 Titelmans had said these words were added in the Greek codices, though he
   considered them unnecessary.

[ER *proficiscor Hierosolymam ministrans sanctis* 'I am setting out for
Jerusalem, ministering to the saints.']
[RESP] *proficiscar Hierosolymam ministrare sanctis* 'I shall set out for
Jerusalem to minister to the saints.'[1] He prefers to change the Greek text
that is entirely consistent rather than admit that the copyists have changed
o to *a*.[2] The present tense is altogether more appropriate to the meaning, for

[Paul] says he is doing what he is already actually doing. In addition my critic informs me, from my *Annotationes*, that the participle is sometimes used by the Greeks in place of the infinitive, as in ἐτέλετο Διατάσσων [having finished teaching] and μέμνημαι ἐλθών [I remember while coming].³ But he should learn that this is not the case with all verbs. For we shall not say πορεύομαι γράφειν [I am setting out to write] in the same way as we correctly say διατέλει τὰ κάλλιστα πράττων [he continues to do the finest things], but γράψων [about to write] would be correct.⁴ So he will have to offer a different little note if he wants to preclude my surprise. And the meaning here is not 'I go to Jerusalem to minister to the saints' but rather that he has been doing this work long since by collecting moneys and making preparation. This is all 'ministering to the saints.'

1   Rom 15:25 'I shall go to Jerusalem, to minister unto the saints'; CWE 56 415–16; *Collationes* 293v–294r
2   Ie have changed *proficiscor* (present) to *proficiscar* (future)
3   Cf the annotation on Matt 11:1 (LB VI 59C), translated as *cum consummasset praecipiens* 'when he had finished teaching' and *memini veniens* 'I remember while coming.'
4   The Greek is πορεύομαι . . . διακονῶν [present participle] 'I am setting out . . . ministering.' Erasmus appears to be saying that while a participle construction, which he uses in his translation, is always possible in Greek, the infinitive one, as in the Vulgate translation, is not possible with πορεύομαι. πορεύομαι γράψων [future participle] 'I am setting out about to write' would be correct, but like the VG Latin this would then be a purpose expression, which is what he wishes to exclude, insisting that Paul is speaking of what he is doing at present.

[ER *in pauperes sanctos* 'for the poor saints']
[RESP] *in pauperes sanctorum* 'for the poor of the saints.'¹ He says *sanctorum* is understood distributively, that is, it signifies those of the number of the saints who are poor. But this form of expression is allowed in Greek, not in Latin. I wanted to point this out.

1   Rom 15:26; CWE 56 416–7; *Collationes* 295r–v

[ER *si spiritualia sua communicaverunt (gentibus)* 'if they have shared their spiritual goods (with the nations)']
[RESP] *nam si spiritualium eorum*¹ *participes facti sunt [gentiles]* 'for if [the gentiles] have been made partakers of their spiritual things.'² He denies that poor saints who were in Jerusalem communicated the gospel to the gentiles. Who suggested that to him? If they communicated nothing, why is this preceded by *et debitores sunt illorum* [They (the gentiles) are in debt to them]? [Paul] is speaking here of the distribution of duties, so that the

one group furnishes spiritual works, the other renews material things. Was there a debt to them on account of the fact that Christ and the apostles were Jews? Yes, if you understand that they [the Jews] are the nation designated, and that nation first announced the gospel to the gentiles. They are said to have done it because it was done by the elders. However, it is likely that saints living in Jerusalem also communicated the gospel to gentiles, either with the apostles in Asia or in Jerusalem, where there was an enormous number of gentiles.

1   VG *illorum*
2   Rom 15:27; CWE 56 417–8; *Collationes* 295v–296v. This response gave rise to an entirely new annotation in *1535*.

From the last chapter to the Romans

[ER *quae est ministra ecclesiae Cenchreensis* 'who is a minister of the Cenchrean church']
[RESP] *quae in ministerio ecclesiae, quae est Cenchris* 'who is in the ministry of the church that is in Cenchreae.'[1] He says I have noted the same things as Lefèvre.[2] But where did Erasmus state that following Paul we should say in Latin *Acyla* for *Aquila*?[3] Since the Greeks do not have the letter *q* they pronounce our words in any case with a κ [kappa].

1   Rom 16:1; CWE 56 423; *Collationes* 298r–v. For Aquila and Cenchreae, see also Acts 18:18.
2   Titelmans does not say this, though his reply, addressed to Lefèvre and Erasmus without distinction, might be taken to imply it.
3   The first of several examples of misspellings of proper names alleged by Lefèvre. Aquila, the name of a person referred to in Rom 16:3, is in Greek Ἀκύλα. In the *Collationes* Lefèvre is said to object to the transcription of Greek upsilon by *i*; the question of kappa and *q* does not arise.

[ER *qui est primitiae Achaiae* 'who is the first fruits of Achaia']
[RESP] *qui est primitivus [ecclesiae] Asiae* 'who is the first [of the church] of Asia.'[1] Chrysostom regularly reads 'of Achaia,' although his exposition provides no certain argument.[2] But if 'Asia' is taken to mean the whole region that is covered by the common term 'Asia Minor,' Achaia is a part of Asia. But if it is taken as that part that is strictly called Asia, Achaia is different.[3]

1   Rom 16:5 'who is the first fruits of Asia'; CWE 56 426–7 (see also CWE 56 424 n2); *Collationes* 299r–300r
2   Chrysostom *Hom in Rom* 31.1 PG 60 667–8
3   Elsewhere Erasmus seems to know that the Roman province of Achaia was in Greece, not Asia Minor. See CWE 56 426 n7.

[ER *item quae in domo illorum est congregationem* 'likewise the congregation which is in their house']

[RESP] *et domesticam eorum ecclesiam* 'and their domestic church.'[1] Here my 'teacher of old men' has a wonderful time exulting and crowing because that very word that I earlier translated as *ecclesia* I now render as *congregatio*, I who have branded the Translator so often for affecting variety. But one may make different allowances for the divine Translator than for Erasmus, since indeed there is nothing in him that is not inspired by the Holy Spirit. But let him not think I have put the Latin word for the Greek rashly: ordinary people think a church is a building, so lest they should understand here a building within a building, I have translated *congregatio*. This is a concession to the thick headed who do not know what *ecclesia* means in Greek. But elsewhere too Paul used *congregatio* in a good sense, as in 2 Thessalonians 2.[2]

1 Rom 16:5 'and the church which is in their house'; CWE 56 425; *Collationes* 300r–301r

2 2 Thess 2:1, where in the Vulgate ἐπισυναγωγή is translated as *congregatio*.

[ER and RESP] *salutate Mariam* 'Salute Mary.'[1] Chrysostom certainly has ὑμᾶς [for you].[2] But why am I at fault if, having stated that there are two readings in the Greek sources, I follow the one that seemed best to me at the time? The meaning is in every respect the same whether you read ὑμᾶς [for you] or ἡμᾶς [for us], except that the first person reflects better the politeness of Paul, who includes himself in this expression so that he might not seem to be reproaching the Romans for accepting the kindness of a woman. And perhaps that is how the Translator rendered it, for *nos* is easily corrupted to *vos*. This, of course, was a good place to declaim against those who correct the Latin on the basis of the Greek, though that is not what I do – I show each can be corrected from the other.

1 Rom 16:6; CWE 56 427; *Collationes* 301r–v, where the cue phrase is *salutate Mariam quae multum laboravit in vobis* 'Salute Mary who hath laboured much among you.' The annotation is in fact concerned only with the pronoun at the end.

2 Chrysostom *Hom in Rom* 31.1–2 PG 60 668–9. Erasmus added a reference to Chrysostom to the annotation only in 1535 but there stated that the scribe included both ἡμᾶς and ὑμᾶς.

[ER and RESP] *ei autem qui potens est vos confirmare* 'now to him who is able to strengthen you.'[1] Here he makes a constant and prolonged clamour because I pointed out that Nicolas of Lyra was mistaken in following Haimo.[2] He does not defend the error but believes I have perpetrated an intolerable crime because I mingled joking with description. And here, in order to increase, by the art at which he is extremely good, the enormity of

my jokes, laughter, mockery, impudence, bitterness, and other things horrible to relate, he makes Lyra one of the sacred and ancient Doctors of the
church, who now reigns with Christ in heaven contemplating with the angels and apostles the face of God. But neither the authority of the church
nor miracles have placed this man among the number of the saints, nor has
the reputation of a life lived in holiness commended his memory to us. No,
rather there are other things reported of him even by the Franciscans that
I would not want to repeat here. Even in learning the theologians do not
accord him a great deal. I, however, do not utterly despise his labours, nor
do I deny that he is in heaven; but I feel the same about many who have
been condemned to punishment for their misdeeds. But neither on that account do I owe as much reverence to their memory as this man requires.
'The dead should be spared.' And I do not accuse them; my concern is with
the books in which they speak to us as if they were still alive. No one ever
venerated the dead so religiously that he was afraid to disagree with them.
If someone who disagrees causes harm, why does this man disagree so often with Valla who died long ago and who is more likely to be reigning in
heaven than Nicolas of Lyra? 'But joking is offensive.' It is a joke, but without bitterness. And was I so stupid hitherto that I did not think Lyra was
owed the reverence that we owe to Augustine or Jerome! Now just as he
sees Nicolas of Lyra as exalted among the greatest saints, so he sets us together 'in this pitiful and filthy stable of a world where everything stinks
and is befouled with ordure.'[3] How full of ordure is this sort of language!
And yet it is in this ordure these books are written in which I occasionally
find some fault. So just as this fellow has exaggerated beyond measure the
mean conditions of those who live in the spirit of Christ (for it is pious to
believe this of everyone unless the opposite is proved), so he accumulates
a ridiculous number of long, theatrical descriptions about Lyra: a king and
priest before God, honoured in the highest degree in the sight of the divine
majesty – though it could turn out that Lyra dwells with those below. But
he had to lay these foundations so that he could slap down to his heart's
content even his dearest Desiderius. 'It is not right,' says he, 'to diminish
the honour of such men, but people who belittle a reputation for learning
diminish honour. Doesn't anyone who disagrees with the ancients diminish their reputation for learning?' What theologian does not do this? Does
Lyra not do this very thing sometimes? Who in fact are these people who
despise Lyra because his language was unpolished? But if the matter is to
be settled on the basis of linguistic resources, is it not those who lack skill
in languages who should be taught? Who in fact are these people who are
skilled only in languages?[4] Was Valla such a one? Was Lefèvre? – for I shall
say nothing of myself. But still in this dispute more trust is to be placed in

those who are skilled in languages than in one who, equipped with skill in
not even one language, handles the business of languages with such confidence, advertising himself in borrowed plumage.[5] How seriously in fact
he seems to take himself, saying that 'the earth is too small for my impudence, which would poke fingers up and stick out its tongue even at the
heavens.'[6] Who cannot see that this young man was born to be a slanderer?
Does a man poke out his tongue at heaven because he has criticized something in Lyra's books? In the first place, it is uncertain whether Lyra is there.
Secondly, I do not speak against him as a heavenly person but against the
books he wrote on earth as an earthly person. This is my critic's truly sublime eloquence. Having thus vented his spleen to the point of satiety against
me, he represents Valla and Lefèvre as speaking in a pious and religious
way. To myself when I suggest – for this is what he pretends – that Paul
did not say simply 'grace' but added 'the grace of our Lord Jesus Christ,'
and thus makes a prayer for the disciples dearest to him, he immediately
makes objection on the grounds that this benediction is intended not only
for those to whom he was writing but for all Christians.[7] Here too I could
disagree. Finally, in his conclusion he represents me as a penitent asking
God for a good heart and himself, as if he had performed a good deed, as
singing us a psalm.[8] But perhaps it would have been more appropriate to
sing some penitential psalm after such annotations in which he goes off his
head so often, blows his own trumpet so much, advertises himself in borrowed plumage, and slanders his neighbour so often without reason – and
a youth to his senior, what's more. He injects lethal venom covertly with a
viper's tooth, as in that passage where someone warns that the next day is
the feast of the Ascension, and he makes me answer, 'I hadn't noticed,' as
if I had no regard for feast days.[9] And again in another place, when there
was a mention in passing of the rightness of faith, he says, 'You will hear
of this matter, since there will be occasion to speak with you separately.'[10]
Again and again he threatens reproaches, suggesting rhetorically of course
that he is concealing marvels for modesty's sake, and other things more
poisonous than these, which Nomentanus would not say about Balatro.[11] If
I wanted to set these passages out, the sensible reader would easily perceive
that all these blandishments, 'kindest of men,' 'dearest Desiderius,' and the
affirmation of his sincerity of heart, are nothing more than honey mixed
with wolfsbane. And he thinks it extraordinarily witty, attacking with these
metaphorical teeth, so that only his fellows, forewarned, might recognize it
and laugh. Where, finally, has he learned these arts, true son that he is of
the humble and very simple Francis? But wherever he learned this trickery,
it should have been avoided here, because people have a very low opinion
of this man's whole brotherhood, and these books can have no other effect

than that they think even worse of it as each day passes. For this work is said to have been printed with the authority of the fathers, from which it is clear how discriminating these seraphic folk are.[12] But now I am weary of this labour. I pray that this young man shall be granted real modesty, real sincerity, real charity, such learning that he can do well what he believes he is capable of, and finally glory solid and lasting instead of empty and counterfeit.

1 Rom 16:25 'now to him that is able to establish you'; CWE 56 436–7; *Collationes* 303v–304r. As with the previous item, the cue phrase is the beginning of the verse, but the point of departure of the note – Erasmus' response to Titelmans' attack on him for his criticism of Nicolas of Lyra – was the inclusion in his translation of the subscription, *missa fuit a Corintho*, which is included in his Greek, but omitted in VG (and DV).

2 Titelmans' reproach runs from *Collationes* 304v–306r. Haimo was mistakenly said by Nicolas to affirm that the Epistle to the Romans was written from Athens, not from Corinth (Nicolas of Lyra *Postilla super totam bibliam* IV prologus f aa r [Strasbourg 1492; facsimile ed Frankfurt am Main 1971]). To explain this, Nicolas imagined that Paul wrote part of it in Athens and the rest in Corinth. Erasmus remarked satirically: 'He would prefer ... that Paul make a journey, however roundabout, just so that Haymo's authority should not be impaired ...' The author in question is Haimo of Auxerre, not, as was supposed in Erasmus' time, Haimo of Halberstadt; see the article by Hermigild Dressler in NCE 6 898–9). Haimo's work, *In divi Pauli epistolas ... expositio*, clearly says the letter was written in Corinth (*praefatio* and f xliiii v, PL 117 361C and 504D, where it is still attributed to Haimo of Halberstadt). In the *Apologia de 'In principio erat sermo'* (29 n61 and 32 n79 above) Erasmus attributes this work, with some hesitation, to Remigius of Auxerre. For Nicolas of Lyra, see the letter to the reader 139 n6 above.

3 *Collationes* 305v: 'in hoc miserando ac foetido ... terrae stabulo, ubi stercoribus foetent ac sordent omnia'

4 *Collationes* 305r: 'What do we take away from their honour? Why do we belittle their reputation for learning? Just because they did not use such elegant language, such cultivated expression, such as those instructed in languages alone judge everything of their own.' At this point Valla and Lefèvre have both declared that they have no more to say. This part of Titelmans' tirade is clearly directed only at Erasmus, whose joke he regards as almost blasphemous flippancy, and who, it is implied, is qualified only in language and not in theology.

5 Another allusion to the *Aesopica cornicula*; see the prefatory letter 141 n13 above.

6 *Collationes* 306r: 'the intolerable petulant spleen of one for whom the earth does not suffice unless he pokes fingers and sticks out his tongue at heaven.' The jibe clearly irritated Erasmus since this is the second time he alluded to it; cf the prefatory letter 139 above with n7.

7 Erasmus is responding here to two passages. In a preceding article on Rom 16:23 *Gaius hospes meus, et universae ecclesiae* (*Collationes* 303r–v), he is quoted as

pointing out that the Greek for the phrase 'the whole church' is in the genitive and as reading it (*et ecclesiae totius*) to mean that the benediction was intended for all Christians (CWE 56 431–2). Titelmans in fact agrees with him, though he adds that 'Ambrose' and the oldest Latin versions put the expression in the nominative (*et universa ecclesia*); Ambrosiaster (I 490–1) in fact has the genitive. The discussion is then prolonged in a closing homily (*Collationes* 306v–307r). The place of the benediction is discussed in a preceding annotation, CWE 56 432–3, and here at *Collationes* 303v–304r. It is also mentioned in Titelmans' prologue [d7]v.

8 *Collationes* 308v, 309r–310v. See the prefatory letter 138 n3 above.

9 *Collationes* 54v

10 Perhaps a rather distant memory of 'I expect to discuss elsewhere at some time at greater length things like this that concern the steadfastness of Catholic dogma' (*Collationes* 134v), in the conclusion of the long article on Rom 5:12, which contains much threatening language.

11 Two parasites in Horace *Satires* 2.8. The second name, also used as a common noun in *Satire* 1.2.2, means a babbler or a buffoon.

12 See the prefatory letter 141 n14 above.

The End

WORKS FREQUENTLY CITED

SHORT-TITLE FORMS
FOR ERASMUS' WORKS

INDEX OF SCRIPTURAL REFERENCES

INDEX OF GREEK AND LATIN
WORDS CITED

GENERAL INDEX

WORKS FREQUENTLY CITED

This list provides bibliographical information for works referred to in short-title form in this volume. For Erasmus' writings, see the short-title list following.

Allen   *Opus epistolarum Des. Erasmi Roterodamii* ed P.S. Allen, H.M. Allen, and H.W. Garrod (Oxford 1906–58) 11 vols and index

Ambrosiaster   *Ambrosiastri qui dicitur commentarius in epistulas Paulinas* CSEL 81 (Vienna 1966–9) 3 vols

Annotationes   Erasmus *Annotationes in Novum Testamentum* LB VI, except where the 1516, 1519, 1522, 1527, or 1535 editions are specified. For these see Reeve I and II.

ASD   *Opera omnia Desiderii Erasmi Roterodami* (Amsterdam and Oxford 1969–)

Asso   Cecilia Asso 'Erasmus' *Apologia de loco "Omnes quidem resurgemus"' Archivio Italiano per la Storia della Pietà* 15 (2003) 165–201

Augustijn   *Epistola de interdicto esu carnium* and *In epistolam de delectu ciborum scholia* ed C. Augustijn in ASD IX-1 3–50 and 51–89 (Amsterdam 1982)

AV   *The Holy Bible . . . AD 1611* (London 1946)

Bentley   Jerry H. Bentley *Humanists and Holy Writ: New Testament Scholarship in the Renaissance* (Princeton 1983)

Biblia latina   *Biblia latina cum glossa ordinaria* (Strasburg: 1480–1; repr Turnhout 1992) 4 vols (These volumes have no page numbers and no continuous sequence of signatures. The copy reproduced has page numbers in manuscript, but these are often illegible. They are given where possible in square brackets, but it is sometimes necessary to search at the appropriate biblical book and chapter.)

Boyle   Marjorie O'Rourke Boyle *Erasmus on Language and Method in Theology* (Toronto 1977)

CCSL   *Corpus christianorum, series latina* (Turnhout 1954–)

CEBR   *Contemporaries of Erasmus: A Biographical Register of the Renaissance and Reformation* ed Peter G. Bietenholz and Thomas B. Deutscher (Toronto 1985–7) 3 vols

Chomarat	Jacques Chomarat *Grammaire et rhétorique chez Erasme* (Paris 1981) 2 vols
Chrysostom *Hom in Rom*	John Chrysostom *In epistulam ad Romanos homiliae* PG 60 385–682
Clichtove	*Propugnaculum Ecclesiae Adversus Lutheranos: per Judocum Clichtoueum Neoportuensem ... elaboratum et tres libros continens* (Paris: Colinaeus 1526) 3 vols
Collationes	Frans Titelmans *Collationes quinque super epistolam ad Romanos beati Pauli apostoli* Biblioteca Apostolica Vaticana M.F. 11–1986 (Antwerp: William Vorstermann 1529)
CSEL	*Corpus scriptorum ecclesiasticorum latinorum* (Vienna and Leipzig 1866–)
CWE	*Collected Works of Erasmus* (Toronto, Buffalo, and London 1974–)
DACL	*Dictionnaire d'archéologie chrétienne et de liturgie* ed Fernand Cabrol and Henri Leclerq (Paris 1903–53) 30 vols
De Jongh	H. de Jongh *L'ancienne faculté de théologie de Louvain au premier siècle de son existence (1432–1540)* (Louvain 1911; repr Utrecht 1980)
De Vocht	Henry de Vocht *History of the Foundation and the Rise of the Collegium Trilingue Lovaniense 1517–1550* (Louvain 1951; repr Nendeln and Lichtenstein 1976)
Digest	*Digesta seu Pandectae* in *Corpus iuris civilis* ed Mommsen and Krueger, with an English translation ed Alan Watson (Philadelphia, 1985) 4 vols
DTC	*Dictionnaire de théologie catholique* ed A. Vacant and E. Mangenot (Paris 1903–50) 15 vols
DV	*The Holy Bible: translated from the Latin Vulgate* [Douay-Rheims Version] rev by Richard Challoner (Rockford, Ill 2000)
ERSY	*Erasmus of Rotterdam Society Yearbook* (1980–)
FC	The Fathers of the Church (Washington, DC 1947–) 127 vols
Friedberg	*Corpus iuris canonici* ed Aemilius Friedberg (Graz 1959) 2 vols: I *Decretum magistri Gratiani;* II *Decretalium collectiones*

Gerson	Jean Gerson *Oeuvres complètes* ed Mgr Glorieux (Paris 1962) 10 vols
Hamilton	Alastair Hamilton 'Humanists and the Bible' in *The Cambridge Companion to Renaissance Humanism* (Cambridge 1996) 100–17
Hugh of St Cher	*Prima [-septima] pars huius operis: continens textum Bibliae cum postilla Domini Hugonis Cardinalis* ([Basel]: [J.Amerbach for Anton Koberger in Nuremberg] [1498–1502])
Kinney	*The Complete Works of St Thomas More* 15 ed Daniel Kinney (New Haven and London 1986)
Latham	R.E. Latham *Revised Medieval Latin Word-List* (London 1965)
LB	Erasmus *Opera omnia* ed Jean Leclerc (Leiden 1703–6; repr Hildesheim 1961–2) 10 vols
Lefèvre	*Commentarii in S. Pauli epistolas* in *Pauli epistolae XIV cum commentariis* Faksimile Neudruck der Ausgabe Paris 1512 (Stuttgart 1978)
Lewis and Short	*A Latin Dictionary* (Oxford 1996)
Loca depravata	Erasmus *Loca manifeste depravata, sed ex infinitis, ut ocurrebant, pauca decerpta* LB VI *[6]v–*[7]r
Mansi	*Sacrorum conciliorum nova, et amplissima collectio* ed Fr J.D. Mansi (Florence 1759–1827); facsimile ed Graz 1960 of repr Paris 1901–27) 53 vols
Mirbt / Aland	*Quellen zur Geschichte des Papsttums und des römischen Katholizismus* ed Carl Mirbt and Kurt Aland I (Tübingen 1967) 2 vols
NCE	*New Catholic Encyclopedia* (New York, Toronto, and London 1967) 17 vols
NRSV	*The Holy Bible ... New Revised Standard Version* (New York 1989)
Oberman	Heiko Augustinus Oberman *The Harvest of Medieval Theology: Gabriel Biel and Late Medieval Nominalism* (Cambridge, Mass 1963; repr Grand Rapids, Mich 1967 and Durham, NC 1983)
OCD	*The Oxford Classical Dictionary* 3rd ed, ed Simon Hornblower and Antony Spawforth (Oxford and New York 1996)

Opuscula	*Erasmi opuscula: A Supplement to the Opera omnia* ed Wallace K. Ferguson (The Hague 1933; repr Hildesheim 1978)
Origen *Comm in Rom*	Origen *Commentarii in epistulam B. Pauli ad Romanos* PG 14 833–1292
Origen FC	*Commentary on the Epistle to the Romans* trans Thomas P. Scheck FC 103–4 (Washington, DC 2001). This is translated from Rufinus' Latin translation of the original Greek.
PG	*Patrologiae cursus completus ... series graeca* ed J.-P. Migne (Paris 1857–86) 167 vols
Pio	*Alberti Pii ... tres et viginti libri in locos lucubrationum variarum Desiderii Erasmi* (Paris: Bade 1531)
PL	*Patrologiae cursus completus ... series latina* ed J.P. Migne (Paris 1844–64) 221 vols
Reeve I	*Erasmus' Annotations on the New Testament: The Gospels* ed Anne Reeve, intro Michael A. Screech (London 1986)
Reeve II	*Erasmus' Annotations on the New Testament: Acts, Romans, I & II Corinthians* ed Anne Reeve and Michael A. Screech, Studies in the History of Christian Thought 42 (Leiden 1990)
RSV	*The Holy Bible ... Revised Standard Version* (New York and Glasgow 1952)
Rummel *Annotations*	Erika Rummel *Erasmus' Annotations on the New Testament: From Philologist to Theologian* (Toronto, Buffalo, and London 1986)
Rummel *Critics*	Erika Rummel *Erasmus and his Catholic Critics* Bibliotheca humanistica et reformatorica 45 (Nieuwkoop 1989) 2 vols: I 1515–22; II 1523–36
Sartori	Paolo Sartori 'La controversia neotestamentaria tra Frans Titelmans ed Erasmo da Rotterdam (1527–1530 ca.): linee di sviluppo e contenuti' *Humanistica Lovaniensia* 52 (2003) 77–135
Soloecismi	Erasmus *Soloecismi per interpretem admissi manifestarii et inexcusabiles, e plurimis pauci decerpti* LB VI *5r–v
Souter	*Pelagius's Expositions of Thirteen Epistles of Paul* ed Alexander Souter, Texts and Studies 9 (Cambridge 1922–31; repr Nendeln and Liechtenstein 1967) 3 vols: II text of Pelagius; III text of Pseudo-Jerome

Theophylact

Theophylact *Expositio in epistulam ad Romanos Expos in Rom*
PG 124 319–560

Valla

Lorenzo Valla *Opera omnia* (Basel: H. Petri 1540; repr Turin
1962) 2 vols

Vander Haeghen

F. vander Haeghen *Bibliotheca erasmiana: répertoire des oeuvres
d'Erasme* (Gand 1893; repr Nieuwkoop 1972)

VG

*Novum Testamentum iuxta Graecorum lectionem ex emenda-
tioribus exemplaribus, et veterum orthodoxorum lectione, cum
versione Des[iderius] Erasmi Roterod[ami] Theologiae professoris.
adiecta vulgari aeditione, quo magis in promptu sit lectori collatio*
(Basel: Froben 1527)

Titles following colons are longer versions of the short-titles, or are alternative titles. Items entirely enclosed in square brackets are of doubtful authorship. For abbreviations see Works Frequently Cited.

Acta: Acta Academiae Lovaniensis contra Lutherum *Opuscula* / CWE 71

Adagia: Adagiorum chiliades 1508, etc (Adagiorum collectanea for the primitive form, when required) LB II / ASD II-1–9 / CWE 30–6

Admonitio adversus mendacium: Admonitio adversus mendacium et obtrectationem LB X / CWE 78

Annotationes in Novum Testamentum LB VI / ASD VI-5–10 / CWE 51–60

Antibarbari LB X / ASD I-1 / CWE 23

Apologia ad annotationes Stunicae: Apologia respondens ad ea quae Iacobus Lopis Stunica taxaverat in prima duntaxat Novi Testamenti aeditione LB IX / ASD IX-2

Apologia ad Caranzam: Apologia ad Sanctium Caranzam, or Apologia de tribus locis, or Responsio ad annotationem Stunicae ... a Sanctio Caranza defensam LB IX / ASD IX-8

Apologia ad Fabrum: Apologia ad Iacobum Fabrum Stapulensem LB IX / ASD IX-3 / CWE 83

Apologia ad prodromon Stunicae LB IX / ASD IX-8

Apologia ad Stunicae conclusiones LB IX / ASD IX-8

Apologia adversus monachos: Apologia adversus monachos quosdam Hispanos LB IX

Apologia adversus Petrum Sutorem: Apologia adversus debacchationes Petri Sutoris LB IX

Apologia adversus rhapsodias Alberti Pii: Apologia ad viginti et quattuor libros A. Pii LB IX / ASD IX-6 / CWE 84

Apologia adversus Stunicae Blasphemiae: Apologia adversus libellum Stunicae cui titulum fecit Blasphemiae et impietates Erasmi LB IX / ASD IX-8

Apologia contra Latomi dialogum: Apologia contra Iacobi Latomi dialogum de tribus linguis LB IX / CWE 71

Apologia de 'In principio erat sermo': Apologia palam refellens quorundam seditiosos clamores apud populum ac magnates quod in evangelio Ioannis verterit 'In principio erat sermo' (1520a); Apologia de 'In principio erat sermo' (1520b) LB IX / CWE 73

Apologia de laude matrimonii: Apologia pro declamatione de laude matrimonii LB IX / CWE 71

Apologia de loco 'Omnes quidem': Apologia de loco taxato in publica professione per Nicolaum Ecmondanum theologum et Carmelitanum Lovanii 'Omnes quidem resurgemus' LB IX / CWE 73

Apologia qua respondet invectivis Lei: Apologia qua respondet duabus invectivis Eduardi Lei *Opuscula* / ASD IX-4 / CWE 72

Apophthegmata LB IV / ASD IV-4 / CWE 37–8

Appendix de scriptis Clithovei LB IX / CWE 83

Appendix respondens ad Sutorem: Appendix respondens ad quaedam Antapologiae Petri Sutoris LB IX

Argumenta: Argumenta in omnes epistolas apostolicas nova (with Paraphrases)

Axiomata pro causa Lutheri: Axiomata pro causa Martini Lutheri *Opuscula* / CWE 71

Brevissima scholia: In Elenchum Alberti Pii brevissima scholia per eundem Erasmum Roterodamum ASD IX-6 / CWE 84

Carmina LB I, IV, V, VIII / ASD I-7 / CWE 85–6
Catalogus lucubrationum LB I / CWE 9 (Ep 1341A)
Ciceronianus: Dialogus Ciceronianus LB I / ASD I-2 / CWE 28
Colloquia LB I / ASD I-3 / CWE 39–40
Compendium vitae Allen I / CWE 4
Conflictus: Conflictus Thaliae et Barbariei LB I / ASD I-8
[Consilium: Consilium cuiusdam ex animo cupientis esse consultum] Opuscula / CWE 71

De bello Turcico: Utilissima consultatio de bello Turcis inferendo, et obiter enarratus psalmus 28 LB V / ASD V-3 / CWE 64
De civilitate: De civilitate morum puerilium LB I / ASD I-8 / CWE 25
Declamatio de morte LB IV
Declamatiuncula LB IV
Declarationes ad censuras Lutetiae vulgatas: Declarationes ad censuras Lutetiae vulgatas sub nomine facultatis theologiae Parisiensis LB IX / ASD IX-7 / CWE 82
De concordia: De sarcienda ecclesiae concordia, or De amabili ecclesiae concordia [on Psalm 83] LB V / ASD V-3 / CWE 65
De conscribendis epistolis LB I / ASD I-2 / CWE 25
De constructione: De constructione octo partium orationis, or Syntaxis LB I / ASD I-4
De contemptu mundi: Epistola de contemptu mundi LB V / ASD V-1 / CWE 66
De copia: De duplici copia verborum ac rerum LB I / ASD I-6 / CWE 24
De esu carnium: Epistola apologetica ad Christophorum episcopum Basiliensem de interdicto esu carnium (published with scholia in a 1532 edition but not in the 1540 Opera) LB IX / ASD IX-1 / CWE 73
De immensa Dei misericordia: Concio de immensa Dei misericordia LB V / ASD V-7 / CWE 70
De libero arbitrio: De libero arbitrio diatribe LB IX / CWE 76
De philosophia evangelica LB VI
De praeparatione: De praeparatione ad mortem LB V / ASD V-1 / CWE 70
De pueris instituendis: De pueris statim ac liberaliter instituendis LB I / ASD I-2 / CWE 26
De puero Iesu: Concio de puero Iesu LB V / ASD V-7 / CWE 29
De puritate tabernaculi: Enarratio psalmi 14 qui est de puritate tabernaculi sive ecclesiae christianae LB V / ASD V-2 / CWE 65
De ratione studii LB I / ASD I-2 / CWE 24
De recta pronuntiatione: De recta latini graecique sermonis pronuntiatione LB I / ASD I-4 / CWE 26
De taedio Iesu: Disputatiuncula de taedio, pavore, tristicia Iesu LB V / ASD V-7 / CWE 70
Detectio praestigiarum: Detectio praestigiarum cuiusdam libelli Germanice scripti LB X / ASD IX-1 / CWE 78
De vidua christiana LB V / ASD V-6 / CWE 66
De virtute amplectenda: Oratio de virtute amplectenda LB V / CWE 29
[Dialogus bilinguium ac trilinguium: Chonradi Nastadiensis dialogus bilinguium ac trilinguium] Opuscula / CWE 7

Dilutio: Dilutio eorum quae Iodocus Clithoveus scripsit adversus declamationem suasoriam matrimonii / *Dilutio eorum quae Iodocus Clithoveus scripsit* ed Émile V. Telle (Paris 1968) / CWE 83

Divinationes ad notata Bedae: Divinationes ad notata per Bedam de Paraphrasi Erasmi in Matthaeum, et primo de duabus praemissis epistolis LB IX / ASD IX-5

Ecclesiastes: Ecclesiastes sive de ratione concionandi LB V / ASD V-4–5 / CWE 67–8

Elenchus in censuras Bedae: In N. Bedae censuras erroneas elenchus LB IX / ASD IX-5

Enchiridion: Enchiridion militis christiani LB V / CWE 66

Encomium matrimonii (in De conscribendis epistolis)

Encomium medicinae: Declamatio in laudem artis medicae LB I / ASD I-4 / CWE 29

Epistola ad Dorpium LB IX / CWE 3 (Ep 337) / CWE 71

Epistola ad fratres Inferioris Germaniae: Responsio ad fratres Germaniae Inferioris ad epistolam apologeticam incerto autore proditam LB X / ASD IX-1 / CWE 78

Epistola ad gracculos: Epistola ad quosdam impudentissimos gracculos LB X / Ep 2275

Epistola apologetica adversus Stunicam LB IX / ASD IX-8 / ASD-8 / Ep 2172

Epistola apologetica de Termino LB X / Ep 2018

Epistola consolatoria: Epistola consolatoria virginibus sacris, or Epistola consolatoria in adversis LB V / CWE 69

Epistola contra pseudevangelicos: Epistola contra quosdam qui se falso iactant evangelicos LB X / ASD IX-1 / CWE 78

Euripidis Hecuba LB I / ASD I-1

Euripidis Iphigenia in Aulide LB I / ASD I-1

Exomologesis: Exomologesis sive modus confitendi LB V / CWE 67

Explanatio symboli: Explanatio symboli apostolorum sive catechismus LB V / ASD V-1 / CWE 70

Ex Plutarcho versa LB IV / ASD IV-2

Formula: Conficiendarum epistolarum formula (see De conscribendis epistolis)

Hyperaspistes LB X / CWE 76–7

In Nucem Ovidii commentarius LB I / ASD I-1 / CWE 29

In Prudentium: Commentarius in duos hymnos Prudentii LB V / ASD V-7 / CWE 29

In psalmum 1: Enarratio primi psalmi, 'Beatus vir,' iuxta tropologiam potissimum LB V / ASD V-2 / CWE 63

In psalmum 2: Commentarius in psalmum 2, 'Quare fremuerunt gentes?' LB V / ASD V-2 / CWE 63

In psalmum 3: Paraphrasis in tertium psalmum, 'Domine quid multiplicate' LB V / ASD V-2 / CWE 63

In psalmum 4: In psalmum quartum concio LB V / ASD V-2 / CWE 63

In psalmum 22: In psalmum 22 enarratio triplex LB V / ASD V-2 / CWE 64

In psalmum 33: Enarratio psalmi 33 LB V / ASD V-3 / CWE 64

In psalmum 38: Enarratio psalmi 38 LB V / ASD V-3 / CWE 65

In psalmum 85: Concionalis interpretatio, plena pietatis, in psalmum 85 LB V / ASD V-3 / CWE 64

Institutio christiani matrimonii LB V / ASD V-6 / CWE 69

Institutio principis christiani LB IV / ASD IV-1 / CWE 27

[Julius exclusus: Dialogus Julius exclusus e coelis] *Opuscula* ASD I-8 / CWE 27

Lingua LB IV / ASD IV-1A / CWE 29
Liturgia Virginis Matris: Virginis Matris apud Lauretum cultae liturgia LB V / ASD V-1 / CWE 69
Luciani dialogi LB I / ASD I-1

Manifesta mendacia ASD IX-4 / CWE 71
Methodus (see Ratio)
Modus orandi Deum LB V / ASD V-1 / CWE 70
Moria: Moriae encomium LB IV / ASD IV-3 / CWE 27

Notatiunculae: Notatiunculae quaedam extemporales ad naenias Bedaicas, or Responsio ad notulas Bedaicas LB IX / ASD IX-5
Novum Testamentum: Novum Testamentum 1519 and later (Novum instrumentum for the first edition, 1516, when required) LB VI / ASD VI-2, 3, 4

Obsecratio ad Virginem Mariam: Obsecratio sive oratio ad Virginem Mariam in rebus adversis, or Obsecratio ad Virginem Matrem Mariam in rebus adversis LB V / CWE 69
Oratio de pace: Oratio de pace et discordia LB VIII
Oratio funebris: Oratio funebris in funere Bertae de Heyen LB VIII / CWE 29

Paean Virgini Matri: Paean Virgini Matri dicendus LB V / CWE 69
Panegyricus: Panegyricus ad Philippum Austriae ducem LB IV / ASD IV-1 / CWE 27
Parabolae: Parabolae sive similia LB I / ASD I-5 / CWE 23
Paraclesis LB V, VI / ASD V-7
Paraphrasis in Elegantias Vallae: Paraphrasis in Elegantias Laurentii Vallae LB I / ASD I-4
Paraphrasis in Matthaeum, etc LB VII / ASD VII-6 / CWE 42–50
Peregrinatio apostolorum: Peregrinatio apostolorum Petri et Pauli LB VI, VII
Precatio ad Virginis filium Iesum LB V / CWE 69
Precatio dominica LB V / CWE 69
Precationes: Precationes aliquot novae LB V / CWE 69
Precatio pro pace ecclesiae: Precatio ad Dominum Iesum pro pace ecclesiae LB IV, V / CWE 69
Prologus supputationis: Prologus in supputationem calumniarum Natalis Bedae (1526), or Prologus supputationis errorum in censuris Bedae (1527) LB IX / ASD IX-5
Purgatio adversus epistolam Lutheri: Purgatio adversus epistolam non sobriam Lutheri LB X / ASD IX-1 / CWE 78

Querela pacis LB IV / ASD IV-2 / CWE 27

Ratio: Ratio seu Methodus compendio perveniendi ad veram theologiam (Methodus for the shorter version originally published in the Novum instrumentum of 1516) LB V, VI

Responsio ad annotationes Lei: Responsio ad annotationes Eduardi Lei LB IX /
ASD IX-4 / CWE 72

Responsio ad Collationes: Responsio ad Collationes cuiusdam iuvenis gerontodidascali LB IX / CWE 73

Responsio ad disputationem de divortio: Responsio ad disputationem cuiusdam
Phimostomi de divortio LB IX / ASD IX-4 / CWE 83

Responsio ad epistolam Alberti Pii: Responsio ad epistolam paraeneticam Alberti
Pii, or Responsio ad exhortationem Pii LB IX / ASD IX-6 / CWE 84

Responsio ad notulas Bedaicas (see Notatiunculae)

Responsio ad Petri Cursii defensionem: Epistola de apologia Cursii LB X /
Ep 3032

Responsio adversus febricitantis cuiusdam libellum LB X

Spongia: Spongia adversus aspergines Hutteni LB X / ASD IX-1 / CWE 78

Supputatio: Supputatio errorum in censuris Bedae LB IX

Supputationes: Supputationes errorum in censuris Natalis Bedae: contains
Supputatio and reprints of Prologus supputationis; Divinationes ad notata Bedae;
Elenchus in censuras Bedae; Appendix respondens ad Sutorem; Appendix de
scriptis Clithovei LB IX / ASD IX-5

Tyrannicida: Tyrannicida, declamatio Lucianicae respondens LB I / ASD I-1 / CWE 29

Virginis et martyris comparatio LB V / ASD V-7 / CWE 69

Vita Hieronymi: Vita divi Hieronymi Stridonensis *Opuscula* / CWE 61

Index of
Scriptural References

This index lists the citations and allusions made by Erasmus, but not those added by the translator for explanation or illustration.

Index of
Greek and Latin Words Cited

This index lists the Greek and Latin words or phrases in Erasmus' own edition or the Latin in the Vulgate on which Erasmus makes some comment, but not other Greek words for which he simply gives a Latin equivalent.

LATIN WORDS

General Index

abstinence. *See* fasting and abstinence
Acacius of Caesarea 50 and n31
Achaia 257 and n3
Adrian VI xxiv
Aeschines 2 n3
Aeschylus 60 n71
Aesop 141 and n13, 261 n5
Amandus, brother 157 and n3
Ambrose xvii, xxi n40, 30–1, 32 n82, 38, 48, 50–4, 58 n68, 66 n9, 143 and n25, 145, 177, 184, 207 n2. *See also* Ambrosiaster
– 'Commentaries on Hebrews.' *See* Haimo of Auxerre
– *De fide. See* Gregorius Illiberitanus
– *Hexameron* 29 and n59
Ambrosiaster xxxvii, 50 and n31, 51 n35, 54 and n51, 58 n68, 143 n23, 177, 178 n6, 181, 182 nn2 and 4, 184, 185 n2, 195–6, 199, 201 n26, 203 nn65 and 71, 205 n96, 210, 211 n4, 214 n4, 215 nn3–5, 216– 17, 218 n10, 232 and n7, 234 n3, 236 n2, 236–7 and n5, 245, 248 and n2, 252–3 and n2, 262 n7; *Quaestiones veteris et novi testamenti* 201 n26. *See also* Hieronymiana
Amerbach, Boniface xxiv
Ammonio, Andrea xxiii n47
Andrew, the apostle 94
Anselm xviii, 31 and n74, 32
Apollinarius of Laodicea 48 and n23, 54, 55 n56
Aquila 257 and n1
Aquinas. *See* Thomas Aquinas
Arians (Arianism) 28, 150 and n6, 230
Athanasius 196, 203–4 n73

Athens 138 n4, 261 n2
Aristotle, Aristotelianism xxx n80, 80 n66
Augustine xvii–xviii, xxi n40, xxxvii, 10–11, 32, 35 n89, 36, 38, 48, 52–3, 143–5, 150, 177, 190, 202 n46, 237, 259
– *Confessiones* 216, 218 n9
– *Contra Cresconium grammaticum Donatistum* 158, 159 n3
– *Contra Faustum Manichaeum* 150, 151 n7
– *Contra Iulianum* 191–3, 197, 199, 202 nn35 and 43, 205 nn98 and 105
– *De civitate Dei* 53–7 and nn46, 52, 56, and 57, 59 n69
– *De correptione et gratia* 221 and n4
– *De doctrina christiana* 225, 226 nn2 and 3, 227 n4
– *De ecclesiasticis dogmatibus. See* Gennadius
– *De moribus Manichaeorum* 111 n34
– *De trinitate* 3 and n4, 4–5, 15 n8, 19, 23 and n37, 34 and nn85–7, 35
– *Enarrationes in psalmos* 24 n38, 180 and n2
– *Epistolae* 66 n9, 70 and n25, 74 n44
– *Expositio quorundam propositionum ex epistula ad Romanos* 207 n2, 208, 229 n3, 234 n3
– *In Iohannis evangelium tractatus* 6 and n13, 8–9 and nn29, 31, and 32, 15–16, 19, 22–3 and nn35–6, 24, 25 n45, 31 nn74–5, 35 and n91
– *Principia dialectica* 36 and n94
– *Quaestiones veteris et novi testamenti. See* Ambrosiaster

The design of
THE COLLECTED WORKS
OF ERASMUS
was created
by
ALLAN FLEMING
1929–1977
for
the University
of Toronto
Press